D1524188

Hindsight

Hindsight

Charlotte Wolff M.D.

Quartet Books
London   Melbourne   New York

First published by Quartet Books Limited 1980
A member of the Namara Group
27 Goodge Street, London W1P 1FD

Copyright © 1980 by Charlotte Wolff M.D.

ISBN 0 7043 2253 6

Phototypset by BSC Typesetting Ltd, London
Printed in Great Britain by The Anchor Press Ltd
and bound by William Brendon & Son Ltd
both of Tiptree, Essex

302/31

Contents

Les moments nous changent plus que le temps.

Natalie Barney   *Un panier de framboises*

Introduction

My first autobiography, *On the Way to Myself*, was published eleven years ago. It is an autobiography with a difference. I selected those aspects of my life which showed the correlation between creativity and outer events. The hazards of 'fate' and a good deal of luck played a considerable part in my life. I had to flee from Nazi Germany, which changed my circumstances and my language. But I was fortunate enough to meet the right people at the right time to further my research and ambitions. *On the Way to Myself* is an autobiography of the mind, and its chronology represents a zig-zag curve, appropriate to the theme. Many aspects of my life had to be left out, for example my childhood and intimate personal experiences which had no direct relevance to my creativity. The book ends in the early fifties because my books on the Human Hand and Gesture had been published, and I had no further research in mind at that time.

This new autobiography, *Hindsight*, is a completely different proposition. It is the history of my life from birth to the present day, and is told chronologically. Here and there I have had to go a step or two forwards or backwards in time to put certain points into their proper perspective. It was, of course, impossible to leave out those events and influences which had been dealt with in the earlier book. But I recount them here in a different way: they are seen from a new angle, and treated in a cursory manner. Looking back on one's life in old age gives one the vantage point of a 'bird's eye view'. One sees oneself in two ways: as the person who has lived that life, and the person who *interprets* its outer and inner happenings – from a certain distance. I do not believe that age necessarily makes for 'detachment'. We are always the same person, and never want to forgo the need to love and be loved, to please and to be pleased (to mention only a few). We are *all ages* at any age. I did not have it in mind to look for 'meaning', quite simply because I don't believe in that either. I wanted to show the trials and errors, the windfalls of good fortune, and the bad presents from Pandora's box. And achievements as well as failures in personal relations and in my profession, are all recorded in the light of hindsight.

I am fully aware of the fickleness of memory. Imagination and emotions change and colour *events*, wrongly thought of as reality. We can only get glimpses of it through our imagination. And the light this most precious gift sheds on happenings and feelings is what counts – the *real* story.

I A German Childhood

Riesenburg (town of giants), where I was born, did not justify its name. It was a small town of about 4,000 inhabitants. Two market places, the Great and the Little Market, were its most lively features. One entered the latter through the Riesenburger Tor (tower), a relic from the Middle Ages which had fallen into ruin, but still served as an archway to the older part of the town, and was a reminder of a more glorious past. In contrast, neither its layout nor its houses suggested anything ancient or remarkable: Riesenburg was merely a dull little township. Its immediate surroundings were fields and meadows. But about five miles to the south one entered a large virgin forest, the Great Forest, and two miles to the north was a small conifer wood on sandy ground, the Little Forest. The former had the attraction of a rich animal- and plant-life, while the latter was a favourite spot for short outings.

In spite of the drabness of the place, the image of Riesenburg had a romantic appeal for me. Close to it ran the river Liebe (love), a tributary of the Weichsel which was the watershed between West and East Germany before the First World War. A lake called Sorgensee (lake of sorrows) flowed into the Liebe, which added the right touch of nostalgia to the image. Both the river and the lake played a considerable part in my childhood.

Riesenburg, a thoroughly German town, lay amidst Polish land and villages, and was a few miles from the Polish border. The German 'face' was stamped on the appearance and character of the inhabitants, which no foreign traits had ever altered.

To the east of the Weichsel lay the province of Westpreussen with its capital, Danzig. The town had undergone mixed fortunes, belonging to Prussia at one time, to Poland at another. And the mighty Deutsche Ritterorden (Teutonic Order of Knights) had held it in its grip during the early Middle Ages. This beautiful town had a unique international position as a Hansastadt and trading centre. Danzig was our metropolis, and it became my second home when I was nine years old.

Westpreussen was German in spite of the Poles in our midst. They seemed to be more a name than a reality. Before 1918 the 'Polish Question' had not come into the open, and people were not conscious that they lived with the insecurity of an ethnic and political problem.

As a matter of fact, a Polish woman had been the most important person in my babyhood. She was my wet nurse, and her milk fed me for a year, if not longer. She stayed with us until I was two, and my mother later said I was never the same again after she left. No trace of memory recalls this earliest period of my life, but a photograph which I treasured depicted a happy, relaxed baby in the arms of a swarthy Polish woman, hefty in build and tender in expression. I only knew from my mother that she had come to us with her baby boy with whom I must have shared her milk. The only reminder of her was this photograph which meant so much to me that I gave it away as a precious present to a Russian woman I loved, and never saw it again.

Westpreussen might have had a simmering Polish question, but no incident in my early surroundings suggested that there was a *Jewish* question. A handful of Jewish families and a few unmarried women lived their lives peacefully as German *Stadtsbürger Jüdischen Glaubens* (German citizens of the Jewish religion), without any perceptible discrimination. History speaks of an innate German anti-Semitism, viciously revivified in the late nineteenth and early twentieth centuries. E. Stöcker, a parson, and K. Jahn, a 'muscular' Christian, who preached against the Jews, were the main culprits, but their influence had not penetrated our peaceful town. I was never aware of anti-Semitism or any personal discrimination until the beginning of the thirties.

I was the second child of middle-class Jewish parents. Their first-born was also a girl, named Thea, which may have had something to do with the comedy of errors surrounding my birth. My father announced the happy event to his only brother by telephone with the words: 'My little boy has arrived.' Perhaps he was drugged by wishful thinking, as the midwife had declared me to be female. I shall never know the truth about it. I heard the story

2

only when I was in my teens. My uncle Josef told me about it with a wistful look and the words: 'You have always been a camouflaged boy.' Whatever the wish of my parents may have been, the 'wrong' sex made no difference to their love and devotion. They took great pride in their children, and my father paraded me with obvious satisfaction before his friends and customers. I felt sure that he enjoyed my company, because he took me with him on his country rides when he visited peasants and big landowners to buy corn. I loved driving in a gig with him. I snuggled up to him. He put his arm around me, and I put my head under the cape of his brown greatcoat. He talked to me as if I were grown up, and he spread the news that I gave him good business advice – at the age of four. His father had been a corn merchant before him, and had left his house and business to his son. An oval-shaped enamel plate fixed close to the entrance with the words, 'C. Wolff, Getreide' (corn), announced this fact. My grandfather, Caspar Wolff, had left town after his son's marriage to live in Zoppot on the Baltic.

Our house stood in the main street, called Lange Strasse, which made a sharp downward bend close by. Consequently, the house looked askew, as one part was on a lower level than the other. Next to us lived a butcher. Then came the baker, who inhabited a corner house bordering on a small side-street from which emanated strong gutter smells. It cut into the line of the Lange Strasse. Then came the grocer's, with one side in our street and the front facing the Great Market. As in all small townships, the market place was Riesenburg's life and soul, with its big stores, a chemist, haberdashery and an ironmonger's shop. Every two or three weeks, the Great Market was invaded by country folk who came with their animals: horses, cattle and pigs. They brought smells and money with them, attracting not only buyers and sellers, but also small children like myself. We stared at the animals and peasants, wandering cautiously around them, listening to their talk and bargaining. The animals always stole the show, but noises and smells came from both beast and man: smells and gossip were hallmarks of our town.

Casual contacts with neighbours relaxed the mind after a hard day's work, and in the evening, when the weather was fine, my parents sat on chairs in the porch of our house and watched the passers-by, exchanging greetings and gossip with them. So did the inhabitants next door and opposite. When the weather was

3

unfavourable, windows served as a less successful substitute for the porch. A small mahogany sewing table with colourful cottons, scissors and other paraphernalia stood at the window of our living room, which allowed a good view of the street. My parents sat on either side of it, looking out, and chatting about business and neighbours. These handsome *Nähtischchen* (little sewing tables) were a customary requisite in bourgeois houses. What a good excuse for my mother, and sometimes a seamstress, to sew or mend, while watching the world go by! I did the watching and staring without the excuse of work. I could not tear myself away from the little table. My interest did not centre on people in the street, but on the garden opposite our house. It was deserted, as if under a bad spell. But in a sharp angle, right in my line of vision, stood a graceful *Akazia* tree which was my delight. I do not know why it attracted me so, except that when it was in flower I thought it was a Christmas tree in summer. The garden sloped down towards a large and more presentable house than those in our street. It belonged to the owner of a sawmill. A narrow pathway separated his house from the deserted garden, a pathway which led to the Sorgensee. On cold winter days the lake was frozen, and we children went skating on it. In the early afternoons my sister and I would visit the frozen playground, and amuse ourselves gliding over the icy surface, either singly or hand in hand. We acquired some skill in the exercise, moving in semi-circles and even daring some clumsy dancing steps. We were close enough to the Baltic to enjoy the healthy climate of cold winters and hot summers. The invigorating winter air made life outside and inside the house worlds apart.

The warmth of the *Kachelofen* awaited those who came in from the cold. It was a large stove, built into the wall from floor to ceiling, simultaneously heating two rooms. People warmed themselves leaning against it. This healthy form of heating can still be found in old German houses. The *Kachelofen* was fuelled with anthracite, coal or turf, and never went out. The cosy warmth indoors in winter months, and glorious summers with high skies and warm winds still linger in my mind like a nursery rhyme. Could all this be a mirage of happiness past, which makes childhood look as beautiful as the Phoenix re-born from the ashes? I do not believe that it is a *fata Morgana*, but a pristine reality, untouched by the deceptions of an adult world.

Our house had a courtyard which signalled my father's profes-

4

sion. At the rear stood a large granary, containing tightly-bound sacks of corn: wheat, rye and barley. Chemical fertilizers, which had already invaded agriculture early in the twentieth century, were stored in another part. Along the wall separating our court-yard from the neighbour's property were three intriguing 'build-ings': next to the granary stood a stable fit to accommodate four shire horses; then came a walled-in manure heap, filled with horse dung and hen droppings. Wooden boards with iron handles covered it, protecting us from unsavoury smells. A closely wired hen house adjoined it, which held about a dozen pullets and a fine cockerel. I have no idea whether pleasure or economy was the reason for keeping hens. Opposite the stable stood the privy with a large hole in a small bench. Newspaper cut into little squares hung on both sides of it.

The cobbled courtyard with its outbuildings was typical of a corn merchant's establishment in a small German town of that time. The nursery looked on to the courtyard, which was a private playground for my sister and myself. We watched the hens, stared at the horses, and played hide and seek behind the sacks in the vast granary. Labourers moved corn in and out and chased us out. But the coachman would lift us onto a horse when he was in a good mood.

I had another playground of my own in the street, where I made my first social contacts, playing with the children who lived next door. Their house belonged to a painter and decorator; it was a modest one, built on one floor. The boy was my age, the girl a year older. The three of us were sometimes joined by the sons of a Colonel of the Kürassiers, Adelbert, Manfred and Rüdiger. They were, however, not allowed to play in the 'gutter', and we were invited to join them in their garden. I had a special contact with Adelbert, the eldest, who pushed me on the swing with obvious pleasure, and was my partner on the seesaw in the middle of the garden. Their father, with his splendid white uniform and black riding boots with silver spurs, patted our heads on his way into the house, but his wife never looked at us, nor were we ever invited *inside*. Yet there were no obvious class prejudices among the inhabitants of our town. They were *de bonne volonté* towards their neighbours, regardless of wealth, class, race or religion. Ideal image of childhood? By no means. The Germany of the early twentieth century was a tolerant country because there was work for everybody. Its social order was simplistic, and reinforced

5

by the commands of the Bible. People still accepted their place in the world as the will of God. Religion had not lost its hold over the poor, and murmuring voices of rebellion did not alter this state of affairs before the First World War. Jewish people could live in peace and comfort. They did well in business and the professions. The best store in town belonged to the parents of my closest school friend, Netty. And in their house I enjoyed warmth, good food and complete acceptance, which compensated for a certain coldness in my mother's temperament.

But, for a different reason, another store which belonged to a friend of my parents was important to me. It displayed boys' outfits which I used to eye longingly. I asked my father to buy one for me because I favoured boy's rather than girl's clothes. I had never been conscious of any preference for the male in my family, I just felt that my clothes were not the right apparel for me. It was only in my late teens and early twenties that I wished I had been male, because the girls and women I loved were attracted to men.

The family is a circle, turning round on itself with little room for friendships. Jewish families were paragons of a closely-knit community, bound together by mutual help and affection. Rarely did they let their relations down, even when feelings were antagonistic, jealous or hostile. Friendships with other Jews were redolent of pleasant family ties but on a rather casual level, and contacts with non-Jews did not go further than acquaintance-ships. A certain separateness between Jews and Gentiles was self-chosen, as no sign of anti-Semitism reared its ugly head in my early surroundings. But I had noticed a kind of condescension on the part of Jews towards Gentiles. There was, for instance, my father, whom I heard say to my mother: 'He is a decent enough "goy" but naïve, as *they* usually are.' Such distinctions, made among adults, luckily did not affect us children. The truth was that German Jews had an emotional affinity with each other, which drew them together and tended to exclude Gentiles. For a long time I have thought that a racial bond was at the back of this pattern. Jews lived for more than 1,800 years in ghettos all over the earth, persecuted and despised. They had no choice but to marry inside their small communities, and families became more and more inter-related. Virtually incestuous bonds preserved a racial identity. The marks of Jewishness were handed down from generation to generation, so long as mixed marriages were the exception rather than the rule. Jews remain Jews first and fore-

6

most, be they equal citizens in a host country or not. The Jews who claimed to be as German as other Germans did not want to see the truth; only the Zionists did, who put their Jewishness first, rejecting integration into a foreign 'body'. They acted in accordance with their beliefs and prepared for their exodus to Palestine. All that was fortunately hidden from a child whose parents never thought of themselves as being anything but German Jews, living in peace with their neighbours. Perhaps because of their stance, I didn't see the error until I was an adult.

Although I felt at ease with all my peers at school, I was drawn to Jewish girls. I felt more relaxed with them, especially with Netty, to whose mother I had taken a fancy. The warmth of hospitality in her home was not evident in the houses of my Christian classmates. I cannot recall any of them except Lischen (Lizzy) Senkbeil. There was a good reason for me to remember her. Lischen lived at the lower end of our street, close to where it ended in a meadow. She passed our house on her way to school and I used to join her. More often than not we also walked back together, and sometimes I accompanied her home. She was different from the other girls because she had red hair, a white face and water-blue eyes. Lischen was a vivacious and clever girl, but I was less interested in her than in her father's smithy. When we reached her house we found the door of the foundry wide open. I used to stand still, staring at the goings on – her father hammering on an anvil, and his apprentices welding iron into strange shapes. The noise was deafening and the sparks were flying. This was a male kitchen, a warlock's den. I had never come across anything like it, and the sight hypnotized me. I felt rooted to the spot. I admired Lischen's father and his work. Jews had neither smithies nor muscular craftsmen.

There was another essential difference between Jews and 'others', which struck me forcefully in my second or third year at school. I was excluded from lessons on religion. I felt left out, and asked my classmates to tell me what they were taught. And so I learned, second-hand, something about Christianity. I was told of Jesus and His miracles, and I got to know that He was the Saviour of the world, who loved everybody, particularly children. I was envious of my Christian peers. I felt a sense of deprivation. I couldn't understand why I should not share the happiness of having a Jesus who loved children and did miracles. I know that I prayed to Jesus night after night, secretly and intensely. I do not remember how long I indulged this nostalgic exercise. It had equalled, if not surpassed, my other frustrated desire: to be dressed as a boy. But neither of these frustrations was strong enough to spoil my enjoyment of life. I felt loved by my parents, and I had a companion in my sister whom I loved and hated as siblings do. I was singled out by my principal teacher during the three years I spent at the Höhere Töchterschule in Riesenburg. It was a private school for pupils with parents of means. Fräulein Lange, the principal teacher, made no secret of her special liking for me. She allowed me to carry exercise books which she had to correct, and to accompany her on her way home. I looked up to her with love and satisfaction, and also with a sense of triumph, having outshone my classmates in her eyes.

There should have been compensation for any religious deprivation in the Jewish Sunday school. This was regrettably not the case. Our teacher, the *Cantor*, did not tell us much about the Old Testament. He gave us Hebrew lessons where we only learnt to read the language mechanically. In the end we could read Hebrew, but did not understand the text except for the routine blessing, which is the model of the Lord's Prayer: 'Our Father, who art in Heaven.'

In my pre-school days, my father was the centre of my world. My mother aroused both affection and fear in me. Once when I still slept in my parents' bedroom, I saw her naked. I was about three years old, and was caged into a small child's iron bed with high drop-sides. The sight of this gigantesque person with large breasts and flabby skin terrified me, and my supine position must have accentuated the impact. I never spoke about this experience but have never forgotten it. A few months later, she gave me another shock. One night, affected by a bad cold, I coughed persistently. Suddenly she stood over my bed and said angrily: 'Stop that coughing, I cannot sleep.' I tried to suppress it, but couldn't. I do know that this event also had a lasting effect. It conditioned me to cringe at the idea that any noise I made could anger other people. Yet I knew that my mother loved me. She addressed me in endearing terms and indulged my dietary idiosyncrasies. As I disliked milk, she rewarded me with chocolate wafers after I had swallowed half a glassful. Spinach, which I, like many children, abhorred, became a treat when she decorated it with strawberries. Sometimes I clung to her, sometimes I withdrew. My ambivalence, which she must have noticed, made her diplomatic: she bought me sweets as a special favour when she wanted something. She had a weight problem which she treated sensibly. One of the treatments was a source of great perplexity and amusement for us children. We saw with amazement a static rowing boat installed in the nursery. Mother, scantily clad, took the oars and rowed on the spot for precisely thirty minutes every day. My sister and I tried to emulate her, but found it much more fun to watch her than to imitate her. Medicine has its own fashions which recur at intervals. About seventy years after my mother rowed her orthopaedic boat, the exercise is again a favourite method of keeping fit.

My mother's need for movement was, however, not confined to the home. She had to go for long walks, and wanted a companion to ease a task she didn't fancy. It fell to me to accompany her. I must have protested at being used against my will. She had to buy me cream cakes to make me comply. Only then did I agree to march with her to the Great Forest, about five miles away. The walk was long and tedious, and the road dusty and dirty from fast-moving carts and horse droppings. But the arrival was a triumph every time. Our long promenade gave a glow to our cheeks. We were both too tired to venture deeper into the forest, and settled down in a *Biergarten* close to the edge. I ate my cakes and drank lemonade, while my mother refreshed herself with coffee. As I was too fatigued to run about any more I passed the time listening to tunes from a juke box. My mother gave me pennies to put into the tall Victorian machine, and out came the hit tunes of the day. I loved their beat and sentimentality, and I still have a soft spot for music hall songs. The return home was agonizing for us both. I was tired and resentful, my mother satisfied with her exercise, but feeling guilty that she had exhausted me.

The Great Forest was a wonderful place for sightseeing. People came from far away to visit it. It stretched for about fifty miles to Marienwerder, a provincial town bigger than Riesenburg. We had friends there, and on crisp winter days went for a four-hour ride packed into fur rugs in a horse-drawn sleigh, to visit them. The Great Forest was part of the large woodland area extending from the Baltic deep into West and East Prussia. It opened my eyes to nature's gifts, and I learned about the many varieties of trees and animals it hid. On summer days the family went there in a landau. We picnicked in a secluded spot, and my sister and I watched the bucks with their antlers, the hares quickly rushing over moss, and the red squirrels climbing trees. We were equipped with light baskets to gather wild strawberries. We glimpsed their brilliant red partly concealed behind their leaves, and their colour attracted us as much as their aroma.

The scent of the sun-drenched woods, the wild strawberries, the bucks and hares, were a *real* picture book, which I preferred to an imaginary one. But the woods were not the only attraction of the world outside. The river Liebe also held exciting promises. The meadows alongside it had a richness of their own, with flowers such as daisies, buttercups and violets. But our interest was centred on the butterflies – cabbage whites, red admirals, tortoiseshells and others. We ran after them to catch them in muslin nets. Sometimes we went into a small bathing hut where we changed into cumbersome costumes to swim in the Liebe. In childhood, time seems to have no stop, and its 'golden' days should not be laughed at as a myth. They are close to that reality we search for a whole life long and never attain. It is the child's prerogative to experience every impression anew, which is the prelude to first-hand living, if society does not succeed in suppressing spontaneity.

I know that Cupid's arrows can get at their target at a very early age, but not as early as psychoanalysts will have it. I know that I fell in love for the first time when I was three years old. It happened when my mother and I visited relations in a small town not far from Berlin. We were led into the house by the back door via a large courtyard, where I saw peacocks displaying their feathers in full splendour. Out of the house came my mother's sixteen-year-old cousin who had not been at the station on our arrival. She passed the beautiful birds to greet us – a lovely black-haired girl with dark eyes in a pale, round face. She walked towards us, her full lips smiling. She had a womanly figure, looked older than her age, and a short neck made her appear smaller than she was. My memory of her is as clear as a photograph taken on the spot. It was love at first sight. The glow of a new feeling had hit me. I recall not only her face, her walk and her smile, but the whole setting of this enthralling experience. During our visit I had eyes only for her. I always managed to sit next to her at table, and cuddled up to her. And I didn't want to go anywhere without her, following her from room to room.

My first love had been preceded by an emotional event beyond my understanding. It might have been the prelude to it. I was not quite three years old when I had a strange experience. Lying quite still in my little bed, I was suddenly compelled to raise myself up. I stood upright, touching myself all over. I felt an intense glow of pleasure going through me. I could hardly bear my happiness, and had to take deep and quick breaths. I think of it now as a process of birth without its pangs of pain. I had been born to my Self. From that moment on, I felt apart from my beloved father and my rather frightening mother. I was I, and in the centre of my life. It gave me the power to direct my eyes wherever *I* wanted to. My sense of identity had been born, and from then on I responded to impressions in my own way, and their focus of reference was my Self.

Love has become a misused word because it has too many facets to be clearly profiled. I had an emotional love for my parents, which filled me with gratitude for their protective care. I was made conscious of its depths when I succumbed, at the age of five, to a bad bout of influenza, and had to stay in bed for a time. They never tired of coming into the sickroom with: 'Are you feeling a little better now? Do you want anything, anything to play with, anything to eat?' I do not remember my answers, only their loving gestures and words. When I had nearly recovered my father gave me a large package which had arrived by post. 'This is for you,' he said. I was thrilled to unpack a woollen dress in tartan tweed, with a red belt. My parents had ordered it from Berlin to celebrate my recovery. I had never seen such a pretty garment and was enthralled. I wore it for years and forgot the boy's outfit I had always wanted. I looked time and again into the mirror, admiring it, and paraded in it before my parents and friends like a peacock. I had made it part of myself, and have never forgotten the pleasure it gave me. My parents pampered, spoiled and over-protected their children. Discipline had no proper place in their educational code. But it had advantages: it gave me trust in people, and considerable self-confidence. On the other hand, spoiling the child can be the cause of disappointment at the lack of response in others. I had the naïve idea that everybody should be inclined to like me. Much later, during my stay in France, when I met the Red Emma (Goldmann), my misplaced expectations were brought home to me. She looked at me with sympathy and a touch of regret, saying: 'You live on hope and expectations.'

11

I had enjoyed the positive side of capitalism in the peaceful days before the First World War. Under a tolerant monarchy, individual strife was legitimate and collective solidarity still in its infancy. The few Jewish families were probably quite unconscious of the fact that their Germanness could never be fully acknowledged by Gentiles, and would not shield them for ever. They acted as all Germans did. On the Emperor's birthday, windows were lit up by candles, and those of the Jewish people were no exception. The Christmas tree stood in their houses just as beautifully decorated as those of their Christian neighbours. Carols were sung and presents were discreetly displayed underneath the tree or on a table nearby. '*Stille Nacht, Heilige Nacht*' rang out from our house, and expectation and excitement grew until the hour of darkness on Christmas Eve, when the presents could be picked up before the festive meal of goose, red cabbage and a heavy Christmas pudding.

Other memorable events were the Kaiser's visits to an East Prussian county. People travelled from far away to have a glimpse of him, and so did we. Wilhelm II loved hunting, and frequently went to the estate of the Graf Finck von Finckenstein, close to Christburg. We went there in our landau for many miles to see him and to meet our relatives from Salfeld (a small town in East Prussia). They were a family of six and in prosperous circumstances. My uncle Bernhard, a corn merchant like my father, had been more successful in business than he. Aunt Emma, a comely woman, blue-eyed and cheerful, called the tune in her family. And my two girl cousins, as handsome as their mother, could twist their father round their little fingers. My uncle had the looks of a boxer, squinted and hardly spoke a word. His sons did not give him much joy because they had not inherited his physical vigour. We were assured that he had a heart of gold, but I never had proof of it. Aunt Emma, who lived to the age of ninety, now and again uttered pearls of wisdom which my parents ridiculed. But I was impressed, particularly by one: '*Es zerkömmt sich alles*'. How often did I wish to believe in her: 'Everything comes right in the end.' It was always a red-letter day for us children to drive to the woods around Christburg to meet our relatives on the day of the Kaiser's visit. After a picnic in the woods, our party drove to Finckenstein. On the edge of a forest, hedged in and set well back from the road, lay the hunting lodge of the Count. The special tooting of the Emperor's car announced the approach of the cavalcade, and our hearts beat fast at the sound. People stretched their necks, leaned forward, nearly trampling down the hedges, while staring at the car bearing Wilhelm II. There he was. One just saw a glittering helmet and a black moustache. He acknowledged the hurrahs of his subjects with a smile and a very light wave of his good hand, and everybody had his or her great little moment of ecstasy. We rode home exhausted but elated by our glimpse of the ruler.

I never experienced a death in the family when I was little, but already then I had a vague understanding of a living death. Two aunts of my father, the only Jewish spinsters I knew, lived in an old and damp house not far from us. I often visited them with food and other treats from my parents. One had to walk through a bad-smelling pathway to get to them. This unpleasant prelude to the visit enhanced the impression that the two old women were outside life. They always wore black, had white faces, frightened eyes, and gestured wildly with their thin hands. They chattered about trivialities without a stop. These scarecrows in the garden of childhood were as kind as they were poor, people with tremendous courage who kept up appearances beyond their means. They fascinated and frightened me because they were good people treated like outcasts. They had come to the end of their lives without having lived. Pictures of failure – *women on the shelf.* Then, during one holiday in Riesenburg, Thea and I were no longer prompted to visit them, but were not told that they had died.

Death was rarely mentioned in conversation, yet it was celebrated as a feast. I could not understand why my mother and her brothers were so jolly after we had watched their mother being interred in the Jewish cemetery. Food and wine was as good and plentiful as at a wedding reception. The animated crowd could just as well have been dancing instead of talking about 'her' and how much she was worth. I couldn't understand this hilarity and preoccupation with money. My grandmother had been good to me, and I wanted her to be alive.

The taboo of death is the other side of the taboo of capitalism. One didn't speak of one's 'capital' either, one kept one's financial position secret, like an extra-marital love affair. Yet the most endearing expressions in Jewish families had capitalistic overtones. My parents called me '*Goldchen*' (little golden dear) when they were at their most tender. Although money meant as much

13

to them as to all capitalists, the health and education of their children had priority, even at the cost of financial sacrifice. My parents wanted us to have a good figure and a good education. 'You might have to stand on your own feet,' they told us. And so we were given '*en pension*' to Tante Auguste in Danzig when my sister was twelve and I nine years old. It seems odd that I had been little conscious of my sister at home, but she became alive to me when we were thrown together in new surroundings. I went through a second separation from people I loved. The first one, repressed and forgotten, was from my Polish wet nurse, the second was from my parents and their world which had been my own. Now I noticed my sister. She was handsome, and had the same upturned nose as my mother, curly brown hair and forget-me-not blue eyes. I further noticed that Tante Auguste's son, a young lout of eighteen, paid attention to her, but never looked at me. I was relieved that he didn't because his enormous frame and large squinting eyes frightened me. And so did the squashed boxer's nose in his fleshy face. I used to look away from him to my aunt, as if seeking refuge, and I soon became very much attached to her. She was a beautiful Jewess of the Sephardic type. She had been widowed at an early age, and was affected by Menière's disease. I don't know whether the loss of a loved husband had contributed to her illness. She had gone almost deaf soon after his death, and developed great skill in lip-reading. But she also used a hearing aid in the shape of a trumpet. I felt greatly drawn to her. I must have been homesick and bewildered by the new surroundings, and often wandered at night in a trance-like state into her bedroom. She opened her arms to me without a word, and I went to sleep at her bosom. She thought it wise that I should see a doctor because of my nightly restlessness and heart palpitations. She took me to an eminent physician who reassured her that I was physically sound, and explained my complaint as acute nervousness.

I had been at school in Riesenburg for three years before I started my new life in Danzig. School entrance was celebrated almost like a birthday. The new pupil had his/her photograph taken, and was made a fuss of. I had been eager to go to school and to please my teachers. I was a good pupil, though never first but always second in class. Perhaps I guessed already at that age the disadvantages of coming first. The second place always allows for something better to come.

14

I was not consciously stricken at leaving home, but my roots were in Riesenburg, and although in time I adjusted to the big town of Danzig and my new environment, I longed for the holidays when my sister and I went home to our parents. I knew every station through which we passed, stopped or changed trains. Before we entered Dirschau I used to stand up and stare at the long bridge over the Weichsel with its massive steel girders on each side.

After the Treaty of Versailles was signed in 1918, Dirschau became an important railway junction, the starting point of the Polish Corridor. Every train was stopped there and all passengers had to get out. Some trains were directed to East Prussian towns close to the Baltic, such as Königsburg or Memel, others to Marienburg.

But in my childhood, Dirschau was an ordinary railway station, and the train went straight through to Marienburg. Here we had to change onto a branch line which went to the then Polish border, stopping at Riesenburg. In an hour's journey we reached our destination. The train had steamed through rich arable country where several stations had Polish names. It seems odd that we passed through them as if they didn't exist, but I remember a sense of sadness when I looked at the drab houses and neglected gardens close to the station. And the people who had to live there couldn't possibly be like us, I thought. Germany was the heart of the world for me, and other countries, other folk, had to be pitied. How early such misplaced nationalism makes itself felt! The innocence of childhood knows no better. The small world of the child is his world at large, where foreign countries and people hardly exist. Nationalism is as natural to him as it is childish in an adult.

Apart from Netty, I had made no close friends at the Höhere Töchterschule in my home town, but I had acquired several comrades during the holidays. They included Lischen Senkbeil and some boys either of my own age or older. My favourite was Arthur, a tall and lanky youth with a long Jewish nose and a great sense of humour. But his chief attraction was his power to provide forbidden fruit in the shape of cigarettes. His father owned a tobacco shop on the Little Market, and Arthur managed to steal a few packets here and there. With these spoils in hand, we went to a secret place to indulge our 'vice' with three or four 'safe' comrades. We used to sit down behind a large barn on the outskirts of the town, smoking with bravado in anxious secrecy. The adventure bound us together in an underground gang. Its members had to provide in turn toffees or chocolates as a blindfold for elders and betters. We always got away with this deception. But we were not so lucky with another. Compelled to try out sexual games as well, four of us grasped the opportunity for such an experiment when Arthur's parents were away on holiday. We went on tiptoe into their bedroom and jumped into their twin beds. We were half undressed, keeping our underclothes on. We thought it the right thing to touch each other, but were embarrassed and didn't know how to begin. It was a fumbling exercise with soft talk and much giggling. It all happened in broad daylight while people were being served by the housekeeper in the shop downstairs. We had taken it for granted that she was fully occupied, but she must somehow have heard us. Out of the blue, she came up the stairs and chased us out of the beds, cursing and threatening to tell our parents how horribly we had behaved. Luckily we were not naked, and easily got out of the house. I don't know how Arthur fared with his parents, but our secret never came to the knowledge of mine, and all was well. But after the damper of discovery, our sex games became a thing of the past. I had no regrets, preferring smoking anyway.

The journeys to and fro between Danzig and Riesenburg, the holidays with parents and friends, became a way of life I could not imagine being without.

My parents' first consideration in sending my sister and me to Danzig had been health. We both had a curvature of the spine which could be corrected through orthopaedic treatment, according to the local physician. My parents took us to an orthopaedic surgeon, Dr Wolff, in Danzig who advised treatment at his institute, to which they agreed. No time was lost. We started exercises immediately on orthopaedic machines designed to make one use one's body properly. One of these was a kind of bicycle. We were strapped onto its seat and ordered to keep our back and head straight. We pedalled on the spot, while our arms had to move to and fro two wooden boards attached to the back of the seat. And among many other monstrosities, we discovered mother's rowing boat! The ingeniously designed machines looked forbidding but fulfilled their purpose: to re-establish atrophied muscular function, to correct a curvature of the spine and re-vitalize the whole organism. The treading machine was a good example of this. One had to concentrate on working with one foot at a time. Both feet were fixed with leather straps to a heavy iron pedal and it was no easy task to press it down. Dr Wolff's Institute was well known and of excellent repute. Trained nurses watched the proceedings, and after an hour's orthopaedic exercises, each patient was rewarded with a twenty-minute massage which was both a treat and relaxation.

We went to school from 8 a.m. to 1 o'clock, then travelled back by tram for lunch. After the meal we went out again to visit the orthopaedic institute. It happened to be in the same street, Poggenpfuhl, as our school. This was quite a distance away from the Pfefferstadt where my aunt had a five-room flat. We returned late in the afternoon to do our homework until the evening meal. Life was full and tiring, with not much time left for play and enjoyment.

Scherler's Höhere Töchterschule was reputed to provide a sound preparation for higher education. Was it because of my nostalgia for Riesenburg and difficulty in adaptation, that both teachers and pupils left a blank in my mind? I only know that I was eager to learn all I could because I wanted to enter the Viktoria Schule, a *Realgymnasium* (grammar school) for girls, when the time came. My mind was set on becoming a university student.

The daily tram journeys took us through beautiful parts of Danzig. Every morning at 7.30 a.m. my sister and I boarded the tram at the Hauptbahnhof (main railway station), rode along the Stadtgraben, crossed the ancient Holz- and Kohlenmarket, and journeyed along the elegant Langgasse which ended at the *Rathaus* (town hall) which was crowned by an exquisite tower, the finest example of medieval architecture of its kind. At this point we got out and walked through the narrow Töpfergasse to school in the Poggenpfuhl. And by 2.30 p.m. we had to repeat the journey. But at that time Danzig's beauty had not yet taken hold of me. I remained unaware of it until much later.

My father's younger brother inhabited a beautiful patrician house in the Frauengasse, which was known throughout Germany and beyond for its unique architecture. This street stood in the shadow of the mighty Marienkirche, an outstanding example of Gothic architecture, a 'show piece' as much as a place of worship. Its most precious possession was '*Das Jüngste Gericht*' by Memling. This, the largest Protestant church in the world, oppressed

17

me as high mountains have oppressed me for as long as I can remember. But my uncle's house attracted me even before I understood its singular distinction. A mark over the porch indicated that it was built in 1632. A heavy door with wood carvings opened into the entrance hall with the staircase on one side and the *comptoir* – my uncle's business premises – on the other. We children were not allowed to enter this temple of Mammon. It was at the end of a long dark corridor which filled me with a sense of awe, as did the high ceilings of the long and narrow rooms. The first floor contained the largest one where the Salfeld boys had been installed. My uncle had taken them in to further their education as a favour to their mother, his favourite sister.

My sister and I visisted the boys on Saturdays and Sundays. They were about our age, and our relations took it for granted that we were suitable company for each other. We used to sit for hours with them in their large room, ill at ease because we had little in common. I know that our spirits rose when the grown-ups joined us for a performance of the magic lantern with its wonders of moving pictures, the working of which was beyond our understanding. They were the first moving pictures we had seen.

Our imposed visits were regularly returned by the cousins at my aunt's home in the Pfefferstadt; the unwanted gatherings prevented us from ever making contact at all. But boredom vanished when the four of us took the tram to Langfuhr to visit my father's youngest sister and her family. Her husband was a civil servant who had all the marks and habits of the decent German official of the time. He wore the proper suit and high collar of that class, had a pince-nez carefully poised over his nose, and his hair parted in the middle. My aunt was a handsome hunchback. She had lively eyes which looked at her husband with reserve and at her children with devotion. Their son, Cousin Leo, could have been a foundling. He seemed to have nothing in common with his parents, either in appearance or mentality. The skin of his face was tightly drawn. His brown eyes looked away from rather than at people. He had a musician's nose, finely cut and pointed, and had shown musical talent from an early age. He became a pupil of Joachim, one of the foremost violinists in Germany at the time. We were, in temperament, two of a kind, and became close friends. His sister, on the other hand, linked up with mine, and both girls made a better contact with the Salfeld boys than Leo and I did.

Langfuhr, a lovely suburb of Danzig, had a wood on its 'door-

18

step' where the six of us walked or ran about, either as a group or in pairs. A blank in my memory affords no detail of happenings on these outings, except that our elders didn't check on our comings and goings. And we were either too young or too innocent to take advantage of such freedom. Most children and adolescents have the desire to gang up in groups, and to favour one or two individuals with their close friendship. I was no exception to the rule until the age of thirteen. From then on I needed solitude, a need which grew with the years.

My time with Tante Auguste and the holidays in Riesenburg came to an end when my parents sold their house and business to move to Danzig. They were still young, my father in his early forties, my mother ten years younger. Ever since he was a young man it had been my father's desire to work hard for a short time and make enough money to live from his dividends in Danzig. He imagined a life of leisure would be an ideal existence, and the idea that he could land himself in a life of boredom never occurred to him. But it crossed the mind of my mother, who only agreed to take such an eventful step if he would join the business of her brother, who was a wholesale grocer in Danzig. He complied, but hoped for a sleeping partnership which would leave him free for the pleasures the city had to offer. He was not a capitalist at heart, but a dreamer and escapist. Of all people, parents are the most difficult to know, because of the taboo of their sex life which children do not want to envisage. They don't see parents as physical beings, but as elders who love and protect them. In my early youth, I never criticized them. My father had worked to enjoy leisure, my mother, never content with what she had, wanted more and more material goods. She had a 'Sisyphus' mentality, and he was a romantic. But both were highly principled people. 'Honesty is the best policy' and *'Tue recht und scheue neimand'*, ('Do the right thing and fear no one') were their favourite mottoes. Such precepts could not be abandoned, as an unforgettable incident taught me when I was about four. Our maid had taken me and my sister for a walk around the Great Market when I suddenly lagged behind, attracted by a barrel full of biscuits with a pink sugar layer. I couldn't resist taking one. The maid had not seen it; she went on with my sister without watching me. I held the biscuit in my hands for a few moments, then put it back in its place. Nobody knew of the conflict I had experienced, and my sense of relief that I had resisted temptation. The struggle must

19

have been considerable, because I can still visualize my furtive action and the place where it happened. My parents' ethical code was my command.

Separation from my parents and reunion with them during holidays had accentuated our mutual affection and pleasure in each other. My life between nine and thirteen years of age had all the ingredients of excitement and fulfilment: the chance of higher education, the successful treatment of my spinal curvature and good general health. When children are totally in the power of their parents, they suppress opposition and criticism. And I was in perfect harmony with mine. Holidays were celebrated as a great event, and young and old friends came to the house to chat and play. My parents were happy enough to have us home to provide special treats for us: excursions by landau to Christburg or Salfeld, to the Great Forest or to friends, the Rosens, in the nearby town of Rosenberg. Salfeld could not be reached in less than seven or eight hours, which necessitated staying the night. My relatives cast glamour over me. They lived in a villa surrounded by a large garden, with an orchard at the back and flower beds in front. My handsome girl cousins impressed me with their fine clothes and their sporting achievements. The grown-ups talked business and food, we children talked school, played table tennis and went swimming or walking. Close to the house was a sawmill which was a favourite 'hunting ground' for games of hide and seek with the sons of the owner. The scent of freshly-sawn wood has invigorating powers. I felt spirits and energy rise to great heights at the sawmill, and still recall the smell of freshly-cut wood in my nostrils with nostalgia.

Rosenberg was only a day's outing. The Rosens had a store in the market place. Their only child, Günther, of my own age, was my special friend. The few hours we stayed with the family were spent in gossip over a good meal, with card games to follow. It was generally poker, but to please us children, the grown-ups gave in to play 'Gottessegen bei Cohn', a stupid game of chance. I could have developed into a true gambler because I liked, above all, to win.

These happy excursions and diversions came to an end when my parents moved from Riesenburg to settle in Danzig. I didn't take long to realize that the loss of my home town was greater than the gain made through our reunion. The first setting of my life had gone, a setting intrinsically linked with the idealized image of my parents and a happy childhood. The impressions and experiences in the town of my birth had made my life. To be uprooted from one's beginnings is a shock, the effects of which can be immediate, but are, as a rule, delayed by circumstances which have a time table of their own.

In the world of our small town I could walk anywhere alone – on the larger streets as well as the lonely side ways with their gutter smells. No limit was set to my wish to explore the world around me. And there was a special day of the week to look forward to – the Sabbath, which was celebrated by my parents. On Friday evenings my mother put two silver candlesticks on the dinner table; food was special and plentiful, and we had a small glass of port wine afterwards. In spite of keeping to this Jewish custom, we thought of ourselves as Germans, and of Germany as our homeland. It was only after a visit to Paris in my early twenties that I had an inkling that other people, other lands, might not only be vastly different, but also vastly more civilized than the country of my birth.

I was a clever child, perhaps too clever by half, and it didn't do me much good that my father had paraded me as a prodigy in front of his cronies. At that time, parents regarded their children as small adults. Psychology had not yet entered public imagination. Only the intellectual *avant-garde* in Austria, Germany and perhaps America knew of a paradoxical man called Freud. My parents had never heard of him. Perhaps it wouldn't have made much difference if they had known about psychoanalysis. The label of the clever child stuck to me. It certainly made me an ambitious person who tended to reach for goals beyond her grasp.

My parents were not well matched. They differed essentially in everything from appearance to *Weltanschauung*. But before they moved to Danzig, their incompatibility had made no impact on me. They were part of the canvas of Riesenburg, my home. They were prosperous enough to give their children all the comforts they could wish for. My father's family had a Mediterranean look, and probably belonged to the Sephardic branch of Jews. My mother's family, blond and inclined to obesity, came originally from Poland or Russia. The two 'tribes' differ as much as chalk from cheese. Since the devastating thirties, I have realized that the Jews are a race. I recognize a Jew from whatever country he or she may come. My mother, blonde, with an upturned nose, blue-eyed and plump, could at first sight have been taken for a

German housewife, but her posture and expressions were Jewish. My father, dark-eyed, dark-haired, with a paunch, looked neither like a Spanish nor a German Jew, but a mixture of both. The *mélange* had not been quite successful. He was as indefinite in appearance as in character. One could not know him; he submitted easily to any suggestion with kindness and the wish to please. But his mother and two of his sisters could have come out of Goya's paintings. They were beautiful and virile women.

The long-standing acclimatization into their host countries has left its mark on Jews of different countries, affecting their appearance and behaviour. Such acclimatization has made some Jews look and behave in an unJewish way. My uncle, the civil servant whom I have already mentioned, was a blatant example of this. He looked and behaved like an old-fashioned German rather than a Jew. Yet he was a remarkable member of his race. He showed outstanding courage when he was incarcerated in Auschwitz, where he gave comfort and help to his fellow inmates in the concentration camp. I only heard by chance of his exemplary behaviour about two years ago.

My father loved beauty, had a thirst for education and travel, and looked on money as a means to an end. My mother, who admired the educated classes, had probably been frustrated in her marriage from the start, because her first love had been an intellectual cousin of hers, a professor of medicine. Her original make-up may have been quite different from the personality she later became. She seemed to be depressed, and in a permanent state of anxiety, particularly after her two brothers had committed suicide during the First World War. No wonder that she appeared to be withdrawn, and was rarely demonstrative in her affection for us children. Her perpetual worry about money made her keen to accumulate more and more in order to be safe. She could never rest, and didn't want my father to idle his life away. She drove him on to be busy and improve his position. While he didn't care if other members of the family were more successful, she hated to be the poorer relation. My father's younger brother had become a rich man, which my mother thoroughly resented.

In March 1913, my parents rented a six-room flat in the Fleischergasse, No. 60, and my heart leapt with joy. How little did I know then about the irretrievable loss I would suffer through removal from my earliest roots! At almost the same time, another change was in the air for me. I entered the Viktoria Schule, which was well known for its high standard of teaching. Its forbidding exterior dated back to the early nineteenth century, when public buildings looked like a mixture of church and workhouse. But the courtyard where the pupils ate their sandwiches during a break between lessons was as pleasant as the classrooms were gloomy. My new abode in the Fleischergasse was only a stone's throw away from the school. Things fitted, and it seemed preordained that I should become a pupil at the famous grammar school at the time of our move. I entered the 'sexta', which is the lowest form. But Latin was already a principal subject. From the sexta to the prima, with two years in the secunda, school took a good slice out of one's life, six years if all went well. I was lucky enough to manage it in the appointed time.

The die was cast, and it seemed as if the stars smiled favourably on me. They did and they did *not*. They were double-faced. I was happy enough at school, but felt more and more uneasy at home. I missed Riesenburg terribly. We now spent every summer holidays at Bad Flinsberg in Silesia. We had healthy and exciting times there, but the void left by Riesenburg could not be filled by any substitute. Flinsberg was a well-known spa, lying at a height of about 600 metres, close to the Bohemian frontier. The town was surrounded by pine woods which perfumed the air. Most of the visitors, ourselves included, stayed in villas, made invisible by overgrown gardens. Oldish ladies of slender means took in paying guests to make ends meet. We walked every morning through the gently ascending *Kurpark*, and promenaded up and down a covered colonnade, drinking the waters of the famous Flinsberg spring through a straw. They were recommended as a cure for rheumatism, anaemia, liver complaints and other ailments. To complete the 'cure', we took a *Fichtennadel Bad* (pine needle bath) twice weekly. They were an aromatic delight and, if nothing else, contributed to our *joie de vivre*. My mother became a different person on these holidays. She came to life. She had not given up the fight to reduce her weight, and climbed the surrounding mountains in the company of new acquaintances. This time I did not have to be coaxed to go with her. I loved these climbing tours over mountain meadows with flowers of pristine purity, and through the pass which led into Bohemia. I caught the excitement of crossing a frontier, and enjoyed the strange atmosphere of a café in the small Bohemian town, where we indulged in strong coffee and cherry tarts with whipped cream. The women who served there carried their corpulent bodies with poise and grace. They wore national costumes in bright colours which made them look even fatter than they were. Their black eyes sparkled with friendliness, and I stared at them as if they were overgrown dolls.

But every time before the long journey from Danzig to Flinsberg, I became ill through over-excitement, and the same happened before the return home. Yet these times brought me closer to my mother, who was at her best, and showed unbridled affection to my sister and me. The nervous tension she aroused in me was forgotten, but it came back in the old surroundings. I felt out of sympathy with the business talks between my parents, mostly instigated by her. They dominated their conversation, particularly at meal times. I remained silent, ate quickly, and escaped as soon as possbile to my room. I wanted to be away, not to hear or see 'them'. They had changed. Their minds had shrunk because their interests had contracted with the loss of a booming business, their house and home. They must have had great difficulties in adaptation: my father to his dream of leisure, my mother to reduced circumstances. She could not reconcile herself to not being as well off as before. The differences between my parents now became unbridgeable. My mother's pride was hurt not only because of narrowed circumstances, but she also suffered from being a 'nobody' in Danzig whereas she had been a highly esteemed citizen in Riesenburg.

My busy life with my aunt in Danzig had not allowed much time for friends. But after my parents' arrival, and our move to a flat close to my new school, things were different. Before that time, my contacts with other pupils were negligible, which increased my nostalgia for Riesenburg, and might have prevented me from making new friends. Now I looked outwards. Soon after entering the Viktoria Schule, I felt much attracted to a Jewish girl in my form, and longed to be with her in and out of class. She had a slim and elegant figure, but was dressed poorly. There was nothing in her demeanour and appearance which diverged from the conventional, except an adult attitude of reserve. She never spoke of herself, and seemed to have little to say otherwise. She either couldn't say No or didn't want to, when I begged her to let us meet outside school. And so I also got to know her family. My friend's mother had been widowed soon after her birth. She was an intelligent woman. A three-room flat in a ramshackle house in the Altstädtischen Graben, a poor quarter of Danzig, underlined

24

the depressing atmosphere of their existence. Yet both my friend and her mother had the poise and manners of people who had seen better days. The mother worked as a secretary, and an elder brother lived with an uncle in Berlin. Lotte E. and I spent many afternoons in the flat. I wanted to hold her hand and kiss her. She said nothing, but submitted. Why had I fallen for her? She was no beauty, with her mousey hair, expressionless green eyes, and a thin mouth which had forgotten how to laugh. And her receding chin added to the attributes of a weak person. Yet I never forgot her, even when I fell in love again a year or two later with Ida, a Russian Jewess, who had the delicate freckled skin of the red haired and the gait of a Siamese cat.

What a difference between these two! Ida's high cheek bones and large grey eyes were characteristically Russian, as was her mouth with its protruding lips which seemed to chew words more thoroughly than did those of German people, and attracted the eye to the lower part of her face. It was like the full stop to a phrase, a definite statement made. I wanted to be in her arms, kiss her, sleep with her, without having any thought as to how or where or when. At the same time I became infatuated with another younger girl at school, whom I searched out during the breaks, which pupils spent in the courtyard. No older than thirteen, she already had a musician's face, with her tightly-drawn skin and a finely-cut nose. Her high forehead dominated her face, which had an altogether transparent look. Her father was a well-known physician, and his daughter's ambition encompassed both medicine and music. I looked out for her, passed her house not far from the Fleischergasse, hoping to meet her, but never dared to speak of my feelings to her. Was it or was it not accidental that every one of my early loves was Jewish? I relate it to the wider context – a natural compatibility of minds. But the centre of my life was Ida, sixteen years old, three years older than myself. It so happened that her parents had taken a flat for the summer season in Zoppot, and invited me there for weekends. Ida was the image of her mother whom I admired, not only because of the resemblance, but also for her generosity of spirit in permitting us all we wanted, and her gift for preparing delicious Russian food. And perhaps I liked her because she was so different from my own mother, always equable, smiling and well dressed. There was never a quarrel in their house. Father, who neither spoke nor appeared to listen, could have been deaf and dumb. He occupied

25

himself with playing patience every day and all day long. He occasionally smiled at us, and ate his wife's delicious *gefüllte Fische*, warm for lunch and cold for supper.

One never knows the real reason why one is attracted to a person or a family. It might have been their humanity and the warmth of the family life of Russian Jews, which was extended to the friends of their children. The Russian Jews I got to know were self-confident because they had not lost their Jewish identity. I compared them favourably with my relatives and Jewish acquaintances who thought of themselves as *Germans*. Neither Ida nor I had ever heard of the term homosexuality, nor did we know anything about love between people of the same sex. We experienced our attraction without fear or label, and had no model for love-making. We just loved. Kissing produced the greatest excitement, and we kissed at any hour. When we slept together our legs were entwined, while our two mouths moulded into one. These were probably the happiest nights of all my days. We had no fear, no sense of guilt, and our parents, well aware of our attachment, either did not see anything extraordinary in it, or did not let us know if they did. They were perhaps as innocent as we were. Later on I realized that my parents knew of my love for women. They never questioned me about it, but accepted me as I am. Their attitude was contrary to everything the Old Testament and the Talmud teach about unorthodox sex. Even to this day, orthodox Jewish men give thanks in their prayers that God has made them male and not female. This puts the male chauvinism of orthodox Jews into a nutshell. They live emotionally in in Middle Ages, still believing that the old prayer reflects the true position of male and female. But liberal Jews had, already then, quite a different attitude. My parents and relatives would have found such outmoded beliefs an insult to nature. In Wilhelminian Germany, Jews lived a free life, acquired a good education, and many followed cultural pursuits, distinguishing themselves in the arts and sciences. The old-fashioned orthodox Jew was to them redolent of the ghetto; they looked on him as an alien. My parents had no qualms about the sex of their children. It never entered their heads that there should be a different education for girls and boys. They wanted us to have the best possible schooling and to go to university if we wished. Many Jewish families had the same approach, and it was not surprising that a great number of female university students were Jewish.

26

My happiness with Ida, however, did not help me to accept the life I had to lead with my parents. While I was fully aware of their understanding and affection for me, I was repelled by their materialism. I felt contempt for the world of business, which I thought of as a form of thieving. The family of my Russian friend was so different. They were idealists of a sort, people who had gone through persecution without being morally diminished. On the contrary, they had grown through it. They had the 'right' values. They knew how little material possessions meant because they had been deprived of them. They had escaped from pogroms in Russia and Poland, and their sufferings had given them a sweet melancholy and open-handedness which was apparent in their faces, their gestures and their actions. Humanity came first. They did not bend the knee before the God of Mammon, yet they knew their trade and business. They had a surprising gift of adapting themselves to a new life, and always seemed to fall on their feet and land in comfortable circumstances.

One day Ida showed me an album of photographs, and pointed to one of a striking-looking girl who had been her best friend in Odessa, their old home. I was struck by her face. She had dark hair and an unusually high brow, large black eyes, a Mona Lisa smile, and a sensuous mouth, redolent of an oriental woman. I asked Ida whether her friend's family had Asian blood. 'No, they are Russian Jews. Lisa's father has remained in Russia, but she lives in Berlin with her mother, a brother and a sister. She is very clever.'

The photograph evoked in me the image of Dostoyevsky's Nastasia Filipovna, a woman to dream about. I had by then read most of his novels, and had devoured *The Idiot* many times. I had fallen for Nastasia, one of the most attractive women ever depicted in fiction. I didn't reveal to my friend how I felt about the photograph. She was the re-incarnation of my female ideal. But Lisa was not fiction, she was alive, a ten hours' train journey away from Danzig. And (D.V.) I would meet her one day. The idea made me wild with ecstasy. From that day on I began to live a double life. I only 'existed' in my own surroundings. I lived mechanically as a schoolgirl in Danzig, while my real life was in my imagination. I day-dreamed of meetings and conversations with Lisa. I fantasized about her day and night with a burning excitement. I sought solitude more than ever because I wanted to be alone with my dream love. But I went on seeing Ida, and tried not to reveal my change of feeling towards her. As time went on, my dream of passion made me ill. I suffered from indigestion, palpitations and migraine, the psychosomatic symptoms of emotional disturbance.

My parents never thwarted the ambitions of their children, and showed understanding of my particular need for solitude. They allowed me to occupy a tiny room looking towards the street, which was the furthest away from the rest of the family. The door to it was a 'Sesam öffne Dich'. I did my daily homework as quickly as possible so as to be free for my dreams, for reading philosophy and poetry, and for writing poems myself.

I still spent a great deal of time with my Russian friend. However, the difficult situation between us was resolved through her departure from Danzig. Her family went to Stockholm during the First World War. How they could choose such a time and actually get to Sweden was a puzzle to me and many others. Although her departure left me with an emotional void, it had liberated me. I don't know how I managed to make my fantasy life fit in with the routine of school and home. But I had acquired the skill to manipulate my parents to leave me to my own devices. They didn't ask questions and let me go my own way,wherever it might lead. I was touched by their trust in me and grateful for it. It may have been loneliness that gave school at that time a new meaning and value. I was keen to acquire knowledge and I learned fast. My teachers saw a promising pupil in me. A special relationship developed between two of them and myself, which became a new focus of interest at school. My Latin teacher, Dr Maynard, must have been surprised and pleased to notice my eagerness to learn the language which my classmates found a bore. He seemed to favour me in a rather clumsy fashion. The class was inclined to ridicule him as a queer and an eccentric. I felt sympathy and admiration for his 'gauche' behaviour. When, one day, he invited me to visit him at home, I had no doubt that I meant more to him than other pupils. I imagined that we were birds of a feather, united by an unspoken bond. He talked to me as an equal, discussing philosophy and education with me. I was proud of the interest he took in me, but he did not touch my emotions. Romana Haberfeld, my teacher of German literature, awoke quite different feelings. I admired her mentality and imaginative power, which fed her pupils with a rare understanding of German and foreign literature. She was a rather thick-set woman, broad-shouldered and sinewy, who walked like a moving stature. The class stood up in an instant when she entered. Her poise and authority made us listen with complete attention and open-mouthed admiration. Not only I, but most of my peers, wanted to please her. When she spoke in her husky voice and her blue eyes lighted up, the drab surroundings of the schoolroom vanished. I was not only immersed in listening to her words, but was intently looking at the strange beauty of her face. Her black hair grew abundantly over a rather short brow, and her full red mouth had a quiver of sensuous enjoyment when she spoke of Lenau, Brentano, *die Günderrode*, or the songs of the troubadours. She was a creative teacher, whose every word had the flavour of something not heard before. She attracted me like Konrad Lorenz attracted his orphan geese, which followed him everywhere as if he were their mother. I promenaded the street where she lived during afternoons or evenings, hoping against hope to see her. Was it calf love, the crush of a girl for her teacher? Stereotyped interpretations of any kind of love are as erroneous as they are condescending. They totally miss the point. The erotic love of a pupil for a teacher of the same sex is a natural passion on which much of the culture of ancient Greece depended. At any time in history, girls and boys who experienced this nostalgic longing for an older and wiser person have been graced by the gods. They have found a model of *being* which can mould their future. It can set the trend for their social behaviour, their moral values and aesthetic tastes. I never forgot Romana Haberfeld: her face, her low brow, her proud gait. And when I read about her in Günter Grass' *From the Diary of a Snail*, old feelings returned. Grass described her as one of those unusual women who never abandoned their post. Like every other public servant, Romana Haberfeld had been dismissed by the Nazis from the Viktoria Schule in 1933. But she went on teaching in Danzig, by then part of Nazi Germany. She had joined another teacher of her race, Ruth Rosenbaum, who had founded a private Jewish High School on the outskirts of the city in 1934. It was, of course, closed by the Nazis in 1939. Ruth Rosenbaum got out of the country and emigrated to Israel. She settled in Haifa where Grass visisted her. But his tale does not report what happened to Romana Haberfeld. One fears the worst.

My love for Romana Haberfeld and my affection for Dr Maynard, so different in quality and intensity, had something in common: I never forgot either of them. Memory is stimulated

29

through emotion and strong feelings. That is why I recall these teachers and not my classmates, who left me cold. But there was still another teacher, a Fräulein Böse (angry), who intrigued me enough not to forget her personality. She taught French and taught it so well that it enabled me to translate Baudelaire's *Les Fleurs du Mal* into German several years later. Fräulein Böse's facial expression did justice to her name. She looked like a warrior, always at the ready to slay an enemy. I never saw her smile. Her lips, tightly pressed together, and her furrowed brow, signified a burdened mind unable to shake off unpleasant preoccupations. She avoided personal contact with her pupils, yet she was one of the best teachers at the Viktoria Schule. Her enigma, her reserve, her obvious isolation, impressed me as much as her method of teaching. Sometimes her eyes seemed to rest on me for a moment, but as soon as I imagined I had caught her glance, she looked away.

I had also created a life of my own in the room away from the family. It was a room with a view. I looked out on the ancient Franziskaner Kloster, dating back to the fourteenth century, which had been transformed into a grammar school for boys. Though young life had invaded the quietness of the beautiful building, it had not disturbed its ancient atmosphere. In spite of the noise of boisterous boys, the splendour of this medieval monument spoke through its stillness. A long colonnade led into the cloister. I could see it from my window on the second floor, though it was almost hidden by several rows of copper birches.

Not long after my Russian friend had left Danzig, we moved from the Fleischergasse to Langgarten, and this change meant the loss of a beautiful and quiet place, which had been a cherished ivory tower. Our new abode in a modern house had a lift and other amenities, which were an advantage for my parents but of no interest to me. Langgarten was a wide and busy street on the outskirts of town. A tram, linking the Werder Tor with the Danziger Hauptbahnhof, passed through the street. We were very close to the pastures of the Werder, a stretch of land with rich arable fields, fruit trees and well-fed cattle. However, I had some compensations for the loss of the Fleischergasse. My new room was again as far away as possible from those of my parents and sister. And my new surroundings also gave me a new field of exploration and experience. We lived near the Langebrücke which was one of Danzig's most ancient streets. It ran alongside the river Motlau, and became the focus of attraction for many solitary walks I started to indulge in at that time. On one side of the Langebrücke stood ancient buildings, symbols of pride and power of the old Hansa town. The other side was occupied by large granaries and wharves, characteristic of Danzig's importance as a trading centre. And other treasures also unfolded themselves through our move. On my way to school I crossed the Langebrücke into the Langemarkt with its Renaissance *Börse*, (Stock Exchange) and other famous buildings of the sixteenth century. The Langemarkt was an architectural jewel of historical significance. Its patrician houses were among the finest examples of Danzig's ancient buildings. Some were privately owned, others converted into business premises.

My way to school was paved with aesthetic treasures of which I had not been aware. Before I reached adolescence, I had sensed distances rather than beauty. I was about sixteen when we moved to Langgarten, and it was then that I began to *see* what had previously passed me by. The opening of my eyes might have been the consequence of a strange experience which happened to me at that time. Before it occurred, I had neither much noticed the Langemarkt, nor the beauty of the fifteenth-century *Rathaus*, with its marvellous tower. I had been unaware of the elegance of the Langgasse which the *Rathaus* graced with such aplomb. This slightly curved street was Danzig's chief shopping centre. Patrician houses were interspersed with buildings of a later date, still imitating the old style. An exception, however, was the post office, which stood half-way down the Langgasse. It was in fact an eyesore. Danzig was a tightly-built town where space was at a premium, and many of its streets were called *Gassen* because of their narrowness. One of them crossed the Langgasse at the post office. A few yards from this crossing point I had an overwhelming experience. One might wonder how it was possible simultaneously to be in love with a teacher, dream passionately about a woman never seen in the flesh, and be physically attracted to younger girls at school. The capacity for emotional simultaneity is youth's privilege and pain. Youth and age make one wonder how much our emotions depend on our hormones. Yet they cannot explain everything, and I do not believe that my 'experience' could be traced to my endocrine make-up, though it might have had something to do with it. I was on my way to school, but on this day I went like a robot through town, unaware of my surroundings. Suddenly I had to stop for no reason whatever. I was unable to move. I had been taken over by an inner power such as I had never felt before. A sense of immeasurable happiness filled me. I breathed deeply and heavily, and in doing so my body appeared to change. I became taller than I really was, my hands, larger than before, stretched out with palms turned upwards. But the strangest sensation was that which affected my brow: I felt a bluish crystal just above my eyes at the root of my nose. I called it the amethyst. I have an amethyst in my head, I whispered to myself, crazy with joy. What had come over me? Where did this power which seized me come from? I felt the whole universe in my head. I had the sensation that I knew everything that had ever happened, and would come about in the future. My mind had become omniscient. I stood rooted to the ground on the right-hand side of the Rosengasse at the back of the post office. I noticed a number of carts in its backyard with their shafts turned upwards. The surroundings are as vivid to me as they were on the day when it all happened. I stood next to a jeweller's shop and noticed glittering stones in its window. I had gone far away from my former Self. Yet I was a pupil in the Secunda of the Viktoria Schule, and just on my way there. I vaguely remember that I reached the Hundgasse close by, but I have no idea whether or when I arrived at school, and I cannot recall how I behaved. My guess is that I behaved as I had always done, and that nobody noticed anything different about me. But everything *was* different from that time onward. The turbulence within me started a psychical revolution. I had never read esoteric literature, and the notion of the 'third eye' was unknown to me. Nor did I have any idea of changes in one's body-image, which can happen to adolescents. The experience was totally my own. I had no model, nor did I know of anyone having experienced anything like this. Powers unknown to me had revealed themselves. One does not know why one person can become sensitive to buried powers of the mind and others cannot. In *The Doors of Perception*, Aldous Huxley wrote about such unknown faculties of the mind which might be the key to the understanding of the event I had experienced. Alienation from one's surroundings, for which one compensates in fantasies of self-aggrandizement, can find physical expression in a change of body-image. One sees oneself as taller and bigger. But psychological explanations cannot do justice to the phenomenon. Endocrine function might throw some light on it. The pituitary which regulates growth could have a hand in the change of body-image, of feeling extended in size. The sense of happiness might be due to the androgenic hormones released through excitement. But these attempts at a rational explanation do not fill the bill. Something irrational *had* happened to me, similar to St Paul's shock on the way to Damascus. I had felt a 'cosmic' energy flowing through me: it made me one with the universe. This sounds high-faluting stuff, but that is how it was.

Although the experience had come out of the blue, it had its precursors. Many colourful stones may one day make a mosaic. And puberty is a phase when wonders happen to a mind which is open, to a body which yearns for experience. A multi-coloured love life, and the alienation from my parents, might have engendered an implosion in the mind at the time of endocrine hyperactivity. But why try to explain a miracle and thus divest it of the miraculous?

Up to that time I had not seen the beauty of Danzig, though it must have affected ny unconscious mind. I had walked through the Grüne Tor which led from the Lengemarkt onto the Langebrücke, and not seen its sixteenth-century grandeur. I had often looked at the Artushof, built in Renaissance style with the Neptune fountain in front, without taking in what I saw. But there had been one exception. When I was still in the care of Tante Auguste, my sister and I used to stand stock-still at the *Rathaus*, waiting for the tram to take us back to Pfefferstadt. The *Rathaus* tower housed a famous clock. When the hours struck, the chimes played a well-known hymn. At the same time one or other of the four Apostles appeared in front of the clock. They came out from their hidden place at the upper part of the tower onto a small balcony, dressed in beautiful colours. We loved these marionettes in the sky, and tried to come back from Dr Wolff's Orthopaedic Institute at the right time to watch them and hear the hymns. The chimes went on with their musical performance as long as I knew my Danzig, long after the Apostles had ceased to cheer us. Back in the tram to the Pfefferstadt we passed many of Danzig's highlights. The driver enjoyed ringing a bell when going full speed, but made a decisive sound at the stops. One was at the Langgasser Tor at the other end of the Langgasse. As we went through it we could just peep at a passage adjoining it, which housed Danzig's finest flower shop. After that we passed the fifteenth-century *Stockturm* on the Kohlenmarkt, a grim place which had once been a dungeon. But that was a long time ago. Its lower part had been made into a large hall which accommodated second-hand bookshops. Then we drove past Freymann's stores and stopped at the ugly Danziger Stadt Theater. The ancient Arsenal between these two modern nonentities was well set back from the street. It seemed far away in its sixteenth-century splendour, looking grim and threatening. But as a child I had hardly noticed Danzig's famous buildings. The tram went with a swoop into the Holzmarkt, passing close to the Kriegerdenkmal on a green square in the centre. The Holzmarkt was a crossing point of many streets. At one corner stood the town's best pharmacy, with green bottles of enormous size in the window, a symbol of alchemy rather than medicine. We did not pass the pharmacy, as the tram made a sharp turn to the left into the Stadtgraben, a newly-built street with the headquarters of the military Commandant of Danzig, General von Mackensen. He *was* a picture of a soldier, and I was duly impressed when I saw him in the flesh. He could have come out of a fairy-tale – in his Hussar uniform with gold epaulettes, gold stripes and an enormous fur hat. His white moustache blended with his water-blue eyes. He greatly distinguished himself as Hindenburg's right-hand man in the First World War. He became Head of the General Staff. It was he who had the brains while Hindenburg held the final command. Danzig rewarded Mackensen for his outstanding service by making him an honorary citizen of the town.

On our four journeys a day, we sped along the lengthy Stadtgraben as if in a particular hurry to reach the terminus at the Hauptbahnhof. A few steps from there was Pfefferstadt, my aunt's abode. Children's capacity for work, pleasure and every kind of change cannot be measured on an adult scale. It is as different from that of grown-ups as their feeling and measure of time. We did not seem too tired after the day's doings when we returned late in the afternoon to do our homework for school.

We did not have enough time to talk to Tante Auguste and she had too much on her hands. She appeared to requite my affection for her. She saw in a flash when I had particularly enjoyed seeing the Apostles and listening to the chimes of the *Rathaus* clock. It was she who told me that a golden sculpture was placed at the very top of the tower. It was called the needle because it was as thin as one. It represented King Sigismund of Poland who held the flag with Danzig's coat of arms high in the air. He was the weathercock who indicated the direction of the winds, shown by the flutter of the flag in his hand.

When I was about twelve, the *Zeughaus* had come out of its glorious past into the modern present. I hadn't noticed it then, other than as a grim building not to be looked at. Now at sixteen or seventeen years old, I saw that the heavy portals were opened up, and the cannons and other weapons in the arsenal had either disappeared or were displayed as museum pieces. But the most amazing transformation had taken place inside the building. It had become a shopping centre. And when I lived with my parents in the Fleischergasse, walking every day through the St Trinidad's Kirchengasse to the Viktoria Schule, I had passed one of Danzig's oldest and most beautiful churches, that of St Trinidad, without being aware of it. It had stared me in the face when I looked out of the window of my little room, but I only saw the Franziskaner Kloster next to it. Why? Because it connected past and present; it was full of life and noise since it had become a grammar school for boys. Before we moved to Langgarten, I had not paid attention to the remarkable St Stephen's house on the Langemarkt, with its gilded gables and sculptures, a piece of sixteenth-century Danzig to be proud of. No, the blindness of youth, concentrated on its personal wants and dreams, could not look outwards, except when some sensational impression pierced it. The scales over my eyes had fallen away after my strange experience, and I became alive to the unique architecture of old Danzig. From then on I found the company of my schoolmates unbearable. I had never taken to them anyway, and had, from an early age, loathed giggling girls and their conversation about teachers and boys. Now I felt like a being from another world, imprisoned in a wrong society. Only my love for Miss Haberfeld and affection for Dr Maynard enabled me to play the game of an adolescent girl when I was in fact an adult. My feelings towards my parents had been ambivalent since our reunion in Danzig, and I had been unable to share with them or my sister any emotional experience, nor talk of my poetry. Yet the alienation filled me with guilt and regret because of our former closeness. My sister had played a comparatively small part in my childhood, and for long periods I had hardly noticed her. Yet there was a bond between us, stronger on her side than mine. She proved it through a generous act which could have brought her into difficulties with my parents. It showed me up as selfish and her as loving. From that time on, I held her dear, and confided in her.

Since my experience I seemed further away from my milieu than ever. I walked on 'wings', and my elation made me well disposed even towards people whom I didn't particularly like. And outside circumstances helped to re-establish a better contact with my parents. The wholesale grocery business which my father had joined occupied much of his time. My mother also involved herself in the enterprise, together with her brother's young wife Recha. The two women had a better business acumen than their husbands, who admitted that the good trade figures were due to their advice and initiative. Recha and my mother saw eye to eye and became friends. The family atmosphere became more relaxed and at times as cosy as in earlier days. Now we were well off again, which pleased my mother, but she still could not get over her resentment of my father's younger brother. His exquisite house and furniture and his great wealth still irked her. She resented his overpowering personality, and saw as little as possible of him and my aunt. It was true that Uncle Josef did lay down the law, and showed condescension towards my father who had not quite 'made it'. His wife, a tall, thin woman with greying hair, was amused by her husband's overbearing personality, and listened to his 'wisdom', tongue in cheek. She did not seem to notice my mother's antagonism, or did not care. She attracted me not only as superior in manners to Uncle Josef, but also through her elegance, her reserve, and her literary interests. My mother disliked her less than her husband, and made up her own jokes about my uncle on whom his wife could look down. He was a small and sturdy man with a prominent chin, a large mouth and a deep voice. His clever brown eyes scrutinized his surroundings in a flash. He rightly claimed to know people when he saw them; his insight into character traits was uncanny. Though a stockbroker by profession, his great interest was music. He went to almost every concert, and had learned to play the flute, an accomplishment which he cherished but seldom exhibited. He had joined the Freemasons, which accounted for his wide circle of acquaintances from different strata of society. I never knew how my aunt Bertha fitted with his gregariousness, but they appeared to be a harmonious couple, living an enviable life with their two children in a beautiful house. On my frequent walks through Danzig, which became a cherished escape after my 'experience', I often passed through the Frauengasse and called on my aunt. She seemed to welcome my visits. She greeted me in her calm and undemonstrative way, but with a smile and a friendly glance in her eyes. We had no small talk, but discussed books and the future. Once she surprised me by asking my advice about one of her children. Her son, four years my junior, caused her much anxiety. He grimaced and was fidgety, and obstinately refused to go to school. I suggested that Dr Freyhan might be the best person to advise her. He had helped me, and recognized the psychological origin of my trouble. She consulted the doctor who couldn't explain her son's symptoms to her, but assured her that there was no question of mental illness. My cousin remained a charmer and a problem child right into adulthood. But the physician's diagnosis had relieved my aunt of the fear that the boy might be psychotic.

The style of life in the Frauengasse had caught my imagination, and engaged me in a pleasant relationship with an older woman who could have been my mother. My aunt either guessed or knew how I felt about Romana Haberfeld, through intuition or a chance remark which might have given me away. She had heard about her as one of Danzig's outstanding teachers. When she told me that she too had been emotionally attached to a teacher in her teens, I spoke more freely to her than before, and she became more forthcoming and lively. But I could not bring myself to tell her that I wrote poetry, for fear that she too might have the prevalent idea that a poet is a social freak. Poetry had been my world since early puberty. I began to write poems at the age of about twelve, modelling myself on the romantics: Heine, Lenau, Novalis and Brentano. Only several years later did I start to find my own voice. Inspired by the Old Testament, I wrote poems on Israel's prophets before I really came into my own, writing from personal experience. I needed a spiritual framework in my uneasy adolescence which the Bible, books on eastern religions, and philosophy provided.

Days of conception cannot be definitely known; therefore one celebrates birthdays. Making tangible events significant is a crude method of verification. It omits a whole world of possibilities. One cannot fathom the fine threads of the web our unconscious needs weave. In spite of frustrations, I lived my life there and then in a hypo-manic-depressive rhythm. I applied my energy to diverse activities and much day-dreaming. But the chasm between reality and fantasy was probably responsible for the precarious balance in my emotional and physical health. Wild swings of mood changed the emotional climate from euphoria to depression, from health to illness. Ever since the disappearance of Riesenburg from the horizon, I had felt the need for 'escape' and adventure to fill the void. It so happened that a health condition came to my aid. I had suffered from sinusitis since I was ten, and not only had to miss school all too often, but also had to undergo unpleasant treatment for it. The E.N.T. specialist flushed out my sinuses with an antiseptic, and the procedure left me weak for days.

My longing to meet Lisa led me in the end to plan a visit to Berlin by hook or by crook. One day I had an inspiration, and knew how to attack the problem. I made it clear to my parents that the sinus trouble gave me too much pain and nervous strain, and impeded my progress at school. I begged them to get a second opinion from an expert. My parents agreed, and a consultation with Dr Jansen of Berlin, a highly recommended specialist, was speedily arranged. On 10 January 1917 my mother and I travelled to Berlin. My mother took rooms in a pension in the Tauentzinstrasse, while I was received into Dr Jansen's clinic nearby. He advised an old wive's remedy – inhalations with camomile tea and linseed poultices. The flushings out had to be discontinued! I thought the result worth the journey, and my mother shared in my pleasure. I had told her of some correspondence about a meeting with Lisa, but didn't mention that a phone call to her house had been a setback. Lisa was in Munich, but expected to return on 12 January. By then I had moved into the pension where my mother was staying. My second phone call was answered by her. Yes, she would come to see me next day about 5 p.m. My mother left before that time to visit an aunt. I walked up and down our two adjoining rooms. Russians have little sense of time, and I was prepared to wait. But I was wrong. Lisa arrived punctually and, with a languid smile, reached out her hand, staring into my eyes. She was three years older than I, a vast difference at that time of life. I felt like a gawky schoolgirl confronted by an elegant Russian woman. She wore a black seal coat and a fur cap. She was a slightly-built woman of small size, and her head seemed too dominant in comparison. I only saw her face – and how I knew it! Those large, melancholy eyes were oriental eyes. But where did her high brow with its two bulbed prominences come from? This was the forehead of a thinker, reminding me of the sculpture by Rodin. It seemed an oddity in a beautiful woman's face. I couldn't take my eyes off her. Yes, the high cheek bones, her large mouth with dark-red lips, and a receding chin were in sharp contrast to the forehead, and a reassurance of her femaleness. How very Russian she looks, I thought. There she was in the flesh as I had imagined her: Nastasia Filipovna – born into reality. I had fallen in love with her photograph over two years ago – and now I was in love with *her*.

I don't know whether she was aware of what happened to me during this hour in the Tauentzinstrasse or not. I have no idea how she felt about me, except that she apparently wanted to know me. She had heard about me from our mutual friend Ida. She suggested that we should write to each other, and laughingly promised to be a faithful correspondent. The day of our meeting was the Russian New Year's Eve. She had to leave me soon after 6 p.m. in order to prepare for a party in their house. She came towards me, took both my hands, and kissed me on the forehead. And she was gone, as silently as a spirit. Had she been there? When my mother returned I spoke little, but I was beside myself with excitement. She behaved as I had always wanted her to behave. No questions, just: 'What shall we do tonight?' 'Let's go to a music hall,' I said. 'Fine,' she answered. We went to a *Bumslokal* close to the Nollendorfplatz, and stayed until midnight. Neither of us wanted to go to bed. Had she met her cousin instead of visiting the aunt? She looked lovely and happy, and I wondered! We listened to the vulgar music and jokes, and ate *Bockwurst* with Sauerkraut. It could have been salmon or caviare for all I cared. We were completely taken over by the noise and gaiety of the atmosphere, the beat of the hit tunes of the period. I had not felt so close to my mother since I could remember. Next day we went back to Danzig, and I was glad to get away, to find myself alone again with time to reflect. It was a visit with consequences. I went to school like an automaton, and only came to life in the lessons of my favourite teachers. I no longer did my homework properly.

Many letters were exchanged between Lisa and me, and a few months after our meeting she invited me to spend the summer holidays with her and her family. I would have a room nearby with friends, but take my meals with them. My parents had nothing against the project if that was what I wanted, and on a hot summer's day I took the express train to Berlin. Lisa awaited me at the Bahnhof Zoologischer Garten. The beginning of my holiday was different from any expectations I might have had. Any arrival in a new place is difficult for a nervous person, but how could I bridge the world I had left and the one I had come to, which was so different from all I knew? I probably never did. I was installed with the Russian friends of Lisa's family, whose daughter Raja became a good companion immediately and a friend later on. Lisa showed herself to be reserved, playing a waiting game. It was not long before I realized that she had a cruel streak. She teased me about my provincial clothes and long hair. 'You look like a schoolgirl,' she told me. I was hurt and bewildered by her attitude, but her family fascinated me from the start. They were like people out of a novel. Her mother, an inscrutable woman, left her three children to their devices while she pursued her own. Her brother, Grischa, a pupil of Busoni, belonged to a circle of artists and littéateurs. Some of them came to the house and seemed interested to make contact with me. Grischa always introduced me as *his* friend. One of his favourites was Walter Mehring, an attractive youth with swift-moving eyes and black hair, one lock of which always fell over his brow. He gesticulated wildly with his hands, which constantly went through his hair as if to keep it in check. He amused me as much with his rapid speech as with his witty and acid asides. Not all his words could be grasped; they chased each other, as if he was afraid he might be stopped midway.

Lisa and I were awkward with each other. After the intimacy of the letters and the poems I had sent her, I felt at a loss in the new situation. It was for her to handle it. She was probably as stunned as I, and we had to play an emotional hide and seek which left me exhausted. She had that hypnotic power of many Russian women who leave one stunned by a mystique which surrounds them like an aura. I had, however, sense enough not to cling to her. Every morning I walked alone or with Raja down the Kurfürstendamm to the Café des Westens, one of the two famous haunts of artists and writers; the other was the Romanische Café next to the Gedächtniskirche. One day Raja and I were joined at our round marble table by an older woman in trousers. She had a sensitive face, which was lined but still beautiful, and her black hair was cut in an Eton crop. I had seen her face, drawn by herself, inside her book of poems. She was Else Lasker-Schüler. I found her glamorous and strange, and though I was flattered that she spoke to me, I felt no shyness with her. I told her how much I liked her poetry. Had she heard what I said, I wondered? Her eyes flitted around the café as if in constant search of something she would never find. Her forehead bore a persistent frown. In the days which followed I used to go back to the Café des Westens alone. Every time she came to my table and spoke to me of her son. Was he the person she looked out for so anxiously? She certainly worried about him. She had the odd idea that I should correspond with him. 'You would be good for him,' she said. I really didn't understand the whys and hows of a proposition without any foundation. I told her I couldn't write to anyone I hadn't seen, and she didn't even know if her son would fall in with her wish. 'You must meet,' she decided. We did, and disliked each other on sight, both of us being determined to have nothing to do with the other. He must have told her that he didn't like me, and would not engage in a correspondence with me. And so she dropped the idea, but remained friendly with me for some years. My acquaintance with Else Lasker-Schüler broke some ice with Lisa. After a week or so, we spent most of the day together, and used to walk arm in arm up the Kurfürstendamm to the local police station, where, as an enemy alien, she had to report daily. And many a time she took me to Willy Jäckel's studio. This overgrown boy with the small head of a Great Dane was strangely inarticulate in conversation. He had already made his name as an expressionist. He showed me some of his paintings, never turning his small blue eyes away from Lisa. He was obsessed with her. His equally tall, platinum blonde wife, who could talk articulately and with much sense, provided the right atmosphere of a well trained hostess. She too seemed under Lisa's spell. When I saw the portrait Jäckel had painted of my friend, I became a fan of his. I thought it one of the finest examples of his art. He had painted her as an oriental version of the Mona Lisa, with a large red mouth, a dark-coloured face, and a white forehead which stood out through its height and contrasting colour. The picture was acquired by the Kunsthalle of Hamburg. I wonder if it has survived the autos-da-fé of the thirties. Lisa appeared to be far more friendly with his wife than with Jäckel. I felt that she was afraid of him. After two weeks or so we had made some way towards each other, that is, when we were outside her house, which was constantly invaded by people. I never felt at ease with her there, and remained bewildered by the variety of the visitors I met. It was Russian mystery all over: there

41

was Lisa's special friend and teacher, the sculptor Lis Gleistein, who mixed well with writers, students of philosophy and journalists. They came to see Lisa and her brother Grischa. On the other hand, I frequently met German officers who were invited to dinner. They came to see her mother. They were as courteous and charming in behaviour as they were intelligent in conversation. Why were they there? But I had ceased to be surprised or particularly bewildered by my unusual experiences.

After five weeks of an extraordinary holiday in Berlin, I returned to Danzig, physically and mentally exhausted. I remained floating in a twilight state for a long time, but my ordinary life went on mechanically. There was still a war on; the Kaiser had abdicated and Germany was in uproar. Some handwritten notices fixed into wooden frames on corner houses in a few streets had reminded me of the war which I had not been conscious of most of the time. I had mainly noticed it in the rationing and deterioration of food. Chickens always had an *haut-goût*, bread contained carrots and swedes apart from other unidentifiable ingredients. Real coffee was unobtainable, and a brew made from plants or even weeds was served as 'ersatz'. But the black market flourished and provided butter, cream and meat if one could pay for it.

Soon after my return from Berlin, Lisa invited me to spend the Christmas holidays with her. On 20 December 1917, I went back to say adieu to her because I had been asked to come before she returned with her mother and sister to Russia – by then a Communist state. This time my parents were set against my journey, and refused to finance an adventurous undertaking which had made me ill the first time round. But they couldn't keep me back. My sister offered me her savings to pay for the holiday. I accepted her generous gift. For some months past, I had taken daily small sums from my mother's purse. The problem was solved. I had enough money to see me through. I departed secretly. Lisa awaited me once more at the station Zoologischer Garten. But this time she embraced me fervently. I stayed with the same friends in the Konstanzerstrasse, but I didn't walk every day to the Café des Westens as before. Lisa called in the morning to take me to a quiet *Konditorei*, where we sat for hours, talking, laughing and looking at each other. The war was not yet over, but Lisa was preparing to go back to Russia, in spite of the Communist revolution. How her mother could face the new Russia was a greater puzzle than her own difficulty in adapting to a Communist state. Lisa neither mentioned any problem which this change in her life obviously entailed, nor did she speak of her father and his whereabouts. She behaved with that excited liveliness which masks despair. 'Let's live for the day!' she told me. When she reclined on her Récamier sofa, she pulled me close, and kissed me over and over again. New Year's Eve came and was celebrated at Lisa's home with her family, the Jäckels and other friends. Lisa's mother could have worn a tiara, the way she looked and behaved. One could not think of her in the new Russia. Lisa's brother, Grischa, on the other hand, had not put on an act. He was his melancholic self. We drank mulled wine, and melted lead into odd shapes from which we 'read' our fortunes. This was a typical German custom. A scrap of the metal hit my left thumb when Jäckel tried his luck. I still have the scar which I wear like a decoration. At the same time we had to concentrate on our heart's wish. Nobody was allowed to know what it was so as not to spoil the magic. My one and only wish was to have my mouth on Lisa's, then and there – and always. For me the kiss was the height of delight, the height of erotic lust, which reverberated through the body and stayed in the mind.

A few days after the feast I had to leave, as my school holidays were over. Lisa and I could not say adieu. We thought of the separation as unreal. I left her at the station with an odd quietude, waving when the train pulled out. When I arrived at a large crossing point midway between Berlin and Danzig, I jumped out and boarded the train on the other side of the platform, which took me back to her. My unexpected return was a sensation. Lisa treated me like a worshipping lover, and we were inseparable during the three extra days my adventure had secured. When we finally had to part, she whispered in my ear: 'You are the person I love.' I went away dazed, and did not feel a sense of loss – then. I had wired my parents that I could not return in time because of a cold. I felt just as uneasy about the lie as about their reaction to my flight. I was back in Danzig three days after school had started. My sister fetched me from the station, and when we arrived at Langgarten my parents were so pleased that I was safe and well that my escapade was not even mentioned. My sister became my closest friend from that time until her early death.

Lisa had gone but her brother remained in Berlin. He was my only link with her for many years to come. I went on as before with my life in Danzig, much helped by my Aunt Bertha. She thought that I suffered from lethargy due to low vitality. She sent me several bottles of port of which I was to drink daily a small glassful with a beaten egg. Aunt Bertha's diagnosis was not on target. I had started a new life with a heightened output of poetry. In fact, I didn't know how to find enough outlets for an emotional pitch which made me restless at home, inattentive at school, bored and boring with other people. At that time I really began to *know* Danzig. Many of Danzig's *Gassen* illustrated its history, their names being related to medieval German guilds. Craftsmen and traders had been clustered together according to their occupation. The public buildings and patrician houses gave a picture of Danzig's historical significance in the world at large. The most outstanding was the *Arthushof*, which reflected signal phases of the town's fortunes since the fifteenth century. Its functions had changed over the centuries. It had first been a *Trinkhalle*, then a court of justice, and finally the stock exchange. The façade, a mixture of Italian Renaissance and German Gothic, seemed right for this nothern metropolis. The painted ceiling of the entrance hall was northern in concept. Each painting was in its own frame, and represented mainly sea- and landscapes. An enormous *Kachelofen* filled one corner of the entrance hall from floor to ceiling. It was an outstanding work of art with tiles, into each of which was moulded a miniature sculpture of a warrior, a sailor or a beautiful woman. A winding staircase with wooden sculptures on each side led to an ornate gallery, with symbols of Danzig's great times as a Hansastadt. Models of different kinds of sailing vessels were reminders that corn and timber had been shipped from Danzig to many parts of the world. I had passed the *Arthushof* every day on my way to school, but now I looked *into* it at leisure on my private walks. I have always wondered if the name of Frauengasse had something to do with prostitution. It was so close to the Marienkirche, and a small pathway called the Pfaffengasse led from the church into it. I never liked to be close to the Marienkirche, and was inclined to turn my back on it. Yet I admired this majestic building because of its history. It had taken 300 years, on and off, to complete and was regarded as the most outstanding church, not only of Danzig but of Germany. But it could just as well have ornamented another big German town, for it was not as typical of Danzig as the *Gassen* and its patrician buildings were. They were unique in layout and style, and their façades had not changed since the Middle Ages. The Marien-kirche has not only stood the test of time, but also the nefarious destruction of bombs, while most of Danzig was wiped out in the Second World War. It is to the credit of the Polish Government that it has re-created the town in its old image, and the illusion is virtually identical with reality. The photograph of my uncle's house reproduced here in the illustrated section is, however, the real thing: it was taken before the war. It shows the craftsmanship of the stonemason of the seventeenth century, and is an example of the narrow patrician houses adorned with unique *Beischlägen*. Those were reached from the street by a few stone steps, at each side of which stood a delicately sculptured column. Iron banisters, elegantly curved, led up to the walls of the *Beischläge*. The relief of a female figure is sculpted on that of my uncle's house and its rain pipe releases its contents through a dolphin's mouth. The *Beischläge* occupied so much space that no room was left for pavements. One could shake hands across the street with people from the opposite houses. There was no room for heavy traffic, which was an attractive feature. I loved the Frauengasse, and I loved my uncle's house, with its narrow spiral staircase leading to the living quarters of my Salfeld cousins. Climbing a few steps higher, one entered a small ante-chamber covered with a Persian carpet, and tapestries hanging from the walls. It led to a spacious dining room, furnished with Danzig's heavy furniture, all in black. The chairs with high and beautifully carved backs stood around a heavy table. And a roomy black dresser with similar wood carv-ings leaned against the wall. The floor above contained an enormous bedroom for the whole family, and a small nursery for the two children. Two maids slept in the attic above. When I was about six years old my parents took us children for a short holiday to Danzig. I slept two or three nights in the family's bedroom in the Frauengasse. My parents and sister were accommodated elsewhere. But I was privileged to share with them the exposed intimacy of sleep, which might have been the beginning of my later relationship with Aunt Bertha.

How much of glamour and inspiration the street and the house provided for me! On my exploratory walks, I used to go through the Frauentor onto the Langebrücke, proceed along the Motlau until I came to one of Danzig's great curiosities – the Krahntor. Once seen never forgotten. It was a mixture of fortress and gran-ary. It had a tilted roof of triangular shape which stuck out like a nose over the Motlau. An enormous anchor on an iron chain like a butcher's hook picked up the wares from ships. It hurled them up into a storing place from where they were transported inland. The Krahntor was both instrument and symbol of Danzig's commercial power. Its lower part built in stone could have been a dungeon. It very likely was. It made me call the Krahntor a beautiful guillotine.

Further on, the Langebrücke became more and more vulgar without losing its spice. When I came to the Häker Tor I changed course, and passed through it to the Häkergasse, a poor and rather forbidding street. Many orthodox Jews lived there in a kind of ghetto. One saw men with long black kaftans and flat broad hats, which they wore in summer and winter. They had locks of hair hanging down the sides of their faces. They seemed to rush along, as if frightened, brushing the cobble stones rather than walking over them. They were like people on the run, looking inward and up to Jehova, but not at the world. I knew that part of the town well from shopping expeditions with my mother. She bought kosher sausages there, but disliked going into the butcher's shop alone.

After a glimpse into the eerie street, I hurried back to the Langebrücke and went to one of my favourite places – the Fischmarkt – where the Langebrücke ended with aplomb. Here was life in the raw. I stared at people who were the very opposite of my kind – the fishwives of Danzig. They were shouting and laughing, selling flounders, carp, hake and herrings. They sat on large stones in all seasons, and talked with a slang and wit of their own. They looked like prehistoric figures, all bosom, belly and bottom. Sometimes I saw them going in and coming out of a cabin-like snack bar. Then their high spirits rose even higher, and their small eyes, buried in their fat faces, cried with laughter. The Fischmarkt was the end of my walk along the river, and I would have been exhausted had my mind not composed lines of a poem, which generally happened on these promenades. Their rhythm moved my legs against fatigue and I got a second wind. I trotted back to the Häkergasse and from there into the poor part of the Altstädtischen Graben, walked up the long street, passed the house of my first 'infatuation', and reached the Holzmarkt. I looked at the pharmacy with its green bottles, at the corner of the Schmiedegasse. The latter led into the Pfefferstadt where I had stayed with Tante Auguste.

In my desire to find Danzig's identity, I looked at all the signs and portents of its past. Close to the Holzmarkt, the Schmiedegasse could have been an illustration to *Fanny by Gaslight*. It had a sinister aspect with its broken-down dwellings which could only house the depressed and the poor. But when one came nearer to the Pfefferstadt one saw a different picture. After crossing the bridge over the Radaune which led from the ugly to the beautiful part of the Schmiedegasse, one entered an enchanted world. The Radaune is a canal traversing several parts of the town. One could see from the bridge a small peninsula with an unkempt lawn full of weeds, shaded by birches and willows, and just glimpse, on terra firma, *Die Alte Mühle*, dating back to the fourteenth century. It was powered by the waters of the Radaune from 1350 to the 1930s. And my thirst for ancient monuments was more than satisfied by the solid beauty of the *Rechtsstädtische Rathaus* next to the bridge. Its history went back to the sixteenth century, but it had been out of use for more than one hundred years.

After such splendid sights, the end of my walk became an anti-climax. But my interest revived when I reached Pfefferstadt No. 73 where Tante Auguste still sat at her sewing table watching the world go by.

In the tram which took me back from the Hauptbahnhof to Langgarten, I looked out once more for beauty spots which I had failed to notice in my early years in Danzig. Before the tram turned into the Langgasse I always glanced at the Synagogue in the Reitergasse. I could just espy the pseudo-oriental building for which I had very ambivalent feelings. We kept the big Jewish festivals of *Rosch-a-Shona* (New Year) and Yom Kippur. Visits to the Synagogue were compulsory on those days. Both the atmosphere and the happenings in the Synagogue almost suffocated me. The religious service was held on the ground floor, which was reserved for males. Women did not participate in it, and had to sit in a gallery above. At Yom Kippur the Torah was taken out of its resting place, and carried round the men's pews. In a sonorous voice, the Cantor recited and sang texts from the Torah. He wore a skull cap and had a 'tallis', a long tasselled scarf, around his shoulders. The women, second-class citizens of God, chatted about children, house and clothes, and paraded their fineries to one another. They didn't understand Hebrew anyway; nor did most of the men I believe, apart from the Rabbi

47

and Cantor. I accepted neither the discrimination between the sexes nor the hollow holiness of the religious service. After my strange experience at sixteen, I refused visits to the Synagogue. But it never dawned on me that the Synagogue and the happenings within it had been a foreign body, not only to a renegade like me, but to many non-Jews also.

After the tram had passed through the Langgasser Tor, my negative feelings had gone. I sat up straight and craned my neck to look at the Grosse Wollwebergasse, centre of the 'Haute Couture'. It was a distinguished street where modernity mixed with antiquity without offending the eye. The style of the shops did not clash with the ancient *Zeughaus* (arsenal), which was well set back from the street. Its severe façade testified in stone and metal that the past is always with us. And I never tired of staring at the stylish Langgasse with its narrow houses decorated with carved gables. But none of them was as striking as St Stephen's House, which I looked at when we came to the Langemarkt. It dated from the seventeenth century, built by a rich corn merchant who traded with Mediterranean countries. The sculptures and beautifully wrought iron banisters of the *Beischlägen* were among the most beautiful to be found in Danzig, but were even outdone by the sculptures and bas-reliefs decorating the front of the house. These were made of gold.

Danzig had a chequered history. The Poles, the Deutsche Ritterorden, the French, the Russians and the Germans, all had a hand in its fate. In its finest days it had been a Hansastadt. For several centuries it was a German town, and from 1920 until the Second World War – a Free State. Now it is a Polish city. It never lost its identity, not even after its destruction. Its houses, its *Gassen*, their names obviously changed, have been re-created as they were before. I last visited the town in 1932. At that time it was certainly its original self. Patrician merchants, craftsmen and tradespeople had combined to create a lasting monument of the town. Their own sense of identity, their great pride in their work and achievements, had left their mark on the city in spite of adverse circumstances in its history.

My solitary walks were a safety valve from an unsatisfactory milieu, but they were also a delightful lesson in history. I needed compensation for the trials of my daily life, both at school and in my family. I clung to these walks like a desperado. Yet in spite of the aesthetic satisfaction the town gave me, I had always felt

48

oppressed by Danzig, a beautiful prison which my mind had tried to change into a fairy-tale world without really succeeding. I therefore yearned to get away from its restricting atmosphere as often as possible. And I did so by taking trips to Oliva and Zoppot, sitting in cafés with 'friends', and breathing the air of pine woods and the Baltic. The friendship with my musical cousin had gone on, but it had not been happy. It had an artificial note: our heads rather than our hearts had kept us together. In the last year at school, a new friendship lifted me out of the inadequate relationships I had experienced with other people. I had met Walli on the tennis court. Tennis was one of the few sports in which I was not unsatisfactory. She was tall, had yellow-blonde hair over a low brow, and high cheek bones. Her small, almost slit eyes were clear and blue. Her family might have come from Finland or Lapland, but they were Germans. Walli was not only intelligent and a talented painter, but she also knew something of the art of living. Both her gift of observation and her aesthetic appreciation were intriguing, and so was her capacity for sensuous love. We were drawn to each other at sight. I was quite stunned by her commanding figure and unusual face, but it was the feel of her hands so lightly touching every inch of my face, my neck, my whole body, that aroused me as I had never been aroused before. I was, however, not in love, but madly infatuated with her. And I was sure that she felt the same way about me. She was so completely there when she was present, yet she had no staying power in my imagination. No words were spoken on our walks through the forest of Oliva and along the shores of the Baltic. We knew where to find secret places on our outings, well hidden from the crowd. We lay side by side, touching, feeling, clasped in each other's arms. The pleasure she gave me had a flavour I had not experienced before. It was totally absorbing, and it left me free from anxiety or tormenting preoccupations. She made my last year in Danzig the happiest, and our relationship went on for a long time after I had left.

The spoilt child's advantage in facing life's hazards is her/his confidence in being favoured, favoured by people and fate. Yet the danger of disappointment in others produces a vulnerability which acts like the night on some plants – closing them up. The risk of neurotic illness is ever present in people who are either over- or under-protected. States of depression and obsessional anxiety always lurk 'around the corner'. The guardian angel of luck can, however, help towards a feasible adaptation to life's hazards. During the last months before the *Abiturium* I had to get a strong grip on myself to face the written and oral tasks set for the final examination. Yet I never anticipated failure because I trusted my favourite teachers not to allow me to fail. For several years I had neglected my homework, and I realized that I could only pass through luck and goodwill. But I never expected to be one of the few pupils who were not required to take the oral examination. The great day came when the results of the papers were declared, and the names announced of those dispensed from the oral ordeal. I could not believe my ears when I heard my name among them. But it was true. I ran home, beside myself with pride and excitement. I caught my mother who was on the point of going out, embraced and kissed her, shouting: 'I have been dispensed from the oral.'

She was delighted, and we went together to buy the red *Mütze* (a stiff red beret with a peak), which the *Abiturienten* wore on their great day. The *Abiturium* was an event in which the whole town participated. The happy school leavers paraded for hours up and down the Langgasse. The boys from the grammar school in the Fleischergasse had their final examination on the same day as the girls of the Viktoria Schule. The lucky ones, who had passed without going through the 'oral', were seen first on Danzig's main street. Girls and boys fraternized, linked arms and shouted congratulations to each other.

A month later I left Danzig for the University of Freiburg. I had intended to study philosophy and literature, but was persuaded by my parents to make medicine my profession.

'It will give you a livelihood,' my father had suggested. And I agreed.

II   Student Days

In May 1920, I boarded the train from Danzig to Berlin, where I changed to one bound for Freiburg in Breisgau. I crossed Germany from the north-east to the south-west. I was to spend the first year of university life in Freiburg. The same year Danzig became a *Freistaat*. The Treaty of Versailles had created the Polish Corridor, which cut Westpreussen into two, and Danzig, in an isolated position, resembled Berlin of today with one important exception: its inhabitants could be supplied with passports of the *Freistaat*. They had been given the freedom to choose either to be Danzigers or German citizens. I had acquired a German passport because my new life was bound up with wider fields than the beautiful 'prison' of Danzig. My choice had been purely practical, without regard to politics. I had been more or less asleep to the events which had changed German history. It may sound incredible today that such great happenings should have made so little impression: events like the loss of the First World War, the socialist revolution, and the Communist Putsch when Eisner took a short-lived command in Munich. Even the murders of Rosa Luxemburg and Karl Liebknecht did not affect either my family or myself deeply. We heard about them but only reacted mechanically: the meaning and impact of these outrages failed to penetrate our minds. And the success of the Bolshevik Revolution in October 1917 was an event of no concern to us. We were not the only ones whose sensibilities were blunted. Many people, Jews and Christians alike, people older than myself, had failed to appreciate the consequences of the historical upheaval in Germany and Russia which involved us all. My Uncle Josef had however seen warning signs, and had started to make preparations to leave Danzig and Germany for good. His warnings were disregarded by my parents.

In June 1920, Rathenau, a Minister of State and a Jew, was murdered by officers of the German Freikorps, a fascist organization. But even then German Jews, my parents included, were not shaken out of their lethargy. At nineteen years old, I was not concerned about anything other than the pursuit of my studies and my poetry. I arrived at the University of Freiburg a very private person indeed.

In spite of fascist clouds on the horizon, the Germany of the twenties was a democratic republic, and did not discriminate against Jews – or women students for that matter. No *numerus clausus* existed against either at universities. The state didn't take a hand in university education, and gave no grants to students for fees or maintenance. It was a private matter. Parents paid for everything, and we were dependent on the money and goodwill of our elders. Without sponsorship or any interference from the State, we were free to organize our studies as we wished. We were responsible for ourselves, and had to show our worth only at the examinations. We had no tutors to turn to and supervise our work. The students profited from this freedom in learning to stand on their own feet, and gained in self-confidence and self-assurance. I consider this position superior to present-day arrangements, which do not entail a proper commitment from the student, making him or her but a cog in a wheel. German students were not only allowed to do as they pleased, but they could also matriculate in two disciplines at the same time if they wished. I took advantage of this opportunity. I had wanted to study philosophy, but had decided on medicine as my profession. At Freiburg I subscribed to lectures in both faculties.

The train journey had been very long and tedious, and I arrived at a Freiburg hotel in a state of exhaustion. Yet, I filled in the necessary forms for the lectures in philosophy, and those obligatory for first-year students of medicine on the day of arrival.

Freiburg was the El Dorado for students of philosophy. The old German university had acquired a new attraction through the rising fame of Professor E. Husserl, philosopher and founding father of phenomenology. He was the forerunner of existentialism. His pupil and assistant, Dr Heidegger, has been given the credit, but his philosophy owed so much to Husserl that he was the messenger rather than the originator of existential thinking.

Husserl lost his Chair at Freiburg during the thirties because of his Jewish origin.

I cannot recall whether I knew in advance how lucky I was to study philosophy with the two most eminent teachers of the time, but I soon became aware of the privilege. I also enrolled to attend lectures in physiology and chemistry, obligatory for students of medicine. But Freiburg's attraction was not confined to the university. Visitors from all over the world came to this lovely city at the foot of the Schwarzwald. No wonder that I had difficulty in finding a hotel room on my arrival, and I realized that I might not get a bed-sitter in Freiburg itself. The place was full to overflowing. While I was looking at a board with advertisements for lodgings, someone tapped me on the shoulder: it was Sonja Lubowski, a beautiful Russian woman I had met at Lisa's some years before. She was in the second year of her medical studies, and had taken rooms with her brother in the nearby village of Günterstal. She offered to ask her landlady if she had a room for me also. She succeeded, and that same day I found myself next door to her and her brother. When a young Persian arrived in her room while the three of us were having supper, I knew at a glance two important facts: he was in love with Sonja and was delighted to have me join the party in order to form a foursome. There was no need for his scheming to get Sonja on her own. Walter and I liked each other as soon as we met, and it was not long before we spent hours without – as well as with – the other two.

The inspiration of Husserl's lectures and the company of my new friends became the two poles of my existence, while I went to my pre-medical lectures with indifference. I shall always remember Husserl's appearance. His hair was greying and his white face was adorned by a goatee beard and a well clipped moustache. His eyes looked with friendliness at his students, but there was authority in his gentle demeanour. He spoke with a calm voice when he demonstrated how to search for first-hand understanding of ideas and objects. I can still hear him saying: 'Do not rely on authority, look at everything anew with your own mind and eyes. Take off the blinkers of second-hand learning.' I was an enthusiastic and attentive pupil. I was invited to join a group of ten chosen students attending Dr Heidegger's seminar during the second term. The two men could hardly have been more different in appearance and temperament. Husserl had something ethereal about him, while Heidegger looked like a peasant. He was churlish and his attitude to us was inscrutable. While Husserl tended to look at his students, he was inclined to stare at his hands or the table. This table is fixed in my mind. It was made of heavy wood, probably oak, and was oval in shape. We students and Dr Heidegger sat around it like a garland. Heidegger's teaching impressed me because of his scrupulous definitions and his sharp judgment of our questions and answers. He did not miss the minutest detail in anything we discussed. He went into every nook and cranny of a subject, sometimes ad nauseam. I admired, but did not like him, because of his overbearing presence. Heidegger's seminar was an elaborate version of what we had learned from Husserl with the important difference of our active participation.

Heidegger came into his own when he took Husserl's mantle in the thirties. This may be the reason why his work was better timed to become a major influence on existentialism. We know little of the laws underlying synchronicity and timing, but they undoubtedly play a considerable part in making works of science and art widely known, or leaving them undetected.

I liked the country around Freiburg, and felt well in its bracing air. Günterstal had been a happy choice and had brought me luck. The village nestled on a hill. It was surrounded by meadows and lay at the foot of the Schwarzwald. Rural life was pleasantly disturbed by the presence of a number of students who, like myself, had not found accommodation in Freiburg, which was within easy reach of Günterstal. One could get to the town in twenty minutes by tram. My three friends and I did the journey there and back every day of the week. We studied at different departments of the university. We sometimes met for a quick lunch and sometimes we did not. Sonja and her Persian poet were inseparable, while Walter and I rather went our own ways. We soon became onlookers at an enchanting love-display, and acted our part with smiles and discretion. But the four of us went on walking tours together into the Schwarzwald, either on shorter excursions or right up to Titisee. The air of the pinewoods was the most invigorating medicine I had enjoyed since I had left the Baltic. The four of us formed a small community without becoming a commune. We were at ease with one another, confident enough to keep silent when we felt like it. The absence of confessional dialogues made it possible to be intimate without taking sides. We reached the highlight of our friendship on a short holi-

54

day in Konstanz-am-Bodensee. The season favoured us, the days were hazy and hot, and we savoured the architectural beauties of this ancient town to which the Council of Konstanz had given historical significance. We lingered in the parks and on the shore of the Bodensee, but most of all we enjoyed long hours boating on the lake. The two men did the rowing. Sonja and I slept or stared at the coast line, breathed the clean air and day-dreamed. Our boat, a cradle for four, took us over the lake of Konstanz, glimmering in sunshine, to Meersburg, and once even to Lindau, the southern outpost of Bavaria. Meersburg, with its hilly, cobbled streets and old houses, had been the home of Annette von Droste-Hülshof, one of the greatest women writers Germany has produced. We felt like happy babes in the small boat paddling along. To me, this was like a dream come true. The Persian poet quoted from his poems, and their rhythm tuned with the rhythm of the boat's movement. His recitations hypnotized us, as good poetry does – even when one does not understand the words. We were young and healthy, and lived in the Weimar Republic, which allowed for almost unlimited freedom. We were privileged in having the means and the time to enjoy a student's life without restrictions. An old hotel with the appropriate name of Hotel Barbarossa sheltered us for the nights. We had two rooms, one for the men, the other for Sonja and me. Dead tired from the journey to Konstanz and a long day's excitements, I went to sleep the moment my head touched the pillow. When I awoke at dawn, I turned to see if Sonja was awake, but it was Walter who lay on the twin bed next to me. I gasped. We laughed. 'Why didn't she tell me that she would change beds with you?' Walter had no answer but: 'She came into our room and begged me to take her place next to you. I couldn't let her down.' I thought it natural that the two lovers wanted to sleep together, and didn't bear the Lubowskis any grudge for the trickery they had used. But I asked them to get Walter a room of his own for the rest of our stay. I was glad to have helped the lovers and to have earned their gratitude. The radiance of these two graceful and happy people was a reward in itself. He, with his black locks and olive skin, moved like a cat. She was of stronger fabric, a blonde Jewess, whose grey eyes, half covered by drooping lids, couldn't look one fully in the face. Her high brow and Grecian nose did not quite match her large mouth and blood-red lips of an ostentatious sensuality. She held herself in perfect poise, and her body, well

55

rounded, had an androgynous touch with its broad shoulders and small waist. A muscular and strong woman, she impressed me as someone whose natural authority blended well with her gift of listening and her human warmth. Walter, on the other hand, had not been favoured by nature: he was fat and flabby and had to wear glasses since childhood. This had made him a slave, not only to his beautiful sister but to everybody else. Yet I liked him greatly. He had considerable intelligence, not only in his own branch of medicine, but also in political affairs and social questions. His wide interests made him a stimulating companion. The odd thing about this blissful life was that it had no staying power in my mind. After I left Freiburg, the contact appeared to have vanished. The relationship had been as insubstantial as it was delightful.

It had been a stroke of luck to encounter circumstances which were best fitted to the needs of the moment. Such insouciance, such happiness without tears, had come to me from comparative strangers. After one year in Freiburg, I left with a sense of gratitude. Destiny had favoured me through my study with Husserl and Heidegger, and it had given me the experience of intimate comradeship without conflict.

My Russian friend, Ida, had returned to Germany from Sweden and the family had settled in Königsberg. She expressed the wish to renew our friendship. And so it came about that I continued my studies at Kant's university. The change from the happy-go-lucky south German town of Freiburg to this grim place in East Prussia was not only a climatic shock to me. It changed my mode of life and study, and it changed me. My friend's family had a flat on the outskirts of the town, and they took a bed-sitter for me in the house next door. My reunion with them was like a home-coming. Ida and I took up where we had left off and continued the old intimacy. We took it for granted that this was the thing to do. But it turned out to be a repetition to fill a gap. She had developed into a woman, and did not hide from me that she wanted to marry and have children. Yet she claimed to love me still. I was not sure whether she did enjoy our intimacy at all, or only pretended to do so. After a few weeks of daily meetings I knew that it had been wrong to re-start a relationship which should have been left as memory. I avoided being alone with her and sought other company. I turned to her younger brother who had become a member of the Zionist movement, which was especially strong in Königsberg.

I became an exemplary student, regularly attending the pre-scribed lectures in biology, zoology and botany. I wanted to get through the pre-clinical examination with flying colours – which I did in due course.

Kant had given his name to this university, but he had no successor there comparable with his genius either in philosophy or any other branch of science. But his memory still gave glamour to the place. I had read his books when I was fourteen or fifteen years old. My writing table had been covered with the works of three philosophical giants: Kant of Königsberg, Schopenhauer of Danzig, and Spinoza of Amsterdam. I now felt an almost personal connection with each of them. I was studying at the university Kant had made famous, I had often walked past Schopenhauer's birthplace in the Heilige-Geist Gasse in Danzig, and I always felt close to Spinoza, the philosopher and diamond cutter, a fellow Jew. I had been fascinated by the combination of his two profes-sions, one enriching material wealth, the other mind and spirit. My studies with Husserl and Heidegger had deepened my per-sonal approach to him. Diamonds have the properties of purity and excellence, and they fitted, in a roundabout way, the morality of Spinoza's teaching.

But, for the time being, I had left philosophy behind. Königs-berg interested me for different reasons. I felt close to my friend's family who treated me as one of theirs. They were Zionists like most of the Jews who had fled from Russia during the pogroms of 1905. They had been 'burned', and had good reason to want a homeland – Palestine. Both the older and the younger genera-tions of Russian immigrants were the hub of the Zionist move-ment in Germany. They had settled mainly in Königsberg and Danzig. Most of the older generation were merchants, and these two cities, centres of commerce with eastern Europe and Russia, were their obvious choice for re-settlement. But their children had gone over to other professions. Jews have always been keen on education. They wanted their children to better themselves. No wonder there were a considerable number of students at the university who came from a Russian Jewish background. But others went into banking or were apprenticed to different crafts in order to prepare for their new life in Palestine. And there were young men and girls who worked on the land for the same reason. They broke the barrier of professional restrictions from which Jews had suffered over the centuries. These were abolished in the

Weimar Republic. The young Zionists of the twenties had finished with a taboo and prepared the way for the Israel of the forties and after.

The Zionist group at Königsberg represented a cross-section of professional people, craftsmen and skilled labourers. All Jews were welcomed to Zionist meetings whether they belonged to the organization or not. I was much impressed by the idealism and sense of purpose of Zionists. They were re-living the Exodus of the Jews from their homeland, so poetically described in the Old Testament: 'By the waters of Babylon we sat down and wept.' I admired their faith in themselves and a better future, but Zionism remained a romantic idea for me. How odd that it never occurred to me at the time that I was in the same boat as they were! Such unawareness is but another proof of the self-protective blinkers which prevent people from realizing the unpalatable truth of their own situation. I had not yet come across anti-Semitism when I was studying in Königsberg, either in my private life or at the university. Now I wish that I had. It might have freed me from the false idea that Germany was *my* country. I could not feel an outsider as they did. Although I loved their company, was inspired by their enthusiasm, I could not join with them, as I believed in the safety of my background. Nobody could fail to see the change in the Jewish type when looking at these young Zionists. Men and women alike could put their hands to anything. I knew Jewish girls who were both students and farm workers. How healthy and strong they were, cocking a snook at the conventional idea of Jewishness and womanhood! *They* were in the *avant-garde* of women's liberation. These young Zionists were the revolutionary pathfinders for an Israel which made the desert bloom, and where science and humanity could find a new home.

Although I could not identify with Zionists, I may have accepted their faith subconsciously because I remembered them vividly when my own time came to find a new homeland. Their image, long before that of the Israelis of this generation, helped to alter the caricatured image of the Jew which had been responsible for his sense of humiliation and a great deal of anti-Semitism.

I disappointed my parents by ending my stay in Königsberg after two terms. They had cherished the thought of having me near Danzig, but I promised to pay them long visits during holidays. I had gone from one end of Germany to the other in answer to a call from the past, which promised the resuscitation of an intimate friendship in a milieu I cherished – that of Russian Jews. But my enthusiasm paled under the veiled rejection of my friend Ida, and I wanted to get as far away as possible. I planned to go to another university in southern Germany to concentrate on my studies and perhaps find new friends. I spent a long time with my parents before journeying south again. There was time for rest and reflection. The old contempt for my father's job, my mother's temperament, returned. I felt the same estrangement from them as in earlier days. Then, I had sometimes imagined I was a foundling, as I could not believe I was the child of people whose interests and values were so different from my own. At that time I had started the search for a new family, a different world. I wanted to find *in* the world what was not there. Unfulfilled desires make people restless and morbidly introspective. I chased after imaginary butterflies for many years, indulging in illusions – not a bad thing as a temporary measure.

The absorption in philosophical studies while still at school was an escape to start with, but became a reality later on. The compulsion to write poetry apparently followed the same pattern, yet it came from a different source. Creative stirrings, which may be innate in all of us, seized me like a physical need. We do not know what impulse forces the mind to listen to inner rhythms, and to shape images into poetry. This was the real life for me. It gave me satisfaction though I suffered the ups and downs of elation and depression, the bed-fellows of creative endeavour. One never knows whether one has shot into the dark or hit the target. Ego-fulfilment does not feed the whole person. The mind has to be fed from outside as well, and what could be more fulfilling than mutual love? The later poems I wrote had all been love poems. Poetry is in its nature nostalgic and the product of half-fulfilled or unfulfilled desires for things seen, experienced and gone. It is banal to mention that words, the symbols of images, have their roots in one's native language. My language was German. The images my mind had formed had come from German books and people. I did not know then that there was a difference between German Gentiles and German Jews. I did not know then that the very ground from which my vocation came would one day be taken away from me, that I had indulged in an illusion.

Most of my poems were love poems to women. My feeling that love was something that only happened between women has been a certainty for me ever since I can remember. This conviction did not change, though I fully realized that it was *my* kind of love, and different from that of many others. The word love has lost its meaning. Although I never experienced the stirrings of an uncontrollabe desire for any man, I had platonic relationships with many, and some had a strong emotional flavour. There was my feeling for my Cousin Leo, the musician, to whom I felt akin. We shared an interest in poetry, and it so happened that he became a physician like myself. But he went out of my mind when I became attached to a woman. Labels like 'lesbian', 'hetero-' or 'homosexual' were out of place in my world. Even after I had studied the works of Krafft-Ebing, Magnus Hirschfeld and others, I never applied them to myself. Having pursued, over the last fifteen years, research in human sexuality, I have realized how right my refusal of labels had been. I have shown in my sexological research that sexual categories imposed by society are erroneous and nonsensical.

But let me return to my young days as a student in Germany. After I had made up my mind to leave Königsberg, I chose Tübingen in Württemberg as my next university. There was more to this choice than geographical preference. My Cousin Leo had nearly finished his medical studies in Heidelberg, not far away. He was happy there, less as a medical student than in his friendships with artists and poets of the Stefan George circle. I did not want to share my cousin's life, and rejected his suggestion to continue my studies in Heidelberg, and went to Tübingen instead. But visits to and from either university were planned, which gave me the best of both worlds. I needed to be on my own as a way of life. Tübingen had attracted me through the association with Hölderlin, whose poetry I knew by heart. His books, together with those by Rilke and Trakl, had shared my working table in Danzig with tomes of philosophy.

Hölderlin, Hegel and Schlegel had been students in the Augustinian Convent in Tübingen at the same time. They became friends, studying theology and philosophy at the Seminary. The little town had preserved the architecture and atmosphere of the Middle Ages. One had a sense of permanence, as if time didn't exist. Part of the town nestled on a hill, another part lay in a valley, and the river Neckar divided one from the other. An avenue of plane trees bordered the river, alive with boats, mostly rowed by students who cruised along the Neckar which also flows through Heidelberg. The beauty of the town and its mild climate acted like a balm on my nerves. The easy access to the Württemberg part of the Schwarzwald was another attraction. I often found myself hiring a boat and rowing along the Neckar, something I had never done before. And I also ventured on my first walking tour with *Biwak* and tent. Tübingen had been a lucky choice. It gave me back health and vitality. The old university was famous for its medical school. Professor E. Kretschmer, whose *Korperban und Charakter* is internationally known as the pioneer study in somatotyping, was Head of the Department of Psychiatry. Professor von Möllendorf, who taught embryology, then a new branch of medicine, also made lasting contributions to his subject. He impressed me greatly. Small in stature, with a pale face, sad brown eyes and white hair, one could divine in this young savant a creative spark illuminating his great erudition. He was an outstanding teacher, as was the lecturer in anatomy, Professor Fischer. The large auditorium was full to overflowing at his lectures on the human body. He made us students actively participate by asking us to reproduce in colour his own drawings on the blackboard. Muscles were coloured blue, inner organs red, bones yellow, etc. Students enjoyed the lessons on anatomy as children enjoy their games. These two men knew the art of teaching, and gave us a good grounding for the pre-clinical examination.

Tübingen had made history as Hölderlin's birthplace, and as a distinguished German university. One could see the theological Seminary on the hill where Hölderlin had lived and studied, and discussed philosophy with his fellow students, Hegel and Schlegel. He had lived in Tübingen as a young man, and died there in a carpenter's house in psychotic silence. People came to the little town to honour his memory. They came on a pilgrimage to one of the greatest poets of all time. Hölderlin's aura and memory was the soul of Tübingen's romantic past, to which modern scientific distinction was added as a bonus. I often looked up at the Augustinian Convent on the hill when I took to the river in a boat, and day-dreamed of the past, wholly enveloped in the atmosphere of the Middle Ages, of Hölderlin and poetry.

Once I ventured on a walking tour in the Schwarzwald with two male colleagues by the names of Lichtenstein and Mendersohn. They had been *Wandervögel* who knew the rules of camping and how to make a long excursion enjoyable. We met with rucksacks at the idyllic railway station of Tübingen and, after a short train journey, entered the Schwarzwald. It was my first exercise in walking over a hilly terrain the whole day long in the company of two students I did not know well. The experience was unforgettable. We were in tune with each other, and walked in step. Lichtenstein could not resist smoking a pipe, but he laughingly allowed Mendersohn and me to take it away from him. The two men made a camp fire on the right spot and after a meal and short rest, we walked on and on until we reached the lovely spa of Freudenberg, which had good hotels, convalescent homes and a sanatorium. I was dead tired and went to bed in a hotel, leaving my companions to themselves. Next day I took the train back to Tübingen, while they returned on foot. The three of us had achieved more than a long walk through the Schwarzwald: the naturalness of comradeship between woman and man. No affectation, no false tone or gesture had marred our time together. There was no hint, and certainly no problem, of a 'weaker' or 'stronger' sex. I had experienced freedom. It was like drinking water straight from the well.

Tübingen had been as happy a choice as Freiburg: each had offered me different possibilities, given me different gifts. Both had broadened the mind and enriched relationships. I had tasted *liberty* without having to fight or assert myself, but I shall never know if I owed my luck to the people I mixed with or to the ease of manner which pervaded the Weimar Republic. It might have been a mixture of both.

It was not until the end of the second term that my contentment and peace of mind became disturbed. Students took their meals in cheap and overcrowded restaurants. There were two close to the university. Once, when I sat at a table with other students not known to me, a red-haired, haggard-looking waitress came to take the orders, but before I could give mine, she glared at me, shouting: 'I am not serving *you*.' 'What is that?' I asked. She did not answer. The other students stared, equally bewildered. One said: 'She is new, I think she is "touched".' I took myself off and went to the other restaurant in the road. But I was shaken by the incident. Had it been my first encounter with anti-Semitism? Perhaps, but I couldn't be sure. The woman, quite young, could have projected a grievance against someone else on to me. I didn't find an answer, but realized that I had been hit by a mental blow because I was different. The event marred the serenity I had felt in Tübingen. I was about to change universities anyway, but now I was eager to depart.

I had chosen to spend the rest of my student days in Berlin, a city which held great promise in many ways. A Berlin university degree opened up particularly favourable prospects, not only in Germany, but also in foreign countries. Apart from professional advantage, Berlin was the focus of Germany's cultural life. Undoubtedly it had profited much from the achievements of the *Bauhaus*, situated in Darmstadt. The *Bauhaus* was the nerve centre of progressive art. Abstract paintings had been executed by Kandinsky and others long before it opened its doors, and experiments in the combination of movement and sculpture had also been known before. But in the Weimar Republic their reputation became worldwide. The *Bauhaus* housed an international community, which gave architecture and the arts and crafts a new face. However, Berlin's magnetic attraction as the metropolis of the new Republic did not only reflect these progressive cultural achievements. It had a special 'draw' through its permissiveness which attracted outsiders of either the progressive political or sexual variety.

The inflation which made Germany bankrupt had not yet become definitely ruinous. My parents still managed to keep me afloat. I had always taken the opportunity to visit the wider fields around my universities, and therefore didn't hesitate to accept an invitation from my cousin to come to Heidelberg before I started a new life in Berlin. I had a great time there. The Neckar runs through the beautiful university town on its last stretch before it flows into the Rhine. Close to Heidelberg lies Neckargmünd, a sight-seeing spot with wooded hills overlooking a wide, green valley, through which the Neckar takes a tortuous course westwards. This little town was also a gourmet's delight. My cousin and I enjoyed exquisite meals there, unaware that these happy days were but a short reprieve before the great disaster of hyperinflation. Leo had spent four years at Heidelberg University, and had by that time withdrawn into a kind of aesthetic hermitage. He had collected choice *objets d'art*, books of poetry and novels of literary merit, without neglecting his medical studies. We shared the rarefied atmosphere of Heidelberg's artistic élite, which was as elusive as it was glamorous. I felt favoured to have a glimpse of that world. Leo introduced me to his friends, poets and artists of the Stefan George circle. One of them was the poet Weismann, a youth of considerable intelligence and wisdom, which spilled over in his Hölderlin-like rhythms. Unfortunately he was already close to the same illness as Hölderlin had suffered from – schizophrenia. But at my visit he was still like a fire ball – his sparks of love and poetry were flying around, delighting and alarming his friends. Once the three of us visited Mannheim to attend one of the last lectures given by Rudolf Steiner. He must have spoken for two hours about the essentials of his teaching, but I cannot remember a word he said. I still *see* him, a small man with a white face, a very high brow and luminous dark eyes. Our vocabulary had not produced at that time the word 'charisma', which Steiner had in a measure I had rarely encountered before. The hall was filled to capacity, and one could sense the spell he cast over everyone present. He really had an 'aura', that rather mysterious radiation which some unusual people give out. The evening inspired me to read his books which, however, fell far short of my personal impression of him. His philosophy is sound in many ways. But he was unable to express it in writing, which diminished the influence he could have had. His books are not only boring but expose him to the suspicion of charlatanry.

The most important event of my visit to Heidelberg was the meeting with Jula Cohen, a close friend of my cousin's. She lived in a studio flat near the Heidelberger Castle, where she worked as a sculptor. She was petite and of nondescript colouring, who moved gently and cautiously in a literal and symbolic sense. She observed her visitors and everything else through a lorgnette with a long ebony handle. Jula was short-sighted and held her head slightly bent, which left one wondering if she was *with* one or far away. But her small, deeply set eyes observed every gesture, shape and expression. Her head was too large for her slight body, and one's attention became fixed on it. The finesse of her whole personality could be read from the fine texture of her skin, her hands and her delicately shaped nose. The corners of her thin mouth went up and down when she talked or teased, and betrayed a sense of humour not without cynicism, which made her company stimulating and amusing. The many freckles on her face and hands made her less different from more ordinary people, and lightened a certain awe she easily aroused. This physical trait accentuated a clownishness which she liked to exhibit when conversation became intense. She was an orphan, and her only brother had been the one compensation for the loneliness of a fragile child. The two loved each other like twins. She had that 'touch' of perceptiveness which attracted intellectuals and artists to her. No wonder that she had been one of the 'chosen' to get near the great Stefan George and his interpreter, Professor Friedrich Gundolf. A woman of quality, my cousin called her.

The word élite had not yet become a term of abuse. At the apex of the élitist hierarchy were poets and philosophers, and those who venerated them had a claim to be accepted into their magic circle. The inequality of man cannot be brushed aside by wishful thinking. It is not surprising that élitists had a kind of telepathic sense for one another.

I did not know how lucky I was when Jula suggested introducing me to her close friend, Walter Benjamin. She wrote to him about me and suggested that we should meet. The fact that she did so meant that I was accepted by her and her circle. Benjamin's name already had the ring of exquisiteness, but I had no idea of his importance before I met him.

About two months after my visit to Heidelberg, I went to Berlin and entered the university. By then inflation knocked loudly at Germany's door, but my parents still managed to pay the fees for my studies and maintenance. They warned me, however, to live very economically as costs were rising sharply week by week. I was no stranger in Berlin. On my visits to Lisa I had made friends with her friends. The Arinsteins, with whom I had stayed, asked me to be their guest until I found a suitable bed-sitter. And so I was back in Lisa's circle. There was Jäckel's pupil, Hella A., who for years had been in love with the master, and could never leave her house, waiting all day long for a phone call from him. She and her mother gave me an open invitation for meals, a chat or just to be with them. I went there daily and became part of the household. I settled happily into Berlin and the most exciting period of my student life began. In the atmosphere of the twenties one breathed the 'permissiveness' of *freedom*. One's sensuous and emotional needs, whatever they were, could be satisfied. The iron bars of the old régime had gone. The lost war and, by now, hyper-inflation made people delirious to savour their lives. It was the old story of the dance of death at the edge of an abyss. At no other time had there been such creative daring among German artists and thinkers alike. Culture flourished while the country seemed at death's door. It was the heyday of erotic pleasures, sophistication and wit, which gave spice to plays, *chansons* and the cabaret. The 'intimate' theatre with its musicals and revues reached a quality never achieved again. It was there that I saw *The Threepenny Opera* by Brecht and Weil. Heaven was not somewhere above us, but on earth, in the German metropolis. Heaven for some is hell for others, and the forces of destruction leered amongst us. The trouble with the Weimar Republic was that it gave a chance to the cultured and sophisticated, but did not speak to the masses of the German people. They didn't know where they were, and their resentment against progress and freedom grew. Rathenau had been murdered, Hitler was to come soon. Some intellectuals and artists saw the writing on the wall, but hated to be disturbed by the rumbling dissatisfaction of 'philistines'. And others either didn't see the approaching danger, or refused to care about it. They had everything they could wish for, and held on to it like grim death. I took advantage of Berlin's offerings. I wanted love, pleasure, knowledge and intimate friendships.

When I telephoned the Benjamins, I had no idea that I would find many of these 'goods' through them. Walter and Dora received me with warmth and hospitality. They needed a third person at that stage of their marriage, and they saw me as the right 'in-between'. I was delighted to fill this place, and took to them at first sight. They lived in a beautiful house in the Grunewald, Delbrückstrasse 23. It had belonged to Walter's parents, and had all the amenities of comfort and space a rich bourgeois family could afford. Walter and Dora stood for everything but a bourgeois life, nor had they the means to live in luxury. Jokes were exchanged between the three of us about the incompatibility of their surroundings with their own financial insecurity. Walter seemed more worried about it than his wife. He made every effort to get a lectureship at a university. Influential people spoke for him when there seemed to be a chance at the University of Frankfurt, but it escaped him because of his Jewish origin. During the whole of his life he had lived 'on a shoe string'. He told me with a grin that he was nothing else but a *Privat gelehrter* (private tutor). Dora took everything in her stride. She had striking looks which alone gave her a 'presence'. But there was more to her than that. A blonde Jewess with slightly protruding eyes, a heart-shaped mouth with full red lips, she exuded vitality and *joie de vivre*. Dora seduced one through her very being. She took to me in a big way, and introduced me to her many friends, mostly men who were in love with her. She was a gifted journalist who worked freelance for a large publishing house. Walter and Dora led separate lives and had different inclinations. I happened to share the interests of both, but it was Walter with whom I had the closer contact. She appeared to be pleased about this, as my frequent visits to him freed her considerably to go her own way. Walter and I used to sit opposite each other at a long oak table, covered with his manuscripts. The walls of his room were made invisible through rows of books which reached from floor to ceiling. There was, however, one large space left on the back wall, to house a picture Walter loved – the 'Angelus Novus' by Paul Klee. He had a personal relationship with this picture, as if it were part of his mind. I was not enthusiastic about it at first though I felt the sensitivity in what seemed to me an unassuming geometry. But in time I understood that it expressed a lucidity in composition and 'touch' which is the essence of the creative process.

I then understood why Walter loved the 'Angelus Novus'. Klee, this sensitive visionary, appealed to Walter who was a visionary himself. He was a poet by nature, and his talk was like no one else's. He took one into the virgin world of first-hand experience. Even things known acquired a new face when he spoke of them. But we did not only have intellectual talks. He loved hearing of my adventures and affairs, and reciprocated by telling me about his own emotions. He was a romantic and a highly emotional man. Behind his work had always stood a person he loved. He had written poems and translated Baudelaire's *Les Fleurs du Mal*. In 1924 his translations were printed side by side with my own in *Vers und Prosa*, a monthly magazine published by Rowohlt. The two years I knew Benjamin belong to the most important of my life. Right at the start of our friendship, I got a glimpse into his originality as a thinker when he read to me, chapter by chapter, his essay on the *Wahlverwandtschaften*. Now he is internationally acknowledged, and the essay has been hailed as a masterpiece. I knew from him that it had been inspired by the woman he loved most, the sculptress Jula Cohen, who had introduced me to him. Walter was not only one of the greatest minds of the century, he was also a wonderful friend. Indeed, he made friendship his principal concern. He was at my side whenever I needed him. In 1923/24 inflation had become astronomical, and my parents could not provide for me any longer. My Uncle Josef still helped for a time, but in the end my parents wanted me to give up my studies and return home. I had not the slightest intention of doing so, and worked hard to earn money by giving German lessons to foreign students. But this was not enough to keep me going. Walter and Dora were determined to help me. He suggested coming with me to Danzig to convince my parents that my studies must not be interrupted. And so we travelled there together. Walter was so strong in his argument that my parents gave in helplessly, not knowing what else they could do anyway. He assured them that he and his wife would leave no stone unturned to get me through my last years at the university. But the *dea ex machina* was Dora Benjamin herself. She persuaded a Dutch physician to give me a *Stipendium* in guilders. I was saved, and pursued my studies which I had neglected while I was busy earning money.

I saw a different side of Walter's personality in Danzig. He not only surprised me by his skill in argument with my parents. He was much alive and wanted to see Danzig's beauty spots I had told him about. He was also eager to visit the casino in Zoppot to play roulette. I had made several successful visits there before, and wanted a repeat performance. And so we took the train to Zoppot. He was in excellent spirits, and looked like a person who has something up his sleeve. A scheme to win? I cannot remember whether either of us won, but we delighted in the atmosphere inside and outside the casino. We went for a promenade on Zoppot's pier which was a mile long. We watched the fishermen landing their boats, and looked at the curved outline of the shore, with Gdingen at its very end. Gdingen, now in Poland, was a German beauty spot in the twenties. I had seen all this for years, but with Walter I saw it anew. This gauche and inhibited man, whom one could imagine at a desk rather than in the open air, behaved as if something marvellous had been given to him. All things were 'new' to him, and at no time had he more resembled a child than in Zoppot. He chuckled with laughter, and his eyes, hidden behind glasses, glinted with amusement. Walter was an eternal student with a flair for discovery. His mind reminded me of a mole, always digging and searching for what lies underneath.

In Danzig and Zoppot, I saw Walter Benjamin as a person without age, for whom life could be a treasure hunt when mood and circumstance allowed. His appearance singled him out; he had not the male bearing of his generation. And there were disturbing features about him which did not fit with the rest of his personality. The rosy apple-cheeks of a child, the black curly hair and fine brow were appealing, but there was sometimes a cynical glint in his eyes. His thick sensuous lips, badly hidden by a moustache, were also an unexpected feature, not fitting with the rest. His posture and gestures were 'uptight' and lacked spontaneity, except when he spoke of things he was involved in or of people he loved. He used to walk around the room when he got excited, a nervous habit which made one feel on edge. His spindly legs gave the sorry impression of atrophied muscles. He hardly gestured, but kept his arms close to his chest.

Walter's other side disturbed many people who found him an unsympathetic person. But we were emotionally at ease with each other, as he too had a homo-emotional side. The way he spoke of his friend, the poet Heinle, could leave one in no doubt about his love for him. He evoked his friend's purity of mind and absolutism when he told me of his common suicide with the woman he loved. Both were convinced that such love as theirs could not withstand the trials of ordinary life. Walter was in full agreement with them. Love and death were Benjamin's constant preoccupation. He never experienced the torments of jealousy, either about his wife or his beloved Jula, who did not requite his love.

Did Walter pretend, or was he really so much more civilized than most human beings that he could dispense with the capitalism of possessive love, I wondered. There was Dora who loved his closest friend, the very opposite to him, an intellectual dandy and womanizer. Yet the intimacy between his wife and his friend did not disturb his peace of mind: on the contrary, it brought the two men closer together. Walter's unrequited love for Jula, and her passion for the man Dora loved, did not interfere with his friendship for him either. The closeness between these four people never waned, and one can only marvel at how Walter's life mirrored Goethe's *Wahlverwandtschaften*. No wonder that one of his best essays was inspired by it. The four people in *this* quartet were bound together in an emotional incest. Their passions ran in cross-currents, but their mutual attachments held fast. Walter reminded me also of Rainer Maria Rilke for whom nostalgia for the beloved was more desirable than her presence, which he all too often found an encumbrance rather than a pleasure. I realized that Benjamin could not face physical love for any length of time, and that he resembled the troubadours of the Middle Ages who

69

loved nostalgic love. He wrote so convincingly in his essay on Surrealism about their 'Minne'. It would be easy to idealize him, but he would have been the last to allow it. His pedantry and inhibitions made him a difficult person to live with. His cynicism alienated many admirers, but those who understood him knew that he had to defend himself by keeping people at arm's length. He was intimate only with a few who were akin to him. Two essays he wrote in *Angelus Novus* bear witness to the intensity of understanding and feeling he had for his friends. In *Die Wieder-kehr des Flaneurs* ('The Return of the Flaneur') he wrote unforgettable words about my own friend Franz Hessel, the novelist; and in another, he spoke with great intensity of feeling about the poet Karl Wolfskehl. Wolfskehl once read a poem to him and Hessel, and he described, as only a poet can, the joy and wonder he had felt. It was like an experience of spiritual love which filled him with ecstasy and stayed in his memory. It reminded me of the delight he had in two books I had found for him while we were visiting my parents. I took him to one of Danzig's landmarks, the ancient *Stockturm*. Its lower part con-tained several second-hand bookshops. There I had seen chil-dren's books of the nineteenth century, with illustrations of breathtaking colours. Walter was a collector of such books. He expressed his admiration of the *Stockturm* and its hidden treas-ures with the words: 'This is *ein Kramladen des Glücks*', (small shop of happiness). My own pleasure, fifty-five years after this event, equalled his when I read in his essay, *Aussicht ins Kinder-buch* published in *Angelus Novus*, the following: 'Primary colour is the medium of fantasy, the heavenly home of the playful child, in contrast to the severe canon of the artist.' (My translation.)

And he quotes Goethe in the same essay: 'The transparent, pure colours are as limitless in their brightness and elucidation as they are in their darkness. They can be regarded as fire and water in their strength and depth.'

In the last resort, Walter's personal life remained nostalgic and sterile. His Self was in his work, fed by inspiration from people he loved unrequitedly. He would not have wanted it otherwise. I believe the key to his work is the realization that he was a poet who happened to be a brilliant philosopher, and one of the most remarkable interpreters of our time. I have often asked myself whether interpretative and creative art are different in essence. Both deal with the same substance, and come from the same source. They are conceived through listening with one's outer and inner ear, seeing with one's outer and inner eye, and giving expression to what one has 'heard' and 'seen'. The shaping of the material is the thing which makes the difference between good and bad art. Art is but the gift of *shaping* material, whether it is mined from one's own imagination or someone else's. Perhaps the agony and the ecstasy are more abundant when one heaves the material out of the recesses of one's own mind, but one cannot be sure of that.

My poems had not only enriched my life on their own account, but they were also instrumental to my friendship with Franz Hessel. He was the editor of the magazine *Vers und Prosa*, and he invited me to discuss the publication of some of them. I met him in his tiny bed-sitter, which was the maid's room. He preferred it to all the others in his large apartment. Hessel looked like a Buddha, gentle and smiling. His round head was bald. His large face, brown eyes, full lips and serene expression combined eastern meditation with French gourmandise. When we had known each other for a time, I called him Hessel, the taster, as he was an excellent cook. He was as cosy as a loving mother – the very opposite to Walter Benjamin. He faded out of my life while Hessel and I came closer together.

Intimate friendships unfortunately do not always hold fast when the preoccupations of love take priority over all else. And that was what happened to Walter Benjamin and me. Walter was swept away into a new life by a Russian woman he fell madly in love with. I had formed an intimate attachment to a German girl. After that we rarely met, until finally we lost one another without any reason I could think of. Walter and Franz Hessel, whom I had introduced to each other, became close friends. They collaborated in the translation of Proust and Balzac into German, which strengthened their bond.

Hessel, a foremost novelist in the twenties and early thirties, was put into literary exile when the Nazis came to power. His novels *Heimliches Berlin* and *Spaziergang durch Berlin* have not only a nostalgic charm, but are documents of the city's cultural history. They were republished in the sixties, but found little echo in the German public. He is now mainly known for his translations of Proust and Balzac which he did with Benjamin.

Walter Benjamin, whose work was little known during his lifetime, has achieved international fame over the last three decades, and has become a legendary figure in Germany. He has not only influenced the philosophy of our time, but also the arts and humanities. More and more of his writings have been dug out and published in Germany and elsewhere; and several biographies about him have already appeared. In the early fifties some of his books were translated into French and English. This country, however, took a long time to understand Benjamin's importance, and as far as I know, only minor works like *Die Einbahnstrasse* ('The One-way Street') have been published in English.

The task of describing simultaneous events is almost impossible. One wishes to have the palette of a painter to juxtapose what, unfortunately, has to remain sequential in writing. While I was still seeing a great deal of Walter and Dora Benjamin, a quite different world had aroused my interest, my sense of adventure and my sensuality. Berlin, with its reputation for being the most 'permissive' town in Europe, had become a paradise for homosexuals. They came from all over the world, but particularly from England, to enjoy a freedom their mother countries denied them. Dr Magnus Hirschfeld, founder of a new teaching on unorthodox sexuality, had already gained an international reputation. His books and his Institut für Sexualwissenschaften had become well known in Germany, Great Britain and America. He enjoyed the recognition of several distinguished psychiatrists like Forel, Moll, Bloch and Louis Marcus who collaborated with him. Already in the late 1890s he gave lectures on sexology at German *Hochschulen* (colleges for further education). He also founded the *Zeitschrift für Sexualwissenschaften,* the first periodical of its kind. He was still inhibited enough to hide his own inclinations behind the mask of an 'ordinary' German Jewish physician. Much about the man himself has come to light only recently. His own homosexuality and transvestism must have broadened his understanding of the wider view on human sexuality hidden from others. His importance as a pioneer in sexology is rated high, but his credit does not stand high enough. He has been too easily relegated to psychosexual history, while much of what he wrote is, in fact, up to date. Was it his influence that made the Germany of the twenties the first European country where sexual freedom was preached and practised, or did the Weimar Republic make a Magnus Hirschfeld possible? In any event, the time must have been right for both. *Schwule* (homosexual) bars and night clubs sprang up not only in the fashionable Berlin W., but also in the poorer parts of the city. One could see Mercedes cars in front of homosexual bars as well as posh lesbian night clubs. Men and women, whose own tastes might have been 'straight', eagerly watched the goings-on in this 'underground world', now known by the hideous title of 'subculture'. Some of those who had come as observers joined in the fun and danced with same-sex partners.

Love for women has been my natural inclination ever since I can remember. I did not think of myself as someone on the sidelines because nobody ever questioned me about my erotic preference. It was taken for granted by my parents, relatives and the circle in which I moved. There was no need for me to pretend, hide or seek subterfuge. The Jewish middle class was, as a rule, ignorant about such things as unorthodox sex, but my parents and relatives were not. I was pleasantly surprised when my Aunt Bertha once remarked: 'I think you are in love with Mrs X.' I answered: 'Not in love, but very attracted.' She smiled.

My uncle had always looked on me as a boy, and never expected that I would fall in with the conventional pattern. The prejudiced attitudes of society didn't affect me because I was unaware of them. I was accepted as myself in my private and professional circle, and I suppose that I naïvely assumed that the whole wide world would do the same. In any event, being oneself carries conviction, and is the best weapon against persecution of any kind. I was self-confident in my approach to others whether they were women or men, because I had never been checked in emotional and erotic overtures. Only the end of the affair with my friend in Königsberg had made a chink in my armour. For a time, fearing that a man would always be the winner when it came to the crunch, I was attacked by nagging doubts about my way of loving. But my youth helped me to repress resentment and fear. It is a well-known assumption that one instinctively selects ideas and people who assist one's inner growth, and rejects those who stultify it. This 'truism' is, however, doubtful. But Berlin was the best place in which to get over disappointment and self-doubt – on the surface in any case. It catered for all and everything. People who don't fit into stereotypes have an uncanny gift of recognizing one another. Mutual attraction and unconventional needs made them create their cosy coteries. They were only forced into minority groups when they were treated by society as inferior. Second-class citizens need a collective identity to pre-

73

serve their individuality. But in a tolerant society, 'outsiders' have no need to be either self-conscious or afraid of persecution, and their togetherness results from kinship rather than social pressure. As far as I remember, the Weimar Republic gave everybody the chance to live their lives undisturbed. It certainly showed its intention to guarantee the sexual freedom of the individual by abolishing the famous Paragraph 175 (law against homosexuality).

The early twenties were Germany's economic graveyard. The events of those years gave a shock to the whole of Europe, and their reverberations are still felt in Great Britain today. In the Weimar Republic, downtrodden by inflation, the citizens had lost all sense of security. They didn't know what was coming to them next. The tragedy of its downfall was, however, only one side of the coin. The other side told a different story, that of cultural advance, personal freedom, and collective tolerance.

A great deal has been written about the Berlin of the twenties, and it is unnecessary to add anything else but my personal experiences of that time. For me, Berlin's erotic climate was exciting, and gave me the feeling of being alive, which I badly needed after an emotional trauma. There seemed to be time and strength again to pursue medical studies, to dance in night clubs, and to cultivate friendships. The Dutch *Stipendium* procured enough money to keep me on the bread line, but for luxuries I needed more. I went on giving German lessons to Russian students. I had a predilection for their way of life where hospitality equalled 'insouciance' about the future. My pupils treated me as a friend, taking me out for meals and surprising me with tokens of gratitude.

In those days the pursuit of love did not mean getting in and out of bed with people. One-night stands were not the fashion. Sex was not a dirty word for my companions or myself. But we must have realized that sex *per se* is a dead thing, which no technical acrobatics can bring to life. Only emotion and sensuousness can. Sex has meaning only as an expression of the erotic imagination. I believed then (and still do) that sex must be put back into its proper place – within the gamut of sensuous feelings and outlets, which have a beginning but no end. To hold erotic tension night and day keeps body and mind in the grip of constant desire and one's sensuality in permanent revolution. The brain, flooded with erotic images, stimulates love, desire and nostalgia which are also the essence of poetry. One need only think of

Georg Trakel's verses, or the poetry of Berthold Brecht and Alfred Lichtenstein to be aware that sex in itself pronounces a death sentence on the imagination and the emotions, while eroticism gives them birth and re-birth. My own experiences witness to this fact. I wrote poem after poem fired by the sensations and emotions of erotic love.

The opportunities for erotic pleasure in a sophisticated milieu were many in the twenties. Clubs and bars for lesbians and homosexual men could be found in Berlin's West End and further afield. There were elegant restaurants on the Kurfürstendamm and its side streets which provided not only food but a dance floor where 'normal' and other tastes could be satisfied. One on the Kurfürstendamm was favoured by transvestites. Soldiers and sailors dressed in female attire looked out for strong men or lesbians to dance with.

Dora Benjamin, who had introduced me to several of her men friends, enjoyed visiting the Verona Diele, a favourite lesbian club in Berlin W. It was customary for men to accompany lesbians to their playgrounds. Once inside they became shadowy figures, sitting like wall-flowers at small tables, looking on. They stared at the sight of lesbians dancing. The intensity with which they pursued their pleasure reached an erotic pitch that enthralled the onlookers as well as the dancers. Although Dora had always been a *femme à homme*, she had a taste for the Verona Diele because, as she said: 'These women are authentic.' Dora's friend Ernst S. frequently came to lesbian clubs with both of us or with me alone. He was elegant and suave, and seemed to be available to go places day or night. He was a connoisseur of the arts, music and women. A 'flaneur' of charm, I enjoyed his company, and didn't mind him visiting the Verona Diele with me. It cast an unforgettable spell over me. The women who danced there in front of many men, oblivious of everybody but their partners, were mostly prostitutes. These lesbian 'habituées' earned their livelihood on the streets, but loved women at home. One could have no doubt that this love was their life when one saw them gyrating with one another, cheek to cheek, as if in a trance. As a frequent visitor to this club, I got to know several of them personally. As a rule we danced silently, but sometimes we talked. One of them visited me once in my bed-sitter. She had been a circus acrobat and wanted to get back to her former job. 'I'm sick of being a prostitute,' she said to me, adding: 'I can't stand always the same idiotic move-

75

ments.' I liked her greatly, and wanted to help her. On impulse, I wrote to Lisa's brother who had a job at the Russian Trade Delegation, asking him if there would be any possibility of her joining a Russian circus. My daring deed proved to be lucky for her. There was a Russian circus travelling through Germany. She joined it, and wrote me a happy card from Düsseldorf. She didn't regret leaving the streets and becoming a trouper again.

In spite of the freedom, or illusion of freedom, in the Weimar Republic, lesbians were watched by the police, and from time tc time lesbian clubs were raided. It was by no means clear whether the police wanted to clamp down on prostitutes rather than lesbians, but both proprietors and visitors were afraid of 'Razzias'. The girls thought they were hunted on both counts. In any event, the proprietors wanted the presence of men as a deterrent. The interest of the police remained a puzzle. After all, Magnus Hirschfeld and his Institute were left in peace by the state. Did they perhaps regard him favourably because his Institute had become a tourist attraction and brought foreign currency into Germany? It was an ambiguous situation all round. Perhaps the police meant to kill two birds with one stone! I had been spared the experience of being caught. The threat overhanging our secret pleasures rather added to their attraction. We looked on the 'Razzias' as a big joke rather than a danger, as not much happened anyway. The police wrote down the names of those present, gave them a warning and left.

Luckily I was unaware of threats to my happiness and my very security. I went to lectures on medical subjects in fits and starts: my life was in my human relationships outside university. I felt specially drawn to Ruth. We were birds of a feather, and companions in the escapades into lesbian locales and night clubs. Her almond-shaped eyes, and the olive skin of her face alone, made her stand out among the German crowd. Short-sighted as she was, she never missed the admiring glances of a male or female, and flirted outrageously with both sexes. As a student at the famous art school in the Hardenbergstrasse, she had escaped from the bourgeois milieu of her parents, and her sense of adventure enticed her into leading a double life. She played the part of a dutiful daughter as well as that of an uninhibited young woman with strong lesbian leanings. She bewitched people with her cat-like grace, her finely-cut features and the odd charm of her personality. Intelligent and observant, she listened with passive

76

attention to discussions and confidences, but became aggressive with people she flirted with, in particular, women. She had modelled herself on Napoleon, and her self-image of a conqueror dictated her erotic behaviour. Her kisses were bites rather than caresses. She always had to be the one who led, be it at dancing or love-making. We were rivals and friends. Sometimes friendship spilled over into eroticism. Sometimes we danced together, but more often we partnered other women. Unfortunately, we were attracted by the same people, which led to jealousy, and on several occasions to physical fights. I loved it all, wrote poems to her, wanted and rejected her at the same time. Yet our friendship remained unbroken, even after she married and settled thousands of miles away. She became instrumental to my first close partnership with another woman. But I am running ahead in time, as this happened at the end of another year which brought a complete upheaval and great happiness into my life, but ended catastrophically.

Ruth was the person I saw most of during my first year in Berlin. Sometimes we went in the evenings with Ernst S. to the Verona Diele, sometimes to Top Keller and a lesbian café in the afternoon without him. We danced, we talked, we were together. We were taken as a 'couple' at the Top Keller, a lesbian club close to the Nollendorfplatz. It had nothing in common with the chic of the Verona Diele, nor did the people who frequented it. It was the real thing, a place where lesbian women of all classes met, danced, and engaged in odd rituals. The fear of Razzias was ever present there. It had a hush-hush atmosphere, and the doors were bolted after a certain hour. Then one felt more happily imprisoned than safe. The names of visitors were carefully noted in an ante-chamber, ruled by two amiable lesbians who were fat and hairy, and kissed every woman on sight. They smoked cigars and exuded cosiness. They had the tenderness one often finds in the very corpulent who enjoy life, and they moved with accomplished grace. This is typical of the endocrine make-up they portrayed. Quite a few of the habituées of the Top Keller earned their living through prostitution. They were probably among those girls who used to wait for customers around the Nollendorfplatz, wearing gamine clothes and long boots. Some had whips in their hands. Masochistic males chose the Top Keller in search of masterful women who would be prepared to beat them up. A brittle aristocrat once approached our table and begged me for a dance and talk. When he offered me an apartment on condition he was bound and whipped twice a week, I laughed unceremoniously, which was the end of a futile attempt. Apart from prostitutes, the women present were dyed-in-the-wool lesbians from rich and not so rich houses: teachers, governesses, students, artists and factory workers. They became an intimate group for the hours they were together. The place had the appearance of a *Bierstube* rather than a night club. The bare boards of the large room had an empty and deserted look before dancing began. The tables along the walls were not covered with table cloths, and the chairs were cheap and hard. The drinks however had quality. One certainly went further here than in the elegant Verona Diele. It was the real thing all right, in spite of the presence of men. Most of them belonged to one or other sexual variation anyway. Their presence was in line with the set-up of all lesbian clubs in the twenties. The love which dared not show its face *quite* openly used men as a camouflage. Yet the fear of Razzias remained ever present, and in this establishment they were definitely thought to be aimed at the prostitutes in our midst.

The highlight of the evening came at the eleventh hour in the form of a ritual dance, known as the *Schwarze Messe* (Black Mass). A strange creature, a tall woman who wore a black sombrero and looked like a man, ruled the dancers with an eagle's eye. She was of a striking beauty. We called her Napoleon. I suspected her to be the owner of the premises. She called us out to join her, and we arranged ourselves like a garland around her. She stood in the middle of the circle and uttered commands in her hypnotic voice. We stepped forwards and backwards, holding a drink with one hand and our neighbour with the other. This went on and on until we got the command to drink and throw the empty glasses over our shoulders. Ruth and I were picked up by married couples on several occasions, but they didn't get what they wanted; we skilfully avoided bed by manoeuvring them into talk about themselves.

1923 was a year of destiny for the German people, when all sense of security was lost in inflation of disastrous proportions. While the country sank into the deepest pit of misery, I experienced a complete upheaval in my private life. I had never before been so full of the bitter sweets of love and creative urges. A number of events led up to this. I had not lost contact with Lisa's brother Grischa, who now and then had news from his family. I had learned that she was married and had a baby daughter. By the beginning of the fatal year, letters from her arrived at my address; they were love letters. Her feelings for me had not changed through marriage and motherhood. She wanted to see me again, and had prepared the way to make this possible. The unbelievable came true – she really managed to circumvent the Iron Curtain and get a visa to visit Germany. In the summer of 1923 she arrived in Berlin with little Irina, two years old. How a town becomes a different place through a presence! Her presence redrew the map of Berlin for me. Before she came, streets had been streets, one more or less like another, looked at with indifference or pleasure. Now they had acquired a life of their own. Those which led from my house to hers became hot lines – one had to run, touching them only with one's toes. They had to be traversed with the utmost speed. I saw Lisa every evening. During the day I had to attend lectures and seminars, while she was engaged on a number of activities which she did not disclose to me. The child stayed with the Arinsteins during the day, and she brought her back to her furnished room at about 6 o'clock. This was the hour when I joined them. We ate a cold supper, the child was put to bed, and we were alone – in a fashion. Little Irina slept, but she was very much there. Her presence did not dampen our emotional rapport. We used to talk much of her past in Germany and her love for Russia. And she translated poems by Alexander Blok for me. She became ecstatic about Russian abstract painters (who were then allowed to exhibit in the U.S.S.R.). She hardly spoke of her husband, but she told me she had married him out of gratitude. He was a lawyer who had saved her father from a frightening predicament. She had not been unhappy in her marriage, even quite content because she had her child. She lived for Irina. I never asked questions, but was puzzled when, a few weeks after her arrival, she had to meet some Russian people late in the evening. This happened more and more often. She begged me to await her return and to watch over the child. Nothing would have induced me to leave anyway. As before, I was hypnotized by her. My maddening love for her made me completely submissive. Every moment with Lisa, at whatever hour of the day or night, was a treasure found. Sometimes I waited until the early hours of the morning, when she returned, deathly white, but refused to let me go. Did she ever go to bed? She gave me no explanation about these appointments, which deprived me of her presence and did her no good. 'You are not deprived,' she replied, when I told her how I longed for her to be there all the time. 'I am with you always wherever I am.' Although I felt the same, I probably did not accept any break in this most precious time of my life. Her visa expired after six months. Was I jealous of those unknown men with whom she had spent hours and hours? It never occurred to me that this could be so, because I was sure that she did not go out voluntarily, but was compelled by some *force majeur*, some political commitment, to do so. Why had she got permission to leave Russia? She had to perform a useful service, to be sure. These reflections did not come into my mind at the time, but I must have felt that it might be a matter of life or death for her and hers, to act as she did. She never looked anxious; she always gave me her full attention and embraced me with fervour. We kissed in a state of exhaustion, but this did not lower the emotional temperature. She clung to me as if I were the only bridge from her past into a precarious present, which made her life tolerable. I soon found out that her protestations of love for Russia had the ring not of truth but of concealed terror.

I had not in fact been deprived by these long hours of waiting for Lisa. The presence of the child, a miniature of her, who was entrusted to me, gave me a sense of belonging. I felt a strange and admiring affection for her, and she became as much a comfort in Lisa's absence as a taboo in her presence. The mystery surrounding my waiting hours heightened erotic tension, and created the voltage which powered the poems and translations I wrote at that time. It was then that I translated Baudelaire's *Les Fleurs du Mal*. Whatever I had written during her absence had to be read aloud to Lisa on her return. 'It makes me feel alive,' she said, 'to know the way you spend the time.' I know that she liked my work. I could see it in her eyes and in the posture of her bowed head rather than in words of praise.

It seems odd that Lisa's brother did not visit her at the *pension* where she stayed. I had no mind at the time to worry about this strange negligence, as I knew Grischa was much attached to his sister. I only saw him once at a dinner party given in Lisa's honour by the Arinsteins. He had a good position at the Russian Trade Delegation. His boss was Adrejewa, the wife of Maxim Gorky, who supervised Russia's cultural exchange with Germany, which, strangely enough, was part of the trade between the two countries. It is more than likely that her brother's position had something to do with Lisa's visit to Berlin, in its political connotation. Four months of her visit had passed. It could have been four years as far as I was concerned: the elasticity of time had been stretched to such an extent that I lost count of days or months. But suddenly, like a bolt from the blue, the illusion of quasi-permanence was broken. Lisa's husband arrived without warning. He came in anger to fetch his wife and child back to Charkow. But he had planned to spend a holiday in a German spa before returning home. Had he too a part in a political mission? Did Lisa know of his coming or not? She certainly gave nothing away to me. From one day to the next, I was thrown from happiness into despair. I did not feel able to face our separation. Her behaviour altered from the day her husband arrived. She spoke to me about her departure with a hurtful detachment. Did she feign this coldness, was she afraid of her husband? Jealousy of her relationship with me had probably been the real reason for his sudden appearance two months before her visa expired. I never met him. Had she prevented such a meeting, fearing emotional storms? She embraced me fervently though, before going on the holiday. We had been alone for barely ten minutes when she begged me to leave. I did not see her again before her final departure to Russia with her husband and Irina. I became ill from the shock.

The last weeks of Lisa's visit had coincided with university holidays. The new term had however started before she left. I had to go to my courses and lectures as otherwise I would fail in my final examination. After a fortnight in Danzig in the loving care of my family, I continued my studies. My resolve to go on with them and not to succumb to exhaustion and lethargy saved me from severe depression. Punctually at 8 a.m. I arrived at the Charité (now Centre of Medical Studies of the D.D.R.) to attend courses in pathology, lectures on interior medicine and psychiatry. I made myself concentrate on my work, and went out in the evenings with colleagues and friends. I succeeded in getting really involved in my medical studies and the whole academic milieu. My impressions of the professors who taught me were vivid enough to remember their personalities and some of their 'aphoristic' sayings. There was Professor Lubarsch, a brilliant teacher of pathology, walking with small inhibited steps around us students investigating cuts of human tissue through the microscope. He was admired and feared for his snide remarks about the way we approached our work. He never minced words and, with a dismissive gesture, told those who failed to learn the technique of microscopic diagnosis that he would not let them pass the final examination if they didn't pull their socks up. But, in fact, he was as kind in examinations as he was grim at his courses.

There was the ebullient Professor Kraus, with a roving eye for lovely girl students. His lectures filled the auditorium to overflowing. This extrovert and charming teacher of interior medicine wrote several standard works on his subject. Jewish women seemed to enjoy his special favour. On occasions he would call one of them out to come down to the podium from where he lectured, to help him demonstrate certain points. Contrary to the belief of many non-Jews, girls were not made to feel inferior to boys by liberal Jewish parents. Intelligent Jewish girls outshone non-Jewish ones in the whole student population, and this was certainly so among medical students. My own parents' pride in my academic career was almost embarrassing, though at one time they had wanted me to give it up and become a secretary.

The most impressive lectures of all were those of Professor Bernhard Zondek, the endocrinologist, whose name belongs among the most eminent in the history of this branch of medicine. He was a quiet man, the very opposite to Kraus, and one of the few *Jewish* university teachers. I have never forgotten the following remark made in one of his lectures: 'It is the pituitary gland which regulates the function of sleep. It can work like a bromide. Its secretions induce sleep.' This was spoken in 1923 and still holds good in 1979.

Professor Czerny, the paediatrician, Hungarian by birth, had the charm of an East European. His teaching also produced unforgettable moments. I still remember his dictum: 'Don't ever allow children to drink large amounts of fluids. Bacteria multiply best in liquids, and particularly when the child's white blood corpuscles are already increased.' I don't know whether this result of his observations still holds good, but it makes perfect sense to me.

My teacher in psychiatry was Professor Bonnhöfer, father of Dietrich, who made such a great impression on the English clergy and public. He was already white haired, had a well-trimmed white moustache, and the general appearance and manner of a higher civil servant, prim and proper as they were at that time in Germany. One couldn't make him out, and my only failure in the final medical examination was in psychiatry. To his question: 'How would you deal with a violent patient?' I answered: 'I would put him into a straight-jacket.' He replied: 'Those days have passed. You would give him an injection of scopolamine.' And this one lapse appeared to be sufficient reason to let me fail. He was kinder, though, at my second attempt, but I only remember the wrong answer I gave when I failed and not the right ones which made me succeed.

It so happened that many of my teachers acquired international fame. The atmosphere of freedom in the Weimar Republic might have been a contributory factor in encouraging progressive research. Even at the time of the German inflationary disaster, means were found to go on with promising experiments in medicine, unfettered by state control. How odd that it did not strike me that, in spite of the new German tolerance, a Jew could only be an assistant professor, not an ordinary one. Even a man of Zondek's great brilliance had not been given that honour.

Work was a constructive antidote for personal loss, and my ever-growing involvement in literature and the arts was another. Ruth and I again started to visit our favourite lesbian clubs, and never missed any of the art exhibitions at the rather academic Berlin Sezession, and the ultra-modern Sturm Gallery. Its Director, Herwarth Walden, had been Else Lasker-Schüler's second husband. Our eyes were opened and we were much moved by the expressionist paintings of Chagall, Franz Marc, and the abstracts by Kandinsky, Gleize, Magritte and others. The international community of artists had found its first sponsors in Germany and Austria.

I had at last been able to regain much of the life which Lisa's presence in Berlin had so brusquely interrupted. Old friendships were revived and new contacts made. And I also took a new interest in fellow students I had met at the Charité. We discussed our courses and learned from one another.

But my heart was not engaged in my medical studies. I longed for the world of the imagination, the company of writers and artists. And I found it with Franz Hessel and his wife Helen who worked as a fashion writer in Paris. Both attracted me greatly, and they replaced the Benjamins – in a fashion. Although my life had found a firmer basis again, my love for Lisa ruled my thoughts and emotions. I had managed to control my distress about her sudden departure, but, as it happened, only for a time. When the university holidays came I felt at a loss without the daily discipline of work, and my despair came back. Two months had already passed since she had left Berlin, and I had not received a single letter. At this time of uncertainty, I met Katherine at Ruth's house. Preoccupied with Lisa, I had not noticed that another person was present. I spoke to Ruth of my uncontrollable desire to see Lisa again, and said I would jump into the Spree if I couldn't find a way. To my amazement, a voice somewhere behind me clearly uttered: 'You are going to. I shall see to it.' I stared, amazed, at the person who had spoken. It was Ruth's bosom friend, the beautiful Katherine. The months that followed proved that she was as good as her word. Her impulsive decision was put to the test at once. She did not hesitate to take me to her bed-sitter the same night. I was too dazed or flattered to object. We slept together, and did not separate for another nine years. My first lasting partnership with another woman had begun.

Katherine, daughter of divorced parents, could not settle to live with either of them. At the age of twenty she had gone through several love affairs and a broken engagement without any visible effect. A woman whom Holbein could have used as a model for one of his madonnas, she conquered men and women alike. Perhaps she was beautiful enough not to care about her physical advantages. Katherine was a romantic at heart, and believed that she had a mission in life. Of an independent mind but not independent means, she preferred poverty to fettered riches. Katherine's intelligence lay mainly in her hands. She was a talented painter, a good dressmaker and an excellent cook. An innate shrewdness helped her to get by where others would have given up, and her intuitive intelligence picked without fail the people who were destined to be useful to her 'missions'. I think it was her romanticism which made her love me. I had aroused her spirit of adventure which she turned into the pursuit of a worthwhile cause. On the spur of the moment she had decided to achieve the impossible, namely, to take me behind the Iron Curtain. She wanted to help this love-sick person to follow her heart's desire. As was to be expected, she succeeded where everybody else would have failed.

Luckily we had no hunch that our journey into Russia would end badly. But the events of those days were as inescapable as Greek tragedy. We went on this crusade of love innocent in heart and naïve in spirit. I often wished that I had resisted the urge to go, yet I would not like to have missed either the strange preparations which made the journey possible, nor the adventures, the happy and bad experiences we went through. My periodic reflections of regret were but a quixotic exercise.

I had never come across such a stubborn devotion as I experienced under Katherine's tutelage. She undertook to care for my welfare from the first night on. And she continued in the same way for several years, which put my physique if not my spirits into better shape. But Katherine did not seem to mind that I was completely preoccupied with someone else. No jealousy or desire to change the course of my feelings disturbed our intimacy, a closeness which gave me the strength to bear what was to come. I would not have had occasion to admire her so whole-heartedly if I had not witnessed her daring actions to get the money for our adventure, which was our first preoccupation. Only with the means to pay for the long journey and other expenses involved could we start on the difficult, if not impossible, task of getting the visas to visit Russia. As fate willed it, my own luck and a bit of ingenuity played a considerable part in getting them in the end. While all this was happening, my friendship with the Hessels grew in intensity, and was extended to Katherine who had found favour in their eyes. Almost at the same time, the circle of our friends became enriched through meetings with several artists of the *Bauhaus*, first and foremost the Swedish painter Vicking Eggeling and his friend Ré Richter. Eggeling's pioneer work as an abstract painter and one of the first to create a new art form in film is now fully recognized in the civilized world. But in 1924 only a small group of progressive artists realized his importance. I did. After seeing his film 'Symphonie Diagonale', which was one of the first abstract films ever made, I was inspired to write an essay about its significance. I recognized its practical applications, particularly in the learning of languages and the design of textiles and other materials. This essay was instrumental in obtaining our visas for Russia. During the wild attempts to make a fairy-tale come true, Lisa had written to me again from Alupka in the Crimea. Her doctor had ordered her to rest in a benign climate because she had contracted tuberculosis. She assured me that she was thinking of me day and night. I wrote to her of our preparations to visit her but, as it turned out, she never received my letters nor the telegram announcing our departure from Berlin. But her professions of love strengthened Katherine's and my resolve to go to the Crimea. The Lisa I knew was thinking of me with the same tenderness and the same nostalgia as she had shown in Berlin before her sudden departure. If I had had the sense to reflect, I would have seen that she was in no way a free agent, and that only away from her husband had she dared to be herself and express her feelings. I would have recognized, too, that her husband had considerable influence in Communist Russia, and might have had her watched if he had reason to fear another person's influence, as he had surely done during her stay in Berlin. I would have foreseen, if I had not been drugged by wishful thinking, that this pattern of events would repeat itself, only more violently. Common sense could have told me that a potential trap would be set for Lisa and me if I crossed him.

Katherine's wit and daring in approaching the 'right' people left me bemused and enchanted, and my attachment to her grew in proportion to her success. Without any legitimate reason she was admitted to industrial bosses and well-known bankers. Her password must have been her beauty. She ended up by getting the necessary cash in dollar notes to pay for our adventure, but we still had to conquer the greatest stumbling block – to acquire the visas from the Russian Embassy. At this point I went into action. Katherine's daring had succeeded. If one wants to achieve the impossible, one must be prepared to take risks and to act unconventionally. Käte Kollwitz, one of the most admired artists in Germany, was highly regarded in the U.S.S.R. because she was not only a great painter, but also championed the cause of socialism. I decided to seek her help, and asked her for an interview. My 'prayer' was answered. Katherine and I were received by this wonderful woman in her modest house in the East End of Berlin, where her husband practised as a doctor. She listened smilingly, while I looked at the structure of her beautiful face with high cheek bones and large, sad eyes. Her hair, already greying, had a parting in the middle. The little room, the coffee and cakes, the damask table cloth, were all marks of the life style of the *petite bourgeoisie*, which seemed at variance with her looks and personality. She seemed taken with our idea to visit the new world of the U.S.S.R., and gave us a letter of recommendation to an official at the Russian Embassy. 'But you must have a good reason to go – something which could be useful to them,' she warned us. These words resounded in my ears, until I thought of Eggeling's film 'Symphonie Diagonale', and my essay which I had called 'Eidodynamics'. I hoped to convince the Russians that Eggeling's film was not only a progressive experiment in art, but had a wide variety of practical implications. I spoke of my plan to Eggeling and Ré, who were enthusiastic about it. After I had received Eggeling's agreement, I asked Lisa's brother to advise me how best to set about it. He promised to think the matter over, and to help me if he could. He was able to interest Madame Andrejewa (Gorky's wife) in my project. She suggested that Eggeling's film should be shown to her, and promised to read my essay. Eggeling complied with her wish and she saw his film at the Trade Delegation. A few days later I was asked to go and see her. I cannot remember her face, but I recall her sonorous Russian voice. She must have had a fine instinct for the usefulness of the unusual. She had found Eggeling's avant-garde film fascinating and progressive, and she thought that my essay 'Eidodynamics' be of particular interest to the educational departments of the universities of Moscow and Charkow. In 1924 few foreigners were allowed to visit Russia, as the country was in the grip of famine. Our friends did not believe we had any chance. But I had faith. I am convinced that Madame Andrejewa's recommendation tipped the balance in our favour to get the visas.

It was about eight months after our first meeting when Katherine and I went on our pilgrimage to Russia. We must have had an angel of protection to guard our steps. We felt quite secure in our dream of wish-fulfilment, and had no idea how exposed we were through our naïvety and ignorance of the Communist world.

On a day in June 1924, we boarded a train which was to take us from Berlin to the Russian border. We passed through the Polish Corridor, stopped at Königsberg, and finally arrived at Riga. Soon after an already very long journey, we found ourselves in a Russian train where we had a compartment to ourselves in the Wagon Lit International. I was surprised at its luxury. I had never seen such a comfortable carriage before. One could settle down as if in one's own bed-sitter. We were served with endless cups of tea and tasty meals. How odd, I thought, to come across the old-fashioned style of capitalism in Communist Russia! After a day and night journey, we arrived in Moscow. Our tickets had been made out for a journey from Berlin to Sevastopol, the gateway to the Crimea. It was a long, long way. When we descended from the train in Moscow we felt dead tired but not daunted. We took a taxi to the Red Square, and paid an astronomical price for the fare, so that we decided then and there to be wary of exploitation.

We were duly impressed by the Kremlin and the golden cupolas of the churches in front of us. At the same time I felt frightened by the severity of the place. We had left Europe. The Red Square, as grim and powerful as an Eastern potentate, was totally 'foreign' in impression and significance. We were not only tired but hungry, and did not know where to find a restaurant. A nice-looking Russian addressed us in fluent German, offering his services. We asked him how to find a restaurant. He knew a good one and accompanied us there. We had a meal together, which took hours as we had to wait unusually long before and between courses. Our companion reminded me of the charming lady who came to join us in the wagon-restaurant on the train to Moscow. She had asked the same questions as he, and my answers were much the same also. I told them both about Eggeling's film, my essay and Madame Andrejewa's interest in both. I mentioned with pride, that I would be giving talks at the universities of Moscow and Charkow. And I was naïve enough to inform them that we were on our way to Alupka to visit a friend before I carried out my cultural mission. Our companion did not leave us until the evening. After the meal, he took us to the river Moskva and into a park. We talked and talked. Eventually, we landed at the station to catch a train to Sevastopol. The life in and around Moscow station frightened and saddened me. There were people with no shoes, clad in sackcloth, waiting for hours, days and nights to get on a train. They looked like refugees who had fled from invading forces. We easily got a compartment in the Wagon Lit International, as Russians could not afford this luxury.

We had crossed the first hurdle on our way to Lisa, steaming towards the south. Moscow had depressed my spirits. We had seen derelict streets and others half in ruin with magnificent buildings set in between the decay. And the famous Red Square had conveyed such a grim power that it seemed like a threat of unimaginable consequence. It was true that I had been overwhelmed by its magnificent buildings, the golden cupolas of the churches and the green patina on the roofs, but so far Russia had frightened me. Yet we were on our way, and the thought of Lisa repressed the forebodings I might have had.

We passed through the endless Russian steppes and the cornfields of the Ukraine. The train stopped at many stations, and people awaited its arrival. Some were beggars, others had come to sell fruit. And lovely-looking gypsies played the fiddle for a few copecks.

When we reached Charkow my heart sank. Perhaps Lisa had already returned home and we were going on a wild goose chase. Yet there was nothing for it but to take the risk and go on. It was odd that she had never replied to my letter telling her of our progress in the preparations for the journey. Of course, letters took a long time – perhaps one had arrived for me after our departure, I comforted myself. The air got hotter and hotter; we saw cypresses and large cacti from the carriage window, and at last we arrived at Sevastopol. It was early in the morning, but the streets were full of people, landaus, and painted carts like those of gypsies. Sevastopol seemed to be a friendly town with darkish men who spoke in husky voices. The Crimea had a full-blown Middle Eastern flavour and a sub-tropical climate. We stared at the ugly memorial to the soldiers who had died in the Crimean War, which stood in the main square, but didn't care for further exploration of the town. We wanted to be on our way as quickly as possible, and hired a car to take us on the long drive along the coast to Alupka. It was a hair-raising trip over a vast plateau. To the right was the Black Sea, to the left cliffs of sandstone with many hollow caves. They were mainly inhabited by young people who were outsiders of society. Even children had sought refuge there, children who had gone wild or were orphans. They were the well-known *bespironiy*, a plague for the government which had no power to tame or control them. The landscape was as arid as the desert, and was strewn here and there with low, white buildings with flat roofs. The air was burning, the sky high and of a light blue, and the Black Sea green. All of a sudden we came to an inn. It stood in a wide-open cave, protected by an overhanging rock from rain and wind. We sat at a wooden table on very hard chairs, and ate an excellent meal cooked on a brazier nearby. After a large portion of roast lamb and vegetables, we finished with cheese cake and Turkish coffee. Then on we went; the driver must have been anxious to get home. He drove frighteningly fast, and late in the afternoon we stood at the door of the sanatorium where I hoped to find Lisa.

Our arrival had not been unnoticed. The front door was opened before we had knocked. A young Russian woman spoke to us in Russian. Katherine smiled at her and said Lisa's name.

89

The woman smiled back and, without further comment, led us to Lisa's room on the first floor. Katherine knocked at the door, but opened it without awaiting an answer. Lisa, very close to her, stared with open mouth. She was rooted to the ground, and too shocked to say a word. She looked at me as if I was an apparition, and still did not move forward to greet us. She looked pale and strained, and her expression of incredulity transmitted itself to me. I could not move either, and stood stock still, waiting. Then it dawned on me that she had not expected us. Katherine's sang-froid saved the situation – for the moment. She went towards Lisa. 'How good to meet you at last!' I saw her relaxing. 'I cannot believe it,' she said in a low voice which sounded unreal to me. Then I approached her: 'Lisa, the unbelievable is true.' And I touched her hair, slightly. I could not kiss her, or say any more. We sat down on her bed, Katherine on the one and only chair. Irina arrived with an older girl who had taken her out. She ran up to me. I embraced her. The ice broke – with a thin surface crack. Katherine and Lisa talked about our journey. No, she had not received my last letter, nor even the one before, and the telegram announcing our coming had not arrived. A mystery!

We were introduced to the physician in charge. He invited us to take supper at the sanatorium and to spend the night there. We would have to get private accommodation after that, but would be most welcome to meals at the sanatorium. I had an immediate understanding with that stocky Russian Jew, who spoke a mixture of German and Yiddish. We met with kind folk at table, mostly privileged workers who had been sent there for convalescence, or as a reward for good work. They received us with the hospitality typical of the Russian people. The odd thing was that they seemed not at all surprised at our sudden appearance on the scene. Had they come to accept the unexpected as a matter of course? They looked healthy and were in excellent spirits. We never saw a sign of the downtrodden poor in 'sackcloth and ashes' who had congregated at Moscow station. Nor did we come across either exploiters or beggars in Alupka. I am sure that Lisa and I needed days to believe in the reality of our visit, even in the reality of our own persons. We floated in a dream, half bliss, half nightmare.

The folllowing day Katherine and I moved into a private house in the village. Alupka lay in hilly country with vineyards and fruit gardens in plenty. Close to the Black Sea were hills with outland-ish trees, which provided recreation and shade from the sun of a sub-tropical climate. The Crimea could have been a favourite place of the gods instead of privileged Communists. Mimosa and passion-fruit trees stood side by side with ancient oaks and white birch trees. Peaches, apricots, olives and wine were in abundance. This landscape was inhabited mainly by muslims, swarthy men and olive-skinned women. The women worked while the men sat outside dirty cafés, drinking Turkish coffee and smoking out of long, crooked pipes. They wore colourful skull caps. Alupka could have been a biblical place, an old village in the Middle East. In its centre stood a mosque with a pointed minaret and, from a balcony around it, the muslim priest called the faithful every hour to say their prayers.

Katherine and I had difficulty in getting used to the climate, and preferred to lie under a shady tree for hours rather than to go to the beach. Lisa had to take her child there which separated us for a few hours daily. I did not mind this during the first few days, as I needed absolute rest to find myself. I lived as in a fairy tale, looked at the southern trees, the sea, and admired the many dolphins jumping up and down in the green waves. The range of sometimes pink, sometimes golden cliffs perhaps attracted me the most. They had seen millennia. I knew nothing of their geological structure, but I wondered about the many runes on their surface, like hieroglyphs engraved aeons ago. Their colour made me think that the sun had once lodged there and left an afterglow.

Lisa and I got closer and closer as time went on. She and Katherine had become friends, and I never observed a trace of jealousy between them, or myself. We spent the day and part of the evening together, but Katherine always went a few hours before me to our room in the village. Lisa and I sat on her bed, whispering rather than talking as we did not want to disturb Irina, asleep in one of the two beds. Lisa had read my pamphlet about Eggeling's film, and had written at once to the University of Charkow to say that I was there and would be available if the relevant department wanted me to lecture. An answer came almost immediately suggesting that both of us should visit an official at the Ministry of Culture who was on leave in Sochi on the Black Sea. We could get there and back on a day trip by steamer. And Lisa was asked to translate my essay into Russian as soon as possible, and send it to the university.

The interview arranged, the three of us set off on a magic tour of the Black Sea – to reach Sochi via Yalta, capital of the Crimea, famous in the literary world through Chekhov. It was not a high official but the Minister of Culture himself who received Lisa and me. We had left Katherine in one of the taverns of this Crimean spa. He spoke German fluently, and we had a lively conversation about art, abstract painting and my pamphlet. He was a courteous and charming person. He wanted me to lecture at Charkow University, and fixed a date for the beginning of September. He asked Lisa to send him a copy of her Russian translation of 'Eidodynamics'. We were enchanted by the visit, and our mutual success might have contributed to a certain recklessness in our behaviour during the days which followed.

Soon after our day at Sochi, Lisa and I were as intimate as we had been in our happy time in Berlin. I had not really noticed that a common balcony linked the rooms of the first floor of the sanatorium, and neither of us was aware that one could see through the thin curtains. One night Lisa asked me to stay. We were lying on her bed, talking, kissing, and outrageously happy to be together. Suddenly I noticed a shadow passing on the balcony. It startled me. I feared no good would come from that ghost on the balcony, but I said nothing to Lisa. A few days later her husband arrived unexpectedly at the sanatorium. He could take a few days off work and wanted to make the acquaintance of Lisa's friends, he explained. He looked shrewd and intelligent, and his bearing was that of a man who had seen the world and tried to make the best of a bad situation, as Communism must have been for him. He had the appearance and behaviour of a successful business man, a 'capitalist' who knew the tricks of the trade. He had a penetrating look and a glint in his eyes which betrayed an impulsive nature. But nobody could take exception to his manners. They were perfect. He treated Katherine and me as welcome guests, and invited us to spend as long as we wished in his house in Charkow on our return journey. Had Lisa told him of my lecture at the university, I wondered. This fat but handsome lawyer, wearing a pince-nez with gold rims, fitted as little into the picture of Communism as the muslims who prayed in their mosque. Another mystery! He stayed at the sanatorium with his wife and child without any payment, but money was no object when he took us on splendid excursions into the hinterland, during his three days' visit. I had no doubt that he was a privileged person, but what was his service to the state, I wondered. The Secret Service was the only answer to that rhetorical question.

Lisa looked stricken by grief and froze again towards me. I know that she could not be herself with me while he was there. I learned the truth about his visit and his feelings only too soon. When Lisa and I were alone for a short time, she told me that we must leave Alupka as soon as possible. Otherwise she could not answer for the consequences. He had obviously blackmailed her. His gallantry towards the beautiful Katherine, his courtesy towards me were but a smoke screen for getting me out of the way. Katherine was just as alarmed as I about such an abrupt end to a wonderful experience. We had been there about three weeks – or was it four or five? I could never remember time in this strangest of all dramas in my life. When I sat in the car on the point of leaving Lisa for ever, I felt feverish and sick. She kissed my mouth, she held my hands, a Niobe who would turn into stone the moment we had gone. I did not look at the landscape, and don't know how we got on the train at Sevastopol. But it was steaming towards Charkow. I was stricken by an infectious disease, and felt so weak that I had to be supported into a taxi at Charkow station. We were well treated at Lisa's home. Katherine put me to bed in Lisa's room, the best in the house. I nearly died in her bed. My temperature had gone up to 103 degrees. An ancient doctor diagnosed malaria and prescribed accordingly. I got worse. Katherine was with me day and night. I had to drink strong coffee, as my heart muscles were weak and my pulse had gone down to forty. Just like Napoleon's pulse, the doctor declared. He had by then realized that I was suffering from dysentery and not malaria. I remained in danger for another two weeks before I slowly came back to life. It was the middle of August or thereabouts. I was still unable to walk unaided, and feared that I would not be able to give my lecture at the university in September.

At that time a letter from Lisa arrived, asking me to leave as soon as my health permitted, and never to get into contact with her again. I was dumbfounded, but too weak to react properly. I just did not believe what I read.

Katherine's careful nursing, and the food she got for me on the black market, saved my life. At the beginning of September, I gave my lecture on Eidodynamics to students at the Department of Education who knew enough German to be able to appreciate it.

All this happened nearly fifty-five years ago. In 1979 Eggeling's film was one of the major exhibits in an exhibition at the Hayward Gallery, London, from 3 May to 17 June, organized by the Arts Council of Great Britain. In the biographical note on

Vicking Eggeling his friend and devotee, Ré Soupault (formerly Richter), wrote the following: 'Amongst his closest friends belonged Dr Charlotte Wolff, friend of Dora and Walter Benjamin, who in her book *On the Way to Myself* gave a detailed account of the trip through Russia where she lectured at the University of Charkow on Eggeling's film. It was she who thought up the name for this new art form: "Eydodynamics" – a name which was also accepted by Eggeling himself.' As in many other instances, the past had returned to me with the showing of Eggeling's film, which had been instrumental in one of the greatest events of my life – my journey into Russia.

A few days after I had given my lecture we left Charkow, a most depressing town. We went via Kiev and Warsaw to Danzig to visit my family and get a breathing space between the Russian tragedy and the life in front of us. My parents and sister were at the station, overjoyed to see me alive; they took to Katherine at once. We stayed in Danzig for about a month, looked after and spoiled by my family. I had not really fully recovered, but went back to Berlin with Katherine to start life anew.

The bliss of having been in her arms could not compensate for Lisa's complete renunciation of me, although I realized that her letter of adieu had been written under duress. It confirmed my suspicion that her husband had always threatened her with the loss of her child in a divorce if she refused to give me up. He intended to proceed if she did not obey. I understood, but I didn't know how to live with it. However, the experience of harmony in a threesome relationship comforted me. It was an unexpected bonus. I had never believed that two people who loved each other could tolerate a third. But there had been no third one because the three of us were in unison. Lisa and Katherine had become friends in no time. The strangeness of the circumstances and Katherine's unselfish love and courage had done it.

I still had to complete my clinical studies and get through the final examination. The old pattern repeated itself. Work became a therapy for the trauma of loss. In between short periods of rest, I finished the set courses, and succeeded in all examinations except that in psychiatry, which I managed to pass a few months later. I was now a physician, but had to spend one year in hospitals to get practical experience in different branches of medicine. To start with, I was appointed to the well known *Virchow Krankenhaus*. I was provided with board and lodging and could regard myself as a self-supporting person and – a doctor.

III   A Physician in Berlin

We had occasion to celebrate my freedom from want, but at the same time my residence in hospital meant restrictions on our life together. This did not daunt Katherine. She assured me that she would find ways and means to spend some nights with me 'inside'. Half amused, half afraid, I decided that she was joking. I should have known better. After I had spent a few weeks at the *Virchow Krankenhaus*, she entered it with me in a taxi, covered by a thick rug, unseen by the watchful porter. The experiment was successfully repeated a number of times, she triumphant, and I terrified of discovery. After six months as a house physician, I luckily got permission to sleep out. My 'practical' year, as it was called in Germany, was a year of re-adjustment in more ways than one. I shed the impenetrable skin of the purely private person, and became first attentive to, then involved with, other people, their health and social problems. I enjoyed the contact with patients, and often listened to their tales of woe and their confidences in my free time. I was made aware of what is now known as psychosomatic medicine. Some patients were touchingly grateful for my personal interest, and this encouraged me. I gained more insight into the importance of psychology for medical and social health. I learned more in this one year than I had in the previous five of my studies. And when the German economy had recovered through the wizard Schacht's resurrection of the German mark, I seemed not too badly equipped to be a physician.

I made easy contact with people and was eager to listen as well as to help. But something plagued me in my new position: my profession was not my real vocation. The shock experience in Alupka had stopped my urge to write poems, but I was not whole-heartedly committed to medicine. I buried myself in philosophical works rather than medical books. And I secretly hoped to find my way back to poetry.

After our reuturn from Russia, Franz Hessel kept hope and faith in my literary gift going. How I enjoyed visiting him in his *Dienstmädchen*'s room! I still wondered about this kind of demonstration by the son of very rich parents. His room was really like a monk's cell – bed, table and one chair. That was the way servants were treated. Perhaps he was protesting to his wealthy parents about social injustice. He denied it when I confronted him with this idea. He loved to disappear into the smallest shell – that was all it meant, he said. We spend many afternoons and evenings together. We talked, he sitting on his bed and I on the chair. Things were different when Helen arrived from Paris. We sat around in the elegant living room, furnished in white, or lounged on easy chairs in her own large and thickly carpeted studio. She had the muscular figure of a young man, and breathed vitality and *joie de vivre*. She was a commanding figure, a person of initiative and drive. She lived in France most of the time, and for some years I saw far more of Franz than of her. Both took much interest in my poems and translations, and this almost dispelled my despondency and sense of failure, which were a legacy of the Russian trauma. Katherine had always been positive and encouraging about my literary ambitions. She saw no difficulty in combining medicine and literature, and I realized that one could nurture the other. A writer *has* to execute another profession, as only a few can earn their living from their craft, and poets certainly cannot. The imperative reason is, however, to be in 'life', which provides for mental and emotional food. I was fully aware of this when I entered university. But the dichotomy of aspirations remained undeniable, and led to depression and nervous exhaustion. As a professional person, I was both dependent on and independent of others. The responsibility for other people's health and well-being could block one's creative power on one hand, but stimulate it on the other. Else Lasker-Schüler's friend, the physician and poet Gotfried Benn, succeeded in finding poetic inspiration in his work as a surgeon. I thought it a difficult job to combine medical practice and poetry, though I realized that different uses of the brain can enrich and broaden the mind. In spite of positive thinking and encouragement from others, I felt wanting in my profession. I was simply afraid of the responsibilities which a medical practice would impose on me. I had little anxiety about diagnosis, but feared making mistakes in the treatment of patients. Apart from my absorption in poetry, I knew that my medical studies had suffered through my emotional life and the need to earn a livelihood. All this had prevented me from being fully equipped for the task of an ordinary doctor. I realized that human warmth and psychological understanding could not compensate for deficient medical knowledge. I clearly needed a medical supervisor at my elbow whom I could consult when my own knowledge failed me. Katherine knew the answer to this 'docotor's dilemma'. A close acquaintance of hers was a physician at the *Allgemeinen Krankenkassen Berlin* (Berlin's Public Health Insurance). He seemed delighted to introduce me to a Dr Alice Vollnhals who directed the Department of Preventive Medicine of that organization. Dr Vollnhals appeared to find in me someone she could well do with, and engaged me on the spot for the antenatal service of the organization. Consultations were held at the *Ambulatorien* (surgeries) of the *Krankenkassen* in different parts of Berlin. Every branch of medicine was dealt with there, and the many physicians could hardly cope with the number of patients seeking help. The activities of the *Ambulatorien* resembled a busy beehive. My work took me to Neukölln and the Greater Frankfurter Strasse (Karl Marx Allee), the poorer parts of the town which I had hardly visited before. It suited me well to see new places and faces, to get to know a different stratum of society. It was a long way from one place of work in the morning to the next in the afternoon, and to make this routine less of a strain, Katherine met me for lunch or a snack in the middle of the day. The women attended antenatal consultations every few weeks from the beginning to the end of their pregnancy, and those in any danger were under special watch and care. But the medical side was only half the job. We were concerned with the women's social condition, and those who were in need of help were referred to the Welfare Officer who worked next door to me. The two of us collaborated closely, and discussed every case in detail. We were concerned with the welfare not only of the individual woman but the whole family. This was a progressive step in the right direction. I had the good fortune to have well trained and intelligent social workers attached to me. Their knowledge and social conscience went beyond the necessary credentials for the job. They did their duty with empathy and our collaboration had excellent results. We soon found ourselves crowded out, which made it necessary to hold more consultations than anticipated. Success spurred our enthusiasm. The contact with a world I had scarcely known before gave me a new and vital interest. I was eager to understand the needs and aspirations, the sufferings and satisfactions, of the lower middle and working classes of the twenties. I saw with my own eyes, and even better through those of my social workers, life in the raw. As work made it necessary for me to travel from one end of Berlin to another, I had the opportunity to see Berlin's many faces at close range. Physicians employed by the *Krankenkassen* had good salaries, paid every month. Our six-hour day suited me well, and after I had finished work, I could start a different life. My responsibilities had been shared and discharged without fear. In cases of the complications which occur in pregnancy, I had access to a consultant. I was freed from anxiety, the curse of many physicians who have to stand on their own feet. The status of employee became my ideal. Ever since my schooldays I had preferred the 'protected' second to the 'exposed' first place, and to get a large cheque every month was a special relief. Never have I experienced a greater sense of contentment and security than in the five years I was a welfare doctor. Looking after expectant mothers makes for a pleasant atmosphere anyway. But it was the collaboration with the social workers which made the work pleasurable and stimulating. I made friends with most of them, and one whom I had liked particularly visited me in London in 1958 – twenty-five years after my exodus from Germany.

The happiness in my service lasted until the beginning of 1931. But I must return to the year 1928. I earned a good salary, while Katherine had started to practise physiotherapy, and we could afford to rent an unfurnished flat in a new building on the Südwestkorso in Wilmersdorf. Her father, mellowed since his second marriage, had made peace with his daughter. He had paid for her training and gave her a monthly allowance. Her interests were divided between her job and her vocation. She was a natural painter, and spent her free time at an art school. We seemed to be as close as ever, and were looking forward to enjoying life, as finances were no longer a worrying preoccupation. Yet as soon as we lived together in our own flat with our own furniture, the spirit of adventure which had brought us together began to wane.

We had not understood that our attachment had deepened

through a third force – my love for Lisa. It held fast during the fateful period after the journey to the Crimea. Katherine thought that she still had a role to play as long as the effects of my illness and the loss I had suffered were obvious. But when I had recovered in health, and was able to suppress my chagrin, a vacuum came into our life. We could still deceive ourselves that our mutual interest in art and poetry held us together, and we remained ignorant of the process which the after effects of the great adventure had started in us. The closeness of that time had, in fact, slipped underground, and we could only be wholly together in emotional emergencies.

Although I had recovered physically after a fashion, I became a victim of one of the most distressing forms of anxiety neurosis – agoraphobia. It attacked me very suddenly. From one day to the next, I had no power to control an overwhelming fear of going out of the house. Having no intention of giving in to this handicap, I asked Katherine to accompany me to and from work. She joyfully agreed, being back in her role of helping me. I no longer enjoyed gregarious outings because of my complaint, but here and there I wanted to visit a friend, and the indispensable Katherine had to come with me. For a time, I managed my life in a makeshift fashion. But I hated the kind of dependency it necessitated. After about six months of dragging myself along, I decided on a change of scene which I hoped might cure me. I took unpaid leave and went to a well-known Kneipp Sanatorium near Innsbruck. Katherine didn't hesitate to accompany me, and we were back in our old closeness again. The sanatorium had an unrivalled position on a wooded slope of the Tyrolean Alps, about 600 metres above sea level. We had escaped into a 'picture book'. The keen mountain air scented by pine woods, and easy walks in gently ascending woodland, was a cure in itself. The cold water douches I had to submit to did me more harm than good, but I tolerated the ordeal because of the expert massages and gymnastic exercises which followed them. And I secretly laughed about the doctor's efforts in psychotherapy which every patient had to endure. After two months of sanatorium life I had the courage to take a day off from all treatments. And Katherine and I went on a spree to Innsbruck. No health-meal for us, but a four-course menu with wine. We ambled through the streets, sat in cafés, and took the last bus back. I suggested to the physician in charge that I had now been cured. I do not know if I convinced him, but I felt sure that I had come out of the 'tunnel'. My symptoms seemed to have disappeared. I had won back my courage to face the streets, and I took up my medical duties with renewed hope and fervour. My agoraphobia was gone – for a number of years.

After Katherine's mission had again been accomplished, our relationship gradually changed. On the surface nothing was different. We wanted to be together, and still intended to share our lives for good. But however much we wanted it, our wish went against the force of more instinctive needs. We started to look outside, yet neither of us confessed interest in other people. We still enjoyed our companionship and mutual interests. She showed the same enthusiasm for my poetry as before, and I admired her individual line in painting. But the seeds of separation had been sown in the year we had moved into a home of our own. Her father and stepmother came to visit us, and seemed to like our way of life. I thought no harm could come to us from anywhere. But just at that moment, I received a severe shock. On the evening of 13 January 1929, a telegram from my Uncle Josef informed me of the sudden death of my sister. She had died during an operation from the effects of the anaesthetic. On receiving the news I collapsed. A doctor was called. On his orders I went to bed for a week, and gave myself insulin injections which he had prescribed. His treatment, which was meant to put me on my feet again, had the reverse effect and made me feel totally ill. I was giddy and trembled the moment I got out of bed. I had lost weight instead of gaining it. Then I took things into my own hands, left off the insulin injections, and after a time regained my energy. Work once more became the therapy for a loss.

I felt enthusiastic about the new outlook on medicine in the *Ambulatorien* of the *Krankenkassen*. They were in the avant-garde of preventive medicine and social care. Physicians who treated private patients, or those who belonged to private insurances, looked down on us – the employees of the public insurances. We were an inferior breed to them, people who had not been able to make the grade. But courtesies between colleagues on both sides were strictly observed. Some even forgot pride and prejudice, and accepted part-time service in the *Ambulatorien* because of the high salary they received. But the crossing over went both ways. Indeed, many of us medical employees were engaged in part-time practice, for reasons of prestige rather than money. I followed this trend against my better judgment. Insecurity about my medical expertise disturbed my peace of mind when I suspected any serious complaint in a patient. My state of anxiety showed itself in insomnia and obsessional worry, not only about patients but also about trivialities. I tried to keep my private practice to a minimum, but dared not give it up because I did not want to admit failure.

Understandably, after money had so disastrously lost its meaning through hyper-inflation, it became over-valued when relative financial stability was re-established. The German inflation alone could have unbalanced the German mind but, combined with feelings of national inferiority and the growing number of people on the dole, ingrained anti-Semitism produced the breeding ground for the Nazi mentality. But even in 1929 I had not yet taken seriously the Hitler Putsch of 1923, as I had ignored other warning signs before that. My own world had been poetry, the arts and philosophy, my own desires those of an individualist in all and everything. It had been a grand and self-centred world. My work as a doctor of preventive medicine became the rung of the ladder on which to climb out of it – up to a point. My close friends were still writers and artists, the best 'divertissements' and pleasure visits to Max Reinhardt's Deutsche Theater, Brecht's plays and the intimate revues and cabarets of the twenties. But I had enlarged my circle of friends as well as my interests. The five women doctors of our service embraced a mixture of racial and political commitments. Minna Flake was a Communist and a Jewess like myself. The Director, Frau Vollnhals, was a Pole who married *en deuxième noce* a Jew. Hella Bernhardt, of German blood, had progressive ideas in politics and medicine, and was married to a Jew. These three women became my friends and influenced me in different ways. The fifth woman, Frau X., courteous and correct in her dealings with us colleagues, kept herself to herself. Her opinions and loyalties remained inscrutable until 1933. She had in fact been an active Nazi since 1924. She had probably watched us and reported her observations for all those years I had been a doctor in Germany.

The social workers attached to our service were in complete accord with my own social and political outlook. Minna Flake, the Communist, gave me many lectures about her creed. Although she did not succeed in converting me, she stirred me into playing a more active part in social affairs. I did not join any political party but became a fellow-traveller of the Independent Socialists,

101

and an active member of the Association of Socialist Physicians who were closely connected with them. I distributed leaflets on their behalf in the streets of Berlin when threatening signals of Fascism appeared. I doubt whether I would have taken any political plunge on my own, because I hated to belong to any organization. I had only joined under Dr Flake's influence. But I never regretted that the veil of political ignorance had been torn from my eyes at last in the late twenties. Up to that time I had not been concerned with the position of ethnic minorities and anti-Semitism. The strange incident in the Tübingen restaurant had shocked me momentarily into awareness of German anti-Semitism. Yet the odd behaviour of the waitress had not really been absolute proof of it. In spite of greater awareness of the world around me, wishful thinking made me still feel safe. My work was successful. The number of my patients increased, I had made good in the service of the *Krankenkassen* and had become a deputy director of the antenatal services. I had also been chosen to take part in the Director's pet venture – the first birth control clinic in Germany. I started this pioneer work with the enthusiasm of a reformer, and not without amusement at the contradiction of looking after pregnancy for some hours during the day, and preventing it during the evenings. The exploration of a new territory in family planning, which entailed psychological consultations, had a strong appeal for me. Already in my student days, I had looked out for unexplored borderline subjects which tended to be dismissed by academic science, like the lectures on graphology by Dr Ludwig Klages.

Little did I know that my consultations in family planning would turn out to be my first lessons in sexology and psychotherapy. Once a week I spent two evening hours at the Head Office on the Alexander Platz, to fit women with Dutch caps and teach them how to use them. I saw every client at least twice to make sure that they had learned the procedure. I also recommended chemical preparations as a double precaution. Soon the two hours allocated to my clinic extended to three or more. Husbands came and wanted a word with me. And psychological sessions grew out of family planning as a follow-up service. The Director, two colleagues and myself couldn't cope, and two more doctors were engaged. The service, free of charge, had become a blessing for the poorer Berliners, and a controversial talking point over the whole town. Dr Vollnhals had again

102

drawn a trump card, but I cannot remember whether she got the recognition she deserved. She certainly got it from me, which she much appreciated, and this led to a personal friendship. Welfare services were also combined with family planning, and social workers looked after people in need in the same way as in the antenatal clinics.

Circumstances had made me an amateur sexologist in the late twenties, who learned as she went along through empathy and experience. I seemed to be in my element, and naïvely sure of my grasp of psychological situations, though I lacked specialist knowledge. Dr Vollnhals assured me that I had a knack for the work, a conclusion she came to through the response to my consultations. Her appreciation had much encouraged me in my desire to tread new paths in social and psychological medicine. I was resolved to make my contribution to this new venture which broke through the frontiers of current social and medical attitudes. The new and speedily developing knowledge of sexology became a pointer to a wider view of the nature of human beings. Its most eminent representative who lived in our midst was Magnus Hirschfeld. His Institut für Sexualwissenschaften, founded a few years before the First World War, was a model establishment of its kind. It is justifiable to claim that both his research and the material he amassed on sexual variations has never been surpassed, not even by Kinsey. But it seems strange that Hirschfeld's interest did not include birth control. He wrote much about family planning in his book *Geschlechtskunde* and in the *Zeitschrift für Sexualwissenschaften,* but did not deal with it in practice. He had proclaimed the paramount need for population control, but did not feel compelled to act on it. He wrote a long treatise on this subject with historical references from the time of Hippocrates to the twentieth century. Population control had always implied birth control, which was (and is) in the interest of the state. Hirschfeld mentioned that it had been carried out either instinctively or ritually over the centuries. And he wrote about Malthus' prediction that society would be unable to feed itself, unchecked by family planning. Hirschfeld was also much concerned with social welfare and individual fulfilment, which could only flourish when these needs were catered for. He stressed these points as imperative, not only for the mental health of the individual, but for the continuation of human existence. He proclaimed in the early part of this century what has become the ideology and practice of the seventies. Typecast as a great pioneer in the field of sexual varia-tions, he is practically unknown for the other aspects of his work.

Among the many highlights in the arts and sciences in the Germany of the twenties, Magnus Hirschfeld was one whose enlightenment affected not only the sophisticated, but also the ordinary people in many corners of the world. Far from becoming specialized through the research which made his reputation, he threw light on the whole of human life, from the egg and sperm to the grave. His book *Geschlechtskunde,* in four volumes, may be the most comprehensive and complete ever written on the sub-ject. It is the result of thirty years' experience. He looked into every 'nook and cranny', and each volume comprises some 700 pages. In Volume II (1928), for example, he treated pregnancy, birth and population control, which I have already mentioned. But as a prophet is but little known in his or her own country, he remained a name and a reputation to me, my colleagues and many others in the medical profession. He was like a gigantic shadow, to be avoided rather than sought out. Yet we were living side by side, followed the same trends in medicine, and held the same views on the pressing needs of population control and indi-vidual freedom. But I had only read his *Die Homosexualität des Mannes und des Weibes*, at the same time as I perused *Psychopathia Sexualis* by Krafft-Ebing. I was fascinated by the case histories in both books, but had not been affected personally by the work of either author. It is well known that Hirschfeld's magnificent oeuvre was destroyed in the grand *auto-da-fé* the Nazis made of books by Jews and other 'degenerates'. His legacy had been murdered. Here and there translations in English could be found, but they were incomplete. His famous *Sexual Pathol-ogy,* in three massive volumes, appeared only as a fragmentary compendium in English, selected and edited by some of his pupils.

Surprises can hit, delight and humble one, as the case may be. How little do we know about the whims of fate which spoil or hurt us with unforeseen events. We are ignorant about the hazards which bring the past back into the present. They fill us with fear and wonder. I experienced a shock of surprise when I received, out of the blue, the whole of Magnus Hirschfeld's oeuvre in Ger-man. The books were found for me in second-hand bookshops in Berlin. These treasures must have been carefully hidden from the eyes of the Nazis. A precious gift indeed! It was the fruit of a long search by a devoted German friend. And so I got to know the original Magnus Hirschfeld more than forty years after his death, and about fifty years after I was engaged in my first sexological consultations. Once more the 'Preacher's' great words spoken over 2,700 years ago, 'There is nothing new under the sun', have been vindicated. The wheel of time had turned full circle.

Hirschfeld's name had already passed the German frontiers when most German doctors and the population at large took him for nothing else but a freak caring for freaks. Although he had described every stage of pregnancy with all the possible complications a woman could suffer, German gynaecologists had not a good word to say for him. And to my shame and that of my colleagues, he was neither referred to nor read by us. His ideas and knowledge of the subject and his wisdom might have given us an altogether wider horizon of preventive medicine. He could have taught and inspired us, but, *hélas,* no contact was established between Hirschfeld and our organization. Although united in our aims, paradoxically, we remained worlds apart.

The directors of the *Krankenkassen* had taken a particular interest in the antenatal clinics and family planning. They decided to instruct the population at large in both, and arranged lectures on parenthood and birth control, with emphasis on their social and psychological impact. I was chosen to organize these talks and give some of them myself. The lectures were attended by women and men who had been to the clinics, and others who had heard about us, mainly people of the working class.

One can only wonder how it was possible to combine all these professional activities with private interests of a very different nature. How did one find time and strength for love, pleasure, friendship, the arts and one's own creative output, as well as the ups and downs of a close partnership? Life as many could live it in the Weimar Republic stimulated one's powers. Berlin's effervescent air and animated cultural life might have had something to do with the exultation of the times, but this is not the whole answer.

One could not disregard the mores of the society one lived in. Though I was ruled by the world of the imagination, I had not been slow to realize that medicine was a highly respected profession which gave one a preferential social status, so important to the German mentality. I was affected by this consideration without, I hope, falling into its trap. Even the tolerant Weimar

Republic was class-ridden because German people identified with their social position to the point of becoming a laughing-stock for other Europeans. The people who produced classics of literature, music and painting had not the courage to value their own identity higher than their position in the world. A sad affair, and a weakness which led to the atrocious over-compensation of nationalism under Hitler and his gang. It was not enough that professional people always had to be called by their title, but their wives shared in their husbands' distinction, and women of 'no importance' in their own right would be introduced to a stranger with their titles. For Germans, individual merit had less value than collective importance.

The late twenties had not only given me a new outlook on politics and people, but had finally changed my feelings for Katherine. The first sign of an obvious estrangement appeared when we started to move in different circles. Walli E. had come to Berlin to study painting, and we renewed our strange friendship. Since schooldays, her presence had held me spellbound. She had been a perfect lover, an instructive savant of the erotogenous zones. But I had already realized then how little sexuality has to do with love. Our relationship followed the same pattern when we met again in Berlin. We had wonderful times together without the pain of nostalgia. As before, I forgot everything else when I was with her. The atmosphere which surrounded our excursions to Dahlem, the Grunewald, and risky visits to the flat she shared with an aunt was charged with that sensuous glow which makes one see the world around through rose-tinted spectacles. Who were we and all those other young women of the twenties who seemed to know so well what we wanted? We had no need to be helped to freedom from male domination. We were *free*, nearly forty years before the Women's Liberation Movement started in America. We never thought of being second-class citizens. We simply were ourselves, which is the only liberation which counts in the end. Freedom of and for the individual was, however, short-lived in the eyes of German history. And the avalanche of suppressive measures which followed it dug the grave of this freedom and all others. In my youth, the Women's Liberation Movement seemed to have neither place nor sense for women of the upper and middle classes. The story of working-class women was another matter. The fortunate crowd of the well-to-do had little in common with them, and people like Walli and myself were probably freaks in the eyes of the majority of German people. The liberation of the lower middle and working classes was a necessity because they *were* still regarded as 'inferior'. Snobism pervaded the Weimar Republic in spite of its banner of socialism, a fact which many of my circle understood. But we thought of ourselves, if we thought at all, as 'different', as members of an international avant-garde who recognized one another in any language. I certainly felt that I belonged with them.

A perfect example of a liberated avant-gardist was Helen Hessel. She could turn her hand to anything – a worker on the land in the First World War and a fashion writer in the twenties and thirties, she was a lover of many and the wife of one. She bewitched men and women alike. Her blue eyes, clear and cold as a frosty spring, her elegance and self-assurance, made her the epitome of the seductive female of the twenties. It was no surprise to her husband and friends when she jumped into the Seine, just for a bet. She wrote essays as well as she rode a horse or drove a car. A dare devil, who passionately loved and hated, worked or lazed about. She walked with a slight limp, supported by a walking stick with an ivory handle which added to her elegance. Her hair had gone white before she was forty, and when her features grew sharper with age she developed a striking resemblance to Frederick the Great. I was fascinated by her, and was delighted to accept an invitation to drive with her from Berlin to Normandy for a holiday. She had rented a peasant's house with her friend Pierre Roché in the small village of Sotteville. The year was 1926 or '27, and the holiday was my first experience of France and the French. I hardly knew when I arrived what I had let myself in for. Helen and Roché shared a room, her son, eight years old, and I had rooms to ourselves. Everybody except me walked about naked, and got in and out of clothes in front of each other. It was second nature and fun and games to them. Helen's son, Paul, grew up in an 'alternative' society which worked well for him. He was a charmer by nature, a favourite of the gods. He was also unusually bright and unusually popular. He later went to the *Ecole Normale* which prepares youngsters of high intelligence for public and diplomatic service. He seemed to be the friend of everybody and surprised at nothing.

In the third week of my time at Sotteville, Franz Hessel arrived on the scene. One might have expected him to be jealous of his wife and her lover. But Roché happened to be his best friend, and

I witnessed the same pattern as with the Benjamins. In both cases, the triangualar situation appeared to be a happy one where love and friendship neither clashed nor wavered. Again I had come across truly civilized relationships, an ideal of human behaviour, which many may aspire to, but few can achieve. In his novel *Jules et Jim*, Pierre Rochè gave a photographic picture of his life with Helen and Franz Hessel. It was made into a film of the same name by François Truffaut, where Jeanne Moreau played the part of Helen. Freedom from jealousy means freedom from possessiveness. Jealousy, envy, competitiveness, are all part and parcel of the capitalistic mentality with which the power struggle of male domination has infected society.

My French holiday became a landmark in my life, which made France and Helen the favoured choice for a new life several years later. The idyllic atmosphere of the village with its rose-covered houses had taken my fancy. And I was much impressed by the pride and courtesy of the French, their vitality and *savoir vivre*. They knew about the art of living because they were made for it, and I was charmed by their light 'touch' and vivacious mentality. When at a later date I read Friedrich Sieburg's book *God in France*, I knew that I had believed in his creed since my first visit.

The German economy had improved since the resurrection of the currency value, yet the number of men on the dole grew and grew, and so did political strife and tension. And in 1930-31 Communists and Fascists started to engage in street fights. One could no longer escape the warnings of an approaching crisis. I began to feel uneasy when, in the spring of 1931, the Physician-in-Chief of the *Krankenkassen* told me that it was dangerous for me to continue my job in the antenatal service and family planning for political reasons. He wished to transfer me to a more 'neutral' occupation, and suggested an apprenticeship in an institute for electro-physical therapy. It would allow him to give me a post in that department later on. After a year of study (with full pay) I became, in April 1932, Director of the *Electrophysical Institute* in Neukölln. After I had got over the first alarm of my new work and position, I enjoyed being in a quiet atmosphere, with no change of locality and fewer patients to cope with. I soon started research in the field of electro-physical therapy with the help of a loyal and devoted staff. But all too soon I was shaken to the core on seeing young men in Nazi uniform, marching through the streets of Berlin, and banners stretching across streets which read: 'Death to the Jews'. Katherine came into her own at the beginning of Nazi unrule. She was with me body and soul, protecting my Jewish face with her Aryan beauty when we had to leave the comparative safety of our flat. A year before, we had moved to a roomier flat in the Laubenheimer Platz. At that time, I had no idea that she might have the intention of leaving our ménage. We still had common interests, particularly as we were both attending a course in chirology, which the remarkable hand-reader, Julius Spier, had arranged. I had heard about him from a colleague who was impressed by his psychological reading of the human hand. He told her that his art was teachable. His course was meant for physicians only, but Katherine was permitted to participate. The new interest inspired us both. Spier understood that the hand resembled a map where a person's character and certain conditons of health could be diagnosed. He had aspired to create a method out of his more or less intuitive gift. He imparted to his pupils his own knowledge of hand-reading as far as it was possible. Everyone admired his pioneer spirit and his talent. He taught us a great deal because he had made some order out of chaos, although he had not been able to produce a scientifically valid method. He was self-taught, trained neither in psychology nor medicine. Nevertheless, we gained enough knowledge from him to realize that the human hand could be an important tool in diagnosis. Spier demonstrated the potential value of chirology so well that I was inspired to take the subject further, which enabled me to develop a scientific method of hand interpretation several years later. I am always grateful to this man who started me on my long journey around the human hand, the results of which were published in three books: *The Human Hand*, *A Psychology of Gesture*, and *The Hand in Psychological Diagnosis*. This work represents a great part of my life. I wrote about it in detail in *On the Way to Myself*, but it will also have a place in the chapters which follow.

1932 was a year of doom for me. Katherine left me in the autumn of that year. Her father had impressed upon her that she courted danger for herself if she continued to share her life with a Jewess. I had to face my last months in Germany alone. At first I despised her for letting me down in the hour of need, but I still longed for her more intensely than before. I did not make any move towards her, standing firm, but emotionally disturbed, on my own feet. I was numb, and walked about like a robot. The

German people around me were concerned and helpful. They did not want me to go away, and promised their protection in any difficulty. But I already had it in mind to leave the country. In February 1933 I got notice to quit my service at the *Krankenkassen* on 1 April, but was asked to leave at once. The blow was a communal one, as all Jews were dismissed from jobs and services, and I could take the disaster in my stride. I went the next day, in a fairly composed state of mind, to Neukölln to say goodbye to colleagues and nurses. I went as usual by underground, but I was arrested before the train reached the station Hasenheide. This outrage revived my spirits rather than paralysing them. I asked the Gestapo officer to show me his warrant, which he did. I asked why I was being treated like this: 'You are a woman dressed as a man and a spy.' I laughed in his face, sternly telling him to leave me alone. And I added: 'What a treatment! One of my ancestors swam through the "Katzbach" for Frederick the Great, and this is what we get from *you*.' He had no answer: his face was stony. When we reached Hasenheide he pushed me onto the platform and led me to the guard's cabin. The guard, seeing me in the hands of the Gestapo, exclaimed: 'But that is Frau Dr Wolff who treats my wife at the Neukölln *Ambulatorium*.' He had saved me – for the time being. The officer had no choice but to release me. When I told my superior at the *Ambulatorium* what had happened, he murmured: 'I cannot tell you how ashamed I am to be a German.' Three days later my flat was searched for bombs! I had been denounced as a dangerous communist. The bombs were supposedly lodged in my cellar. My books and papers were scrutinized. Nothing was found because my loyal maid had been able to warn me of the event, as an official had called earlier. And a patient who lived nearby had spirited away 'dangerous' material. These happenings stirred me into action. Events had been like the strokes of a clock, announcing every hour – this is the last hour. The day after the house searching, I not only decided but arranged my exodus from Berlin to Paris. Until the last day, neighbours tried to dissuade me from becoming a refugee. I acted fast, driven by a compulsive command of fate. I got a passport valid for five years at the nearby police station. I want to put on record again that the sergeant who dealt with my case looked at me with great sympathy. He shook hands and said: 'I am sorry that you are leaving. My wife always says Jewish doctors are the best.' I said goodbye to my friends, and informed Katherine by telephone of my departure for Paris in a few days. She promised to come to the station. On 26 May 1933, I stood at the Bahnhof Zoologischer Garten waiting for her. A few minutes before the train was due to leave, Katherine arrived, looking a picture of health and beauty. She said: 'Bon voyage, and do come back in five years.'

I had followed my instinct in trying to escape an evil régime determined to destroy the Jews. I occupied a corner seat at the door of the compartment. Did I imagine I would jump out – in case? I could still be arrested as long as I was on German soil. Never have I lived through such a vigilant strain, before or after. The back of my head seemed to hear and 'see' if the Gestapo was coming. Every minute could be the prelude to life or death – until we had passed the frontier at Aachen. Aachen came. We stopped, I got out, opened my trunk and suitcase. The steely eyes of a Nazi official stared at me and my passport. He let me go back to the train. I was free, and a few hours later arrived at the Gare du Nord in Paris.

IV In Paris

'*Place du Panthéon, s'il vous plaît*', I told the taxi driver. '*Quelle adresse?*' '*L'Hôtel*', I answered. Did I or did I not know of the Hôtel du Panthéon? It had been a good guess. We stopped at the very place – a small hotel, not very clean, where I got the smallest room. I didn't mind, swimming as I was in the twilight of past horror and new hope. I went to bed still in the nightmare of the journey, yet hope for the future must have got the better of me because I slept right into the next day. I ordered my first French breakfast – '*café au lait et une tartine*' – in a café on the Boulevard St Michel, but as yet had no mind to make contact with anybody. It was already late in the afternoon when I telephone Helen Hessel who lived close to the Place du Panthéon. Her voice was like a caress, and her urgency to see me a spring of hope. She begged me to come at once. I was quite overwhelmed by her reception, so terribly pleased was she to see me. The feeling of being wanted acted like a charm on me. But my emotions were out of gear, and in the months which followed my arrival I went up and down like a yo-yo, from elation to despair, from despair to elation.

Helen and I were an odd couple of friends. I had always been attracted by her, not without fear of being suddenly rejected. But now I basked in her warmth. Her friendship and wish to see me settled in a new world was the rock to which I clung. Her son Paul, now fourteen years of age, embraced me with the same spontaneity as his mother. The two loved each other like twins rather than mother and son. This boy had the wisdom one sometimes finds in the young who are well-loved companions of their elders. These two shared their lives in an almost obsessional concern for their mutual well-being. There seemed to be no secrets between them; they teased, talked, kissed, and scolded one another in turn. Paul had struck me as an enchanter when he was still in short trousers. His brown eyes smiled at everyone in constant amusement. His soft mouth, his long arms with their jaunty movements, and his gift of mimicry gave him the appearance of a jester. He got under another person's skin in no time, and knew what people wanted and needed. His identification with his mother made him *ipso facto* a friend of mine, but there was more to it than that. We had a similar approach to people, as we both liked to please wherever we went. His mother was of a different breed, more interested in doing things with others than in reflecting or worrying about them.

The two made immediate plans for my future, and I enjoyed being taken in tow, relinquishing the need to make decisions. For the time being, I was able to stand on my feet financially, but depended for all else on my friends. A few days after my arrival Helen had placed me in a Pension in the Rue Froidevaux, not far away from her flat. She was the fashion reporter of a German newspaper, and had an international circle of friends and colleagues. She soon introduced me to one of her dearest friends, Baladine Klossowska, a German Jewess who, though slightly hunchbacked, was a woman of delicate beauty, sharp intelligence and acid wit. I took to her as to an older sister. She, too, made immediate contact with me, but some months passed before we had occasion to become well acquainted. Helen's life had undergone a great change soon after my arrival, which put everything else into the background. She and Paul left their studio flat from one day to another, and joined me in the Pension. A traumatic event had made her leave her surroundings: a long-standing love affair had come to a catastrophic end. And the break with a man she passionately loved had taken its toll on her. The force of circumstances forged a new bond between us. It brought me nearer to her than ever before, as I was able to give her the kind of comfort she needed. A new situation developed for the three of us. After we had shared life at the Pension for some time, Helen decided that we should live together in a flat of our own. Search for a suitable apartment began on the spur of the moment. At that time modern flats could easily be obtained and, in August 1933, we were installed in a top flat of an apartment house on the Boulevard Brune. It was a few yards away from the Porte d'Orléans, in between an elegant suburb of Paris and a lively part of the *vrai* Paris, the Paris of the people. We wanted to enjoy both worlds. Helen had put her own furniture into the flat as a provisory measure. We would acquire additional pieces later on and make a home to our taste. We planned to get what we wanted at the *Marché de Puces* (the flea market) in about six weeks' time. A holiday spirit had taken hold of us, particularly of Helen who had been seized by the understandable impulse to get away from Paris. She seemed ready for any adventure, suitable or unsuitable, and put forward every good reason for a holiday. She was persuasive enough and the time seemed just right, before Paul had to go back to school late in September. We decided to drive to the south of France. Helen fancied a small place like Sanary on the western Mediterranean. The Côte d'Azur was such a tourist hell – she argued that one wouldn't be comfortable. And Sanary had acquired a new cultural image, as writers and artists from different countries had settled there to find either refuge or peace or both. I was prepared to accept everything Helen suggested, even a holiday from my present life which was nothing but a holiday.

Off we went in Helen's old Ford, on a tour through riveting landscapes and arresting towns. The country around Aix-en-Provence, the country of Van Gogh and Cézanne, was so different from anything I had seen before that I felt quite drugged with enthusiasm. We had passed through Orange, a small town in Provence with an ancient Greek archway and luscious plants everywhere. Orange was a languid place, a sleeping beauty. It was famous for its large amphitheatre, redolent of ancient Greece or Rome. I didn't know whether plays or circuses still brought it to life, or whether it was a relic of the past only. Another surprise had awaited me when we came to Vienne, where we stayed overnight. This city mysteriously links Provence with North Africa, both in the style of its houses and the looks of its inhabitants, out of character with other Provençal towns. Our next stop was Aix-en-Provence itself, and we were back in Europe again. We spent a few hours only in this civilized city. There was a noble quietness about the place in spite of the many tourists passing through during the summer. We refreshed ourselves sitting on the terrace of an elegant café in the main avenue, shaded by plane trees on both sides. After Aix-en-Provence we drove straight through to the coast, and reached Sanary late in the afternoon. The fact that it was much less spoilt by tourism than the Riviera was a recommendation in itself. Toulon, close by, had an international flavour. Merchant ships and destroyers from many lands anchored in its harbour, and the town was always full of sailors, white, brown and black. Business flourished in Toulon with its colourful markets, amusement parlours, and choice restaurants which we frequently visited while in Sanary.

Years later I wondered whether Helen had chosen Sanary because an old friend of hers had made her home there. This friend, of whose existence I had been ignorant, came to play a considerable part in my life. There was more in store for us than we could possibly have anticipated. The 'hand of destiny' had led us to Sanary, whatever Helen's motive may have been.

On entering the main square with its many hotels and cafés, one was reminded of a theatrical scene. It seemed a disappointing place at first sight. We stopped in front of the largest café, when Helen informed me that she had a friend called Lisa M. living in Sanary, but did not know her address. At that very moment, a good-looking blonde stared at Helen, which may have been the reason why she asked her if by any chance she knew where Madame Lisa M. lived. The young girl smiled and said: 'I think I know you. Aren't you Helen Hessel?' 'Indeed I am.' Suddenly Helen recognized Sybille von Schönebeck (Sybille Bedford), Madame M.'s daughter. She gave us her mother's address and encouraged us to call on her straight away. We did. We were warmly received and, as if this was not enough, invited to join a party at her house the same evening.

We met writers and artists of Sanary's cultural colony at this unforgettable gathering. Thomas Mann, his wife, their sons Golo and Klaus had come, and so had Aldous and Maria Huxley. Aldous stood out because of his height as well as his beautiful head. Maria, at his side, seeming smaller than she really was, looked at me with an interest which I didn't understand, but found encouraging. Later she explained that she had heard of my studies of the human hand, which had been one of her liveliest interests for a long time. She was very pleased that chance had brought me to Sanary. She very much wanted to see me again and to get to know me. I was pleased, though rather bewildered to be 'taken up' by her all of a sudden. But her straightforward behaviour rather appealed to me, and I admired her vivacity and her Latin beauty. She impressed me as a woman of whom too many people expected too much. She had the figure and grace of a dancer who might have distinguished herself in any modern ballet.

I recognized at once how highly strung she was, and wondered whether she had not too many duties and problems in her life to

115

cultivate a new acquaintance. But I was wrong. She really insisted on knowing me because she needed an interest of her own, an inner island. She told me that she had always been fascinated by people's hands, but had never found anybody who could instruct her how to interpret them. She felt that hands were the key to a person's character and personality, and revealed more than the face; they might also tell a good deal about health conditions. She was convinced that this was so, and she considered me to be the person best able to teach her. I readily agreed to fill the part she wanted me to play. I liked her and was taken by her charm, and I had not been impervious either to the glamour of the Huxleys or the interesting life they obviously lived at the Villa La Georgette. Things happened quickly at Sanary. The day after the party, Maria called for me at the Pension to spend the day with her and her family. We got on well, and during this holiday I spent much time with Maria, her sister Jeanne (Madame Jeanne Neveu) and Aldous. As a rule, Maria and I were closeted together for several hours in the sitting room. I taught her first of all how to make reliable hand prints. Luckily I had brought the necessary material with me. After this first lesson, practised on our own hands, I showed her by degrees how to interpret them. Those of herself, Aldous, Jeanne and others present served as examples. Our occupation aroused considerable excitement in our 'victims'. And the Huxleys talked about Maria's lessons to their friends and acquaintances. She was an excellent pupil who asked the right questions, and she learned a good deal of the method of hand-reading which I had so far developed. At that time I was still at the beginning of a methodical study, and I insisted on making this clear to her and Aldous. I realized that her interest had given me an unexpected chance, because I was shrewd enough to see that her friendship could help me to find my feet in France. Yet I wasn't a schemer, except in so far as a person in search of security has to be. Maria had a sympathetic personality, and her enthusiasm for the 'lessons' reduced a certain unease I felt in her presence, though I wanted nothing better than to have her as a friend. All too soon I thought she had really become one. She appeared interested in my welfare as well as in my work: I didn't realize that her care for me was not a personal favour, but part of her character. She could not help caring for others. I had obviously indulged in wishful thinking. After I had returned to Paris, I asked myself whether she was a friend or a benefactress only. Whatever her feelings for me may have been, she was, for a time, one of the principal figures who influenced the course of my life.

Already in Sanary Maria had advised me to interpret hands professionally. She knew that this would be my only chance of earning a livelihood in France. It was impossible for refugees to get work permits, but an unorthodox profession such as chirology would not infringe French regulations. However, the time to take her advice had not yet come. Even Nazi Germany strictly observed contracts, and mine guaranteed that my salary would be paid for six months after I had received notice to quit. And so I was well provided for during the first half year of my exile. My prime object had been to pursue a scientific study of the hand, which I wanted to carry out as soon as possible. Chance favoured me. I had made contact with the Society of Friends which spared no effort to help Jewish refugees. I frequently went to their modest establishment in a poor district of Paris. The President, Henri van Etten, soon became a personal friend, and several members of his staff also took a personal interest in me. Through the Quakers' good offices, I met Henri Wallon, Professor at the *Ecole des Hautes Etudes*. He thought that my project for the scientific study of hand-traits had considerable promise, and immediately offered his help. He invited me to study the hands of mentally defective children at a mental hospital of which he was the superintendent. He also made my project known to his colleagues and other medical specialists who reacted favourably enough to interview me. And some asked me to pursue my studies at their clinics.

It was a foregone conclusion that I would free my subject from its superstitious aspect. I wanted to investigate the hands of all manner of people in different age-groups, and had it in mind to include the extremities of apes and monkeys if I got the chance to do so. A few years later I was able to carry out my plan in the London Zoo.

But at the start I not only needed the help of the medical profession in order to study the 'abnormal', but also the general public to learn about 'normal' hands. Only the combination of both could provide a diagnostic map of personality in health and disease. The Quakers came to my help again. They were able to persuade about 200 refugees from different countries to have their hands read by me. I went at the investigation with great fervour, and became completely absorbed in it when I discovered whole families among my subjects. In some cases, I saw three generations of the same family. These were of particular interest because of a possible genetic significance in hand-traits.

Either through a stroke of luck, or the persuasive power of Henri van Etten, I had the opportunity to take hand prints of twenty-four newborn babies in a maternity clinic, a process as difficult as it was thrilling. One such print was reproduced in *The Human Hand*.

Professor Wallon and Henri van Etten soon became the pillars of my research work. I do not know through which of them I had the opportunity to study the hands of twenty-five boxers and thirty film actors in different age-groups. But the most important source of material was Professor Wallon's weekly surgery for people who suffered from emotional and nervous disturbances. The first visible progress of my research dates from these consultations. Professor Wallon compared my diagnostic estimates with his own and found the results encouraging. Other psychiatrists at whose clinics I worked followed the same method as Wallon. I owe it to him that the endocrinologist Dr Gilbert Robin gave me the invaluable opportunity to study the hands of his patients. My first insight into endocrine conditions as mirrored in the human hand came from there. It was of particular importance because the endocrine glands provide a key to the knowledge of emotional reactions. Much groundwork had still to be done before the results of my research in Paris could be assembled into a meaningful pattern. But I had learned the basic lessons of a holistic view of hand-diagnosis through my work in France.

As was to be expected, I had to earn my living side by side with my research sooner or later. Maria Huxley's advice had proved right. After less than a year had passed, I took the uneasy step of giving private hand analyses. The Huxleys were the first to send me friends and acquaintances. Among the former were the Vicomte Charles de Noailles and his wife. They were intrigued by my work and recommended me widely. A snowballing effect through word of mouth produced the core of a substantial clientele. In a relatively short time I seemed to be established as a chirologist. My customers were mainly writers, artists and members of the aristocracy. A profession on the borderline of the sensational is a magnet for people who need help and are attracted by the unorthodox and mysterious. But my own role in the proceedings did not tally with my professional values and etiquette. And this led me into a state of depressive anxiety. I was thrown into a world perplexingly different from my own. I acquired a considerable reputation for psychological insight and sensational revelations of my clients' past. I became intrigued and frightened by the influence my consultations could exert on my customers. I had no possibility of changing the situation: it was a question of sink or swim. I also had to get used to visiting the grand house of French aristocrats, and magnates in fashion and industry. I used to arrive breathless with anticipation but, to my suprise and relief, once inside I felt better. Nervous tension returned, however, the moment my 'divinatory' capacities had to be engaged in tracing decisive incidents of my clients' past.

I had been intrigued to find that the French aristocrats were not encapsulated in a superior ghetto as I had feared. They did not live in a golden cage of *les temps perdus*. The prerogative of birth and considerable wealth (in most cases) did not prevent them from mixing freely with the world outside their ken. And several of my 'high class' clients impressed me for different reasons, which I want to illustrate in the following thumbnail sketches.

The Vicomte de Noailles was a lover of the arts and literature, which probably inspired his friendship with the Huxleys. His quiet manner and his courtesy could not hide his intense curiosity about human beings. He was of medium height, with that alert expression in his quick black eyes and mobile mouth which showed him to be a good listener. He probably made mental notes of everything he heard and saw. Was he a frustrated writer, I wondered. His aloofness made it impossible to ask direct questions. Perhaps he admired Maria Huxley because she provided him with that freshness of the imagination and spontaneity which he seemed to lack. His wife, Marie-Laure, as liberal and progressive in her views as he, had much of Maria's vivacity and naturalness. There was nothing stuffy about her. A great admirer of modern music, she seemed to have limitless energy to enjoy the works and the company of musicians and other artists. She had the sensuous beauty of a colt that could bolt or dance, and one never knew which 'turn' would come next. One certainly could not feel in awe of her, and neither she nor her husband were snobs. I had assumed that the Noailles were exceptions, in no way typical of the French aristocracy, but this was not the case.

The princely house of the Comte de D. with its *objets d'art 'en fleurs de lys'* seemed a world apart from that of the Noailles. I had never come across a staunch royalist before, and had forebodings about the meeting. I stared in amazement at the chandelier in a palatial room I passed through. The many electric bulbs were covered with crystal shades in the shape of *fleurs de lys*. This symbol seemed to pervade the whole place. It appeared even in the design of the wallpaper. The devotion to a lost cause displayed here could have been pathetic. But I found it glamorous and breathtaking. I was transported into the seventeenth century, where such splendour and demonstrativeness of loyalty to the throne might have been commonplace.

A middle-aged man of small stature gave me a warm handshake and a nervous smile. His developing paunch seemed to be corseted by a stiff and well-studied upright posture. The person I met was as shy as he was disciplined; two signet rings on his fingers suggested a desire to attract attention, and his demonstrative amiability, a wish to please. Le Comte was everything I had not expected. The displayed virility of his posture did not tally with the softness of his face and hands. He moved slowly and spoke quickly. He came from one of the oldest French families, and obviously identified with his heritage. He needed the support of a great past to strengthen a weak ego. After a scientific education he had entered industry, but his interests were music and the arts. 'I am open to everything new – in the arts and science,' he told me. He had problems in coming to terms with his bisexual nature. Conscious of a marked female streak, he felt emotionally unfulfilled and restless. He could not concentrate for long on anything, and needed luxury and comfort around him to nurse his indifferent health. He also liked luxury, he confessed. He had never thought of consulting a psychiatrist. 'I need a mother, not a doctor,' he told me. 'You have made the right diagnosis,' I confirmed. He asked me to see his wife, who also wanted to consult me, and so I met La Comtesse de D.

A tall and slim woman greeted me with a charming smile. Two cups of coffee were brought in, and I felt that I was being entertained rather than consulted. La Comtesse was too vivacious to keep still for a moment. Her light blue eyes were slightly bulging, and her facial expression conveyed an eager expectation which I soon discovered had always been both a blessing and a curse to her. She never lost hope and always expected too much. She had the very qualities her husband lacked. She was a virile woman with highly-pitched emotional reactions. Her intelligence made her hold back from action when passion and energy would have induced her to engage in adventures she might have regretted later. She was an idealist in search of the right cause. Sensitive or

120

aggressive as the case demanded, she could be a protectress as well as a fiend.

La Comtesse did not seem to consider the *fleurs de lys* to be of particular importance. She mixed well with all sorts of people, and regretted only one thing – not to have been born a man. 'I would have been a mountaineer or a diplomat, perhaps an ambassador,' she said, laughingly. 'I am a perfectionist,' she told me. She was gregarious, seeking the society of interesting individuals, irrespective of class. She asked me about my work, and immediately grasped its possible application as a diagnostic tool. The royalists' palatial house was inhabited by people who were both privileged and deprived – and definitely human.

When I was asked to visit La Marquise de B., I expected a similar milieu to that I have just described. La Marquise belonged to the family of the Pretender to the throne of France. But there were no *fleurs de lys* in a comparatively modest though beautiful house. The butler led me to a small room which I remember well. Two mirrors opposite each other on the side walls made it look bigger than it was, and next to them were several tall book-cases with sliding glass doors. La Marquise looked as one imagines an elegant French woman to look. She had entered the room with those quick and graceful movements of the Latin race. Her black eyes, though, looked tired. Her manners and personality reminded me of the Comtesse de D. Her interests were wide; she collected *objets d'art* and post-impressionist pictures. 'I live in my imagination,' she said. 'I fulfil what is asked of me, but it does not satisfy me. I am never satisfied, and I have not enough staying power to finish what I enthusiastically start. It makes me feel inferior.' She had written detective stories – 'Not published', she added with a smile. She wanted nothing more than to be a professional writer, and she admired nothing more than the creative mind.

La Marquise had considerable gifts, but her place in life did not allow her to make use of them as she would have wanted to. She had no right to be herself, she told me. 'But I do not allow myself to suffer.'

The apartment on the Boulevard Brune was luckily big enough to accommodate my many visitors, who soon included Italian and English people. My new profession could easily have become a barrier between Helen and myself, but this was not so. She and her son rejoiced in my success. It was not in their nature to resent the intrusion of other people into their home. Helen herself had added to the number of my clients through her connections with the world of fashion and the arts. All went well, as friendship and tolerance outweighed possible irritation when the telephone did not stop ringing.

But neither my growing reputation nor the warmth of my friends could compensate me for a feeling of persistent anxiety and rootlessness. Although I was, at times, carried away by the excitement of success, I was unable really to enjoy my good fortune because I had achieved it in a false position, which clouded my sense of integrity. But the recognition of my research by Professor Wallon and other members of the medical profession was an antidote to self-doubt, and I clung to their assurance of my 'worth' as to a certificate of legitimacy.

My friends followed their own bent. Paul went on adolescent adventures, Helen cultivated her own circle of friends and professional colleagues. She showed no sign of resentment when her closest friend, Baladine Klossowska, turned more and more to me. Baladine treated me like one of the family, and on my frequent visits to her flat I also found congenial contact with her son Pierre. He had a high regard for my research and wished to help me. His brother, the painter Balthus, soon joined the three of us, and made me his confidante. The two brothers were as different as chalk from cheese, but both gave my life a new verve, and Baladine herself became not only a close friend but a woman who inspired me. She fed me with Rilke's poetry on one hand and Jewish homeliness on the other, as well as being an echo of a cherished past. Balthus had inherited his mother's talent for painting and, as is well known, later reached the top of his profession. I had, of course, studied the hands of all of them. Balthus intrigued me greatly. This young man, tall and gaunt, was tormented by obsessions and violent likes and dislikes. He searched me out as he had apparently found comfort in my understanding of his problems and my admiration of his work. I felt attracted to the world he lived in, much of which he generously shared with me. We often went together to the Café de Flore where we sat at the same table with Picasso, the beautiful Dora Marr, Man Ray, Antonin Artaud and other surrealists. What was it about the unique atmosphere at that table? The burly Picasso, next to Dora Marr, just sat and stared, drank coffee and hardly said a word.

Antonin Artaud grimaced and made one feel uncomfortable. Only Balthus and Man Ray talked in fits and starts to each other. One evening, Artaud seated himself next to me. He had searched me out to ask for professional help. I agreed to see him. I had been repelled by him when I first met him, but I liked him as soon as he became a 'client'. I wish that the company at that table had been painted by Balthus as a record of some of the most important exponents of the arts before the war. But as it was, Picasso's table at the Café de Flore remains a personal 'possession' which my memory has perpetuated with the sharpness of a snapshot.

It was, however, not Balthus but Pierre Klossowski who interested the surrealists in my work. He told André Breton about me, and he became instrumental in starting a new chapter of my life in exile. Through him I became closely connected with the surrealists and surrealism.

André Breton was soon one of my most ardent supporters. I had 'read' his hands which confirmed his faith in the importance of my work. He spread the word around his circle, and other surrealists came to see me. They accepted me as one of them, and several became my personal friends. They saw in me someone who had lifted new knowledge out of irrational gropings, which put me in line with surrealism. But I soon realized how far away I was from their ideals.

I had no idea that I would enter a revolutionary world of 'absolute' freedom when I became acquainted with André Breton and the 'movement'. The surrealists had slashed the barrier between the consicous and the unconscious mind, between logical and automatic thinking. They saw the world as a *tabula rasa* to be made anew. Their iconoclasm did not halt at the arts and literature. It tore to pieces the whole imagery behind a civilization which had been in its death thrces ever since the First World War. They thought that psychoanalysis pointed in the right direction. The unconscious was the field of discovery they wanted to explore, but they went much further than their model. Their verbal imagery and associations were neither censored nor interpreted, but used as they came – automatically, like reflexes. They rejected the strait-jacket of the 'conscious' mind. Walter Benjamin called surrealism *'Die letzte Momentaufnahme der Europaeischen Intelligenz'* ('the last snapshot of European intelligence'). After Bakunin, so Benjamin said, absolute freedom had been lost, until the surrealists gave it new life again. He called their movement the most integrated, the most absolute and

123

definitive (from Walter Benjamin's 'Der Surrealismus' in *Angelus Novus* published by Suhrkamp, Frankfurt am Main, 1966).

Benjamin had, at the time, been close to communism, which he thought to be the road to freedom. But the surrealists did not take to that creed because of the fetters it laid on the individual. The only surrealist who joined the Communist Party was Aragon, but he didn't stay in it for long. Walter Benjamin criticized their attitude as a lapsus in discipline, but they believed in no other but self-discipline. They were élite-anarchists. There was nothing in the past, present or future that they did not look at in their own fashion, without bias or prejudice. Hidden forces were their spice of life. They saw mystique everywhere, and believed, as I do, that scientific discovery depends more on surrealist thinking than logic. André Breton regarded poetry as the height of mysticism, as well as the highest form of art. Who could quarrel with that?

E. Teriade, the editor of the surrealist magazine *Minotaure*, invited me to contribute an article *'Les Révélations Psychologiques de la Main'*, with analyses of the hands of artists and writers. I proudly accepted and saw it published in the late autumn of 1935. A year or so before I had met my prospective subjects at the modest offices of the *Minotaure*. The small room became more and more crowded with avant-garde French artists. The ageing Ravel arrived, dwarfed by his friend Valentine Hugo, a most impressive lady, six foot tall. The two held hands. Pierre Klossowski stood at my side as protector and interpreter when my French failed me. I talked to Antoine de Saint-Exupéry, Man Ray, Max Ernst, Dali and others. They went without preamble to the point, and impressed me with their manner and naturalness. The sensitized but not rarefied atmosphere which emanated from them made the evening an unforgettable event. Saint-Exupéry had brought his cousin, Madame de Vogué, to meet me. She was in some ways essential to the *Minotaure*, either in its production or selection of contributors. A brittle and beautiful woman novelist, Louise de Vilmorin, introduced herself to me as a contributor to the magazine. Both women stood next to the tall figure of Saint-Exupéry. The tiny Consuelo, his wife, appeared to be left somewhat outside, as if she were not as close to her husband as she should have been. She was a South American princess, languid and anxious, not happily transported onto foreign soil. She didn't fit into this group, and her awkward position drew one's eye and attention towards her. It so happened that I became well acquainted with her later. We met, with or without her husband,

124

at the hotel in which they had made their home, and I saw her many years later after Saint-Exupéry's death.

André Breton had been instrumental in making my work known among surrealists and the progressive intelligentsia of France. But other surrealists had also given me their full support. The following short vignettes reflect my personal impressions of a few of them whom I particularly liked for different reasons.

André Breton and Paul Eluard: I called André Breton and Paul Eluard, always seen together, mental twins. They were as different in appearance as they were identical in ideas. Breton, a gregarious extrovert, hypnotized people with his oratory and charm. He was entirely himself, never put on an act, never used diplomatic devices. He looked at – and through – one with the uncompromising glance of a person who was sure of himself and his *Weltanschauung*. I never observed any slackness in his demands on himself or expectations of others. He applied his surrealist vision to his whole life. The same could be said of Paul Eluard, but he, a poet, had a more hidden personality. In fact he looked rather like Breton's shadow, a disciple of the master rather than a master himself. But his self-effacement in Breton's presence was a façade for his hypersensitive nature. Eluard's innuendoes were just as impressive as Breton's directness of speech. He had less vitality, and needed solitude because of his health and work.

André Breton's physique fitted his mind so well that one could *read* him straight off from appearance and gestures. His broad and athletic body carried an 'imperial' head. His strong chin suggested determination to the point of obstinacy. He would fight with his fists, if necessary, in defence of his beliefs and loyalties. Nothing was good enough for him except the integrity and freedom he stood for. I admired his wholehearted outspokenness, which left no doubt about his stance. He was the most convicing representative of surrealism I had met.

Paul Eluard was not an iota less pure and strong-minded in his surrealist commitment than Breton. Yet his modesty and rather indifferent health made him a less obvious fighter. One had to get to know him by degrees, before the strength of his convictions revealed itself. Both were angry men, indignant about anything that smelled of lethargy or pretence. I got to know Eluard quite well, as I went to see him and his delightful wife, Nusch, several times in their home. She lived entirely for him and I think that her care prolonged his life. He was already unwell during the thirties when I knew him. Eluard struck me as a romantic who became a revolutionary because of his intelligence and convictions rather than natural inclination. He knew himself well enough to recognize the split between his head and his heart. He lived for love. The eroticism of his poems proclaims his very nature. Yet he stands side by side with André Breton as a leading surrealist.

He wrote a book of poems, *Les Mains Libres*. Hands had a special fascination for him, which stimulated his interest in, and appreciation of, my work. He gave me his book *The Public Rose*, with a dedication. I found his signature striking; I reproduce here one of his letters to me followed by one from André Breton. The sabre-like strokes with which Eluard signed his name indicate an intelligence as sharp as a knife, and extreme aggressiveness which was part and parcel of his revolutionary zeal.

When I met Antoine de Saint-Exupéry at the office of the *Minotaure*, I had no doubt that he wholeheartedly belonged to the surrealist movement. But after I had got to know him, I wondered why he had joined. He was so utterly on his own and didn't fit into any group.

Who was he, this tall man of majestic build, and a curiously asymmetric face? It was disconcerting to look at him. His eyes were so different in shape that they did not seem to belong to the same person. When he looked at one vis à vis, one had the feeling of being scrutinized by two people. He was a disconcerting person to be with through this physical oddity alone. And his hands posed a puzzle also. They were not as muscular as his physique would have warranted, and had sausage-shaped fingers with long, sensitive upper phalanges. These fingers revealed an endocrine defect of which he was well aware and talked about to me. Saint-Exupéry, fearless about life and death, was much afraid of himself. And he thought that his hormonal imbalance might have something to do with it. I could only confirm his suspicion of a complex thyroid dysfunction which affected his emotional climate. He had to combat periodical hyperactivity on one side and lethargy on the other. He told me about his constant changes of mood, and his frequent depressions which made him flee human contact. 'I am like an animal – I go into a corner when I am out of luck or ill,' he said. His manner could charm and fascinate one, yet one felt a void with him because of his difficulty in relating to

15 Juillet 1935

Chère madame,

bien entendu, je serais ravi que l'analyse de mes mains parût dans votre livre.

Pour René Crevel, il est parfaitement inutile de demander l'autorisation, à qui que ce soit. Sa famille (ses sœurs) se désintéressent de tout ce qui constituait sa véritable personnalité.

Ma femme et moi, nous serions très heureux de vous voir — et souvent. Je vous téléphonerai ces jours-ci pour que nous prenions rendez-vous.

Croyez-nous, tous deux, très amicalement vôtres,

[signature]

...uard
4, rue Legendre

Paris le 7 janvier 1936.

Chère Madame et Amie,

Je vous retourne en hâte l'analyse, avec tous
mes remerciements. J'éprouve un très vif remords à l'id[ée]
que j'ai omis de recopier et de vous faire parvenir
les notes sensationnelles me concernant que j'avais prises
sous votre dictée. Il m'est arrivé pourtant maintes fois
de les interroger à nouveau et j'ai rendu grâce toujou[rs]
davantage à votre faculté de divination. Je les conserve
très précieusement et elles sont à votre disposition si
jamais mon nom doit reparaître dans un ouvrage de vo[us].
    Vous savez que ma femme et moi, nous sommes
toujours enchantés de vous voir et que si même un jour
vous avez le temps de desserrer les poings de la petite fille
dont vous avez entendu parler, nous vous écouterons
une fois de plus passionnément. Pierre Mabille dit que
tout est déjà tracé dans ses mains, mais elle le cache
mieux que les grandes personnes ne savent faire.
    A bientôt, j'espère. Croyez, chère Madame, à notre
affectueux souvenir.

André Bret[on]

others. He knew this and was sad about it. It seemed a contradiction that he had such an unusual gift for observing people and everything around him. Every change of colour, of light and shade, was caught by his unusual perceptivity. Was it the very dichotomy of feelings which gave him a hypnotic influence over people and animals? One could have imagined him as a lion tamer! But it was clear that this world could not give him the scope he needed and dreamed of. He was a dare-devil of a pilot, and a poet of considerable stature, whose imagination blended with a dream world rather than with what we call reality. I realized, either from his hands or through 'intuition', that he was accident prone, and I suspected suicidal tendencies. Perhaps he chose the tiny South American princess as his wife because she looked like a fantasy, and with fantasies he *could* make contact.

Saint-Exupéry believed in chance, having no use for free will. 'I don't know how I go or where I go,' were his words which I noted down when I looked at his hands for the second time on 20 March 1936. He had the tenderness of a woman, an irresistible urge to help people and animals in suffering. He could not say 'No' to those who wanted his support, and is supposed to have had a hand in the books of several women writers.

A man of his innate nobility could dispense with social masquerade, and his questions as well as his answers had the same ring of complete freedom as I had found in Breton, Eluard, Walter Benjamin and Aldous Huxley.

Consuelo de Saint-Exupéry whom I met again in 1948 had asked me to write something about her husband to be included in a biography she was planning. I don't know if she ever wrote it, but I do know that I refused. She may have been the only person who knew him who was really enigmatic to others.

Antonin Artaud was introduced to me as an actor. It surprised me that a man of such unprepossessing looks, who grimaced involuntarily, should have chosen this profession. I don't know whether he had already written about the theatre in 1935, the year I met him. In any event, I had no knowledge of his iconoclastic ideas, and I did not foresee his eminence as an innovator who would revolutionize the stage. This ugly man did not strike one as mentally sympathetic either. Yet I found him touching in his obvious helplessness and feelings of inadequacy, which made him tongue-tied. When I looked at his hands, I realized he was a real fanatic and an ardent revolutionary, who had every intention of making his fantasies come true.

I told him at the time that his hands did not indicate acting as his profession, but rather that of a writer. Yet I had no idea of his vocation as a theorist of drama.

He looked like an adolescent and behaved like a child. He was highly suggestible, and his hunted expression reflected a state of panic-like anxiety. In his terror of himself and others, he took refuge in drugs (hashish). He was a clinging person, unable to stand on his own feet. I thought him lacking in ambition, and was therefore much surprised when I later learned of his achievements. I realized that he was on the borderline of mental illness, but did not know that he would pass the point of no return. The knowledge of his tragedy and his appeal for help are illustrated in the letter he wrote to me (see following page).

Women were in the minority among surrealist artists. Male supremacy persisted among them in spite of their illuminating insights into human beings and proclamation of absolute freedom. Surrealism had not helped to give women a platform to show themselves in equal measure to men. As a matter of fact, they could be counted on the fingers of one hand. Those I met were the painter Valentine Hugo, the writers Louise de Vilmorin and Madame de Vogué, and Jaqueline Breton, physical artist and poet.

Feminism is as old as the ages, and there can be no doubt about bisexuality, which has existed from prehistoric times to our own.

An unanswerable question recurred to my mind: how was it possible for women to become the second sex instead of leading the evolution of mankind? Yet eminent women have always been stared at, as if they were the ninth wonder of the world, from Sappho to Virginia Woolf and Simone de Beauvoir.

Women are renowned for their flexibility of mind, which equips them for easy adaptation to new and unexpected circumstances. Their mental and emotional reactions are quick. Men, on the other hand, are inclined to stiffness in physical postures and emotional reactions. Stiffness predisposes to stubbornness, as well as emotional and mental blinkers. Women certainly lack the brute muscle power of men, but other differences between the sexes are the result of stereotyped ideas and education rather than 'nature'. The bisexuality of human beings appears to be more marked in

130

74 rue des Moches

Lundi

Chère madame,

La justesse de tout ce que vous m'avez déjà dit, les précieuses indications dont je vous remercie encore, font que, au risque d'être indiscret et d'abuser de votre amabilité, je dois vous avouer que j'aimerais beaucoup, si cela n'est pas trop vous demander, connaître les résultats de l'analyse que vous comptez faire de mes mains. Aussi me permettrai-je de vous téléphoner un matin de cette semaine pour savoir si, sans vous importuner, je puis à nouveau me rencontrer avec vous et entretenir avec vous des relations qui m'apparaissent infiniment précieuses.

En vous remerciant encore, en vous priant d'excuser mon indiscrétion, je vous prie, chère madame, d'agréer l'expression de mes respectueux hommages,

Michel Arnauld

women than men because they are closer to nature. And women *artists* illustrate the difference more strikingly than others.

Jaqueline Breton was a perfect example of bisexuality in the round. She was one of the most impressive personalities of the surrealist circle. She had the body of an athlete, and had been a circus acrobat as well as a champion swimmer. I called her an artist of the body. She was a bisexual woman whose mentality and temperament perfectly matched her physical make-up. She had the restlessness of someone whose curiosity could never be satisfied. Her sharp intelligence and quick wit made her a stimulating companion and a prominent exponent of surrealism. In spite of her enthusiasm for the unusual and the absurd, her critical acumen sifted the authentic from the false. She shared her husband's ideas, and they resembled each other in their love of travel and adventure, always prepared to come face to face with the unexpected round the corner.

There was another side to Jaqueline Breton, which she saw as her other Self. She suffered periodically from a twilight state of mind, when fantasy took over, paralysing her physical energy. While the rhythm of her body seemed to get out of gear, she found herself listening to an inner rhythm which she translated into poetry. At those times she felt isolated from the outside world, and withdrew from her friends, but she returned to them in the same spirit as before when she came out of these phases. Jaqueline Breton was far too strong a personality to be either beaten or 'eaten' by any force outside or inside herself.

The imaginative introvert has a better chance to adapt to new circumstances than the 'outgoing' extrovert. Imagination helps to get under other people's skin; it is the basis of the actor's art of identifying with the people he portrays. Introverts have much to be grateful for when life plays violent tricks on them.

Destiny lies in ourselves, while fate decides our social setting. The events in Nazi Germany made the past in the Weimar Republic look like a fool's paradise. The future had looked blank, if not bleak, at my departure from Germany. But fate dealt me a good card. It gave me a chance in a million through the people I met. The new milieu I had been thrown into held great promise for my life in exile. The pattern which evolved was complex, even contradictory. My new profession brought me into contact with people utterly different from my previous experience. Luckily I was kept on safe ground by the friends with whom I lived, the benevolence of the Wallons and the Huxleys, and the congenial sympathy of the surrealists. I was thrown into different worlds which did not easily mix, or didn't mix at all. How could one see an underlying structure in a chaotic picture of strident colours? It seemed a daunting task. But it was an exciting adventure to live on the edge of things, often not knowing how to tread. It stretched my energies and aroused my curiosity. The wheel of fate had turned in the right direction to further my research and human experiences.

La Princesse Edmond de Polignac, American by birth, famous hostess and Maecenas, gave much time and help to Jewish artists who had fled from Germany to Paris. After I had seen her professionally, she favoured me with some private invitations. On one such occasion I met Armande de Polignac, her niece by marriage. I was struck by both her appearance and her eccentric personality. I was intrigued and pleased when she asked me to come to see her and read her hands, and we fixed an early date for my visit. She was very interested in what I told her and a long conversation followed. A few days later she asked me to tea, and there could be no doubt that we were not only in sympathy with each other, but had close affinities in tastes. From then on she telephoned me, first from time to time, then frequently, to ask me to tea or dinner. She looked on me as an understanding companion who was, as she said, a comfort to her. She had no '*goût*' for society, and had reached an age when one neither makes friends easily nor indulges in love affairs. She lived with a faithful servant in an apartment close to the Place St Sulpice, and seldom left it except for visits to her aunt. It was an open secret that once upon a time *les deux Princesses* had been intimately involved with each other. When I met her she was already an old woman with a very lined face, and the grey-green eyes of a pedigree cat. Armande seemed to be delighted with our droll friendship. We used to sit on a long sofa covered in black velvet, in a narrow room made bigger by the reflections of several mirrors. We sat, ate, drank and held hands. She spoke German fluently, and though I hated the language, I liked speaking it with her. Armande was a composer of music and had been a student of philosophy. She explained her artistic bent through her descent from Goethe on her mother's side. No wonder I was swimming in sentiment and romance, having found an intelligent fairy princess with whom I could communicate. Armande de Polignac had been married to the Comte de

Chavanne la Palice, but she used her maiden name and never spoke of her husband. She never told me whether she was separated, divorced or widowed. This may have been understandable, but the complete rejection of her only child, a daughter, was not. She only once referred to her, saying: 'I don't know her, and don't want to know of her.' The subject was closed. She lived in the ivory tower of her mind, an eccentric splinter of the society she had belonged to. I saw her as a woman in a glass house, into which I stared, fascinated. The brittleness of her existence moved me. I certainly reacted to the glamour of her social status, but I also became emotionally involved with her.

During the summer months Armande went with Jeanne, her maid, to Yugoslavia where her family had an estate. At one of our meetings in early June 1936, she had mentioned the date of her departure. She had no idea that I would come to the station to see her off. But that is what I did. I went to the Gare du Nord to throw a bouquet of flowers into her compartment a few minutes before the train left, because I knew that I might not see her again before I left for England.

Unfortunately, this intense friendship had not been welcome at the Boulevard Brune from the start. Helen resented Armande's daily phone calls. She found all this quite out of place. Paul, on the other hand, thought it very amusing. He could take few things seriously. How often had he stood behind my back murmuring: 'The Gestapo is arriving – beware!' He could not take the Hitler business seriously either, and wanted me to get over my fright of the Gestapo through teasing. I had had little time or inclination to reflect on the events which had brought me to France not so long ago. But my experiences before I left Germany had not died. They had only been superficially buried and could easily be resurrected from an uneasy slumber.

Although I felt averse to going into restaurants frequented by German people, hearing the language and seeing their faces, I had always accepted invitations from Helen's German friends with pleasure. Was not Baladine living with a German journalist, a man younger than herself, and devoted to her with no thought of leaving her? All too often, his work took him back to Frankfurt am Main, but he never changed towards her – at that time anyway. Perhaps a healthy instinct prevented me from being unaware of the volcanic ground of my relations with 'good' Germans. I had no doubt about Helen's anti-Nazi position. She was married to a

Jew and her two sons were half Jewish. But I had not lost a sharp ear for any anti-Semitic remark or gesture, however slight they might be. The real position between Jews and *all* Germans only became clearer to me at a later date when my life once more took a new turn.

Helen was a well-known figure, not only in the French 'Couture,' but among surrealists and the less conventional members of French society. It was she who had introduced me to the Princesse Edmond de Polignac. It may have been irksome to her that the Princess's niece aroused strong feelings in me. Although my hand-interpretations had made me financially independent, my emotional dependence on my friends had not changed, and my sense of security with them had not been flawed so far. I did not realize that a German woman, even when she was closely connected with Jews and anti-Nazis, could have ambivalent feelings about them. But this was the case with my friend Helen. She became more and more reserved towards me. Her irritation about my attachment to Armande may have got the better of her, inducing her to make diminishing remarks about Jews. Paul did not want to acknowledge the growing rift between his mother and myself. He behaved as if nothing had changed, but the day came when she insulted me with an unmistakably anti-Semitic remark. I stared at her, but uttered no word. I just went to my room, packed my belongings, and left.

Luckily the Hôtel du Quai Voltaire had accommodation for me. Paul had helped me with the paraphernalia of my departure. He saw the taxi drive off before turning away to join his mother. I did not see her again for another thirty years, but met Paul in London eight years later as an officer with de Gaulle.

After two years of happy-go-lucky sharing with Helen and Paul, I was alone again. The years of home life with them had given me a store of experiences, progress in my research, new friends, and financial independence. But I realized that the new turn of events was a step forward rather than a loss, because it had strengthened my willpower and self-confidence. And it made me reject everything German. Other events in the wake of the broken friendship prevented a possible reconciliation.

Not long after the separation from Helen, her German friends who had invited me to their houses bade me adieu because contact with me boded danger for them. Baladine's German partner had been recalled to Frankfurt, and she never heard from him again. I had finally left a half-way house. The wrench seemed almost painless, a liberation rather than deprivation. I started to ask myself whether I had been blind in holding on to German people for so long.

My mind went back to my departure from Berlin, with Katherine's arrival at the Bahnhof Zoologischer Garten at the last minute. Why didn't I hate her, tell her to go to hell, she who had left me when I was in danger? Why did I, so perversely, long for her love which I had not really wanted when she gave it? Loss had attached me to her, against pride and self-protection. Then I remembered some odd goings-on at the Boulevard Brune. I saw the three of us sitting around a card table playing 'spiritual séance'. We pretended to do so with tongue in cheek – but did we? I must really have been taken in by the happenings. The table had spelt out Katherine's name. Could Paul have cheated and moved the table, I wondered later. In any case, I was besotted enough with Katherine to be in earnest, and I had asked the spirit a few questions. When it 'told' me that she had gone back to her family because she was ill, I was truly alarmed. Helen's occult curiosity appeared to be strong enough to find out whether we had really received a message. She encouraged me to telephone Katherine's home in the Rhineland. I did so with some trepidation. Her rather irate stepmother answered the telephone, telling me that she did not know Katherine's address, but could assure me that she was in good health. Although I was not completely cured of my masochistic indulgence, spiritual messages held no credence for me from then on. Not long afterwards, other fancies, other people, preoccupied me, and Katherine was put into the museum of buried memories.

I had been so busy making a new life that I had not looked at my recent past, the Germany I had left. Germany under the Nazis had become a freak country, and I did not want to think about any individual living there. But after the débâcle with Helen, overdue questions about Germany and the Jews came into the forefront of my mind. I began to question my former identification with Germany, which I had had, at all events, to abandon because it had been a false identity. The break with my German friends had not only been a personal and a racial shock to me; I had become aware of what it means to be a Jew – that no nationality bestowed on me would make any difference to my Jewishness. I was an international Jew for good, whether I was a stateless person or a citizen of another country. I was not only prepared to accept this status, but rather liked it. I have stuck to it ever since, without fear or hesitation, and when now asked about my nationality I answer: 'I am an international Jew with a British passport.'

I could not hate or even dislike Helen or the Germans who had said goodbye to me for reasons of self-protection. They had helped me, in an indirect way, to realize my Jewishness. Why had I been so blind before the German disaster as to deny myself the privilege of being different from these Germans, instead of thinking of myself as one of them? At last I recognized to the full what had been amiss with my ideas about German Jews. The Germans had always been a danger to the Jews, not the other way round as they proclaimed. But the Jews must be blamed for their eagerness for assimilation, and their lack of collective identity. I realized now that differences between Germans and Jews had been too obvious to be discarded as insignificant. I remembered how I had been drawn to my own kind rather than to Germans from childhood on. Yet it could not be denied that Germans and Jews had been attracted to one another by a kind of love-hate. Alienness had rather added spice to relationships between them.

The hostility of Germans towards Jews and other minorities was complete in the Nazi period. The Germans had never realized the civilizing influence the Jews had had on them. I remembered how disgusted I was when, before my departure, I perused German newspapers. One was confronted with the rape of a language, the brutalization of words through neologism, easily applied to this flexible language. The Nazis had made a mockery of the works of Goethe, Wieland, Hölderlin, Novalis, Brentano – in fact, the whole gallery of their poets, writers and thinkers. The sinister signs of a horrible change in values and morality dated further back than the days of Hitler. I had first noticed a striking brutality in German faces about two years before I left the country. It struck me like a thunderbolt. Max Ernst might have experienced something similar when he expressed the emotional depravity of human beings by putting animal heads on their trunks. I remember that I told Katherine about my experience at the time, and said I would prefer to live in France. I cannot recollect what her answer was. Yet even then I still felt reluctant to see myself as anything else but a German Jewess. But the ground under my feet must have been shaky. I remember feeling very uneasy when a Jewish nurse, after her marriage to a Jewish government official, was introduced by her husband as Frau Oberregierungsrat. Why had the Jews pushed themselves into high government positions, I wondered. Why did they imitate ridiculous social mores which so blatantly demonstrated the German inferiority complex? Why did they play the same stupid game as the Germans? One had to hold one's breath not to burst out laughing or crying about Jewish imitations of other Teutonic customs, such as duels, producing sabre cuts on students' faces, which were welcomed as marks of honour. The Jews had lived in a fantasy world and didn't watch the danger signals. Many Jews lost their humanity and warmth in the process. When, after the 1917 Communist Revolution, Jews from Eastern Europe 'invaded' the country, German Jews either turned a blind eye to their needs, or openly wanted them out. They were apprehensive of their own brethren, fearing that they might spoil their image as good Germans. It was quite true that some of the Eastern Jews had succeeded in buying property and making money, being bad landlords to boot. Such proceedings were rightly detested by Jews and non-Jews alike, but they increased German anti-Semitism to a high pitch.

Only the Zionists had woken up to reality, long before Hitler. On the other hand, German Jews shared their mother tongue with the German people, and had been reared in their culture. Their vocabulary and imagination were nurtured by the same source. And Jews who were addicted to the word, as writers and poets, felt even more acutely about their bond with the German language. The crux of the Jewish predicament was the loss of their native tongue which nothing else could ever replace. Apart from this obvious difficulty, they did not want to have a closely knit Jewish community, as that might re-create a Jewish ghetto.

The Jewish question is a conundrum and there is no solution to it. I have been much impressed by the fact that Isaac Bashevis Singer, the Nobel Prizewinner for literature in 1978, writes his books in Yiddish. He knows the pitfalls of a borrowed language. In an interview (*Observer*, 17 December 1978) Singer proclaimed that he put his faith in the Yiddish language and spirit. To him, Yiddish is not a dying, only a sick, language. He is not only a survivor from Nazi terror, but brought this Jewish identity as a writer with him into exile. He has remained a 'whole' person. As he says: 'A Jewish writer, if he has no topic, can always sit down and write about the Jewish problem, because he can write a million articles and the Jews will still have a problem.'

My reflections about the Germans and the Jews were both depressing and salutary. Delving into the past did not prevent me from enjoying the freedom I felt after my departure from the Boulevard Brune to the Hôtel Voltaire. I loved being there. The beautiful Quai with the bookstands of street traders amused me. The Louvre on the opposite side of the Seine made me fully aware that I was living in Paris – city of culture. A few weeks after my arrival, Sybille Bedford took up residence in the hotel: we met, we conversed, until we gradually became closer acquainted.

Earning one's living in strange circumstances, pursuing research, meeting journalists and photographers from abroad, were not only time-consuming, but took most of my energy. The rewards were considerable, but at the expense of my nervous energy. Symptoms of over-strain were disregarded because I could not stop in mid-stream. Many appointments had to be faced in dread of collapsing in the middle of it all. It was not my research and meetings with the medical profession that affected me so. On the contrary, they had a therapeutic effect. But luncheons at big restaurants with bigwigs from different countries were daunting, and could only be endured through autosuggestive efforts and a good deal of wine. I often sat among high-powered persons who were calm and well fed, rubbing my temples in order to get the blood back into my brain. And on many occasions I feared that I would fall under the table rather than sit at it! The strain of keeping up conversations, particularly in English which I hardly knew, was a travail in itself. The ménage with my two friends, who knew all this well, had saved me from a nervous breakdown. For a long time, two years or so, they cosseted and comforted me, gave me food and drinks to restore me after these trials. But one cannot go on overtaxing oneself without damage, even when young, and I felt the need to get away from it all. I yearned for distraction and fun, and some casual erotic fireworks. Helen knew what I needed. She introduced me to people who had nothing to do with Haute Couture and French society. They belonged to an American coterie of intellectual women, liberated before their time. Most of them were lesbians who lived a kind of community life. They had enthusiasm and zest for new experiments, and they gave me the relaxation and amusement I wanted. One of them, Paula, belonged, like some of

139

her circle, to the Gurdjieff Group. She told me enthusiastically about the goings-on at these gatherings. The members of the group were taught many lessons by their guru, Gurdjieff, with the aim of increasing their vitality and nervous energy. There was quite a swarm of these American lesbians gathered round the great man. They enjoyed the lessons – from drinking armagnac (a very potent liquor), to the dressings-down they received about their many sacred cows, their habits and general lack of awareness. The guru was a true 'he-man', and his educational scheme was worked out in accordance with the Yin and Yang, the male and female principles. According to him, Yin and Yang dominated all aspects of life but particularly human sex. How odd, I thought, that these lesbians should swallow teachings which denigrated them without so much as a murmur of protest! But there it was: they had found a new religion which kept them going, if not happy. Paula begged me to go and see the Master, with a view to becoming inspired to join the group. I refused. But on her insistence that I should at least have a look at Gurdjieff, I promised to do so. He always lunched at the same hour at the Café de la Paix. There I stared at his bald head and his devouring eyes in a square and badly shaved face. He was a bull-necked giant of a man, who repelled me to such an extent that I ran out of the Café de la Paix without finishing my meal. My God, I thought, how can they trust that old devil! My aversion to Gurdjieff led to the end of an affair with Paula, and my contacts with his American 'pupils'. My claustrophobia in restaurants increased after I had left Helen. It appeared to be the only trauma the separation had inflicted on me.

Maria Huxley had suggested that I should write a book on hand-reading. Her interest in my work made her promise a bit more than she could manage – namely to help with the translation. Aldous Huxley had agreed to write a foreword to the book in which Chatto & Windus were interested. After some months of trying to translate my German text, Maria took fright. She did not really know German well enough, and was afraid to be burdened with something she found too difficult to combine with her full life. It must have been awkward for her to wash her hands of the project, but this was her intention. When I reacted with considerable alarm and distress, she promised not to let me down. At this point Sybille Bedford, who knew the language, offered her help. But even so, Maria worried that the book would not turn out well enough if the translation was not professionally done. In the end, Olive Cook took on the task.

Maria Huxley felt guilty that she had caused me anguish at a time when I depended on her support. On one of her occasional visits to Paris she joined me for a meal at my favourite restaurant close to the Hôtel Voltaire. I felt ill at ease with her. We made conversation, but could not talk away the tensions between us. And I was quite at sea when she sprang on me an invitation to visit her in London. The Huxleys had a flat in the Albany, Piccadilly, and generally spent the autumn and winter there. I recognized her wish to help me, but thought that her generous gesture was an atonement of guilt rather than a token of friendship. Yet, her invitation was made with a show of warmth which calmed my mind – superficially. She wanted to prepare for my stay: she would get rooms for me near the Albany, and I would spend most of the time with Aldous and her. I could see their friends, who were prospective subjects for my book, at their flat, and clients in my rooms. I was touched by her generosity and thanked her profusely. Yet after she had gone, I felt unsure about a visit to London in a few months' time. I couldn't visualize my place in the Huxley milieu. And I thought it inappropriate to meet their friends with a view to making use of them. My ambivalent relationship with Maria weighed heavily on me, and I was much preoccupied with my conflicting feelings about her. My admiration for her intriguing personality had not been affected by doubts of her steadfastness. She impressed me by the way she observed the world around her with the eye of a painter. She looked at and listened to people not only out of innate curiosity, but for Aldous' sake. Her love for him had a sublime quality. She had become the bridge between him and the world outside – his eyes. He was nearly blind, and needed her help to get about town. But she did not only get him along in the humdrum of day-to-day life. Her mental eye illuminated his imagination. She provided the fascinating reports and gossip about people which fed Aldous' mind. Her Latin sense of practicality was counterpoised by a vivid imagination which he lacked. One could not help falling under Maria's spell, however much one might criticize her. She bore the admiration of others as lightly as a feather, and seemed quite unaware of the magnetism which made all men love her. Women were not impervious to her charms either. But she always looked worried and preoccupied, like a clown who has the public 'in his pocket', yet carries, underneath the laughing face, the burden of a melancholic nature. Maria, beautiful and slim, didn't think of herself as either, and tried, to the horror of her friends, to lose weight when she should have put it on. She came into many people's lives like a comet, but one would have preferred her to be a star, and not go away as suddenly as she had come.

The Wallons lived in a small house close the Place de Trocadéro, and with them I regained my enjoyment of life which Maria Huxley had temporarily dampened. Wallon came from Brittany and, at first glance, looked true to the Breton type, except perhaps for his carroty red hair. He had penetrating blue eyes, a lean face and a mobile mouth which articulated his speech with expressive movements. His gestures were altogether swift and staccato, characteristic of an impulsive and impatient person. He certainly did not suffer fools gladly. He was a tall and lanky man, who spoke with a very low voice in a racing tempo, which made it difficult to understand all he said. His wife, Germaine, of peasant stock, was a stout woman with a small, almost ape-like forehead. The dark colour of her eyes looked even darker because of thick brows which crossed the bridge of her nose, as if made by the heavy stroke of a paint brush. She could look forbidding, but emanated warmth, equanimity and benevolence. I knew that both of them regarded me as a personal friend. I had passed the preliminary stages of our contact speedily, because they asked me to meals in their house only a year after we had met. In French society, this is a great favour, shown to close friends rather than old acquaintances. Professor Wallon made me feel at my best because I was sure of him. He had given me his full support, and even asked the board of the Rothschild Hospital to engage me as a psychiatrist, proposing a special plea to circumvent French regulations. Luckily he didn't succeed. It might have prevented me from leaving France a year later. Looking back, I find it amazing that he tried, as France has the most stringent rules against the professional activities of foreigners.

The worlds of Professor Wallon and Maria Huxley were poles apart, but each had launched me into a new life with equal conviction: Maria into the world of her literary and aristocratic friends, and Professor Wallon into that of science. The surrealists had received me into their 'brotherhood', and had provided the first platform from which to make my work known in France and beyond through my article in the *Minotaure*.

142

Although I knew that the *Minotaure* represented a landmark in the history of surrealism, and was treasured by many people all over Europe and the U.S.A., I only became aware of its lasting significance three years ago. I happened to visit the exhibition 'Hommage à Tériade' at the Royal Academy, London, a few days before it closed. After I had admired the paintings of biblical scenes of the Old Testament by Marc Chagall, I entered a room devoted to the drawings of Picasso. And my eye fell on a glass-covered table. It contained exhibits from the *Minotaure*. One showed two pages of *'Les Révélations Psychologiques de la Main' par le docteur Lotte Wolff.* I walked away on air.

My mind went back to the autumn of 1935, the time of its publication. Good stars had smiled on me then, which had lifted my spirits and self-confidence. About the same time, I came to England on a visit to Maria Huxley on a misty October day. The feeling which got hold of me after I had set foot in Dover can only be described as a sense of enchanted unreality. On boarding the train to London, I had a feeling of liberation redolent of my flight from Berlin after we had left the German frontier at Aachen. The comfort of the compartment, the quiet voice of the waiter, acted like a tranquillizer. His courtesy was enhanced by the quietness of the passengers, who seemed to be engrossed in reading newspapers, or just sat still. No noise, no unnecessary words or movements disturbed the peace of this English train. Silence is bliss to strained nerves. Perhaps the mist of the season, perhaps an altogether symbolic mist, kept crass reality at bay from one in this strange country. Apprehension about my visit was simply forgotten. During the days which followed I formed a wholly idealized picture of England: I seemed to have landed in a fairy tale, walking around Piccadilly and meeting some of the country's privileged citizens. My impressions were largely illusory, yet not without relevance to the puzzle the English pose to a foreigner. After my life in Germany and France, I was struck by a difference in attitudes and atmosphere which made England look vastly superior to the Continent.

I came into luxurious surroundings, luxurious not in the sense of material riches but of mental quality. My bed was made. Maria Huxley had organized this venture to perfection: from renting a suite in Dalmeny Court, Piccadilly, to meetings with the famous, the rich and the 'lion-hunters'. Aldous, the eternal stranger, and the vivacious Maria were the focus of attraction for writers, artists and others I got to know during this visit. I never ceased to marvel at Maria's intelligence, her unfailing enthusiasm for the whole undertaking, and for every meeting I had either at the Albany or Dalmeny Court. How much expense of energy, how much fatigue, she must have suffered! Aldous' good humour and his tolerance of 'intrusions' must have meant a real sacrifice of his own needs. I always stood in awe of him, but I felt his goodwill, his desire to help, as an honour bestowed on me, and a sign of his human warmth. At this visit I noticed in Aldous the same independence from any conventional consideration which had impressed me in Walter Benjamin. When he once spoke of 'the bad poetry of Humbert Wolfe, a good man who should have stuck to politics', I stared at him in surprise. I was aware that he had made this damaging statement without rancour or malice, simply as a matter of fact, a statement of truth. The absence of hypocrisy or false sentiment made me admire him even more. Aldous Huxley was the living example of the inequality of man.

The Huxleys' disregard of 'what the neighbours might say' was exemplary. The door bell rang often at their Albany flat to admit people whose faces must have been well known to some of the neighbours. As if this was not enough, passers-by could watch me staring through a magnifying glass at the hands of the 'famous'. Aldous left the house before I started and, after she had received my clients, Maria disappeared quietly into the kitchen downstairs, or else went out.

Maria had laid particular emphasis on an analysis of Virginia Woolf's hands. 'She is a star – our greatest writer,' she had told me, who had paltry knowledge of English and practically none of English literature. A shrewd observer of people's weaknesses, Maria had soon discovered my vulnerability to snubs. She warned me about Virginia Woolf's haughty air and sharp tongue. She had asked her to tea to loosen tension before I looked at her hands. Up to the last minute before she was due to arrive, we both feared that she might cancel the appointment. But Virginia Woolf came punctually at the allotted time. She wore a black overcoat and a brown hat in the shape of a boat. Her manner was reserved and somewhat suspicious. But her curiosity to meet a member of the medical profession who read hands had obviously intrigued her enough to have a look at me and my doings. I found her neither beautiful nor attractive at first sight. It was just as well that she did not awe me and so put me at a disadvantage. In less than ten minutes she had achieved the opposite – she put my hackles up with the cynical question: 'You really believe that there is something in hand-reading?' 'I don't believe, I know,' was my answer. For the first time she looked into my face with a smile of surprise. A hard woman, I thought. I had been apprehensive of her tightly-closed lips and the lines round her mouth, suspecting that she was holding back unpleasant thoughts and feelings. But the moment she looked straight into my eyes and I saw hers, I felt more comfortable. Maria realized that this was the moment to leave us alone, and suggested that I should interpret Virginia Woolf's hands at once so that she could judge for herself whether there was something 'in it' or not. 'You had better sit next to the window to have the full light,' she said before she left.

And so we sat by the window. My magnifying glass in hand, my reading glasses over my eyes, I reached out for Virginia Woolf's left, and after a while for her right, hand. I now had command of the situation. I spoke to her about herself, but didn't say anything about her work as I had read none of her books. I saw, either by intuition or method but probably a mixture of both, a deeply disturbed person, fighting for emotional balance and sanity. She paled at times, took in every word (I spoke in French), and after a long period of listening, she asked questions. Darkness fell while we were talking; perhaps two hours had passed when Maria gave a sign that she was there. She had returned some time before but, seeing us so engrossed, had left the room. The interview ended apparently to Virginia Woolf's satisfaction. She asked me to come to tea the following Sunday at her house in Tavistock Square. I was only too pleased to accept. Maria was delighted and couldn't wait for me to tell her about my personal impression, and what I had seen in her hands. I cannot recall the answer I gave, but Sybille Bedford remembered that I told Maria: 'I think that Virginia Woolf is mad.' If so, I would have blatantly offended against medical ethics. Some time later I learned that Lady Ottoline Morrell had advised Virginia Woolf to consult me.

Before I set out on my visit to Tavistock Square, Maria had warned me to be on my guard. 'She's bound to ask you all about yourself, and she might use your tale whenever it suits her book'. I laughed, as I was quite impervious to such designs. I was not quite sure why I had been invited to tea, except perhaps as a follow-up of my hand analysis. I was led to a room on the top floor of a high and narrow house, where Virginia Woolf sat at a table with all the paraphernalia of an English tea. This seemed quite incongruous. But she was a perfect hostess. She didn't regale me with small talk, but went straight into questioning me about my experiences in Nazi Germany. I wondered whether her desire to hear first hand about the Nazi terror had had anything to do with this invitation. I told her a great deal, about my arrest as a spy suspected to be a man in woman's clothing, the house searching and my disquiet and loneliness after all that. 'My husband is a Jew,' she said after I had finished. 'He is the most humane person I know,' and much later during the afternoon she told me: 'Leonard is my mother.'

But she had not been inquisitive about details of my personal life. We sat at the table for quite a time. There was a hiatus between having tea and what happened after, which has escaped my recollection. But I vividly remember that she rather hesitatingly said to me: 'Let's sit "dos à dos"; it is easier for me to relax.' And each of us sat in an easy chair facing a wall. She wanted to know how I would treat people with nervous tension and anxiety. 'No advice should ever be given by a psychologist. No therapeutic shortcuts exist for anxiety states, and nervous tension has many causes.' When I did however come forward with the suggestion that one could use common sense to alleviate such symptoms, she nodded in complete agreement. 'Have you thought of doing things with your hands, like crocheting or knitting?' I asked. No, she would be too impatient, was the answer. 'What about typing? Just let energy flow out mechanically, which is a possible help against cramping one's postures and stiffening one's limbs.' 'Yes, it makes sense,' she replied. Pause. The silence lasted for about a minute, or may be two. Then she asked hesitantly: 'What do you think of psychoanalysis?' 'You mean Freudian analysis?' 'Yes.' 'I cannot judge it as I had a Jungian analysis. I can only tell you that it is costly and takes years. It may help some people but not others. In certain cases it is contraindicated.' She jumped in. 'You mean, in my case?' 'Yes, I would think so.' 'Tell me about the Jungian analysis.' 'I can only speak about my own experience, and cannot judge its general value,' I answered. 'It did me good, but not for the reasons one might expect from psychotherapy. It is a matter of luck if you find an analyst you like. And real contact between doctor and patient is, to my mind, the *sine qua non* in any form of therapy. I liked my analyst greatly. I went to her because I was lonely, and did not want to burden my friends with

146

my "lost territory". The Nazis threatened to take away all I had. The help I got was like a drug, an escape for some hours a week from a terrifying reality.' 'Tell me more,' she insisted. 'Six months before I emigrated to France I became so depressed that I consulted a Jungian analyst who later recommended me to a colleague in Paris who would continue her work. I did as she bid me. The two women analysts certainly did me good because I liked and trusted them. Their personalities had a healing influence on me.' No answer from the back for a while. Then: 'I have misgivings about psychiatry.' 'Many people have,' I said, avoiding a real answer.

I wonder whether I had noticed that the walls of the room were covered from floor to ceiling with books, before my hostess rose from her chair. She went straight to one of the shelves, took out a book and wrote something in it. It was *To the Lighthouse* in the German translation. 'I want you to have this,' she said, and handed me the book. How beautiful she looked! Her tall and slim figure bore a high and narrow head with a face of classical design. She was in mind and body an aristocrat. With all her understanding of the false and humiliating position of women, she would never have been a Suffragette. She was an élitist, whose feminism remained intellectual.

I had put her precious gift into my briefcase before saying goodbye. I walked down the flights of stairs into Tavistock Square. A few yards from her house I noticed that I had left my briefcase behind. I must have been in a sort of trance when I ran back to the house, anxious and embarrassed. There she stood at the entrance, waving and holding up the briefcase. She handed it over to me and smiled, a vacuous smile. Then she turned her head away and looked at the people who were walking in the Square, and said: 'All these people, all these people – sometimes I lose myself, walking and walking through the streets. And I don't know where I am.' She turned round again to me, waving her left hand in a goodbye, and went into the house. I never set eyes on her again.

I also paid a home visit to another friend of Maria's, Lady Ottoline Morrell. It may sound ridiculous, but it is nevertheless true, that Lady Ottoline and I were friends at first sight. I had come, of course, to analyse her hands, but this time everything was different. She did not focus on what my analysis did or did not reveal about her. She appeared to be far more interested in

147

my life as a refugee, and how I came to take up my present work, which she thought was rather depressing as I was a doctor of medicine. I remember her saying: 'It could be so easily misunderstood.' She asked me to come again, but not for professional reasons. This I did two or three times before I left London. A lively correspondence followed my visits to Gower Street. She wrote me many letters during my remaining year in Paris, and sent me the Bible in German as a token of affection. I only read it because it came from her. I knew that she found solace in the New Testament, and she may have thought it would do the same for me. She had recognized a point of contact between us when she told me: 'You and I are very lonely people, and the people around us have no idea of it.'

In one of her letters Lady Ottoline spoke of a visit she had just paid to Virginia Woolf, which had left her with much sadness. She was very fond of her but distressed by her malicious tongue and depreciation of most people, whether they were friends or not. Her remarks about her were as pertinent as they were empathetic. She referred also to Virginia's adieu to me, which she saw quite differently from my own impression. 'Her gesture of holding up her hand towards you after she had handed you the brief-case was a gesture of defence. She just does not want to acknowledge *real* people,' she wrote. Had I indulged in wishful thinking? Virginia Woolf had been friendly and appreciative towards me from the moment we sat at the window at Albany. Probably Lady Ottoline's version and my own were equally true. Virginia Woolf's illness conditioned her to such ambivalent feelings.

Aldous and Maria shared my view that the study of monkeys and apes would add a new dimension to my work on the human hand. And Julian Huxley was the very person who could help me to realize this plan. It seemed best to go and see him about my project and, shortly before I left for Paris, Maria and I called on Julian and his wife at their home in the Zoological Gardens. As it happened, he agreed about the importance of investigating the extremities of our earliest ancestors, and invited me to carry out such a study at the London Zoo when I had the opportunity. This last-minute visit became seminal for my future plan to leave France for England.

International organizations are an anchor for the persecuted. One need only think of Amnesty International. And a number of religious as well as philanthropic organizations, such as the Society of Friends, helped refugees from Nazi tyranny. They handed their protégés on to their representatives in another country in case of a second emigration. But I do not know why my friend Henri van Etten had notified Bertha Bracey of my visit to London, as I was not a refugee in need and had not by then planned to leave France permanently. He had suggested that we should get acquainted, and Bertha Bracey came to visit me at the Huxleys' in the Albany. Aldous knew her quite well as he shared with the Quakers a mutual concern – pacificism. Bertha Bracey, small, stout and bespectacled, combined a fine intelligence with acute observation and maternal warmth. One year later, she became instrumental in assuring my smooth transfer from France to England. I also went to see *her* at the Refugee Centre in Woburn Place. The business-like atmosphere and the drab streets around the Centre made me see London in a somewhat different light. I had formed a romantic image of the town, having been blinded by the glamour of the West End and those beautiful houses I had visited with Maria. No wonder I had been impressed by the streets and the people around Piccadilly and St James's Square. It seemed natural at the time to project my naïve idea of privileged living onto London and England as a whole. But I had some real justification for thinking that England was a very civilized country. I had not seen anywhere else such a well equipped, and indeed elegant, post office as that in Pall Mall. Here was a definite point of comparison between England and the Continent. Post offices in France smelt like neglected railway stations. Everything there was rough and unfriendly, from the bare dirty floors to the bellowing voices of men and women behind the counters. German post offices had been less noisy, but were lacking in London's style and courtesy.

One could look on the English policeman, the smiling bobby whose reputation for helpfulness was known all over the world, as a public institution. But to see such a representative of the law in person was like a lovely dream for someone who had been afraid of his opposite number in France and particularly in Germany, let alone been in their hands.

The pleasure I felt in walking through the streets of the West End had a different ingredient from the pleasure of Parisian boulevards. In spite of their narrowness and traffic disproportionate to their size, the quietness and courtesy of drivers and pedestrians sealed my conviction that London was indeed the most civilized city in Europe. Europe? England seemed to be far away from the Continent, for which its island status was an insufficient explanation. The autumn with its seasonal mists could have encouraged the idea of England hanging in the air instead of standing on firm ground. The veil of silence and the veil of mists gave London an aesthetic quality of its own, but made it look ghostly. And Londoners didn't appear to stand on quite firm ground either. Twice I had to ask strangers to direct me to a certain street, but they could not do so although it was next to their own. Did the English go so far in minding their own business as to shut their eyes to everything but their own concerns? Aloofness and detachment can become exaggerated, I could not help thinking. One could not reach these kindly people; one could hardly see them in their 'foggy' presence. One would never be able to come close to them, was the obvious, if superficial, conclusion. In famous stores, saleswomen, even more than salesmen, languidly sat or stood around without any obvious wish to sell their wares. They had to be approached, a fraction against their inclination, before the transaction could start. But English people's involvement with themselves also had a pleasant side: they neither stared at one nor were they aggressive. One was left in peace, whether one liked it or not. This was so different from the Continent where people made rude remarks quite openly about anybody, where they shouted and stamped their feet, where life was crude, aggressive and three-dimensional. English people kept their 'third' dimension well hidden, so that they appeared like Disney drawings rather than full-blooded human beings.

These were field-days for a romantic: London and its people within my orbit had fired my imagination, but I realized that there were many gaps in my impressions which one day would have to be filled in. One nagging thought preoccupied me on my visit to London and afterwards: how could the British have become so powerful and rich while working apparently little and with reluctance? They seemed to live for weekends, when shops were closed and they could go off somewhere. To take weekends off was, at that time, neither a German nor a French habit.

And so I left England after a successful 'treasure hunt'. I took a nest egg with me – enough to live on for a whole year in Paris. But the more important treasures were hopes for the future, and some potential friendships.

My return to Paris was an anti-climax. I made comparisons

between the way of life in England and France, and found Paris wanting. I still met my surrealist friends in the same spirit as before, and saw Baladine Klossowska every few days. And there was no ebb in the number of people who sought me out for consultations. But Paris had lost much of its attraction, and I became more and more preoccupied with the possibility of a life in peaceful London. The unwelcome but irresistible thought that Germany would go to war with the West in the foreseeable future lurked at the back of my mind. The possibility that France might be invaded simply terrified me. I saw the concentration camp coming closer and closer to where I was now. I decided to discuss the matter with Professor Wallon, whose political acumen had greatly impressed me. He was not surprised about my fears, as he himself anticipated another war in the not too distant future. He said: 'I think that you have good reason to feel insecure in France. You would be wise to leave for London if you have a chance, to get established there.' He said something else, equally to the point, though difficult for me to accept. 'The trouble with the Jews is that, unlike you, most of them lost their natural reflexes. Otherwise they might have shown more resistance against the Nazis.'

'I know that many of them behaved like hypnotized rabbits, but what could the Jews do against a brutal S.S. who had them completely in their hands? You have not experienced the plight they were exposed to.' He looked thoughtful.

During the last year of my stay in Paris, I saw a great deal of the Wallons, and, in the end, it was parting from them and Baladine that made me feel sad to leave France. Professor Wallon had invited me to contribute an article on scientific chirology for the *Encyclopédie Française*, for which he would write a foreword. In 1938, my contribution 'Les Principes de la Chirologie' was published in Volume VIII of *La Vie Mentale*. This seal of recognition of my work was an appropriate finale to my life in France.

By the summer of 1936, I had started preparations for my departure. I saw fit to invest the rest of my London nest egg in clothes and a new typewriter. It seemed wiser to have a good outfit than to save money. During my last year on French soil I was still much occupied with research and private consultations. I also finalized my book *Studies in Hand Reading*. It was not an easy task, and involved much correspondence with my French and English 'subjects'. I had to obtain their permission to publish the analyses of their hands before the book could be given to Chatto & Windus. Luckily they all agreed. The book appeared in the autumn of 1936 in London, and A. Knopf published it soon after in the U.S.A.

In possession of an affidavit from the Quakers and the Huxleys, I crossed the Channel on a bright October day. My second uprooting involved almost as much preparation as the first, but without the heartbreak. Leaving a country for good means shedding possessions, like cutting weeds away. But I could not leave my books, my typewriter, or my clothes behind. Burdened, as on my previous emigration, with the same metal trunk of German origin, and a cheap brown suitcase, I set forth for England. My brown German passport, valid until 1938, made me feel like an impostor, travelling under false colours. Before reaching Dover, foreigners had to pass through an examination by the immigration officer. It was the emigrant's last hurdle before being allowed or refused entry into the promised land. My knees shook when my turn came. The man at a small table opposite me was middle-aged and bald. As was to be expected, he wore the inscrutable mask of a detective. The image he wanted to project was like that of the English policemen, friendly and human. I soon felt at ease and seemed to answer question after question without difficulty or apprehension. He appeared to take a long time over the interview and, in the end, professed his personal interest in psychology. This not enough, he did something out of turn for a man in his position. He told me that he would like to see me again, and asked me if I could meet him one day for lunch at the Kardomah Café in Piccadilly. I had no option but to agree. We shook hands, and a week later I went to the café at the appointed time. He was already there. He asked many questions about my studies and myself, but reciprocated by telling me a good deal about himself, whether true or false. I am still at a loss to understand his unconventional approach. It had crossed my mind that he might have been a C.I.D. officer who was looking for information about other refugees through me. I shall never know, but my instinct rejected such a suspicion. And so I took him and the sympathy he professed at face value and as a good omen for the future.

First day at school

Danzig in the thirties (map from
Danzig so wie es war by
Hans Lewald, Droste Verlag,
Düsseldorf)

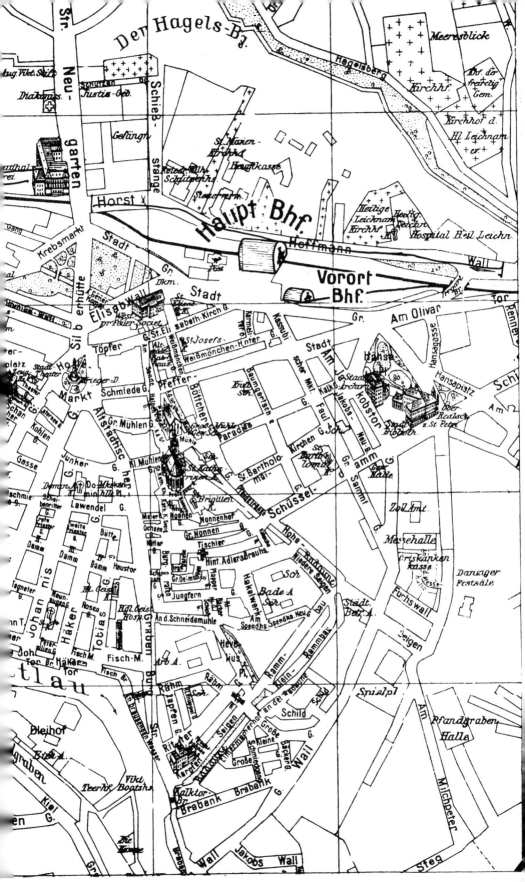

Uncle Josef Wolff's house in Danzig (from *Danzig in 144 Bildern,*
Verlag Gerhard Rantenberg, Leer)

1932, as a young
doctor in Berlin

Photograph by Georg von Hoyningen-Hüne, 1936

Photograph by Man Ray, 1935

Photograph by Man Ray, 1935

A television programme in 1937 about Charlotte Wolff's work on the extremities of monkeys and apes at London Zoo (from an article in the *Listener*).

Photograph by Edeltraut Lemke-Veidt of the author reading her works at the American Gedenk Bibliothek, Berlin, 7 April 1978

V   Trying to Settle Down
in England

Maria Huxley had secured a small room with bath for me at
Dalmeny Court, Piccadilly. It cost four guineas a week which I
could ill afford, but I had friends and expectations as well as a
good deal of self-confidence. The sensation of gambling with fortune appealed to me anyway. Most of my savings gone, I had to
start earning my living immediately. Lady Ottoline Morrell
showed her helping hand at once, and persuaded her friends to
consult me. I received my clients in a tiny bed-sitter, which they
didn't seem to mind. And my elegant visitors, sometimes arriving
in a Rolls-Royce, increased my prestige at Dalmeny Court. I was
very uneasy about it all because I was forced into a double life. I
could be myself only in my research. I started investigations of
monkeys and apes at the London Zoo practically at once. A few
weeks later, the Quakers arranged a meeting with Dr Emmanuel
Miller. He invited me to research the hands of his patients at the
Jewish Child Guidance Clinic in the East End. At the same time,
I had to play the role of a 'chirologist', a role which went against
the grain.

No refugee can make long-term plans for anything until permanent residence has been granted. For new arrivals that lucky
day was a long way off. Life had to be on a provisory basis as the
permit to stay in England was valid for one year only, if that. But
in spite of obvious drawbacks, a temporary position can be an
advantage. It presents a challenge, the challenge to prove oneself,
to take every opportunity in one's stride, whatever the cost. But
the nervous strain of a hand-to-mouth existence produced in this
refugee a severe anxiety state. I discovered the not unusual
human experience of being given presents with one hand and

having them taken away with the other. However, in time I became used to a haphazard life because I had the support of the Huxleys and Lady Ottoline Morrell. And I could count on Bertha Bracey's help if I should be in financial difficulty. It didn't take me long to see the fun of my position, hiding my real profession under the cloak of an odd occupation. I even managed to play a cat-and-mouse game with the authorities. I had been given permission to do hand-interpretations, but was strictly forbidden to engage in any medical activity. But I applied my professional training in the psychological consultations with which I concluded my hand-readings.

The Huxleys were at their most helpful. Aldous had mellowed, and I found him less awesome. They lived at the Mount Royal Hotel with their son Mathew but, in spite of their unsettled life and serious preoccupations about their future, they kept an open door. I saw a great deal of them during the six months they still remained in England. Pacifism had by then become Aldous' main concern. Sybille Bedford has related in her biography of Aldous Huxley (Volume I, *The Apparent Stability*, pp. 328-9) that he realized the inevitability of a second world war, which gave his pacifist activities acute urgency. He had lectures to deliver, articles to write, and much correspondence to deal with. He shunned publicity and a large public. He became worried about his capacity to speak to large audiences, and feared he would not come up to expectations. He badly wanted to reach a large public, but believed that he had insurmountable difficulties in making contact. I was much honoured when he consulted me about his dilemma. I remember the hour of consultation well. I told him that a desire of such intensity implied a *love* for humanity which would reach his audience through its own authenticity. I do hope that I was able to encourage him.

The publication of *Studies in Hand-Reading*, with a preface by Aldous Huxley, had not been a commercial success, but had enlarged my clientele, which from then on became self-perpetuating. The froth of success carried me over financial insecurity and even loneliness – for a time. But I became apprehensive about the many private invitations due to a sensational interest in my work, which I could not refuse for fear of losing clients. I resented being sought out for the very reason which made me feel at loggerheads with myself. My social life became an anxiety-ridden pleasure, leaving me always tired and, more often than not, depressed. My move to England had probably saved my life, but it had left my spirit in the wilderness.

I coped with a life of chance and insecurity, expectation and fear, with a show of bravado. I saw myself as someone who could easily gain and easily lose, both people and money. No wonder that I became wasteful in both directions. I lived next door to Fortnum and Mason, and made this establishment my regular restaurant. Invitations to meals by my wealthy acquaintances were sometimes reciprocated there, probably to the astonishment of my guests. But I indulged in the hope that one day my problems would 'go away'.

London still conjured up the image of my childhood in Germany, which had been happy and secure in an atmosphere of booming capitalism. In any event, my idea of England as the last haven of stability did not change until after the war. I had always believed that English people played fair, but most important of all was my conviction that Hitler would never reach these shores. Great Britain was an impregnable fortress against any aggressor from overseas. Such reflections compensated for the ambivalence of my situation.

Socially on the crest of the wave, my first years in England were flawed by the Jekyll and Hyde nature of my work. I knew that I had to manage this contrary situation like an actor playing a part alien to her nature. I felt more and more lonely in London. I missed Paris, I missed Baladine Klossowska, and the supportive friendship of Professor Wallon, the like of whom I had not encountered in England. As long as Maria and Lady Ottoline Morrell were there, I had some recourse in case of need, although I would have been reluctant to use it. But the Huxleys departed in April 1937, and Lady Ottoline became seriously ill at the end of the same year and died in April 1938. With them I lost the mainstays of my second immigration. Their disappearance made an incision in my life of which I was not fully conscious at the time. Now I see that with them vanished a cherished dream – to be part of the cultural élite to which they belonged.

Lady Ottoline's death was a personal blow to me, which became amplified through Maria's disappearance from London. I had been emotionally attached to her, and I knew that nobody like her would ever again come into my life. Her enthusiasm for my work had been in line with the fervour she showed for new ideas wherever she came across them, be it the philosophy of her friend and lover Bertrand Russell, the poetry of James Stephens, or the endocrine discoveries of Dr Wiesner. It would be futile for me to speak about her other than in a purely personal way, because she has been written and talked about by many others. Lady Ottoline always had a favourite among those she gathered around her, and for a short time it was me. When Maria introduced me to her I was plainly frightened of this gaunt and tall figure. Her hands should have belonged to a man's body. Her lips protruded as if she were attempting to blow a trumpet, which was an unfitting trait for such a statuesque representative of the aristocracy. But the moment she looked at one, the moment she reached out her hand in the gesture of welcome, one was spellbound. Here was a person who didn't fit any familiar model, whose generosity and 'appetite' were of another age. She had constantly to hold herself back, to make herself small, in order to adapt as well as she could to our times, discordant with someone of her calibre. Luckily she didn't succeed. In this country she was one of the few people who showed me warmth and tenderness without the reserve or embarrassment typical of the English. Her gestures were over-emphatic, and often over-reached themselves. They frequently appeared to miss their target for the simple reason that her intensity of feeling was expressed in an unconventional code. On arrival at her small reception room at Gower Street, I sat on an easy chair in front of her. She was seated on a sofa, but I was at her side in no time. She wanted to know every detail of my daily experiences, and particularly of my work. She enquired whether my studies were progressing, and if there were new openings on the horizon for me. Lady Ottoline was an ideal listener because she was a religious woman who believed in the divine, which made her attentive and supportive to her fellow beings. She rarely spoke about herself. But it was obvious that she filled a yawning void with a circle of friends and protégès. She was already at an advanced age when I met her, but age had not damped her enthusiasm. In her biography of Aldous Huxley, Sybille Bedford tells a charming story of how Lady Ottoline broke a string of pearls when talking excitedly at a party. The pearls fell all over the floor, but she remained quite unruffled by the event. Everybody crawled on the carpet to pick them up, which took quite a while. Lady Ottoline hardly noticed what was going on, and when at last, all effort spent, the guests handed the pearls to her, she just put them in a string bag as if they were nothing of importance. Before she wrote this story about Lady Ottoline's insouciance, Sybille had given me a different version. She had told me that Lady Ottoline, walking about the room, had spoken of her pet concern, Virginia Woolf, and how she wished I would have been able to help her. At this point her excitement had got the better of her, and she pulled the string of pearls hard enough to break it.

Events changed as quickly as the English weather in my unstable existence. Therefore attention had to be directed to the present and future rather than things past. A profession with sensational overtones had necessarily an uncertain rate of reward, and was no solid ground on which to build a future. Such a predicament makes one sensitive to every crumb of applause and every critical slight. The need for a secure basis in my existence became a priority, more urgent than ever. Luckily my research went well, and gave me some assurance of a more congenial and better life to come.

Whether we like it or not, patterns in our lives repeat themselves, and I found myself in a situation in England similar to the one I had experienced in France. I had to cope with the same conflict in the double aspect of my work, and I found assistance and solace in powerful friends, another of whom was Bertha Bracey whom I met frequently. There was a certain similarity between Henri van Etten's and her friendship for me. And it so happens that Quakers have been my closest friends from the time I left Germany. Bertha Bracey tried to get a university grant to finance my research, but in spite of support from Julian Huxley she was not successful. Her failure discouraged me from ever trying again to find help from outside sources, and I decided to rely entirely on my own earnings to finance my study on the human hand.

I became a permanent resident in England in November 1937, with an adjustment to my professional permit. I was granted permission to practise as a psychotherapist, but was still forbidden to do any medical work.

The year 1937 had brought me another piece of good fortune. I came into much closer contact than before with Sybille Bedford. It happened like this. The Huxleys' apartment at the Albany had been vacated after their departure, but the lease had still a few more months to run. Sybille moved in, and we met regularly once a week while she lived there. Two people, affected in different ways by the Nazi upheaval, became a comfort to each other. We established a kind of routine in our meetings. I went to the Albany to fetch her for a culinary evening out 'chez' Joseph in Greek Street near Soho Square. It was a small restaurant with tables close to the walls. It had the atmosphere and furnishings of a French bistro. Soho, a foreign island in London, attracted at that time the gourmet rather than the erotomane. Sybille, connoisseur of food and wine, approved of my choice of restaurant, and as regular customers we were especially well treated and well served. We generally occupied a corner table at the furthest end, where we sat eating, drinking and talking. When I looked sideways at Sybille, I saw her eyes and mouth smiling. Nobody else I have known has managed to have such a worried and amused look at the same time. Her rapid speech was something one had to get used to. I often became nervous when, on some occasions, she could not keep still and walked about the room, talking; but 'chez' Joseph she spoke in a quieter voice, relaxed by the good food and wine.

I had interpreted her hands at intervals ever since we met in the south of France. They were small and elegant, of little gesture. It amuses me greatly today, that when Maria Huxley once asked me whether I could see literary talent in Sybille's hands, I answered: 'Yes, particularly as an interpretative writer.' I frequently had to tell Sybille what her hands disclosed. She apparently believed in my 'intuition', and would secretly have liked me to stick to it as a second string. Like most artists, she had faith in the irrational, and was very superstitious.

Superstition? The word is not adequate. It is wrong to elevate the rational at the expense of the irrational in which superstition plays a considerable part. What are we to make of synchronicity, coincidence, of all those events which come as surprises because they have neither been foreseen nor planned? I do not believe in free will, as mood, health and endocrine workings control the decisions we make, the actions we take. We are blessed and threatened by the unforeseen, outside and inside ourselves. In life there are fruitful and fallow days, fruitful and fallow years. Our life and work is bound up with the favour and disfavour of unknown agents. Some people know how to listen, ear to the ground, and can hear whether something good or bad is rumbling underneath. We call them intuitives or seers. Superstition is a form of extra-sensory perception, and it is a mistake to laugh it off as a childish hangover from primitive religions. Artists and writers are predestined observers of the unusual and uncanny, and it is worth while to take their 'visions' and superstitions seriously. They may indeed be better recorders of history than professional historians. Superstition is ingrained in all of us. Everybody longs for portents of luck. The phrases 'good luck' and 'bad luck' proclaim a deep-seated fear of the unknown, the intuitive knowledge that we are led by forces we cannot control.

The acclaim of my hand-readings was to some extent rooted in people's superstition. It makes one feel good to escape the dullness of daily life by having a peep into the mysterious. To be able to give a record of the past and an outline of the future based on former events appeared to many people to be a mysterious gift. The future is grounded in the past. I made this clear to my clients so as not to be classed as a fortune teller. And I insisted that the hub of my work was the diagnosis of constitutional tendencies and personality. It did not occur to me to question my intuitive gift – I took it for granted. The odd thing was that I totally failed at Dr Seoul's famous experiments with E.S.P. at the Psychological Department of University College, London. It was a kind of card game. Dr Seoul asked his subjects to guess from a pack of cards he displayed on a table, some they could not see. I didn't guess one card right, and it made me wonder about my intuitive gift and E.S.P. But I did not try to get to the root of the problem. I might have thought it a waste of time, as no conclusive answer could be given by anyone to such an elusive subject. Did I 'guess' the information I imparted to my clients? Was it all a great fraud on which I had to build my livelihood? Not at all, was my immediate answer. But I remember a nagging unease about date-reading from hands. I tried to comfort myself with the idea that I probably made contact with my clients in a state of self-hypnosis. It was perplexing that I could indicate events in their past which they had forgotten, but recalled when I mentioned them. I was in a kind of trance when the door of my unconscious opened to reach the unconscious of the other person. It was the only explanation I could find for these awkward happenings. But an element of chance always underlies intuitive mind-readings, which in itself exhausts nervous energy. I felt drained after each hand-interpretation. Most of my clients walked on air when they had left, but some did not and were tired for days after.

In June 1957, Sybille Bedford, who had come back to London from France, invited me to meet someone I had known in the past. An Edwardian beauty, dressed in the latest fasion, looked at me with radiant eyes and a wistful smile. 'You recognize me?' 'I do. You are Madame Anonyma.' She nodded and handed me a book with the words: 'This is for you. You have been its god-mother. Do you remember that you advised me to buy an exercise book immediately after leaving you, adding: "I hope you will write something in it every day"? I did. This is the result.' I looked at the title page: *Madame Solario* published in 1956 by Heinemann, London. This beautiful novel was written anonymously, and as the authoress had kept her name secret, I shall do the same. We went on reminiscing about our meeting at Dalmeny Court in 1937. Suddenly she said: 'I don't know if you will remember this. At the end of the consultation you were so exhausted that I had to take your arm and lead you to your bed. You had come out of a trance, dead to the world.' I had not remembered this incident, but it fitted well into the pattern of my ideas.

My meeting with Anonyma had been a complete surprise. It left me bewildered and weak, delighted and sad. Surprises can open old wounds or initiate new beginnings. This one made me reflect once more on my false professional position in the past, and the conflict I had had about it since my Parisian days. I felt its reverberations even after my research work had been widely recognized, and I had regained my place as a physician. Yet I still worried that I had once been engaged in an 'illegitimate' job. In the early years of my exile, Maria Huxley had warned me not to be over-ambitious about finding a scientific method of hand-interpretation. It was self-preservation rather than ambition which had impelled me to take every opportunity to further my research, even at the risk of a nervous breakdown.

Discrepancies and contradictions are part of the human make-up. They can also be symptoms of a neurotic illness, but how can one decide whether they are the one or the other? It needs the mental eye of a psychologist as good as that of a watchmaker, to recognize whether the psyche mirrors proper functioning or faulty working. We are many persons in one, and contradictory drives can bring spice or confusion into one's life. I had enough spice and a great deal of confusion in my early days in London. Life was like a motion picture, constantly changing in scenery and faces. I did not want to miss the luxury of the exquisite surroundings of the many acquaintances who gathered around me, but the contrast between social glamour and scientific aspirations threw me into confusion. I could not resolve these contradictory feelings, and they never left me in peace. They did not fit with my basic needs. I needed the attention and care, encouragement and love, of another person. A child's need for a mother? A mother in many shapes and forms? Yes. People who live uneasily in a world of their own need crutches to get along in the world around them. Their sensitized vulnerability makes them inevitably mother-bound. But every human being depends on maternal support in one way or another. Psychoanalysis proposes that human beings go through stages of development resulting in 'maturity' – when all goes well. This theory is as unsafe as a house of cards. Maturity is no value-measurement. All of us remain emotionally vulnerable because we carry every stage of development with us for good. And in happiness and sadness, we cry out for a mother's love and support. The roles of woman and man have started to be interchangeable, which will lead to a better, balanced society in the future. But in the social plight of our age we have to reconcile ourselves to half measures. We are forced to use our multiple personalities like players acting different plays. We have to hide our authentic Self under a mask, and act a part in order to come to terms with a stereotyped social code.

It was not surprising that women took me under their wing by inviting me to meals, the theatre and cinema. Complying with the existing convention, they assumed a protective role, while the interest of men usually centred around themselves. They wanted to know whether I could advise them how to succeed in business or love. But some had a genuine interest in my research and wanted to further it. I enjoyed the 'care' of women and the 'brotherhood' of men, while I was groping to find a place in a new world.

Yet even in those days, when people accepted stereotyped roles as virtually unbreakable, there were exceptions to the rule. Take, for example, the case of my friend Hermann Schriyver. He was the foremost interior decorator, a famous wit, and extravagant host. I had met him in Paris at the Klossowskis', and had been much taken by his gaiety and outrageous witticisms. I had made an analysis of his hands, which had consequences. I never

161

asked him for any help, but he gave it in good measure from the time we met. He made my work known to his friends and customers, and when I moved to London he insisted on providing me with funds. 'You must have something behind you,' he said, handing me a large cheque from one of the Rothschilds. His mother had been a Rothschild. He might have inherited from her his Jewish warmth, which made him such an attractive companion. Hermann was a Dutchman who never changed his nationality and during the Second World War he had a part-time job of national importance at the B.B.C. He climbed the heights in his own profession when the then Prince of Wales entrusted him with the interior decoration of the Belvedere. Hermann had the gift of meeting with princes and commoners on equal terms. He made no secret of his homosexuality but was nevertheless accepted everywhere. The English admire individuality and excellence, and eccentrics of any kind were welcomed in exclusive circles of society if they had something exceptional to give.

Hermann was a small and fat man. He had short legs and fleshy hands. His movements and gestures were mannered, yet had a touch of elegance. He looked a standard 'queen'. If he invited ridicule, he did not care. He came towards his guests with measured, dainty steps, and a smile on his face. He went through life apparently constantly amused, though I was never sure whether or not he was acting a part. He loved to please, and he did. He was short-sighted, and his blue eyes glinted with amusement behind glasses. His high forehead ended in thinned-out hair which was, nevertheless, redolent of a *Lockenkopf*. The mixture of Jewish and Dutch blood had given him the material appetites of the latter and the humanity of the former. One could never be sure which of the two would win the day, but his friendship for me seemed stable. Hermann was a sybarite; his table was as perfect as his witty entertainment. His guests were writers, artists or wits, but none of those I met there could beat his own *savoir vivre* and delightful exhibitionism. But beneath the debonair persona, he was a lonely man who craved for love, and because he never found the affection he needed, escaped into erotic adventures. I saw a great deal of him in confidential tête-à-têtes. One barely had time to sit down before he asked: 'Now tell me all about yourself.' I usually replied with: 'Let's do it the other way round.' And he would hold forth about his exploits of seduction, and gossip about those of his friends, either seriously or maliciously, and always amusingly. He was a snob and a lion-hunter who readily admitted to being both. Although he did not care about other people's opinion, he wanted to be liked by all and sundry. I am not sure to this day why he took it upon himself to help me so much. I enjoyed his company and his generosity but, in the end, found myself unable to bear the burden of gratitude. And one day I ended the friendship abruptly. Perhaps I had the good sense to resign rather than be fired? Perhaps I did not trust his steadfastness? The amazing Hermann, who cared, helped and spoiled, had nevertheless been more like a distant relative than a true friend. The emotional ingredient was missing. Yet the gifts I received from him had been most welcome – for a time. And he had rendered me an outstanding service in bringing about my meeting with the then Mrs Wallis Simpson, later The Duchess of Windsor, whom he had told about my hand-interpretations. It happened a few weeks after my arrival in England, shortly before the abdication of Edward VIII, that Mrs Simpson wanted me to come to her apartment at Bryanston Court. Some time in November 1936 I went to see her there. I remember the large room into which I was led. I had not long to wait before she came in and shook hands with me. I felt even more nervous than before my session with Virginia Woolf. And I was tense during the interpretation of her hands. But the moment I passed over to the psychological résumé of my findings, I was myself again and relaxed. What was she like? I can only describe the general impression she made on me; everything else must remain buried under the oath of professional secrecy.

She was just *there*, quick in movement, self-possessed, intelligent and natural. She was friendly but didn't smile, she was polite but didn't make conversation. Her body had an androgynous attraction. Her face has been photographed and described so often that I resist remarking on it, except for the expression of her eyes. They conveyed not only a considerable gift of observation but also of accurate judgment; I felt sure that she was a woman who would be herself with anybody. I liked the way she listened to what I had to say, and the few replies she made were intelligent and to the point. She was interested in nothing else but the *reality* of things. She asked me to come once more to Bryanston Court to see her and meet a friend of hers. On that second visit she asked me a number of searching questions which I hope I answered satisfactorily. Then she introduced me to her friend, Madame S.,

LOU VIEI
CHEMIN DE VALLAURIS
5.59. CANNES (A.M.)
CRUMWOLD. CANNES

Wednesday, January 27th

Dear Dr. Wolff —

Thank you so much —
for your letter — It was kind of you —
To write me. At the moment I can't
feel that life is a great success —
but a clear conscience is a great help.
and that I have — knowing that —
I did everything in my power — to
prevent the tragedy that occurred —
I hope we may meet again some day.
Yours sincerely,
Wallis Simpson

who wanted to consult me. She was an American woman of great beauty, who moved her tall and graceful figure in the languid rhythm of people born in a sub-tropical climate. After an hour alone with her, Mrs Simpson returned, and the three of us talked in general terms. I left in a state of elation. Hermann wanted of course to know 'all about it'. I told him nothing except that I had had the time of my life. After Edward VIII's abdication, I wrote to Mrs Simpson in Cannes. She replied in her own hand. Here is her letter.

Limelight did nothing to help me feel settled. I had no real faith that clients would always come to my door, and I could not trust my benefactors either. They blew into my life like whirlwinds. On occasion, their 'affection' ended in erotic adventures which I had not foreseen. I was surprised by such an approach, but whether I liked it or not, I didn't demur because I couldn't afford to lose support. Their way of going about reminds me of the spectacles one sees today at football matches where players jump on each other's backs, kiss and hug, exhibiting erotic reactions which prove that any major excitement can end up in sexual display. It was fortunate that I could laugh about the advances of some of these 'friends'. One form of prostitution is as good as another, I told myself.

Refugees who make good are objects of consuming interest to many English people, but their help has never lacked an element of charity. It was no good telling myself that this Christian virtue was an asset which kept exiles like myself alive and well; I resented being an object of charity. It was mainly middle-aged women who were moved to protect and even spoil the strangers in their midst. But they were fickle, and easily changed the objects of their favour. Real contact with the glittering circle seemed unattainable. The shutters went down the moment one had hoped for a solid friendship. The English have a high reputation for their discretion and loyalty. These fine qualities, signs of truly civilized behaviour, mask in fact an exaggerated self-protection. They stem from a need for self-sufficiency, which is averse to emotional involvement and results in coldness of heart. One doesn't expose others because one doesn't want to be exposed oneself. The weight of one's own sense of independence does not allow one to take another person in tow. The typical English virtues are but the other side of English narcissism. The English care for their own kind because they are of the same

165

mind. An alien always remains an alien in England. A foreigner's life is an easier matter in France, except for getting a permit to work. The French mix well with foreigners, and have a talent for integrating strangers.

My friendship with Hermann Schriyver and Sybille Bedford had given me some relief from the play-acting I had to engage in with admirers and protectors. Unfortunately I did not see much of Sybille after the end of 1937 when she left for France. In February of the following year I left Dalmeny Court for a bed-sitter in Strathmore Gardens, Notting Hill Gate. By that time 'business' had gone down. I was still in demand, but had reduced my consultations voluntarily. Feeling safer as a permanent resident in England, I pursued my research at the price of my practice. My investigations on apes and monkeys of the old and new world had stretched over a period of eighteen months, and their results were published in the *Proceedings of the Zoological Society*. While this was still in progress, I matriculated as a research student at the Psychology Department, University College, London. The then Dr William Stephenson, later Distinguished Professor at Chicago University, arranged and supervised my investigations on students to test the scientific value of my method of hand-interpretation. I worked under 'laboratory' conditions. The subjects were hidden from me by a thick curtain with a hole for their hands to be put through. The results of the research were encouraging, and were published in the *British Journal of Medical Psychology*. Dr Stephenson took great interest in my work and continued to do so when he became Assistant Director at the Institute of Experimental Psychology of Oxford University. I did the same studies on students at Oxford as I had done in London. Every few weeks I went there and stayed overnight with the Stephenson family. Dr Stephenson had become a friend. The dour, red-haired Yorkshireman did not hide his emotional temperament. He was impulsive, generous, and did not suffer fools gladly. He wanted to do all he could for me because, as he once confessed, he had once received much help from someone of my race. He expressed his opinion about my work in the Preface he wrote for my book, *The Human Hand*.

Side by side with my research at the universities of London and Oxford went a large-scale investigation of the hands of mental defectives at St Lawrence's Hospital, Caterham. I looked at about two thousand of them during four years of weekly visits. A Green Line bus took me to Caterham for the day, and I tasted once more the atmosphere of hospital work. My previous research with Professor Wallon was an excellent recommendation to the then Superintendent, Dr Earle. Soon he and other colleagues not only gave me every assistance, but became fascinated with the study itself. Later on, one of them, Dr Rollin, joined me in writing a paper on the subject. I learned a great deal of substance about the hand of the mental defective and psychotic patient, and continued to visit St Lawrence's Hospital through the first years of the war. Dr Earle had left the hospital for another position in 1940, which I felt as a personal loss. But I went on pursuing my research there, and was asked, in June 1941, to serve as a locum at the hospital. Although rather afraid of a return to medical responsibility, I accepted with pride, though not without misgivings. On account of my war service I was put onto the provisory register of medical practitioners.

My brown German passport had expired at the end of May 1938, and I had no choice but to visit the German Embassy to have it renewed. One of my new friends accompanied me on this trying visit. We sat among masses of other down-trodden women and men, most of whom hated to be German. My passport was in fact renewed for one year , but I felt so humiliated and depressed by the treatment we received at the embassy that I preferred to be a stateless person rather than have a wrong nationality. I resigned German citizenship and managed to get a Nansen passport. This document and the permanent residence in England relieved me of the fear of being chased away from its shores. I now had a more secure basis for the future, but still had to go on fighting on two fronts simultaneously. But one stroke of luck is often followed by another and yet another, confirming the old superstition that good or bad things 'always come in threes'. One of my clients who visited me in my bed-sitter near Notting Hill Gate was Esther, a grey-haired English lady of German parentage, who had her domicile in Santa Fé. I never suspected that she would change my life. After I had seen her a few times professionally, she sent me a cheque of £100, begging me to accept the money as a gift from the heart. She introduced me to her friends, among them the Misses Anne and Margaret Tennant. Esther was a spinster in tweeds, and already in her sixties when we met. Her large eyes, with their expression of constant despair, had seen too much misery among her nearest relatives. She had tried to escape it all by leaving for China where she worked as a jeweller. With her inventive gift and sure taste she soon became an expert in making jewellery using semi-precious stones. Museums became interested and bought her wares. Some of her family still lived in Germany. Perhaps her origin had something to do with the generosity she showed me. She insisted that I should accept a stipendium of £100 a year from her, and expenses for food and accommodation as well. She persuaded, not without difficulty, her friend Anne Tennant to buy a maisonette in Tregunter Road, and make a home for me there. She succeeded in the end and, in December 1938, I moved into two rooms of my own. Esther had by then gone back to Santa Fé. I liked her well enough but was not attracted by her. She had never married because nobody wanted her, so she said. I felt sure that she did not want to marry, as she could not have lived with anybody on account of her mental state. She was a depressive who could not endure the responsibilities of a 'coupled' existence. She certainly did not lack friends, and was admired for her talents and her generosity.

Anne Tennant, known as Nan, had not lost with age her appetite for pleasure. She could change from a grande dame into a gamine or a *Hausfrau* like a chameleon. Her small and narrow head reminded one of a greyhound, and so did her gait. She walked with swift, elegant steps, but her hands did not tally with her racy appearance. They were a man's hands, large and heavy. Nan's eyes were perhaps her greatest asset. They were slightly bulging, of a light blue colour, and looked like glass marbles. She was much loved and loved much. Her salty sense of humour and her intelligence made her a centre of attraction. She was born and brought up in the family home, No. 19 The Boltons in Kensington. This is now a home for old people, run by the Servite Catholic organization. Her parents had a religious outlook and a liberal tradition. Nan had been educated accordingly and, as was the custom of the well-to-do in Victorian times, she was widely travelled and spoke French and German fluently. Nan never abandoned her sense of duty and an underlying sense of guilt about 'pleasure'. She seemed safely anchored in the code of behaviour where *'noblesse oblige'*.

Our contact became pleasurable enough to arouse some jealousy in the household. But I was sufficiently content to laugh off those pinpricks designed by her servants and friends to make me distrust Nan. During the first years at Tregunter Road, I imagined that I had at last found a home, but I had deluded myself, believing that I had landed in a haven of security. My unconscious must have been aware of the fact that the ground under my feet was unsafe. My former symptoms of agoraphobia returned and should have warned me to watch and pray, instead of assuming that I had settled down. All was well when I saw people in my own surroundings, but I experienced again a paralysing anxiety every time I ventured outside. I should have remembered how these symptoms had handicapped me before. Yet I tried to conquer them through will power. I forced myself to get on a bus but after a short while had to leave it, fearing I would faint. I fled into the porch of the nearest house, rubbed my temples, and used Coué's method of autohypnosis by repeating the words 'I'm all right'. After some time had passed, I boarded another bus, and arrived at my destination without further incident. But many a time my nerve failed me when I tried to use public transport and I took a taxi. The desire to pursue my research, the over-riding need for a proper professional status, drove me on. I told nobody of my suffering, which I managed to hide more or less successfully.

To be an alien without a nationality was an advantage during the war. I was freer than many other refugees, but still needed police permission whenever I wanted to leave Greater London.

Nan and I had listened to Chamberlain's announcement on the radio that Great Britain was at war with Germany. She cried, not only for her country, but for her friends in Germany. If I felt anything at all it was hope rather than despair. My faith in British invincibility had never been shaken, and a war could be the end of Hitlerism. I might have been aware of being an alien in Great Britain, but not of being in danger of my life from a possible German invasion.

I soon awoke to the fact that a new world was in the making for *everybody*. My circumstances changed simultaneously for the worse and for the better: a contradiction in terms but not in events. In the summer of 1940 Nan retired to her cottage in Suffolk, but came up to London for frequent visits, and continued to translate the bad English of the manuscript of *The Human Hand* into good English until she left her flat for good. I had hoped that our collaboration would strengthen the bond between us. I loved her company and believed that she requited my feel-

169

ings. I must have been as blind as a bat. She had, in fact, taken herself away from me. Her departure changed my home into a boarding-house, where the staff, strictly English, had misgivings about their refugee charge.

No restrictions had been imposed on my research work at St Lawrence's Hospital, Caterham. After I had finished my locum tenens there, I began a study of the hands of psychotic patients at St Bernard's Hospital, Southall, and at the endocrine clinic of Willesden General Hospital. I never lacked the willing cooperation, and indeed the special interest, of the physicians and nurses I worked with. I was always treated as a colleague, and many times as a friend. The superintendents of both mental hospitals invited me for meals and talks, the house physicians, occupational therapists and nurses participated in my work. As I had already the publication of several papers in scientific journals to my credit, I was well on the way to being recognized as a pioneer research worker. On account of my work at University College, London, and at various hospitals, I was made a Fellow of the British Psychological Society in 1941. Two years before, I had started to organize the results of my findings into a comprehensive whole, to be published in my book, *The Human Hand*.

The years of research had been years of many discoveries. They were highlights which sent me into states of ecstasy, and made me grateful to pursue a creative adventure which enriched human knowledge. Such moments were as illuminating and gratifying as the birth of a poem. My opportunities to widen the orbit of research were greater here than in France, and I felt that destiny had led me to the right place at the right time.

While one half of my life enjoyed the smile of the 'stars', the other was darkened by clouds of misfortune. Nan's concern and affection had turned away from me to two young men, both refugees from Nazi Germany. As if this was not enough, in 1941 she abandoned her quarters at No. 9 Tregunter Road, and let her flat above my rooms. The tenants were a couple on the brink of divorce, and the air was filled with the noise of their constant quarrels. Doors were slammed and screams heard all over the house. Peace had gone with Nan. And I had to look after myself, to shop, cook and clean, which, however, turned out to be a blessing in disguise. But before the final separation, the antagonism of Nan's housekeeper had made my life a misery. The loss of peace at 'home' affected me more than the loss of peace in

Europe. I wanted a lifeboat, not a raft, to fight the high seas of insecurity. My 'prayer' was answered, but not in the way I had expected. Alan White, then the Managing Director of Methuen and Co., accepted *The Human Hand* for publication. He had been first intrigued by, and then enthusiastic about, the book. He became a staunch supporter of my work and a friend. I was soon part of the family, consisting of him, his wife and their two young sons. They provided me with a new 'niche', through which the breach with Nan lost something of its effect. The highlights of the new friendship were weekend visits to the Whites at their home in Hildenborough. Alan White, lanky and tall, looked like an over-grown boy. His bulging blue eyes pointed to an over-active thyroid gland, responsible for his ever being on the move. He seemed to be indefatigable in discussion of many subjects, and particularly the works of H. G. Wells. But he applied himself with similar zest to gardening and mowing the lawn. Quick in mental and physical movement, sharp-witted and kind, he was an ideal companion. His wife, Marjorie, a home-maker whose only thought was the well-being of others, calmed the waves of conversational excitement with good sense and food. Weekends at the Whites' had the sweet taste of congeniality combined with maternal care.

After *The Human Hand* was published in 1942, our contact grew ever stronger. My book had a good response, and Alan White, who had 'discovered' me, was much encouraged by this success. But there was more to this friendship than a publisher's patronage. This lanky intellectual of about thirty, with a lively mind, a great reader of novels and philosophy, loved discussions on both subjects, and saw the right partner in me. Marjorie, knitting, cooking, and listening to us when time permitted, was a relaxing influence, restoring the balance between mental exuberance and physical well-being.

It seems paradoxical that the war years were the most fortunate for my professional advance. The response to *The Human Hand* made my publishers commission another book for which I had already collected material. I had watched the expressive movements of psychotic patients at meals and occupational therapy while I was studying their hands, and these observations formed the experimental part of my next work, *A Psychology of Gesture*. It was published in 1945. Now I had two trump cards in my hand. A pattern of destiny similar to that of the early twenties repeated itself – in a fashion. In the Germany of hyper-inflation I had the best time of my life. Now, in England's most difficult years, I sailed on the crest of the waves again, as researcher and author. I felt favoured by fate and grateful to Great Britain. Her sense of freedom for the individual in all circumstances, even in a war, was a sign of moral superiority. With the terror of bombs close to my abode, abandoned by my protectors, I had reached a professional height, while my personal life limped sadly behind, a discrepancy only too familiar to artists and scientists of all time.

Nobody can claim to know reality, or the reasons for success or failure in human contacts, which depend on inner reality. Great minds like Walter Benjamin recognized this dilemma more than sixty years ago. He thought, rightly, that the surrealists had come nearest to solving the problem. They put old wine into new bottles, by creating new images out of the age-old wisdom of unconscious forces. They realized that 'reality' is the missing link in human affairs. They came close to it because they preached and lived a life without role-playing and preconceived ideas. The surrealists insisted that the world of man can be seen upside down as well as the right way up, and that the absurd is a better teacher of 'reality' than rationality and logic. Their image of freedom was unadulterated by social codes of the past or present. They envisaged it as absolute freedom, which *is reality*. They realized that imagination is its very basis. They also knew that images are in the forefront as well as at the back of human relationships and achievements, and determine their success or lack of it.

A nation's image is fixed in the eyes of its members and other nations. And in time it becomes a stereotype of considerable impact and little reality. Over the last fifty years the power of the image has been immensely increased through the media, television and radio in particular. To project an image is the catch phrase which characterizes the unreality into which society has fallen. We have been driven further away than ever from those glimpses of reality we might have been able to catch, had we reflected on the gap between the artifice of stereotype and the spontaneity of truth. If we could measure the significance of an image in relation to the latter, we might be less confused about both.

I had been taken in by an image of the Englsh which was partly of my own making, partly tradition. It was conceived through the physical need to survive and the emotional need for love. It took

172

me a long time to correct it. I had placed too much emphasis on the image which glamorous surroundings had suggested, and had been hypnotized by an illusion which blurred my self-image. Behaviour depends on self-image, and mine was erratic. I had to live on the resources of intelligence and wits. Although I identified myself as a Jew, I had not a Jewish collective to turn to. And thus I remained an isolated outsider.

The collective image of the British people has its roots in an aristocratic concept of themselves. The aristocracy ruled the country's past, and though this past had been hard and unjust to many, it had made the country great. This has never been forgotten. The aristocratic self-image, as stereotyped as it might be, is still alive, even if facts to the contrary stare one in the face. In the past, aristocrats could be themselves without fear or hindrance, which allowed for authenticity in word and deed. In the era of egalitarianism things have changed, but has the image? Authenticity is still rated as the most attractive quality in human beings, although it has now been demoted to a romantic attitude rather than part of a code for behaviour. The aristocratic image has been passed on from generation to generation, in the face of everything denying its social value. Many, if not most, English people have made it look ridiculous, but has it vanished or been destroyed? There is no evidence that it has gone. It was certainly very much alive in September 1939 when, at the first roll call of national emergency, the old virtures, symbolized in the aristocratic image, came to life again. It had resisted the cynicism of the socialists and the outrages of the fascists. And even in our day, the secret longings of many workers, formerly called the 'lower classes', eagerly turn to the glamour of privileged living which they try to imitate. And they secretly value authentic and 'noble' behaviour in spite of demonstrations to the contrary, witnessed almost daily in the last decade. The most loyal royalists can be found among the 'working class'. Royalty and glamorous stars alike exert power over many people, independent of their place in society, but more strongly over the have-nots than the haves. The powerful aristocratic image has survived the facts of a total social change. Its persistent presence is perhaps the only chance for this country to climb out of a threatening totalitarianism, with its inhumanity and disregard for individual freedom.

Most of my early contacts with British people had been with members of the aristocracy and haute bourgeoisie. They reflected

173

the 'English image' more authentically than the rest. Yet their behaviour had adapted to the uncertainty of the country's destiny, and exhibited the negative aspect of a former 'superiority', namely utter selfishness. The Christian religion, though, made them still sanction obligations and duties but they waved goodbye to both when their narcissism was threatened.

It was during the war that I found another brother- and sisterhood, not among those I had mixed with before. They belonged to the 'lower classes'. The butcher, the grocer, the baker, showed me a special courtesy, if not favour, during the war. How often did I get the best pieces of meat without asking, just a bit more of the butter than was due to me, and a double ration of bread? The 'providing' class couldn't do enough for me. I saw in them the stalwarts of humanity, and was touched by their concern. They treated me as a friend, and I responded likewise. My transfer from the upper floor to the basement of life was a happy one in both the literal and symbolic sense. I had been forced to spend my nights in the basement of our house with a few members of the staff who had been left behind together with me. We were a happy company. The fact that I was a refugee from Germany seemed forgotten. Their sense of humour, sensitivity and consideration, made me forget that I was separated from people I had thought my friends. Those nights, and the tired days which followed, inspired me to engage in a new venture. In the many waking hours in the cellar's dormitory, I passed the time translating Shelley's 'Ode to a Nightingale' and other poems of his into German. Basements became part of my life, and not only at night. A Jewish acquaintance in the neighbourhood, Sophie, a seamstress by profession, invited me every week to a meal and a laugh in her basement flat opposite the house where I lived. I could relax in her company.

But other faces and other voices had a different complexion and tenor. There were people in the street or in a shop who insulted me either as a German or a Jewess. I could discard the anti-German remarks but anti-Semitism struck me to the heart. One day, when I was nearly attacked physically by an anti-Semite, I felt such despair that I dared not go out of the house for some days. In the end, my subconscious commanded me to let my sorrow go as I was unable to cope with it. And I shall never forget how suddenly I prayed, and gave this problem over to whatever power there might be to take it on. I said in my prayer: 'I am committing this to a "higher court".' From that day onwards I was free. The release had been instantaneous, and the effect has been lasting.

My healthy entry into life 'below stairs' was a welcome change. It altered the pattern of my life. The canvas of England's fragmented society had presented me with some new design after all. At last I had made contact with *people*. My attachment to my new friends went far enough for me to go and see them while I was a locum at St Lawrence's Hospital, and journeys up and down to London not an easy matter.

In the second year of the war, Esther's stipendium had stopped. I had to provide again for the basic necessities of life through my own earnings, though Nan did not accept any rent from me. My financial position was still too insecure to allow me to feel settled. And, as a stateless person, I remained out on a limb. The last two war years went by in the routine of taking shelter, congratulating oneself on not having been hit by Hitler's doodle-bug bombs, and working. Survival had gone hand in hand with contentment through comradeship and solidarity with my neighbours. The royalties from *The Human Hand*, together with clients who came in its wake, kept me afloat.

I slept through the razzmatazz of VE-Day. I didn't seem to be interested in the arrival of peace, but the relief of being able to sleep in my own bed again was wonderful. I soon started to wake up to peace and visualize a wider future. I could get abroad, see Paris again, *if* I had a British passport. I filed an application for naturalization, and about six months later, in May 1947, I got the precious certificate which made me a citizen of this country. Soon after, I procured a passport, and on the first day of July I went on a nostalgic journey to Paris.

I was going as a survivor with a heart full of fear and anticipation. What would the city be like, the city I had loved? Would I perhaps find some – perhaps all of my friends again? Bad omens before my departure seemed to confirm my apprehension that I might be disappointed. I fell ill three days before the journey, but didn't want to postpone it for fear that it might not come off at all. I had always dreaded going back to my own place once I had left, or postponing arrangements. I was frightened but held fast. I tried to rationalize my phobia of the journey, and of the shock which Paris after the occupation might inflict on me. I realized that the root of my anxiety lay in the fact that I attached too much importance to this visit to Paris. I would surely meet Professor Wallon because he had written to me immediately after the war, suggesting a visit as soon as it was possible. He had mentioned a new psychological journal, *Enfance* edited by himself, and had asked me to contribute to it. He assured me of a warm welcome from him and his wife at their house. His offer of professional collaboration gave me a new incentive for the future. I had been starved of the right kind of encouragement and care. Not that I had been deprived of either in this country, but both Wallon and his wife gave me a caring friendship and a professional esteem which put me on my feet in every sense of the word, and gave me a sense of 'balance'.

Many friendships I had made in England had been spoiled through the undertones of sensationalism. Except during the war years, I had hardly ever been allowed to relinquish a mask. All this went through my mind during several nights when I was ill and feverish, but determined to travel. I had ordered a car to take me to Victoria Station. It didn't arrive at the appointed time. I anxiously waited for some minutes, then took my suitcase and ran into the street. I don't know whether I got a taxi or a bus, but I made it at the last minute, and boarded the Golden Arrow gasping for breath.

And I did arrive at the Gare du Nord. Nobody was waiting for me, but I was in Paris. It was not a mirage after all. I went to the Hôtel du Quai Voltaire, which was still there, though looking a bit battered. But the proprietor and the staff had changed. The Seine, the Louvre, the bistro at the corner of the Rue Bonaparte greeted me once more. I found my way about in no time. But Paris had become its own ghost. Paris had survived, but no hand had been busy to repair, to paint the sad-looking, sometimes dilapidated houses, with the dust of the Nazi past still hanging about them. It had not been wiped off by the liberation. Paris had not found herself again. Had my Jewish friends survived? I had not dared to enquire, but after a day or two I telephoned Baladine's flat in the Rue du Canivet. Pierre answered. Baladine was alive and well and would be desolate to have missed me. During the war she had been with friends in the Dordogne, and was at present back there on a holiday. He invited me to meet his wife who had survived a concentration camp in Germany. They were the only people, apart from the Wallons, whom I saw on this visit. Pierre looked the same, but had changed his way of life. The agnostic of former days had become an ardent Christian. He was one of those French intellectuals of mixed blood who, immediately after the war, got in touch with German pastors, to start a dialogue between the two nations. He was well equipped to be a liaison officer, with the task of healing wounds on both sides. His mother, Baladine, was a German Jewess, his father a Polish aristocrat, while Pierre himself was a French citizen by birth. His Jewish wife had been trained as a social worker. She agreed with his ideas of reconciliation, in spite of her own sufferings in a concentration camp. Pierre's divided self managed to combine Christian faith and practice with erotic curiosity. He was a connoisseur of erotica, and a bibliophile of the subject. The evening with them gave an answer to my feeling of being an alien in the Paris of 1947. There is an enormous difference between the actual and the imaginative experience of persecution. The British people know nothing of the *real* inflictions of Nazi brutality, in spite of the devastation through bombs which they suffered. I saw the difference in Pierre's and Denise's – and other French faces. There was the waiter at the Café de Flore whom I had known in the thirties, looking aged beyond his years, and forcing a smile out of a depressed countenance. He was like a revenant, and I probably looked the same to him – two survivors were meeting. I saw in his eyes that it was a comfort to him to meet someone who had gone away before all that horror had happened, and returned. His presence *made* the Café de Flore for me anew. The few customers read newspapers, rushed to the telephone, smoked Gauloise cigarettes, drank coffee, as they had always done. All this was comfort because it was familiar. And I looked around without the feeling of being in a 'no man's land'. I visited my favourite bookshop with a new hope of finding my old Paris there also. It was still open, and still stood in the Rue de l'Odéon. Was it Sylvia Beach who served me? I could not say. We had met often, but there was no recognition on either side – unless she was someone else? The uncanny sensation of walking on unsafe ground got hold of me again. At that moment I thought of leaving Paris as soon as I had seen the Wallons. I vacillated about making an appointment with them, so uncertain did I feel about the whole situation; it was three days before I telephoned.

My bewilderment was not the only reason for my hesitation. I also vaguely expected Dr Earle from Birmingham to join me. He admired Professor Wallon greatly, and his letter of recommendation about my research had assured me of his warm welcome at St Lawrence's Hospital. When he left for his new job he asked me to feel free to continue my research at Monyhull Colony, where he was to be the superintendent, whenever I wanted. And shortly after the war I went there. My time at Monyhull Colony, a home for mentally defective children, had been more than a professional benefit to me. It had consolidated my friendship with Dr Earle. I felt in contact with this fiery Irishman, who spoke his mind under all circumstances, and was liked and feared for it even by the Board of Deputies at the Mental Health Service. He tolerated no nonsense, slackness or injustice, either in his staff or from the authorities, and would move mountains to get what was needed. He came from a Catholic family, and had remained a Christian in practice though not in creed. He had a mind like a kaleidoscope, shimmering in many colours. One was always held in suspense as to which colour would pass before one's eyes and disappear as quickly as it had shown itself. His moods were as changeable and varied as his interests. He was an erudite man, who knew all there was to know about psychological medicine. He happened to be one of the best psychiatrists I have met, but his abiding interest was poetry. When he recited a poem, it came over as if he had written it himself.

Because of over-use, the word magnetism has lost much of its meaning, but it could be fully applied to this strange man. Having many conflicts within himself, he not only felt empathy with his patients and friends, but was also a healer and a hypnotist. From him I learned the technique of hypnotism, as far as it can be learned. His sensitivity and intuitive understanding, qualities usually attributed to the female, made him a natural healer. He had an androgynous mind, and was homosexual in inclination. Dr Earle could be a brilliant actor, but he never used this gift in his relationships. He treated everybody with his authentic self, be they his patients or his friends, brilliant or mentally handicapped. He had an old aunt living with him in a separate apartment, who was partially paralysed. I was allowed to visit her several times. She was a woman of 'old world' charm, who radiated serenity. Was this, I wondered, his doing? He treated her like his mother, giving her the care and reverence of a devoted son.

Dr Earle never got too close to anybody. He expressed his feelings and emotions through innuendoes and actions, which made his company so comfortable. I was well aware of his

178

homosexuality, and he of my disposition. There was no need to speak about it. He was a staunch supporter of my work. He had already given me every help as superintendent at St Lawrence's Hospital, and provided at Monyhull Colony considerable 'material' – mentally handicapped children and adolescents – for my study. He followed the same method of diagnostic comparison which Professor Wallon had applied to my hand analyses of neurotic and neurological cases. He often referred to Wallon's work, which he thought equalled that of Piaget. And he expressed the wish to meet him one day. I had already mentioned my work with Dr Earle in a letter to Professor Wallon. And it occurred to me that I could be instrumental for the two to meet during my visit to Paris. When I mentioned the plan to Dr Earle he gave me an enchanting smile, and thanked me as if I had given him a wonderful present.

He arrived two days after I had touched French soil after nine years' absence, and his presence changed my outlook on Paris for the rest of my stay. It also eased the meeting with the Wallons, of which I had been apprehensive. They had invited both of us to dinner at their house.

The thought of the Wallons in Paris had frightened me during the occupation by the Nazis. He was a Communist sympathizer who had visited the revolutionaries in Spain during the civil war. I had feared for his and Germaine's life – unless they had fled the city. But I wondered! My only question to Wallon about the war years and the occupation was: 'Have you been all right?' He looked at his hands and curtly answered: 'We have been very busy.' I knew that I must not touch that subject again. But the meeting between the four of us was a present from the gods. I have no recollection of what was said or what happened, I only remember the atmosphere of the evening. I can still sense that excitement in the air, as though we were experiencing a reunion of people who had hardly thought it possible to meet ever again. I had found something precious which I could so easily have lost. The only words I remember were said by Professor Wallon when we took our leave. He said: 'I would be very glad if you would give a lecture on the progress of your research at the Ecole des Hautes Etudes, as soon as you can visit Paris again.' Although he had asked me before to contribute to *Enfance Revue Bio-Psychologique* the invitation to lecture was an accolade. I felt proud, encouraged and reassured that the bond which had

179

brought me back to Paris had been strengthened for good.

Professor Wallon had not told me anything about his activities during the Nazi occupation, but some time later I heard that he had been the coordinator of Resistance at all French universities. And he had been Minister of the Interior for a time immediately after the liberation of Paris.

Dr Earle and I returned to England together. He recited Yeats over the waters of the Channel. We thanked each other repeatedly for a grand trip. Each had made Paris come alive for the other in different ways, and we shared the joy that France was open to us again.

1947 had been a good year for me all round. My article 'The Hand of the Mental Defective' had been published in the *British Journal of Medical Psychology*, but best of all was Wallon's invitation to speak about my subject at the Ecole des Hautes Etudes. I was particularly sensitive to recognition of my work at university level. No British university had as yet bestowed on me the same honour as I had received in France. It is no secret that learned bodies in England take a long time to accept new ideas, but I resented their reserve towards me.

Dr Earle and I went our different ways after our arrival at Victoria Station. I was disinclined to return to my room in Tregunter Road, and went straight to the flat of my friend the seamstress. She was not surprised to see me on her doorstep, and was pleased that I had come. She gave me a meal and asked me to stay the night, but I decided to face the trial of sound pollution in my own place. I waited, however, until late at night before I took the plunge. She carried my luggage and brought me to the door of No. 9 Tregunter Road. 'I shall never settle down in England,' I whispered in Sophie's ear before she went off. Destiny, with all my good fortune, had not provided me with the basic need – that of a peaceful home life, and has not done so to this day. The same pattern repeated itself with variations wherever I lived in London. Quarrelling couples, slamming doors, ballet dancers practising tapping steps on a parquet floor above me, a pianist strumming loudly, have all invaded my 'territory'. It has always disturbed my peace of mind and done no good to my state of health.

One wonders why there are always shadows following one through life. One cannot catch, let alone eliminate them. I took this misfortune as a reminder that I was, and always will be, an alien, not properly welcome in this country, a British citizen by adoption only. My self-description as an international Jew with a British passport meets the case perfectly. It was long ago, in the late twenties, when an old Russian woman who had fled to Germany during the pogroms of 1905 said to me: 'The worst fate ever is to be an exile.' I still see the lost expression on her face. The wisdom of her words impressed me deeply enough never to be forgotten. I don't know if I felt quite the same as she did. I identified the problem of alienness with the problem of being a Jew who can never feel absolutely safe anywhere – even in Israel.

Nature favours youth, but luck does not discriminate between the generations. My research progressed well after the war, and took me away a great deal from uneasy home conditions. I completed the long excursion into the territory of the hand with investigations in schools. I visited the Greycoat Grammar School for Girls and the Merchant Taylors' School for Boys, where I interpreted the hands of children of different ages. Their teachers also came forward as subjects and even as helpers. A science teacher at the Greycoat School prepared statistical and graphic illustrations for my book, *The Hand in Psychological Diagnosis*. I was successful in my practice as a psychotherapist, but tried to keep the number of patients low because of my research, and the unprepossessing surroundings in which I had to see them.

I could almost believe in astrology. I was born under Libra, the sign of balance, and the good and bad influences of fortune have held their balance in my life. But my mind was not a well tempered instrument. Unfortunately my circumstances were better balanced than my emotional self. Perhaps good fortune has to be paid for, as the Ancient Greeks so well demonstrated when they called the dangerous Black Sea the 'Clement Sea', in order not to offend Neptune.

VI   A Wind of Change

I did not understand my English friends who had come like comets into my life. Their dead-pan humour and sense of the macabre were like Chinese to me, and so was their compulsion to gamble and addiction to crime reports and detective stories.

Back in 1938, Nan and her sister took me to see *Arsenic and Old Lace*. They were galvanized with amusement, and laughed every time a victim was bumped off. I stared at them in bewildered naïvety. I was unable to find this play a laughing matter. I thought my friends quite inhuman and indeed perverted. They laughed even more when I told them in the interval that I neither liked the play nor understood their reactions. 'But it is marvellously funny and the acting perfect. How odd that you can't laugh!' they said. We went back to our seats. By then I had got quite depressed. They took no notice of me. 'They don't take notice of what they don't want to know,' I told myself. 'They are inhuman, in spite of their kindness and immaculate behaviour.' At that time I did not realize how safe these English women felt, how sure of themselves they were. It was their sense of security which made it possible for them to laugh at crime.

I needed my English friends, but I did not believe in them. Time went on. The publication of *The Human Hand* had brought many clients into my consulting room. But with the exception of a Swedish-born doctor, physicians did not refer patients to me. The only intimate friend I had was a South African woman, and my greatest supporters, Professor Wallon and Dr Earle, were French and Irish. I began to wonder whether I was prejudiced, or right about English attitudes. The time came when I seemed to have been proved wrong. It happened like this.

My lecture at the Ecole des Hautes Etudes was arranged for a date in October 1948. I badly needed a holiday before then, and in July of that year I went to the picturesque village of Mousehole, in Cornwall. I was the only guest in a private guest-house, owned by two sisters. One of them, Irmgard, not only accompanied me to the village pub, but also on walks on the beach and in the surrounding country. The guest-house was on an ascending road which led to the top of the village. One morning we were climbing up the hill to get a breeze from the Atlantic. While we were ascending, the tall figure of a woman descended and stopped on seeing us. Her eyes, animated by an amused smile, rested on me with a question mark. When my companion had introduced me, she turned to me: 'Would you like to see our house up there?' 'I certainly would like to; how kind of you.' 'Come to tea – both of you – tomorrow.' That was how it started. Irmgard told me all about the amazing Quaker family who lived 'up there'. Gossip was rife in the village, the more so as artists and eccentrics had settled in Mousehole, and gave the inhabitants unusual entertainments, some outlandish, some sad. The Quaker family had gone through an unbelievable tragedy only a few months before. The whole community had been shocked by the disappearance of the youngest daughter Elizabeth – without trace. Fishermen had searched the sea, police the land around Mousehole, in vain. She was a beautiful girl, intelligent and artistic, Irmgard said. She had gone for a swim with her dog, never to return. The dog came back to the house alone. People were puzzled as to what had happened, and some thought it was suicide.

Next day, Irmgard and I sat in a neglected garden with Caroline, her parents, and Isabel, her friend. The property looked out onto the Atlantic, and the smell of the sea mingled with the aroma of roses and lilies. The air went to my head. I stared at Caroline's commanding figure, sitting upright and looking anxiously at her father, ninety-four years of age, who sat a few inches too close to Irmgard, a handsome woman in her thirties. Malevolent tongues whispered that he still had a glad eye for the girls. The mother, who was ninety-two, had a square face with few lines in it. She had an expression of quiet amusement, took no notice of us visitors, but looked at her husband with some disapproval.

Caroline had reached the late fifties, but traces of suffering in her face made her look older than her age. Her watchful eyes took in everything around her. Some sideways glances fell on me;

183

enquiring glances. Her eyes were unquiet and searching. I had the impression that she was looking for something to divert her mind. The family lived in a ramshackle house with a neglected garden; she obviously cared for her parents lovingly, but she was far away from it all. Her complexion worried me. She had dark rings under her eyes, matched by other signs of illness or distress: a yellowish colour to her cheeks and tight lips. Her friend Isabel sat next to me, never speaking a word. She had an air of absent-mindedness and detachment from the scene around her. Was she afraid to open her mouth? Without Caroline, she would have attracted one's attention. She stood no higher than five feet, and looked squat with broad shoulders and a short neck. Her eyes had a stare which could bewilder. They were large and black. She obviously took great pride in her appearance with special emphasis on the coiffure of her grey locks.

My eyes had been drawn to a small garden house in a neglected state, which turned out to be a studio. How forlorn it looked, as if nobody wanted to go in there or give it a clean! The outside needed fresh paint, and the roof, repair. Caroline must have read my thoughts. 'It is my sister Elizabeth's studio,' she said. 'She painted there, and used it as a bed-sitter when she wanted to be by herself.' Was the ice broken? Before we took our leave, she asked me if I would like to see the house inside. We went through a conservatory with outlandish flowers, the names of which I didn't know, into a big dining room with a wooden table fit for the dining hall of a castle. 'I won't show you the upstairs, the roof is leaking and we have to put buckets there whenever it rains. The place needs maintenance and I can't arrange to have anything done now. My brother is going to see about these things when he visits us next month.' Before I left, I looked at the abandoned studio again. 'Come again before you return to London,' Caroline said, 'I shall show you the studio.' 'I'd love to,' I answered, though no answer had been expected.

I went back to say goodbye, and Caroline showed me the studio. It was a small place with a cement floor and fluorescent light tubes on the walls. I saw a drawing of an egg on the easel and a few abstract efforts on a dusty table. After a while, Caroline took my hand and said: 'I would like to see you again.' 'I too.'

Letters went to and fro, and one contained an invitation for a long weekend. Two months after we had met, I took the train to Penzance. Caroline and Isabel fetched me from the station. I

184

looked at Isabel as if for the first time. She had a wistful smile, and a gleam of excitement in her large eyes when she shook hands with me. 'So glad you could come. It will do Caroline good.' The latter tried to stop her from making further remarks, as if afraid. She took my arm. 'You must be tired. Let's go home quick, the taxi is waiting.'

The long dining table was covered with flowers, and there was macaroni cheese, fruit and lemonade for dinner. Isabel was a vegetarian, and no alcohol was served in this house whose inhabitants were Quakers of the old school.

We went into Elizabeth's studio after dinner, and sat on two uncomfortable chairs. Isabel had tactfully disappeared. 'I thought you wanted something from me,' Caroline said, 'the way you looked at me.' I bent over her – we kissed. Then she told me that she had a friend in a neighbouring village, a Hungarian woman who had taken refuge from the Nazis. She looked after her so that she could go on with her painting. 'I visit her about twice a k into the garden. A smiling woman, white-haired and full-bosomed, asked to be introduced. She had just come back from an outing. 'Aunt Emma, Dad's sister, who has come to live with us,' I was told. At ninety-two years of age, she had all her wits about her, and an engaging disposition to boot. She had not left the Edwardian era in the way she dressed and the courtesies she bestowed on me. Her skirt covered her ankles, and a white blouse of fine wool bore a diamond brooch.

This old house, ivy-covered from top to bottom, with a faulty roof and peeling ceilings, was inhabited by personages out of a fairy tale. Aunt Emma picked and arranged the flowers for the house. Father took Elizabeth's dog for a walk, painted landscapes from memory, but mostly sat in the conservatory talking to himself. He looked as spruce and well kempt as his sister, but his mind was not what it had been, he told me. When reflecting in the conservatory he imagined himself to be in Menton or Nice or the Tropics. Mother still cooked and kept the housekeeper and everybody else in order. She thought that the world had become a sadly funny place. Isabel alone did not fit into the idyll. She always seemed to be on edge and far too humble. 'I am leaving soon for Kenya, to live with my brother,' she announced at dinner. Dad murmured: 'A good thing too.' 'She is always threatening to leave,' Caroline told me, 'she does not like Gertrud.' But Isabel gave me her own version. 'You see,' she said, 'Caroline cannot help picking up lame dogs.' 'Oh God,' I thought, 'what about me?' She continued: 'This painter woman exploits her and tries to take her away from me. I am so glad that you have come to us. It takes Caroline's mind off that woman.'

Isabel never went to Kenya. She thought she had found an antidote against the poisonous influence of Caroline's friend. The antidote was myself. She looked at me with increasing tenderness. When she and Caroline brought me to Penzance station, she asked, before I boarded the train: 'May I call you Charles, please?' 'Of course,' I said and smiled. She kissed me.

After the weekend, letters from Cornwall arrived daily, sometimes twice daily, and my own were dispatched just as often, frequently with poems in bad English.

In October of the same year, I went to a Paris resurrected from death. I stayed in a small hotel close to the Jardin de Luxembourg, and within walking distance of the Rue du Canivet, which was Baladine's little street. She had returned, sound and well, from her private exile in the Dordogne. Friends of Pierre had looked after her during the black days of the war. We sat together in her room again, full of her paintings and memories, as if time had had a stop. But the other rooms of the flat were no longer hers. She had given them over to Pierre, his wife and baby son. She adored little Mathew, but didn't care for her daughter-in-law. 'Why did he marry a Jewess out of a concentration camp?' she said, a question I could neither answer nor understand. Later on I realized that Denise had brought back her own worst fears – the yellow star, the concentration camps and death. Baladine had retired from the world outside, and did not live in the present. Her mind stayed with her memories of Rilke, and looked at the future through her love for her baby grandson. Again and again she read me unpublished poems Rilke had sent her as well as extracts from his letters to her. While she was reading at her small regency desk, my eyes wandered from her face looking down, to the portrait of Rilke above the writing table. She had painted him. She told me of those meetings many years ago, when she had installed Rilke at Musotte in Switzerland. I drank in every word, though I had heard it all before. No wonder, I thought, that Rilke had been bewitched by her. Her presence cast a spell over one, so that one forgot all else.

When I returned to my hotel from my first visit to Baladine, a telegram from Caroline awaited me. She was with me all the time, and I knew it. Yet I felt as far away from England and from her as if I had gone to Australia. The two worlds of France and England were incompatible.

My second visit to France had been much more easily accomplished than the first, though it had an awe-inspiring purpose – the lecture at the Ecole des Hautes Etudes. I had less anxiety about the journey itself, but had been apprehensive about preparing my text, and even more of standing in front of a large audience. I anticipated stage fright, particularly as my French vocabulary had shrunk through lack of use over the years. I could only hope to turn into an actor who would play the part all right in spite of, or inspired by, 'first night nerves'. The studies at St Lawrence's Hospital and Monyhull Colony had provided indisputable evidence that the human hand reflects abnormalities of the brain. I intended to demonstrate these points in my lecture. They were sound and safe, and indicated at the same time that my method of hand analysis was clearly mapped out, boding well for other research in progress which would widen its application. The large auditorium at the Ecole des Hautes Etudes was filled with students and members of the staff. Professor Wallon was in the chair. I stood at the lectern. My stage fright vanished after the first few minutes. All went well. After the hands of mentally defective children, and prints of the extremities of a chimpanzee and a gorilla, were projected on a large screen, I had won the day. My audience clapped and stamped their feet with enthusiasm. Professor Wallon expressed his thanks with much appreciation of my work. He invited me to spend the following evening with him and his wife. After the lecture, I went immediately to Baladine in a state of elation.

But I could not hold on to a happy state of mind for any length of time. Doubts as to my good fortune in days to come were ever present. The favourable happenings on this visit didn't convince me that I had really turned a corner and was on the way. Wallon proposed a transaltion of *The Human Hand* into French. He already had a translator in mind, and suggested writing a foreword to the book himself. I showed gratitude and pleasure, but the foolishness of disbelief was still stronger than a realistic appreciation of events. Even Wallon's invitation to contribute another article to *Enfance, Revue Bio-Psychologique* made little

187

difference to the stone wall of resistance against trust in my good fortune. Too many gifts from Pandora's box had been thrown at me, and I was afraid that more were in store. Caroline sent telegrams and wrote to me daily. Her love gave me a sense of emotional security, and helped me to enjoy Paris, especially the meetings with Baladine. *She* had made my second visit to Paris which, as I realized between doubts and fears, had been *meant*. Before lunch we sat on the terrace of Les Deux Magots in front of the Eglise de St Germain. This café had always been one of my favourite spots, where I liked to sit and stare. The terrace was as full with tourists and French people as before the war. Old acquaintances passed by as if reappearing from the grave. Some sat down at our table and chattered as they had done in 'old times'. One of them was Consuelo de Saint-Exupéry, a *triste* little figure who looked utterly lonely. She had made her home on a boat, moored to the banks of the Seine. 'No more fixed abode for me,' she said. She looked like a miniature in stone. I did not accept her invitation to see her on the boat. I had been very friendly with her in the past, but now she was so far away that I could not reach her.

Some evenings I spent at Baladine's home. One was now rather subdued there, walking on tiptoe, talking in a low voice, in order not to disturb the sleeping baby. At other times we dined at Lipp's on the Boulevard St Germain, and once she took me to a famous restaurant on the *rive gauche*, where well-known artists used to dine. We went into a narrow side-street where one could expect to be mugged rather than to see distinguished people enjoying culinary art. We sat at a table on the upper floor, close to a balustrade. We looked down on the crowd as if we had balcony seats in a theatre. We didn't care much for the spectacle below – too much humming and moving – but we cared for the delicious food and excellent wine in front of us. Suddenly, the unexpected happened at the next table to our right. Baladine's son Balthus had entered and sat down with three or four companions. He looked at us without a sign of recognition of either his mother or myself. He just stared, turned to his companions, called the waiter – as if we did not exist. Baladine did not turn a hair or give any outward sign of discomfiture. I sat with my mouth open with amazement at the event, yet I too seemed to accept this absurd behaviour as if it were natural. We didn't hurry our meal, nor did we wish to go away. We went on eating and drinking. Baladine and I talked as lively as ever, looking nonchalantly at the quick-moving waiters and the well-dressed guests. If we had been numbed by this bolt from the blue, it had not changed our behaviour. But when in the end we left the restaurant, I could not hold back. My anger broke through the barrier of inhibition.

'What has happened to Balthus to make him do this?' I asked.

'Oh he can't forgive me that I am a Jewess, who has made him half a Jew. He does not know me in public. He has done this before now, but he comes to see me from time to time, and is as affectionate as ever. You probably don't know that he has adopted the title of his father's family and calls himself Balthus, Count de Rolla.'

'Does he know how you feel about this?'

'I'm sure he does, but it makes no difference to him. I can't throw him out when he comes to see me. I leave things as they are. He has always been very difficult and lonely.'

'I shall never speak to Balthus again.'

'You probably won't have the opportunity,' she answered.

It left me wondering. I asked myself whether I had foreseen such capricious behaviour when I had looked at his hands. I should have known. Perhaps I did? I remembered the simian line in both his palms, which points to emotional imbalance. His divided Self had driven him into a cul-de-sac. No, his anti-Semitism had nothing to do with the unhappy fate of France, with the Nazis or any outer circumstance, as Baladine had said. I said: 'Baladine, I should not have been surprised because I looked at his hands many years ago, and saw the simian line of emotionally disturbed people. One finds it in imbeciles and in geniuses, and I know that I told him about it.' She smiled because neither of us doubted that Balthus was a painter of genius. 'He inherited his talent from you,' I continued. 'Does he recognize this?'

'He might, but it wouldn't make any difference. His rejection of my Jewishness overrules any other feelings he may still have for me.'

Nothing had ever been good enough for him, a perfectionist in everything. He wanted to belong to the élite, not only of painters, but also of society. Snobbism had been his blind spot which made him despise the very root from which his talent stemmed.

I returned from Paris to London as though I came from home into exile. But when the telephone rang every day from a kiosk somewhere in Cornwall, it made things look different. I had always equated intimate friendship and love with security and well-being, in spite of evidence to the contrary. I had put my faith again and again into the conviction that love was the all-powerful saviour. Will you never learn, I had asked myself at the end of an affair of the heart, only to forget the lesson on the next occasion. I thought that this time I had met with the exception to the rule. I did not listen to the small but clear voice inside myself – that the uncomfortable position in alien surroundings should be conquered by one's own efforts and not by protective love. I did not want to hear the warning signal of experience and fell for the illusion once more.

Caroline's entry into my life filled me with the delight of a swimmer who has been close to drowning. She gave every sign of commitment, and I responded in the same vein. But powerful as my emotional attachment was, another motive had driven me to her: the hope of finding a new home where I could rest and be restored from strain and struggle. I was impelled by nostalgia for the lost paradise of childhood which only the loving care of a maternal figure could provide. I could stand on my own feet in the ways of the world, but I became emotionally bound to another woman.

Caroline and Isabel visited London on 14 February 1949. It was a warm spring day when I arrived in a hired car at Paddington Station to fetch them. I wore my best outfit, a tailored suit in marine blue, and had discarded my overcoat. They were duly impressed by the hired car, and thought me much better off than I really was. They did express surprise at my extravagance. They had taken rooms in a hotel in the Cromwell Road where I left them with the promise to join them for dinner. This, however, did not come off, as they changed their plans at the last minute. Caroline telephoned to say she would come to see me at Tregunter Road, while Isabel was visiting an old friend in Hampstead. This put me into no small dilemma about dinner 'à deux', and I found the prospect of having her all to myself rather oppressive. I can't recollect how I managed to prepare for this meal, but I do know that I was able to procure a bottle of Nuits St George. She looked radiant when she arrived. I greeted her with: 'It's St Valentine's Day'. 'Oh, as good as any other day,' she answered.

That was the beginning of an enchanting evening. Being a Quaker, she was not used to alcohol, and couldn't drink more than half a glass of wine. After the meal she looked even more radiant than before. The atmosphere became electric, and sparks of verbal and non-verbal excitement filled the air. I have always loved the atmosphere of unspent eroticism. The glow goes on for a long time when the tensions of love are not discharged in sex. The word romantic does not quite convey the meaning of unspent desire, which electrifies the emotions and the imagination. They are at the root of love, the essence of living. We embraced, let go, embraced again – for hours.

'Don't let's have anything else,' she said. 'I want this to last. All things end if the beginnings are not kept intact. Don't let's have flowers, let's have buds.'

The wisdom of innocence, as old as the ages, as simple as the ABC, touched me as if it were a revelation. This evening was the beginning of a relationship which lasted for more than three years, and the friendship which followed for another twenty-five.

Next day, Isabel came with her to visit me, and found my surroundings attractive. She was a passionate gardener and liked the view from my window on well-kept gardens and a mulberry tree. We spent the following days sight-seeing in London, and evenings at the theatre. Caroline came once more to my abode. and didn't want to go.

'Isabel is buying a small property in Malvern,' she told me. 'We lived there with her mother in a large house before the war. It was situated in a beauty spot; you would have loved it. I am happy that we shall be within easy reach of each other; you can come for weekends and holidays, and I could visit you – that is, if you would like me to.'

In April of the same year Isabel acquired a house at the foot of the Malvern Hills. I could not understand what Caroline had meant by a 'small' property. The house stood in a large terraced garden which ended in a little wood. The property was unusually attractive. When I told them so, Isabel smiled: 'I am glad you like this ugly house'. They had not only started a new chapter in their lives, but also in mine. But little did I realize how much I would be involved.

The house, named 'Hazelwood', was protected from the noise of the road by a thickly planted hedge of yew trees. Only a small entrance gate allowed a glimpse of the property. But nobody could see far enough to perceive its terraced layout, its rhododendron bushes and a small summer house. The little wood at the bottom bordered on a stretch of water. A rock garden, with alpine flowers side by side with those of English clime, greeted one on entrance through the wooden gate, and to its left stretched a gently descending lawn. A copper beech tree shaded it on one side, while a small column bearing a sundial was placed in the centre. Frequent weekends and long holidays during the summer made Hazelwood indeed a kind of home for me, but I tried not to take it for granted, though both friends made it quite clear that they wanted me to come. I was not left in any doubt of an open invitation and enthusiastic welcome. It seemed not to be presumptuous, therefore, to think that I might belong with them. I knew that Caroline wanted me for herself. Isabel was keen for me to come for another reason also. I seemed to amuse her, but she welcomed my visits because I took Caroline away from her 'painter friend', who disturbed Isabel's peace of mind. She was a thorn in her flesh, as Caroline had not agreed to separate from her and had arranged for her to move to Malvern also. Caroline's ties with Cornwall were completely dissolved when both her parents died a year after she had moved to Malvern. I knew that I would always remain desirable to Isabel as a deterrent, if not as a friend.

Luckily my work did not suffer from my emotional preoccupation. On the contrary, it stimulated my efforts. By the end of 1949, my studies had run for seventeen years, since starting in an underhand fashion at the Institute for Electro-Physical Therapy in Neukölln. I had collected a great amount of material, and had been able to find a method of hand interpretation which could assist in psychological diagnosis and also indicate certain health conditions. I remembered how, as a student, I had been inspired by the fact that the Hippocratic finger was recognized as symptomatic of tuberculosis. It might have been the first stimulus to interest me in other revelations of the human hand. Perhaps it was Hippocrates in the first and last resort who had encouraged me to take up a maligned and discredited subject as a scientific study.

I would have become stale in my 'good fortune' had it not been for the emotional attraction I felt for Caroline. She changed the circumstances of my life. Hazelwood and the English countryside around were an unexpected extension of my urban existence. I was enchanted by the gentleness and grandeur of that part of England. The Malvern Hills of very ancient origin, the hilly

192

Cotswolds with their spruce villages, and the idyllic byways and sideways of Herefordshire and Worcestershire, all that took my fancy. But I could not be sure whether or not I lived in a fantasy when I stayed with my friends at Hazelwood. I knew, however, that I liked it that way. I loved the dream-like atmosphere as I had once liked the fog which made London a veiled and ghostly city, hanging in the air. I had been impressed by the dream-like quality fog gave to the town, and I had walked on air, fantasizing about it. I felt the same way about the house at the foot of the Malvern Hills and its inhabitants. A veiled vision which perhaps hid a mystery – that was what I really wanted. The desire for a second home was superimposed on an even deeper need – that of the imagination.

The movement from or to Malvern for short or long visits, interspersed with Caroline's stays at my flat, became a cherished habit. The two women gave me much, and I must have meant a good deal to them, as we were in constant contact with each other. Caroline counted the weeks and days before our next meeting, and Isabel had the undoubted satisfaction that Caroline would be at Hazelwood and not with her painter friend, when I stayed with them. By no means did I underrate the health benefits of my visits. When I arrived, worn out from work with patients and writing a new book, the hills and the house, the clean air and the maternal care restored body and mind. I became attached to the whole setting: the house with its view of the hills on one side, the Evesham plain on the other. Built in ragout style at the beginning of the century, the outside had not much to recommend it. But the position was perfect, and the ten rooms afforded comfort and beautiful sights of antique furniture and other treasures. A special feature was a rectangular dining room, with a long oak table taking up most of the space. The large kitchen next to it led, on the other side, to an outbuilding containing the housekeeper's flat and Isabel's bedroom, which was small, cold and uncomfortable. She was a woman of spartan habits, and enjoyed the hardship of a cement floor and absence of a stove. This civilized and rich woman loved to make herself inconspicuous. The centre of the house was the drawing room, full of light from a bay and side windows, and furnished with regency furniture. Portraits of Isabel's ancestors decorated the walls, looking down, slightly menacing, on the beholder. The terraced garden could be reached through a French window from the room next door, which was

Caroline's studio.

These two unusual women had created a world entirely their own. Both were artists, Caroline played the violin and Isabel the piano. Both loved literature and had travelled widely. The fact that we were from opposite poles, in background, experience and social attitudes, added to the mutual attraction. Our differences never jarred; they amused us, and made us look at each other like colourful birds from different lands.

Caroline had a small flat of her own upstairs, but slept on a couch in her studio when convenient. The guest room which I occupied was next door to it. It was not long before she paid me early-morning visits, without a word, creeping into my bed, putting her face against mine and an arm around my shoulder. The excitement of her caresses took my breath away. She acted as if in a dream, not quite herself. I was flattered. Between the caresses, there was talk, sometimes anxious talk. She did not want to be drawn into emotions she did not really understand (so she said). I had always liked to please and to be loved, and nothing could have given me more satisfaction and assurance than this strange situation. But I foresaw that it could not last, that the days of this kind of enchantment were numbered. It was unlikely that she could continue for long to give way to such urges. Her upbringing, her religion, her love for Isabel made this permissiveness a taboo. One day she would come into conflict about going 'against nature'. And perhaps the Hungarian friend would get wind of her feelings for me, and try to make her feel guilty. At the time I was too engrossed in our attachment to allow myself to doubt her. But an incomprehensible inhibition prevented me from enjoying her morning visits to the full. Perhaps I had been apprehensive from the start, but had pushed away unwelcome thoughts. As a matter of fact it was a long time before negative reactions did set in. The time of bliss lasted for years. All the while, daily letters and presents of love arrived at my door: the first of her garden's snowdrops, then the anemones. She wanted to give and give. She sent drawings by Elizabeth and her father, golden Worcester porcelain, fine cutlery, and pots and pans for my household.

Once, during a visit to my flat, Caroline spoke of a holiday she was planning in her mind with Isabel and myself. She wanted to get herself a car with her own money, and drive us to the Dordogne. And that was what she did.

Caroline's foresight had been total. Her preparations were

complete by the end of August 1950, a few days after I had finished writing *The Hand in Psychological Diagnosis*. 'You could not give me a more welcome present,' I told her. She had acquired the oldest car to be found in the Midlands, according to Isabel. All she could afford was an ancient Standard, more a pram than a motor, but she would get us safely through France – to be sure. The Standard had no boot to store luggage but, undeterred by such a trivial inconvenience, Caroline fixed some metal constructions to its back. Some suitcases could be tied on to them with string. Another metal contraption was fixed to the roof which secured the rest of our luggage. Isabel was not amused but, as usual, gave in to Caroline's whims and became reconciled to 'this oddity' of a car. And one warm September day, we left Hazelwood for the Dordogne.

We must have been a fine sight – an ancient Standard filled with three old women. Some English people stared at us, yet didn't utter a word of astonishment. But in France we became a sensation. We were laughed at from Dieppe to Périgueux, and from Périgueux to Montignac, which was our port of call for a longer stay. We wanted to visit the Lascaux Caves at leisure. The car was as good as her owner had predicted. Caroline had the route worked out to perfection. After a night in Le Mans, we made for Angoulême. We were intrigued by its cathedral in the middle of a busy street. A church tower nodded dangerously to one side, perhaps in sympathy with the tower of Pisa! But the ramparts, remnants of ancient fortifications, were the town's greatest attraction for me. I thought it poetic to sit on a bench, staring at the valley below, imagining that Paul Valéry, a native of Angoulême, might once have sat here, enjoying the same view.

The three of us were in high spirits and generally tolerant of each other's idiosyncrasies. Isabel had to get out at every church we passed, and I wanted to sit outside a café in every town we went through and drink real French coffee. Caroline itched to get out at every beauty spot for a walk, but always accommodated herself to our preferences. But a minor storm threatened the harmony between us when it came to the choice of a hotel. Isabel didn't want to look like a well-off lady. She bought her clothes in cheap shops, and made sport of being parsimonious as well as inconspicuous. She liked to stay in second- or third-class hotels which I abhorred. She enjoyed the inverted snobbery of some rich people who appear poor, while I longed for a room with bath in the best hotel. Caroline succeeded in reconciling our differences, wanting to please us both. It was decided that the choice would be alternately Isabel's and mine, while Caroline was content either way.

It was a grand holiday. We stared at the imprints of hands, those first signs of man's identity, made some 30,000 years ago in caves at Les Eyzies. Because of my research on the human hand, I preferred them to the amazing record of the prehistoric paintings at Lascaux. We went again and again to Les Eyzies to make pencil tracings of the most ancient hand-prints ever.

The Standard took us through the mountains of the Cevennes, the valleys of the Garonne, the Lot, the Dordogne and the Tarn. We passed famous old towns on our way from Angoulême to Périgueux, and further west to Albi. Before venturing south, we had devotedly visited the colourful cathedrals and an early basilica in Poitiers. But more hidden places had affected us through their mysterious stillness, and were stored in the memory as precious stones are stored in the earth. There was Cordes, a small thirteenth-century town in the Languedoc. It nestled on the summit of a hill as if it had grown out of it. Safely tucked away at the end of a steeply ascending road, cars had difficulty in entering it. The town itself is a museum piece, with well-preserved fourteenth-century houses. But where were the inhabitants? Had they turned to stone? Or did they stare at us from behind green shutters? We had passed another timeless place on our way to Montignac, where life stood still. The little town of Brantôme occupies a small island in the river Dronde, and one enters it over a bridge bent like an elbow. Both the water surrounding it and the suggestive bridge evoked in me the image of birth. My friends were also struck by the place – 'Out of this world, where waters run "deep",' Caroline remarked.

Names have a suggestive power, particularly those of towns in foreign lands. One expects to see something fascinating there. Names are promises rarely fulfilled, but the red town of Albi appeared to be an exception. It is a mundane place, filled with tourists on their way to the Pyrenees and Spain, but not attractive enough in itself to those who are in search of memorable treasures. Not that we looked down on the comfort, elegance and excellent food to be enjoyed in the modern restaurants, but we found the real thing in Albi's *ancient* buildings. The thirteenth-century cathedral particularly appealed to my friends, while I was most impressed by the Archbishop's Palace. Both are built in red brick like many of Albi's houses. The grand clergy had long ago left the palace, and its massive interior had been transformed into a museum. The most erotic paintings produced this century were exhibited there: Toulouse-Lautrec's pictures of black-stockinged women, and of chorus-girls who emanated a sensuality no strip-tease could ever suggest. The Archbishop's Palace had gone a long way from the sacred to the erotic, both touching the divine. The palace seemed to me as grotesque as Toulouse-Lautrec's physical appearance. The clash of centuries had produced a remarkable freakishness.

When we made for Cahore we passed through Rocamadour in its dramatic setting. It lies high up on a plateau, with a wide view of the Dordogne valley and steep hills behind it. The town looked grey, not only because of its stone buildings. It had the 'deadly' greyness of a spectre. Its inhabitants seemed to be hiding behind the green shutters of their rooms. But sightseers were abroad in force. They did not want to miss the town's unique layout, nor the guide's tale of its legendary history going back to biblical times. One had to climb endless steps to the twelfth-century Crypt de St Sauveur, which is its greatest showpiece. It was not the church which took my fancy, but the grimness and the dirt of this ancient town – a shrouded monument rather than a place for the living. Its ghost-like mysteriousness impressed me more than the civil-ized town of Cahore, with its ancient bridge and its truffles and wines, famous beyond the borders of France.

It was, however, the small town of Soulliac which perhaps made the greatest impact of all on me. It looked a sleepy place, where people and nature were in an equally somnolent state, with the Dordogne moving gently by. We picnicked close to the town in a quiet place by the river. The reason for our visit was Soul-liac's twelfth-century cathedral, where Isabel had a field day of discovery. But my interest was the statue of Jesaias at the portal. When I looked at him I felt that I had met a person I knew. He looked at the world with large and smiling eyes, as if he wanted to impart something of his poetic wisdom to the beholder. He *was* Soulliac for me, perhaps because I had tried my hand at biblical poems when still at school. 'Jesaias' was one of them:

Jesaias-ist ein Dichter
Durch die Sohlen seiner Füsse

Brennt das Herzensblut der Erde
Wehdonnerleid und Jubelsüsse.

Sein Haupt dringt in die Tiefe
Jedem Stern
Darum ist ihm Geheimes offenbar
Er steht in Demut lauschend
Vor dem Herrn.

Jesaias is a Poet
Through the Soles of his Feet
Beats the Heartbeat of the Earth
Thunderous Pain and sweetest Joy.

His Head reaches into the Depth
He knows the secret of every Star of all times to come
He stands and listens in devotion to Jehovah.

It was silently agreed that Caroline and Isabel shared a room and I was on my own. It turned out to be a happy arrangement. Caroline visited me every night while Isabel made her 'toilette'. She allowed her rather a long time, and Isabel did not object. Did she or did she not know about her friend's emotional upheaval? I shall never be sure because of an extroardinary näivety and contradiction in her make-up and feelings. Nobody could revile love between women more than she did, and I doubt whether she knew the words lesbianism and homosexuality, let alone their meaning. The fact that she passionately loved another woman made no difference to her rejection of a 'vice'. She loathed not only the Hungarian painter, but other women friends of Caroline. 'They are all hermaphrodites,' she had told me with contempt. She called me Charles, but this gave her no hint about the varieties of human love. In any event, we got on famously and agreed that ours was the holiday of a lifetime. Every evening we sat in their room and wrote a diary à trois. We noted down what we had experienced during the day, for example, the dinner we had had at Mende or the gloves I had given Isabel in Millau. And we emphasized our personal preferences in what we had seen. We wrote of the people we had observed or talked to, and amusing incidents we had enjoyed. On one of these we were in total agreement.

After our Standard had safely negotiated the fantastic mountainscape of the Cevennes up to Le Rozier on the river Tarn, we stopped at the best hotel (on my recommendation) for a few days. While we were sipping coffee on the terrace, a strange sight confronted us – the smallest car we had met with on our journey. 'My God,' said Caroline, 'she is worse than ours.' Out of the oldest model of Austin Seven came two young Britishers, who stared at our Standard, which still stood in front of the hotel. They looked at us and we looked at them. The four of us roared with laughter. The young men came to our table in the certain knowledge that the Standard must be ours, and said: 'Yours is one better than ours.' 'Yes, yours is far worse, far worse,' Caroline replied laughingly. We all drank to each other's good journey in the two vehicles which had given us much pleasure, and great amusement to the French people we passed on the journey.

Le Rozier was one of the last highlights of our holiday. We were struck by the women sitting at the wayside, making lace, old women dressed in black, with parchment skins, much lined. They reminded me of birds of prey who knew what they wanted and got it. One finds them also in other mountainous regions of France. They are industrious and seem to be indestructible, matriarchs who hold things together.

We had been away for nearly six weeks. I returned to London after two nights at Hazelwood as a respite between one world and another. A week later, Caroline informed me that she was going with Gertrud to Amsterdam for a week to look at the Rembrandts. 'I had promised to take her there before we left for France,' she wrote. I had only met her Hungarian friend once, but guessed that she would have to be 'paid' for Caroline's holiday in France.

Gertrud, a stocky woman, growing fat, had small black eyes which glinted at the slightest provocation. Bad-tempered and very intelligent, was my verdict. Her hospitality and manners had been impeccable, but her dislike of me was in the air. However, at that time I had no qualms, as it was obvious where Caroline's heart was. During her absence, Isabel telephoned me several times in distress. 'That woman is using blackmail,' she said, 'Caroline is wax in her hands, and she will try to get her away also from *you*. Do come here as soon as possible. Only you can spoil her schemes.' I promised a visit over Christmas, and I stayed at Hazelwood until after the New Year. Gertrud had to join the three of us on Christmas Day. She looked at Caroline and me with obvious misgivings, if not hate. She had either grasped the situation or had forced Caroline to make a confession. But nothing had visibly changed between us. Caroline looked out for me when I walked on the hills by myself, she came to me in the mornings, and her tenderness was even more intense than before. When I had to leave for London, she fixed the date of our next meeting saying: 'In three weeks I shall see you again, if you would like me to come.' On arrival at my flat, she asked if she could make a phone call at once. It was not Isabel she talked to but Gertrud. 'I promised her. She gets so worried when I drive up by myself to London,' she explained. At the beginning of 1951 the signal of danger had come through to me. Isabel had been right. Some form of emotional blackmail was being used by Gertrud. I challenged Caroline by saying just that. She denied the charge, but admitted that she felt worried about the state of mind of her Hungarian friend. I retorted: 'You should be worried about Isabel's state of mind. She is very depressed.'

'Isabel knows full well that she comes first. Gertrud is a job I have taken on and I cannot let her down. And nobody can take me away from you,' she added.

She could not wait to see me again every time we had to part, so she told me. And I suppressed unwelcome thoughts once more. Neither of us wanted to look further than the present. We succeeded for another year or so. Luckily I had been much taken up with my practice and the forthcoming publication of my book *The Hand in Pscyhological Diagnosis* in September of that year. By that time we had known each other three years, probably the happiest years of my life in England. My book was the crowning of nineteen years' search and research, with trials and errors, discoveries and achievements. Its publication had an unexpected result. It led to my permanent registration as a physician in Great Britain. But this happy event was accompanied by all the symptoms of a difficult birth.

A national newspaper had drawn sensational conclusions from my findings and, as if this was not enough, had reproduced material from my book together with erroneous comments. My publishers and I were alarmed and sought the advice of my solicitor. She got an immediate injunction against further reproductions from my text and illustrations by the newspaper concerned. This mishap caused me considerable worry and fear. I was afraid that I might lose the chance of being taken at my real worth as a research worker, and never be allowed to practise medicine in

England. My solicitor had shared my serious view of the matter. She immediately wrote to the General Medical Council, explaining the whole situation. The answer came soon, and came as a surprise. It said that I could certainly be granted the status of a registered physician if I made a special application. I had missed my opportunity some years before, when a notice had been published inviting foreign physicians who had served as locum tenens during the war, to apply for permanent registration. I had not seen the relevant journals, having been completely absorbed in research and personal affairs.

Early in 1952 I became a physician again. My new situation overwhelmed me to such a degree that I couldn't believe in it. Was the permit real, I wondered. I even went so far as to ask the General Medical Council if it was all right for me to put the letters M.D. after my name. The reply assured me that I could.

Re-instatement as a physician changed not only my professional, but also my social position in this country. It strengthened my self-esteem, and relieved me of an ambiguous professional situation which had been a nagging worry ever since I had left Germany in May 1933. At the same time, the re-instatement into my proper place, which I had so desperately wanted, led to an odd backlash. It underlined rather than relieved my sense of alienness in this country. I thought that my colleagues would look askance at me, regarding me as an outsider who had dared to invade their territory. Nevertheless, a heavy burden had fallen from my mind, and my self-assurance and confidence grew in the knowledge that my professional position had been put right. With my new status, I had regained my stature. I was freed from a sense of inferiority in social intercourse and psychological treatment. On the other hand, my medical knowledge had to be revivified to equip me fully for my new task. Fear of failure, never absent in people with responsibility for the sanity of others, irked me. But I hoped that the considerable progress in my research would compensate for possible lacunae in specialist knowledge. I assured myself that it would favour me in the eyes of the profession also. My self-appraisal became a useful antidote to self-doubt, but a residuum of uncertainty persisted.

Nobody can rest on her/his laurels. And I started to question myself about the meaning of achievement. Thinking of my long drawn-out efforts to find a scientific method of hand-interpretation, I realized full well that only the 'eternal moments' of discoveries had stayed in my mind. I realized that it was better to travel than to arrive, and the expectation of reaching a goal was better than having actually got there. We are all travellers upon the earth, and *expectation* is our vital emotional equipment. It is ingrained in the human mind, despite disappointments on the journey. Any desire to find a place in which to stay for good and enjoy rest and tranquillity is but a mirage. It must end in loss of desire. Resting for good makes for restlessness, unless one has arrived at the final station of travel – death.

Moments of elation about discoveries, successful endeavours or any kind of happiness, are but soap bubbles, gone in a second or two. They cannot be ends in themselves. A goal which is not the springboard for another one stifles vitality and initiative. Our longing for security is embedded in our sense of time. One cannot live in the present until one has made it the past. The great moments for child and adult alike are before the curtain rises on the stage, when we are filled to the brim with anticipation and expectation of the play to come. At those moments we live in the future. After the play has started we have already put the future behind us, but we are by no means in the present. We cannot grasp the events before our eyes, until they have become the past. Reflection about impressions is practically simultaneous with the impressions themselves, which means that the past has caught up with a present that never was. All talk of living in the present is false comfort for people who believe that they must possess what they desire and hold on to it like 'grim death'. This misconception has led to false ideas and ideals, which are unhealthy and danger- ous. They contribute to destructive personal and social values. To be in the present, as some great minds would have it, goes with a negation of tensions which are the source of energy. The perma- nent revolution of thought and emotion is the essence of living. Already, in about 540 B.C., Heracleitus taught that life is continu- ous motion. The ideals of our time, geared to getting instead of striving, have made individuals and society lethargic, emotionally numb, and often inhuman. Until people understand the differ- ence between the futility of existing and the permanent revolu- tion of living, true contentment and love are out of bounds.
1952 came in like a whirlwind, sweeping away much which I had believed to be safe. The unexpected happened, bringing new con- stellations and problems; the inner landscape altered in relation to the outer.

202

It seemed to be a good omen that I was able to acquire a ground-floor flat close to Tregunter Road, at the time of my professional re-instatement. But as it happened, I jumped out of the frying pan into the fire. Ballet dancers and 'tiny feet' produced a hullabaloo above my ceiling. Luckily my patients were not disturbed by the noise pollution, but I was. I endured it with a stiff upper lip, alien to my nature. Research on the human hand had come to an end as far as I was concerned, and I did not venture on any other field of investigation. I was too much taken up with my consultations and my personal attachment at Hazelwood, to have either the desire or energy to cultivate new pastures.

Time had not stood still in Hazelwood either. The tragedy of an incurable illness which had afflicted her sister had changed Caroline's life and relationships. Her sister remained with her in the upstairs flat until her death, which turned Caroline more and more towards religion. Both sisters had been 'believers' since childhood, but now religion became the life-blood of Caroline's existence. Though she had relapses into secular feelings, a sense of guilt poured poison into any physical intimacy. Communications between us had slowed down since her sister had moved into the house; and her death had left Caroline numb. I went to Hazelwood for long holidays as before, but she ceased to come to London. She seemed to like having me around, but she had aged and her mind was preoccupied with other things. She still went through the motions of tenderness, but with a sad face. There was a hollowness about her caresses. At that time Isabel turned to me in a new way. Gertrud had been helpful in the time of need, and Caroline saw more of her than before and no longer abstained from visiting her when I was there. Isabel resented that the two women were constantly seen in Malvern together. Once again, she felt left out. 'They are now a twosome,' she told me. 'She won't go and stay the night in Malvern when you are here,' she added. And Caroline commented to me on Gertrud's occasional visits to Hazelwood when I was there: 'I cannot forbid her to come. You have so much in common with Gertrud, I wish that you would make friends.' 'I would not mind,' was my diplomatic reply. Caroline, between the devil and the deep blue sea, had lost her grip on life, and I had not the heart to distress her. I was surprised about my lack of resentment towards Gertrud, but I minded her sarcastic and diminishing remarks about others. Her jealousy made, of course, any rapport between us impossible. I appreciated her intelligence, taste and talent, but appreciation leads nowhere in an atmosphere of mistrust. At the same time, I looked on her as a safety-valve against Caroline's persistent over-concentration on me, which had by then become a burden. Hazelwood had undergone a change in the geometry of relationships. But I was determined not to give way to Gertrud's machinations to get rid of me. While Caroline became somewhat remote, Isabel came closer to me. I agreed to her flights from the house when Gertrud's presence had put her out of countenance. We went on drives into the countryside in her second-hand car. Caroline was anxious about us both. 'She is not a safe driver; you take your life in your hands,' she told me. 'Well, she has it in hers,' I answered laughingly. Isabel was an erratic driver, but I felt quite safe with her because I trusted any driver, having no knowledge of that skill myself. However, it suited me to solidify our friendship, and to keep a firm hold on Hazelwood and Caroline. I had no need though to fear that I might lose her. She still hung on to me, even when denouncing our intimacy as a wrong step in her life. One day she had the courage to talk about it.

'I am not a homosexual, you should know that,' she said.

'I don't know why you put a label on emotions,' I answered, guessing that it was Gertrud and not she who had spoken.

'We shall always be close friends,' she continued, 'but I have deprived the other two. They have suffered because of us. They are very close to me, and I must not have any preferences.'

'Well, Isabel did not mind about your "preference",' I retorted, 'on the contrary, she supported it.' Whereupon Caroline laughingly said: 'You aren't as stupid as you pretend to be, knowing full well that she helped us for a purpose.'

'Naturally, and it was welcome to the three of us.'

'Things have changed,' she said, 'and her design, touching as it was, has no sense any more.'

'I know,' I replied, 'because you have changed.'

'That is not quite true. My feelings for you are always the same, but human emotions go through certain changes. You belong here and I want it so. We shall be close friends and nothing else.'

'Yes,' I agreed meekly.

It was through Isabel that I got to know the little town of Malvern. After taking a morning coffee at a well-carpeted but gloomy café on the Belle Vue Terrace, we either went to the Priory or shopped in Malvern's hilly main street. Isabel gave me a history lesson about the Priory, which fitted into the town like a heart into a body. Malvern had been built around it as its life-giving centre. Its modest reddish-grey façade hid a precious interior, where I was fascinated by some thirteenth-century tiles in the apse, on which the eagle with two heads was painted. They intrigued me more than a chapel dating back to the eleventh or twelfth centuries, and other famous historical hallmarks enshrined in the Priory.

We were determined to get right away from Hazelwood, and make a real day of our outings. We drove either along the Malvern Hills to Upton-on-Severn, or ventured as far as Hereford and lunched at 'The Feathers'. Isabel could not resist visiting the cathedral, which was as familiar to her as her own drawing room, but left me cold. Our frequent absenteeism had the desired effect; Caroline, unquiet and angry that she had driven Isabel to indulge in escapes, and missing me in the house, decided on a welcome change. Gertrud was to visit Hazelwood no more during my holidays. As a concession, I had to accompany her from time to time to Gertrud's flat in Malvern.

'Hazelwood has become a cuckoo's nest,' I had told Isabel on one of our days out.

'There is only one cuckoo,' she protested, 'the Hittite from Hungary.'

'What do you mean?' I asked laughingly.

I knew of her conversion to the beliefs of the British Israelites, but had not taken it more seriously than any of her other diverting eccentricities. But she was in earnest. She vehemently told me that Jews were really Hittites; only a few were true Israelites. The great majority were British people. I suppressed any criticism of this astonishing statement. She went on: 'You are one of the true Jews and belong to us.' I had no choice but to accept the honour – with pleasure.

The trouble spot removed, Caroline firmly took command over Isabel again. Excursions to Cheltenham, Painswick and Stratford-on-Avon with her at the wheel gave a renewed spate of pleasure to the three of us. But I knew that Caroline had not really recovered her former *joie de vivre*. We played rather than felt the intimacy of earlier years. But Isabel was more reassured, and I more at ease with both of them. As time went on, Caroline's letters became more and more stereotyped – letters anyone could have written or read. Her decision to turn away from an intimate involvement had been final after all. But I was taken aback when, one day, I received an urgent request to return all her letters of the first three years. I telephoned my surprise and objection to this deprivation of a cherished past, recorded by her own hand.

'You must let me have them. I cannot bear the thought that anybody could ever read them.' She was adamant, and I had no choice but to comply. It was obvious that she had to destroy the record of a 'mistake' which she could not forgive herself. When I asked her which method of annihilation she had chosen, she told me: 'I burnt them together with all those you wrote to me – in the garden.'

This *auto-da-fé* of despair and guilt had a curious edge of comedy. I could not help laughing at her confession and said: 'It reminds me of the Nazis, burning the degenerate books of Jews and other "vermin".'

'You are hurt, I am sorry, but it had to be.'

'Do you think you have burnt the past?' I asked her.

'Of course not, but I have demonstrated my repentance of it.'

'To whom – God, Gertrud, yourself?' I teased.

'Myself in the eyes of God', was her strong and definite reply. And she added: 'My real feelings for you have never changed and never will. When you are ill, I shall look after you; when you call me, I shall come.' Up to a point, she kept her word until she died.

While my personal life had almost reached a nadir, my professional life became enriched through a new facet to my practice. I was asked to write psychiatric reports for the Probation Service of a Magistrate's Court. One of the senior probation officers, who happened to be a Quaker, had made contact with me, and had arranged that some female 'delinquents' should be interviewed by me, to give the magistrate a specialist's opinion of their mental state. Several of them to whom probation had been granted were referred to me for psychotherapy. This new aspect of my work stimulated me greatly. I liked the contact with my 'delinquent' patients, and welcomed the chance to do some social service for this country. Some of the girls were lesbians who had either been models or prostitutes. They had been arrested for soliciting or abusing the police. Their gratitude and attachment to the probation officers and myself opened my eyes to certain psycho-social conditions, and also to some aspects of homosexuality. The older generation of probation officers were still inspired in their work by a missionary fervour. This was certainly the case with the Quaker who had introduced me to the Magistrate's Court. She became a personal friend who brought me into contact with her colleagues in other parts of London. And one Sunday she took me to the Westminster Meeting of the Quakers. I attended Meeting many times, but from the wrong motives. I was not spontaneously drawn to it, but did so because of gratitude to my new friend, whom I didn't want to disappoint. Unfortunately, these Meetings for Worship had a perverse effect on me. Silences and odd utterances in between gave me a sense of unreality and claustrophobia. And the idea of the spirit either giving tongue in abrupt speeches or ordering long silences didn't strike a sympathetic note in me. On the contrary, I found it unreal, if not ridiculous. I persisted for about a year, trying to overcome my discomfort, but had to give it up in the end. On the other hand, an intimate Quaker group to whom she introduced me did the opposite for me. The group met once a month in the home of Dr Isabel Wilson, a distinguished psychiatrist. The level of discussion was high, and the famous Quaker tolerance made it possible to air divergent views, from Eastern religions to humanism. But most important was the congenial and committed atmosphere between members. Once more, a professional beginning had led to a personal benefit. Friendships started there which were made to last.

London, instead of being a kind of chimera from which one preferred to look away, had regained many of its desirable qualities. I had taken against the city because of the unpleasant home conditions which had followed me everywhere since Anne Tennant had left me. But the renewed presence of my old friend Ruth made a difference. She had settled in London after her husband's death. My eyes were no more turned exclusively to the romantic atmosphere of Hazelwood, and the green fields and granite hills around Malvern. But holidays were spent there twice a year without fail, a custom I indulged in until Caroline's death in 1976. Sparks of the old feelings between us lighted up from time to time. A driving holiday through the Highlands of Scotland re-established something of the old intimacy. But these were moments to be treasured like windfalls, and not to be taken too seriously.

Ruth was both practical and unromantic. After she had met Caroline on one of her rare visits to London, she told me with a disapproving look: 'What contact can you possibly have with that old woman? Do you want to live in a fairy tale? You have absolutely nothing in common with her. You should know better – being a psychologist.' I was quite charmed by this outburst, and of course took no notice of it. I knew what I needed and, fairy tale or not, she and Isabel had done more for me than anybody else in this country; they had healed the painful impression that English women cannot be friends with foreigners, and are fickle when not bound by their peculiar social code.

Ruth had changed from an oriental beauty into a handsome middle-aged woman, whose olive skin was now dark brown and slightly wrinkled through tropical climates. She was a frustrated artist, forced to earn her living in an advertising agency. The blind develop an extra senstivity to touch, and the deaf a special kinetic awareness which enables them to become lip-readers. Substitute functions also develop when outlets for a talent are blocked. Ruth, who had not excelled in intelligence when young, had become a woman of considerable brain power, with literary interests and acumen. She happened to be the only Jewish person in my English orbit. Our common roots and mutual interests made for a family tie rather than friendship. She found a bed-sitter close to my apartment, and her presence was a constant reminder of the pleasures and pains of our German past. But the 'new' Ruth had an air of ambiguity about her; she was inclined to diplomatic double think. One could not get hold of her; she slipped through one's grasp like an eel. Yet I preferred her evasiveness to a mental twinship, easily indulged in between two of a kind.

Sybille Bedford's return to London in 1956 meant more to me than I had anticipated. It not only led to an intimate friendship, but infused into my life the warmth and inspiration I had been starved of. Her friend, the American writer Eda Lord, shared her several abodes in London and Essex, and, in the end, close to my quarters. Our friendship automatically included Eda. The three of us shared the same taste for *conversazione*, which has been so shamefully neglected since the war. The considerable success of *The Sudden View* and *A Legacy* had made Sybille more unassuming than ever. But her eyes still looked as amused and worried as before. Eda had Mexican blood which her beauty reflected in her large dark eyes, and a body, athletic and flexible, made for dance and acrobatics. She was not given to much speech, and only got a word in edgeways. But when she did speak it was with a perceptiveness and wisdom that made one prick up one's ears. Sometimes our evenings extended into the early hours of the morning. The mutual give and take cemented this friendship and lifted our spirits onto a plane of inspiration. The two stayed for seven years in this country, before they left for the south of France after the terrible winter of 1963. I was sad and angry about their departure. Another seven years passed before they settled in London once more. During the long period of their absence, I went from time to time to the south of France. Thus the horizon of holidays stretched from the Midlands to the shores of the Mediterranean. I stayed in the quaint house of an English friend near St Paul de Vence. The almost incestuous contact between women of the English upper class who live on the Riviera stood me in good stead. My friend knew Sybille and Eda and Allanah Harper in whose property they occupied the ground-floor flat. We continued our uplifting conversations *à trois* in the balmy climate and vivacity of the Riviera.

It would, however, have been wrong to conclude from these fortunate circumstances that I had settled down in Great Britain. I had not. I took an empathetic interest in my patients, enjoyed individual contacts, but was unable to regard myself as other than an adopted 'child' of this country, who had to be careful in word and deed. I was, and remain, an outsider, neither able nor wanting to change this position. I look at events and circumstances in Great Britain with the same empathy which I feel for my patients. I cannot help realizing that the collective mind of the British people had undergone changes which I consider symptomatic of 'ill health'.

It is not for me to take an active part in propagating either my own ideas on society, or my political stance. I prefer, on the whole, to remain silent. But the current misuse of the word democracy, and its consequent misapplication, concerns me as much as everyone else inside and outside this country. The welfare state has not been a healer of social ills, but an educator in emotional spoonfeeding. Many English people have learned to take much and give little or nothing in return, like spoilt children. They demand as their right what they should acquire through their own effort and initiative. The decline, if not fall, of a great nation often makes me itch to go on a rostrum and talk about these matters, but I do not feel appointed to give warning signals.

The misuse of a word obviously distorts its meaning. And my

plea for self-discipline and a give and take in *all* relationships might be criticized in the name of democracy as being naïve or fascist. It is neither. My point of view is close to that of the surrealists who stood for the pursuit of absolute freedom in ideas and relationships. One cannot love others before loving oneself. One cannot discipline others before disciplining oneself. And one cannot, or should not, give or take without reciprocating either way. Otherwise the freedom to be oneself and to create a 'free' society will be damaged, and destroyed in the end.

There was another matter to which I *could* apply my time and energy: the problem of homosexuality. It concerns all humanity. I wanted to investigate the joys, sorrows and conflicts of homo-sexual people who do not fall in with stereotyped emotional behaviour. I knew from the start that many problems they have to face are not of their own making, but are produced by the people who look at them with either contempt, ignorance or condescend-ing tolerance. The majority of heterosexuals regard them with disdain, which badly hides the fear of their own homosexuality. My interest in lesbianism as it was lived dates from my student days, but became a different preoccupation when I made it my new field of research in the sixties.

The beginning of this study goes back to the first draft for *On the Way to Myself*. The book was commissioned by Methuen in 1960, but I only started to write in consecutively in 1967. The reasons for the delay were changes in my personal life and heavy professional obligations. I had made a number of unsuccessful starts, though, but only managed to finish one chapter – an essay on female homosexuality. I realized that ideas alone were not enough; they had to be justified or disproved by experimental research. But at that time I was not ready to pursue such an investigation.

In April 1962 Isabel died. I mourned her to an extent which surprised me. I may have divined that a complete change in Caroline's life was in the air, a change which would affect my whole life. She had bought the house in which Gertrud had set-tled twelve years before, and finding herself unable to manage Hazelwood she sold the property and moved into her red brick semi-detached in a quiet street in Malvern Link. For many months she had been unable to come to terms with the 'come down' in her circumstances. Caroline's loneliness after Isabel's death sealed her devotion to Christ's teaching, and religion ruled her life even more firmly than before. In her sadness and depression she expressed doubts that I would find it worth while to visit her, now that Isabel and Hazelwood had gone. This was the one shaft of light in the new situation. I knew that she wanted me to spend my holidays with her as I had done all these years, and not be put off by the modest surroundings and the presence of Gertrud. A new era began for me also. I had not ceased to want and need a 'second home', and I had no intention to be deprived of Caroline and Malvern, but the change of circumstances was not easy to bear. Gertrud received me grudgingly. She resented my visits, but had no power to prevent them, which she resented even more. I stayed in the tiny attic room without a view, which was too hot in summer and too cold in winter. After some time of uneasy adaptation, I was fascinated by the provincial aspect of Caroline's new life, and particularly by the milieu into which she had moved. The neighbouring streets and the neighbours themselves aroused my curiosity, which soon extended to the whole town and its inhabitants. Malvern became a fresh territory of discovery for me. My presence in her house seemed to do Caroline good. She devoted herself to my welfare, and wanted to give me as much pleasure and 'health' as she could. We went for picnics on the river Wye or into the Cotswolds, and visited the three festival towns of Worcester, Hereford and Gloucester. And we drove onto the Malvern Hills and walked on the gentle paths which lead to the British Camp and the Worcestershire Beacon. Gertrud was a professional painter who never missed a day's work, and thus refused Caroline's invitations to join our expeditions. Rainy days and days of rest from driving made the town a new treasure hunt. The atmosphere of a leisured rhythm of life gave neighbours the chance to show good-humoured courtesies and mutual assistance to one another. The exclusiveness of Hazelwood had been exchanged for lively contacts with other people. I was invited to look over their houses and gardens. They were something out of a picture book of the past. The romantic glow of an era long gone enchanted me. I was transported into the Edwardian (or Wilhelmian) age of my childhood. Malvern was, and still is, a garden town, with trees redolent of a much earlier period when forests had occupied its space, leaving their traces hundreds of years later. Many streets all over Malvern have large gardens, hiding big houses built for families at the turn of the last century. The peacefulness of the town was underlined by the fact that many of its public buildings looked like Gothic churches. They gave a religious flavour to the town's atmosphere. Streets of such nostalgic beauty were the essence of Malvern, which the addition of ugly houses with pocket-handkerchief gardens could not destroy.

Caroline's street exhibited in a singular way the social change which had taken place. One side belonged to the well-to-do who had lovely houses with large gardens; the other was inhabited by the 'lower classes', with semi-detached houses and little gardens not worth the name. Her house stood on *that* side of the street. After a few months of homesickness for Hazelwood, Caroline welcomed her new status as one of the less privileged citizens of Malvern. Like Isabel before her, she enjoyed looking ordinary and being inconspicuous.

Nothing can stand still, not even a conservative little town like Malvern. It had, indeed, been the chosen place for the latest scientific enquiry. Malvern had been 'invaded' by a wave of scientists and their staff when, during the war, the famous Institute for Electronic Research was stationed there. They had discovered radar which, as many Malverners maintain, had won the war. Yet the peace and strength of the past had shown itself resistant to any streamlining influence. Scientists bought houses all over Malvern, while most of their staff lived in a modern ghetto close to the institute. The scientists mixed freely with the local inhabitants, sharing their amateur theatricals, Bible-reading clubs, etc.. But neither the sophisticated knowledge they brought with them nor their specialist education had the slightest effect on the life and the people of the town. On the contrary, it was they who civilized the scientists, as some proud Malverners assured me. They had welcomed the newcomers on *their* terms, and the scientists found a rhythm of life and a peace of mind they badly needed. Some of them might even have retraced their childhood happiness in these surroundings, just as I did. They became so well integrated into the new milieu because their overworked minds needed the antidote which Malvern provided.

No wonder that people, in the healthy air of the hills, the commons and gardens with many old trees, lived very long lives. The number of ancient inhabitants must have beaten many records. Women in particular enjoyed an unusual extension of their life span. They seemed to be as indestructible as the spirit of the town.

Caroline's attempts to foster a better understanding between Gertrud and me had some success for a short while, but ended in failure. She could not reconcile herself to me. Her cultured Jewish background and her progressive political views could have made her a sympathetic companion under different circumstances. But our refugee status alone called forth suspicion and fear, as people fighting for the same nest are natural rivals. I had met with this fear among refugees before. In this instance our emotional attachment to the same person swung the balance at the outset against an unbiased relationship. In the end, Gertrud won precedence over me as Isabel had done before her. I had enjoyed a favoured place with Caroline for some years only. I had come into her life as a third person, who was tangential rather than essential to an established pair. The few blissful years with her could not deceive me about this fundamental pattern. After Isabel's death, I fully realized that I was again the outsider in a trio. I was therefore not surprised when Caroline made Gertrud her first and foremost concern, concentrating care and love on her, particularly after osteoarthritis had been diagnosed, with increasing immobility and pain in the joints. From then on Gertrud ruled the roost. But Caroline still insisted on my visits. I understood her dilemma and we managed famously. Her relationship with me was now motivated by affection and religion, and mine with her by affection and need.

The couple at Hazelwood had had much in common with the *Ladies of Llangollen*. Neither would have believed that their love was an 'oddity', something unnatural and rather regrettable. They had probably not been aware of the character of their attachment, or had not the courage to admit it to themselves. The case of Gertrud and Caroline was different. Gertrud, a lesbian born and bred, knew all there was to know about love between women. How much of this knowledge she imparted to Caroline remained an undisclosed secret. The difference between Caroline's feelings and hers must have been a bitter pill for her to swallow. And her frustration might have added to her resentment of me, and also aggravated her progressive arthritis.

I had met with lesbianism years before I started my investigation on it. I had seen the beauty and pain of such relationships. Isabel and Caroline were 'hidden' lesbians. One can never catch those in the net of statistics. Their number is certainly considerable, even in our permissive age. 'Conscious' lesbians pity them, but I am by no means sure that they are not misguided in doing so. Those I knew had an inner richness which outweighed the danger of nervous and emotional disturbances.

Gertrud's death in 1967 did not change the fundamental pattern of Caroline's relationship with me. She was 'spiritually' united with Isabel and Gertrud. I remained an outsider who took her mind off the set routine of a peaceful life. She had devoted herself to doing good and 'loving her neighbour'. I visited her in greater comfort, freed from Gertrud's jealousy, and occupying her former flat to boot. The remaining years of my friendship with Caroline were relaxed and content. She was an amusing and stimulating companion, and did not resent my teasing her about her religious fervour, her idiosyncrasies and spartan way of life. She took a somewhat cynical interest in my research on the subject she regarded with such disfavour – female homosexuality.

VII   Sexological Research

The prelude to my research in sexology was the essay on female homosexuality which I wrote in 1961. It was meant to be part of *On the Way to Myself*, but it could not be integrated into an autobiography which related to achievements rather than ideas. The plan to undertake research on lesbianism had, however, taken hold of me. I knew that I would carry it out after I had given *On the Way to Myself* into the hands of my publishers. In 1967 I managed to do so. I now wonder what the real motives were which so greatly involved me in the subject. Neither my own emotional history, nor the experiences and observations I had gathered among friends, strangers and patients, had enough substance to explain my singular preoccupation with it.

I had read little on female homosexuality, and had only heard of, but not seen, the film on lesbians by Brian Magee. A friend of mine had joined the first lesbian collective in this country founded in 1963 and known as Minorities Research Group. She regularly passed on to me their monthly publication, *Arena Three*. But I have to admit that I had not been particularly interested in either. I was probably rather prejudiced against lesbian groups which, in my view, were bound to lead to a ghetto. And nothing was more alien to me than a 'professional lesbian' – the likely result of forming groups of this kind. It seemed to me insensitive and uncivilized to make a focal point of a perfectly natural way of loving and living. On account of such reflections and sensibilities, I do not believe that the then existing lesbian movement can have had much to do with my own inclination to *know*, rather than feel, something about love between women. My motives came from other sources. To disentangle them completely would be

215

like untying the Gordian Knot. I can only recognize some relevant strands which influenced me to undertake the research. Society has created artefacts of man and woman. The consequences of this 'unnaturalness' are manifold. The emotional alienation between the sexes is one, and the suppression of woman's innate capabilities is another. False valuations were therefore made of the nature and place of both sexes in society. As a result, women could (and can) find emotional ease and harmony with other women better than with men – a conclusion homosexual women had clearly drawn in theory and practice. Although I personally had never suffered any discrimination because of my sex, the power wielded by men over women, emotionally and socially, was one of many reasons why I turned my intimate affections towards other women. Since childhood I had believed that love was a 'thing' between women. And as an adult I realized that the false position between the sexes had to be changed completely, if female potentials and identity were to be established. I had probably been inspired, in the first place, by *feminism* to study female homosexuality. I had realized, before Women's Liberation came into being, that feminism was inseparable from lesbiansim. The lesbian woman is a feminist by nature because she is free from emotional dependence on the male. But society forces her to make up to men for professional and social reasons. She has to play a role in order to stay 'alive', often outraged by her false position. These reflections have been crystallized in my book *Love Between Women* (1971). They can be seen as a leitmotiv of my understanding of lesbianism, which I hoped might contribute to a 'correction' of the falsified *Weltenschauung* on which our social codes and behaviour are built.

In a life, full to overflowing with professional work, friendships and love, the impulse to take up once more research in a pioneer field must have been very strong indeed. But research was the life blood of my mind, and for many years I had suffered considerable frustration through not following my bent. I had to venture again on the quest for new data in an unorthodox field, but could only do so by reducing the number of my patients. The windfall of an inheritance enabled me to realize my wish. The substance of such a study was, of course, the 'subjects', and I realized that it would be no mean task to find enough of them. Last but not least, I would have to secure the collaboration of a university department to put the results into statistical tables. I look at these as a kind of

216

shorthand, of which I understand nothing. In planning ahead, I felt like the author of a first novel, looking at an empty page, bewildered and full of self-doubt. Fate favoured me again to go ahead with my plan. While I was studying the human hand, I had met the right people to assist me at the right time. And something similar, though less glamorous, happened to put me on the way once more. Ruth had met Antony Grey, then Director of the Albany Trust, and had been much impressed by his personality and intelligence. 'You must consult Grey,' she told me, 'he might be the person to assist your research.' She arranged a meeting with Antony Grey at the Café Royal on a November day in 1967. Her prediction turned out to be correct. I knew in the first hour of conversation with him that his great knowledge of the legal and social issues of homosexuality was unsurpassed. He is probably the most knowledgeable person on the subject of male homosexuality in this country. His dedication to the 'cause', his unending efforts to better the lot of sexual minorities, made him the very person who could advise me how to find the material for my study on lesbianism. In January 1968, I visited the Albany Trust for the first time. The three small and cramped rooms it occupied were seething with activity. Homosexual men and women arrived to be seen by either Antony Grey or Doreen Cordell. She also was a dedicated person, who gave her time beyond service hours to her work, which she had to execute in unsuitable surroundings. Men and women came in great numbers to seek her help. She was very interested in my research and promised to help. She did so without delay, and advised lesbian women who were willing to be interviewed to get in touch with me. I became a regular visitor to the Albany Trust and, at many luncheons at a nearby restaurant, Antony, Doreen and I made far-reaching plans for research and discussed ideas on educating the public about homosexuality.

The Albany Trust had provided me with the first batch of subjects. But the obvious agency to support my research was the lesbian Minorities Research Group. I asked them to advertise my request for volunteers in their monthly magazine *Arena Three*, but owing to changes in their organization the advertisement was delayed, and I almost lost heart about getting the material I needed for my study. Luckily, at this time of doubt, I heard of a new lesbian group, Kenric, which had been formed in 1968 by Diana Chapman, Cynthia Reed and others. My approach to them was well received. They were most interested in my undertaking,

217

and advertised my request in their newsletter and by word of mouth. About a month later, *Arena Three* printed my request twice running, and lesbian women came to see me through the agency of both groups. In spite of the considerable number of subjects which their combined efforts produced, I still needed more. When, in February 1969, *On the Way to Myself* appeared, Diana Chapman suggested that I should give a talk about it to Kenric members at Caxton Hall. She was in the chair when I spoke about my life and work in a room full of women who seemed to like what they heard. I had jumped the last hurdle in the collection of my material. 108 lesbians finally arrived at my consulting room to be interviewed at any hour of day or evening. I had a marvellous time, and learned more than I thought possible. And I became a personal friend of several of them. After 125 control subjects had also been interviewed and filled in questionnaires, I started to write the theoretical part of *Love Between Women*. At the same time I had the good fortune to obtain the personal help of Dr Clive Spicer, then Director of the Statistical Department of the Medical Research Council, who took on the statistical work of my research.

I had learned a great deal about the personal and professional life of lesbian women, the games of hide-and-seek they had to play with their employers and colleagues, their parents and heterosexual friends. The interviews confirmed some insights into female homosexuality I had held before, and added others I had not thought of. The autobiographical records every woman had written as part of the research were particularly enlightening. They showed the same individual differences as any other female group, i.e. my controls, with one difference: they were people with a stronger need for independence, and altogether sharper emotional profiles.

But it became clear to me that individual courage and integrity cannot move the mountains of stupidity and prejudice in society. The power of the individual had diminished in the age of egalitarianism. It seemed to me as though the Rhesus monkeys had taken over from the great apes. Contrary to the belief of ardent Marxists, unorthodox loves are less tolerated by left-wing governments than by conservative and old-fashioned ones. One need only think of the ruling about homosexuality in the U.S.S.R. which first 'played' tolerance and then decreed the opposite. The autocratic and 'archaic' governments of the Middle East, on the other hand, had (and have) no objection to *male* homosexuality. On the contrary, it was (and is) practised as a natural way of man's sexual and emotional life. The fact that female homosexuality was (and still is) not only banned but condemned in the most cruel way by these same régimes is quite another matter. It is related to the most atrocious male chauvinism, which dictates complete subordination of the female. The oriental man knows full well that the lesbian is the truly liberated woman, and threatens not only his power complex but also his sexual absolutism.

In the Western world, mental persecution of both female and male homosexuals had come to a pitch when the fetters of other restrictions on the population had been loosened by 'tolerant' governments. Only the financially independent and the mentally brilliant could afford to show their psycho-sexual divergence from the stereotype.

It now became clear to me that lesbian women in this society *needed* to band together, to create a sub-culture in which they could breathe freely and be themselves. Society, disregarding the individual more than ever before, was blind to *real* tolerance of sexual variations, while preaching equal treatment and protection of minorities. Clearly the plea for equality had to be made through collective representation. The Albany Trust, the Campaign for Homosexual Equality (C.H.E.) and the Gay Liberation Front (G.L.F.) were the major organizations caring for homo- and bisexual people. They were founded by men, and most members were male. The formation of lesbian groups became necessary to redress the balance, and to find a way of their own to establish a collective identity. But they have remained on a smaller scale, and are less powerful than those of their male counterparts. The Law Reform Society, the Albany Trust and the C.H.E. contributed a great deal to the change in the law against male homosexuals. And they made some strides in influencing professional groups towards a clearer understanding of unorthodox sexuality altogether. Lesbian groups, particularly Sappho, have the merit of making the media give some, albeit reluctant, consideration to their cause.

I joined Kenric in 1968, and Sappho since its beginnings. The Minorities Research Group, later called Minority Research Trust, folded up in the early seventies. When Sappho asked me to be patron of their magazine I gladly agreed. A few years later they apparently did not want my patronage any longer, as many members were hostile towards psychiatrists. This attitude seemed to me rather odd because of my own life and stance, but I went on supporting them. Kenric, on the other hand, made me an honorary member.

My work on lesbianism made me aware of the gross misconception that lesbians are more acceptable to society than male homosexuals. True enough, the sword of the law has hung over their heads since biblical times, while homosexual women have been free from punishment, certainly since the middle of the nineteenth century, though some idiotic law against them still persists in name in Austria and several American States. The situation has been turned topsy-turvy by professional and lay people alike. I have already mentioned that lesbianism is the backbone of feminism. The liberation of women from the stigma of the 'second sex', inferior to men in most ways, is unthinkable without emotional independence from them. This first lesson of female liberation can only be taught by the homo- and bisexual woman, as *emotional* freedom from the male is the condition *sine qua non* for the freedom of all women. It became clear to me that men cannot allow themselves to be tolerant of lesbiansim because every pillar on which their self-esteem stands would be destroyed by it. The heterosexual feminist can still be caught in the stereotyped net of male domination because her sexual and emotional preference makes her vulnerable. The lesbian is man's most dangerous enemy. She threatens him on every level: emotional, social and sexual. 'Normal' men can tolerate the homosexual male because they can feel superior to him, but they cannot abide the homosexual female on any account. Their horror of her, though often concealed by arrogance and false tolerance, is as deadly as that of the poisonous bite of a snake. Why? Ever since Judaism and Christianity ruled the bodies and minds of people, woman has been put on a pedestal. The human mind is fed by images. The image of woman created by man depicts her as supporting and serving him in every way, and being entirely dependent on him. Any change in this image would make it tumble from the pedestal, and make the male desperate and helpless. He would lose his sense of *power* which rules him, distorted artefact that he has become through the dictates of society over the centuries.

There is another weighty reason for man's hostility towards

liberated women: his envy of their reproductive capacity, which extends to the lesbian as a potential mother. The male can never be as close to his offspring as the female, even if he undergoes a complete personality change. The intimacy of the prenatal bond between mother and child cannot be overcome by a reversal of man's image of himself and his behaviour patterns. He is something of an outsider through the *force majeure* of nature, which imprisons him in a cul-de-sac. His only chance lies in becoming a woman's child himself, which he has done through the ages. But it does not save him from the loss of self-esteem and the lack of instinctual intimacy with his children. It makes him *inferior* to women, the very condition he has always tried to deny through over-compensation, culminating in so-called 'masculine' virtures.

Women's Liberation has been the necessity of our time, but Man's Liberation is the necessity of the future. Man has to change and become what nature meant him to be – a bisexual person. The position of the sexes as outlined here induced me to study bisexuality closely during recent years. In any event, these reflections were part of the motivation which inspired me to undertake my latest sexological investigation.

There have always been women who knew their own worth. They were the feminists of old. I believe that many of them were bisexual or lesbians, whether or not they were conscious of it. Yet only today has the collective drive for women's freedom become an international revolution which male hostility is bound to strengthen.

But what about the women who are satisfied with the stereotyped roles allotted to them? They are afraid of a freedom which does not suit their wants, and have a particular dread of the lesbian, a dread which also affects many feminists. Yet during the last years, a change of mind is slowly taking place among heterosexual liberationists. The realization of psychological bisexuality has become more and more widespread, and female bisexuality as a way of life is on the increase. This trend points to woman's search for her true identity, rejecting the strait-jacket of a stereotype forced on her by society.

The publication of my book *Love Between Women* in February 1971 was a landmark in my professional life. It brought many women in conflict about their homosexuality into my consulting room. They wanted to consult me rather than their G.P. or other psychiatrists. Enlightenment on the subject of unorthodox sexuality has, unfortunately, come slowly, if at all, to the medical profession. With the exception of the Royal Northern Hospital, London, I have not been asked to speak about lesbianism by any medical school in this country. But in November 1970, the lesbian film 'The Important Thing is Love', in which I played the part of the psychiatrist, was shown on I.T.V., and earned high praise from the national press. Any idea, however, that this was the prelude to a lessening of prejudice against homosexual women turned out to be an illusion. The general public was not moved. Some burly males throught it madly funny; others were either cynical or went so far as to attack lesbians physically. At about that time Sappho began its long march against the darkness of public opinion, as the flag-bearer of feminism indissolubly wedded to lesbianism. This helped their cause with progressive women and men who saw the point. Sappho managed to get some recognition from newspapers and television, but Radio Four firmly shut its doors against lesbianism.

In December 1971, I had been asked by Tony van den Bergh to be the consultant in an hour's radio programme on lesbiansim, based on my book. He had already recorded speeches of several lesbians who told of their love, their conflicts and the masks they had to wear in their surroundings. Some 'experts' commented on these stories, and expounded their theories about lesbianism. I gave my own comments throughout. Alan Burgess produced the programme, which was to be presented as a documentary feature of educational value on Radio Four. It was recorded in January 1972, but has never been broadcast. Male homosexuality, however, got a hearing on the same radio station some years ago, which confirms my conviction that female homosexuality is a taboo subject.

But the first stimulus for my study of lesbianism was neither its impact on feminism nor the social dilemma of all homosexuals. I wanted to find out whether biological causes played a part in it. Professor von Möllendorf, who taught embryology at Tübingen University, was godfather to this biological quest. How well I remember his lectures and chalk drawings of the stages of foetal development! The fact that for over three months the foetus is sexually undifferentiated shows that life starts with bisexuality, not only in humans, but in the whole of nature. Homosexuality and heterosexuality are secondary developments, like branches growing out of a tree. I therefore asked my lesbian subjects about their relations with both sexes. The following quote from the questionnaire illustrates the point.

Emotional Reactions
1. Are you emotionally attracted to:
   a) women only?
   b) men only?
   c) women and men?
2. Do you prefer men friends to women friends?
3. Are you physically attracted to men?

The answers of lesbian women confirmed the underlying bisexuality in female homosexuality. By far the majority had sexual relations with men.

People become either hetero- or homosexual through biographical events rather than constitution; others express their innate bisexuality in their own way of life. This realization put me on the way to research on bisexuality *per se*.

The social problems of homosexual people in our society compelled me to participate in the fight to change their lot. And I eagerly accepted Antony Grey's invitation in 1972 to join the committee of the Albany Trust, the first organization to throw down the gauntlet to prejudices against sexual variations. It is an agency for counselling individuals and educating the public. I wanted contact with people, people who needed professional help, but simply being a member of the committee left me out on a limb. I therefore gladly agreed to counsel some homosexual women of the Trust's clientele. And Antony Grey arranged courses on homosexuality for social workers and probation officers which offered me another opportunity for active participation. It gave me satisfaction to take part in this important educational scheme where I talked about my study on lesbianism. The courses were well attended, and, hopefully, have done something to broaden the mental horizon of those who still felt ambivalent about the subject. But they had realized their ignorance of homosexuality, which had a direct bearing on their work. The plan to educate the public step by step, starting with professional groups, seemed the right way to go about it. Their influence on public opinion had more weight than that of homosexual organizations which are suspect of biased views. The courses took place in the roomy home of the Albany Trust in Camden Street, close to the Oval. The Trust had gone through a chequered career. Financial difficulties had forced its move from Shaftesbury Avenue to out-of-the-way addresses. Losing the easy access to the heart of town had been a blow to furthering its main aim: counselling. The number of clients shrank when addresses changed and were difficult to reach. But the house in Camden Street, with many large and well-appointed rooms, gave it a new look and started a revival. Unfortunately, the lease came to an end a few years ago, and the Trust is now in Strutton Ground, Victoria Street.

Antony Grey was again helpful in getting subjects for my research on bisexuality. The first announcement of this study was published in the newsletter of the Trust. It asked for men and women who *thought of themselves as bisexual* to get in touch with me.

I had lain fallow for three years after the publication of *Love Between Women* before starting the new investigation. I needed a rest. The work had tired me out, and an inner voice told me to change course. I had suppressed but not abandoned my literary bent. The time had come to do something about a long-standing plan to crystallize a lesbian theme in fiction, and I wrote my first novel *An Older Love*, which was published in 1976, more than two years after the manuscript had been finished.

The return to my first love, literature, had an odd effect on me: my scientific research, which had been a substitute for poetry, had now taken its place. And I looked forward eagerly to my new study which I had had in mind since the early sixties.

While still in the process of interviewing and sifting through the material of research on bisexuality, I gave talks on the subject to the Family Planning Association and counsellors of the National Association of Youth Clubs. The vivid interest and searching questions of both audiences surprised me. Was bisexuality more acceptable to 'normal' people than lesbianism, I wondered? I regretted that the Albany Trust had not planned lectures for physicians on both subjects. Many still regard sexual variations as undesirable, if not pathological. Even psychiatrists are not free from reservation and embarrassment with 'such people,' in spite of the new stance of the Royal College of Psychiatrists. And I doubt whether the bulk of the medical profession can accept that bisexuality as a way of life is natural.

Psychological bisexuality, however, has become respectable all round. No thinking person can fail to recognize male and female characteristics in people of both sexes. But when it comes to looking at bisexuality as a way of life, most 'ordinary' people are repelled. They cannot come to terms with what is to them a paradoxical situation. Why does the thought of loving both sexes strike such terror into the heart? Love relationships should be exclusive. They concern two people. A third one is bound to spread chaos and emotional confusion to all concerned. But the truth of the matter is different. Threesome love is not unnatural *per se*, but the age-old habit of capitalistic thinking rejects it for reasons of its own. Possessiveness has so deeply gripped the imagination that love for people of both sexes can only be conceived as a devil destroying human bonding and happiness, and would be a death blow to the nuclear family. Homosexual people do at least stick to the intimacy of two, and their love can be understood from that angle. Intolerance of bisexuality is one of the many signs of society's de-naturalizing influence on the human being. I suggested in my book *Bisexuality: A Study* that only a *bisexual society* can free us from sexism and the whole gamut of psychosexual and social suppression. The equation of heterosexuality with maturity, and the male with physical and mental superiority, is leading to the destruction of the human race. The idea that procreation could keep humanity going for a long time yet does not take political power-games into account.

Bisexuals are in an isolated position. They are thrown back on themselves, being unwanted by homo- and heterosexual people. They bear the stigma of having no proper identity. But they have a particular advantage over others: a relaxed relationship between the sexes gives them a wider horizon in understanding others and their needs. Homo- and heterosexuals are disadvantaged through their polarized positions, where inhibitive influences or isolation are inevitable. Bisexuals are not group-builders, and many miss the collective unity of homosexual organizations. In spite of explicit invitations to join them, they are invariably regarded as hangers-on. Yet attempts to form their own groups have failed.

Resentment against the bisexual way of life comes from both ends of the sexual spectrum. Heterosexuals envy them for having their cake and eating it, and homosexuals despise them as cop-outs.

The bisexual women of my research struck me as emotionally

more independent than the men. Yet their greater freedom did not divide the sexes in essential reactions and interests. Both sexes had a stronger emotional attachment to women than men, and the same desire to be accepted by hetero- and homosexual people. Bisexual males and females were at ease with each other because the men were less phallus-fixated than homo- and heterosexual men. Some belonged to the organization Men against Sexism.

Because of male sexism, efforts by homosexuals to form mixed groups have been unsuccessful. It is a fallacy to believe that a natural sympathy draws homosexual men and women together in friendship, which is, in fact, the exception rather than the rule. The female ideal of homosexual men is the maternal woman, who is generally heterosexual. Homosexual love between men is phallus-fixated, while lesbian love is first and foremost emotional. They stand on different ground, and are in unison only in their fight on global issues. Members of the G.L.F. have made a gallant effort to overcome the arrogance of false male superiority. They proclaimed their fight against sexism, and declared themselves in line with the Women's Liberation Movement. They believe in sexual equality, which alone can unite men and women in a harmonious community, but how far they live up to their programme remains doubtful.

Transsexual people are extreme examples of the difference between gender and sexual identity. Their condition throws a spotlight on bisexuality. Twelve transsexual men participated in my research. They felt as women but functioned as men. Many were married and had children. They were loving fathers though they would have preferred to be mothers. In any event, they were a living proof that no definite line can be drawn between female and male qualities and reactions.

Unfortunately, no transsexual women answered my advertisement, and therefore I can only speak of the transsexual male. He lives in a world of his own, and does not fit into groups which cater for homo- and bisexual people. Unlike the homosexual, he hates his genitals and wants to get rid of them. He completely identifies with the female sex, and his desire to become a woman overrules all other considerations, including health hazards. Transsexuals are very courageous people, and I think them exemplary in their genuine search for psychosexual identity. They are often attached to lesbian women, and I knew two who wanted to live their lives as lesbians. But as a rule, they are engaged in their attempts at sex-change for a conventional reason: the desire to live with a man as a 'proper' woman.

Lesbians are inclined to reject them because they don't know where they are with them. Unconventional on one hand, and old-fasioned on the other other, transsexuals are not trusted by homosexual women. The fact that most of them are married and have fathered children adds to the confusion about their place in the psychosexual conundrum. I know of a German transsexual who wished to become a member of a lesbian group, but was refused.

It is obvious that generalizations about sexual minorities do not tally with the character and behaviour of the individuals concerned. But individuality is the very touchstone for understanding idiosyncratic behaviour. For this reason nobody should be pigeon-holed into separate compartments, either ethnic, racial or sexual.

A teacher who does not learn from his pupils fails in his task. A research worker who does not learn from his subjects is not worth his salt. I did not rely on questionnaires alone, however fully answered they may have been. They served as illustrations of my material only, like short-hand or a musical score which gives a bird's eye view over a large territory. The 'meat' had to be extracted from personal interviews and autobiographies. My study focused on the meeting point between individuality and type. But how can one guard individual uniqueness and develop typical traits at the same time? Does the onslaught of social pressures herd non-conformists together in a common mimicry-behaviour? I have no doubt that it is so, which accounts for certain resemblances in their way of life, their expressive behaviour and social attitudes. This question goes to the heart of psychological research. It deals with a paradox. We are used to thinking of paradoxes as mutually exclusive, but this is not so. Human beings are paradoxical in emotional reactions, impulses and even actions, yet they are comprehensive wholes.

Boys and girls falling in love for the first time think that their love resembles no one else's – that it is unique. They are right in their assumption. Of course, individual perceptiveness and emotional intensity can never be measured; they are different in every person. But the underlying nature of love is the same, and the ways of expressing it are similar. Research can get hold of a

227

common ground in a special group of people, through question-naires and interviews. Fixed data of background, family circum-stances, etc., are definite. But the finesse of a person's make-up can only be fully understood through empathy and intuition, the *subjective* endowment of the investigator. The subtlety of indi-vidual differences can only be conveyed through interviews and autobiographical statements. For this reason I used a three-fold method in my research on bisexuality and lesbianism, to get as close as possible to the truth.

Research is an open-ended quest; I called my book *Bisexuality: A Study* because of it. I intended to make a further investigation on this theme after some time had elapsed. But my concern with the effectiveness of organizations designed to help sexual varia-tions is ever present. Perhaps the legal recognition of a person's gender identity in preference to his/her sexual identity is a very remarkable social and legal advance. The reform of the law on homosexuality comes a close second. Laws are structural direc-tives of human behaviour, but they have loopholes. They are pointers in the right direction, but I don't believe they have changed prejudices and hostility in the general public. The organ-izations concerned have had a hand in legal progress, but have hardly scratched the skin of the social organism. They have, how-ever, been useful to many individuals. The Albany Trust and many other counselling agencies have helped numerous people in legal and emotional trouble.

The collective identity of homosexuals reached a pitch in its declaration of gay pride, paraded at a mass meeting in Hyde Park in July 1979. This rather naïve expression of togetherness had the sharp edge of defiance, and exhibited as much insecurity as self-assertion. Yet homosexual organizations have given self-confidence to their members, and have done much to dispel their sense of isolation. The lesbian groups, particularly Sappho, have also taken a definite step towards doing away with the ghetto mentality which beset female homosexuals in earlier days.

The homosexual minority includes many millions in this coun-try. This fact has not escaped the notice of either the government or local councils, and in a few instances they have done something to alleviate the financial burden of 'helping' organizations. Their decision to do so relied on scientific opinion which, in the early seventies, had changed its tune. By then, the Royal College of Psychiatrists had accepted, though not without misgivings, sexual

228

variations as part of the human family. Certain political parties have made a point of supporting homo- and bisexuals, the Liberal Party in the first place. And the British Communists also promised to safeguard the rights of homosexuals. Did either or both do so out of conviction, or rather as a means of vote-catching? What would they do if they came to power, one wonders! The U-turn which the Soviet Union performed in first legally permitting, but later forbidding, homosexuality, is a painful reminder of the unreliability of 'official' promises and the law. Laws can be made and changed.

The unreliable attitudes of official agencies is not the only hazard which threatens the integration of sexual variations into society. By far the greater danger is the persistent prejudice of 'philistines' who are regarded as its backbone. It is common knowledge that people all over the world have a steel-like resistance to giving up stereotyped ideas. As long as male chauvinism rules human societies, bisexuals and homosexuals will be regarded as enemies of the people, certainly in Europe. Democracies will persecute them by subtle, and fascistic régimes by gross, means. Any authoritiarian state can call the populace onto the ramparts to fight the 'degenerates' or make a kill of them. The fact that feminism is an international revolution, and might be very difficult to put down, would not alter the position of the lesbian, particularly in a totalitarian society. In Russia, feminism still exists after a fashion, but lesbiansim is despised, if not worse.

The homosexual movement was strong when it was still in danger from the law, and in the first elation of a new chance. By now a certain relaxation of vigilance has entered the ranks, which could be the prelude to defeat through a backlash in official attitudes. I have lived through the permissive age of Germany's Weimar Republic, when Magnus Hirschfeld was a celebrated figure. Many psychiatrists supported the psychosexual liberation he had initiated. He and his fellow workers were the most advanced sexologists in the Western world. They were free to practise their method of helping sexual variations, and to publish their 'revolutionary' literature. The *Frauenbewegung* and socialism blossomed in Germany. One would have thought that the Golden Age had returned. Instead, a few decades later, Hitler broke out and annihilated both – homosexuals and feminists. It is a historical fact that about two million homosexual men were thrown into concentration camps and frequently killed. The fate

229

of lesbians was probably similar. No doubt many among them were bisexual people, because no clear differentiation had so far been made between the two groups of 'degenerates'. The fate of homosexuals under the Nazis has been depicted in films and plays up to the present day, to be sure that their deeds are not forgotten. Forgotten they won't be, but revived they could be – when another totalitarian madness grips a country. And why was National Socialism and the annihilation of freedom possible? The answer can only be found in the ignorance and the silent or vociferous agreement of the *Masse Mensch*. In different shades of intensity the same could happen anywhere. If it does, the real responsibility lies with the citizens themselves.

I have suggested that only a bisexual society could bring to an end the persecution of sexual (and other) minorities. But how can such a society ever come to pass? A promenade on the moon was utopian in the nineteenth century, but became a reality in the twentieth. The question is how to create an alternative society. The answer lies in *education*, the teaching that the future of mankind depends on a new mentality which devalues materialism, and makes culture and love the pinnacle of its aspirations. The first condition of freedom is absolute tolerance in collective and individual relationships. Tolerance and empathy lead to caring for others. Members of the G.L.F. believe that political radicalism alone would guarantee true equality for sexual minorities. They recommend the fight for a Marxist society. I believe that they are barking up the wrong tree because the exercise would be fruitless. No political change can alter the 'philistines' – the dinosaurs of society – who have been conditioned into stereotyped moulds for thousands of years. Only a cultural revolution can change the world we live in into a new and tolerant one. The acceptance of pscyhological bisexuality is already widespread enough to be the basis of understanding the many facets of love, which would be the tenets of a bisexual society. Bisexual relationships are obviously not a way of life for everybody. They would be optional, but claim neither preference nor superiority over homo- or heterosexual love.

But how could one possibly bring about an iconoclastic change of society? People hang on to old habits, symbolized in stereotyped ideas. They like to live from 'dead' images, which have an age-old 'life' of their own. But I believe in a cultural revolution because of the need to preserve humanity. It may take

230

several generations before this truth is grasped. But the people who are aware of the miseries we live with are numerous, and they are the enzyme which can bring about change. Their number is growing all the time. Bi- and homosexual people, outsiders in our society, have a vested interest in an alternative one. The younger generation of my study were examples of a new way of life which approximates to this ideal. And change is not only desired by those who are directly affected, but also by many progressive thinkers who are sensitive to the human condition. They realize that an alternative society is necessary for the survival of the human race. It falls to them to educate the masses about the necessity of a cultural revolution. The subject of the first lesson is the need for a permanent *inner* revolution, which prevents any slackening in self-awareness and care for others, under the umbrella of an alternative society.

Gabriele Dietze, a young German feminist, has expressed similar ideas, and I want to end this chapter by quoting a relevant passage from her foreword to *Die Überwindung der Sprachlosigkeit. Texts aus der Frauenbewegung* which she has edited. (Luchterhand, Darmstadt, 1979.)

Keine Revolution in einem einzelnen Sektor- schon gar keine ökonomische allein – kann das komplizierte System der psychischen, socialen und ökonomischen Konditionierung zur Unterdrückung sprengen. Alles bedarf der Veränderung: wie gedacht wird – der Herrschaftsdiskurs – wie gelebt wird – die Familie – wie gearbeitet wird – der technisch/industrielle Komplex – ja, wie gelacht, geliebt, geweint und getraumt wird, muss sich andern.

No revolution in one sector alone – and certainly not an economic one only – can break through the complex system of the psychical, social and economic conditioning of suppression. Everything has to be changed: the way of thinking, the way of governing, the whole way of life, the family, how to go about one's work – the whole technical/economic complex – yes, how we laugh, love and cry, and even how we dream – all this has to be changed.

The Conquest of Mutism. Texts from
the Women's Liberation Movement (My translation)

VIII   Interlude

One needs an interlude between major efforts, a time of reflection and rest: *Il faut reculer pour mieux sauter.*' Reflections are bird's eye views, where chronological time has no preferential place. Looking at the past as memory plays it back on the screen of the mind teaches us something of what our life was all about. But no compass can circumscribe such an extensive space of time. Only fragmentary highlights can be picked out from the stream of inner and outer events. They might reveal a comprehensive pattern, illustrating how we coped in the battle for survival, love and self-esteem. It is only through hindsight that we can understand anything. The moment of experience is already the past, and the thousands of million moments which have made *it* and *us* are de-robed of their presence from the start. Yet when the past is focused from a distant view, it can teach us a lesson, sometimes readily accepted, sometimes going *contre coeur*. Patterns have a tendency to tell a story, which conveys the reality behind the endless number of events and feelings we have gone through. We are fortunate if we can get even a few glimpses of that reality, because it is the most precious and elusive of all goods.

In his book *Essai sur une Psychologie de la Main*, Dr N. Vaschide writes: 'Man's characeter is the result of a fight between forward and withdrawing impulses.' Dr Vaschide, Professeur de Philosophie à l'Ecole des Hautes Etudes at the end of the nineteenth and beginning of the twentieth century, was the first to formulate a scientific theory of hand interpretation. He was the most important influence on my work on the human hand. But the mathematical lucidity with which he compressed the complex subject of character into a simple formula affected me for good in my psychological understanding in general and that of the language of gesture in particular.

232

The opposing impulses which shape us are the basis of emotional tension and relaxation, of psycho-physical life as a whole. They are like the waves of the sea: tension driving us up to the crest of the waves, and relaxation letting us rest in their valleys. Vaschide thus telescoped our psycho-physical the life in a nutshell. Almost at the same time as his book was published in 1905 (after his death at the age of thirty-seven), Wilhelm Fliess stirred a wide circle of the intelligentsia with his theory of periodicity, which went hand in hand with his concept of bisexuality. There are apparent similarities between his and Vaschide's ideas. But while he became internationally known, Vaschide's importance found only limited recognition, and he is virtually forgotten now. Fliess, on the other hand, has made a comeback. I pointed out his importance as a visionary theoretician in *Bisexuality: A Study*, and recommended his work on periodicity for further scientific research. Today some American psychologists have taken it up, and biorhythm (unfortunately with the psychical aspect left out) has become a commonplace idea. A superficial and sensational slant on the subject in the low currency of popular psychology does not, however, do justice to the thorough and profound pioneer work Fliess has done. Its essential message, that fruitful and fallow periods occur at rhythmical intervals, can be verified in the life of every human being. Perhaps the failure to give Fliess the credit he deserves comes from a superficial comparison of his theory with astrology. In both instances, predictions can be made. But while Fliess's interpretation of significant dates is of scientific value, astrology cannot claim the same.

How often did I feel wrung out, suffering from states of exhaustion as a student and doctor in Germany! Yet I had a good life, and was well established in my profession and society. The fact that my sense of security was an illusion never dawned on me until obvious signs appeared on the horizon.

My brain had never been stretched to its real limits before the days of exile. Then a new biorhythm altered the pattern of life I had been used to. It affected health and nervous energy. New influences made a *tabula rasa* of old habits, and developed new tenets of behaviour which led to relationships never dreamed of before. Although dangerously exhausted, I had to hold on to what came my way. I had to keep on trying to find a more solid ground, away from the shifting sands of insecurity. The consuming effort to secure a proper place in the world left little time for rest and reflection.

233

After I had terminated my research on hand and gesture, I felt the need for rest. The mental vacuum after many years of exciting investigations had led me into a state of depression. People become morose when they are left with an empty inner space. Any diversion can be a welcome drug, but nothing but the care and love of a maternal person heals the root of the trouble. I wanted to put my head on a pillow not my own, and to live a slice of life borrowed from a friend or lover. I had been close to a nervous breakdown several times, and the threat that this could happen again never left me. Then I met Caroline. Emotional opportunism becomes the way out of circumstances too difficult to tackle by oneself. The need for escape directs a person's attention and curiosity like a life-belt preventing one from drowning. I had been, unconsciously, on the lookout for someone who would 'take me on'. People scan their surroundings, or travel and do all sorts of things, propelled by the desire for self-preservation, that is, preservation through others. In the search for opportunities, when eye and ear are geared to find the right circumstances to prevent breakdown, signs and signals may be misinterpreted. Judgment is banned and any warning voice squashed. But good fortune can also favour an imprudent and helpless person who accepts love too easily. It is a matter of luck. I have always thought myself lucky to have fallen into the arms of the two strange women at Hazelwood. I did not know at the time that my attachment to Isabel and my love for Caroline had been, in the first place, a safety valve. The romantic atmosphere, the well-being they could provide, the beauty of their surroundings, had been a bonus of fate. I could stretch my legs in peace in their home after the accumulated strain of life as an exile, thrown onto dry land like a fish out of water. The two saved me, and after Isabel's death Caroline took on the task by herself. I have been saved for the better part of my life in England, namely twenty-seven years, by two women and the town of Malvern. Only imagination can touch reality. Mine invested them and their milieu with a sense of security and emotional satisfaction, which are the best food for soul and body. I found rest, time for reflection, and – more important – the tonic of self-assurance because I was wanted. Obviously, a peaceful life only exists in the abstract, and the seesaw of ups and downs in an emotional relationship is part of it.

And so it was in our case. But my favoured position with both held fast. They proved to be true to me, guided perhaps by religious principles as much as their own unconscious needs. I could not let go the one and only island of security I had found in England. It was of little or no importance whether I indulged in an illusion or stood on safe ground with them. I shall never know the truth, but suspect that it was a mixture of both.

Apart from my personal involvement, the 'Ladies of Hazelwood' had a fascination for me through their very existence, which filled me with wonder. Never before had I met a couple of such innocence, integrity, and eccentricity. I loved it all. I had come across a virgin land of the emotions, where I observed new gestures of love and fear. I don't know whether I was aware of the privilege of having entered an unknown territory. My time with them was a time of discovery, and tallied with the need which had instigated my whole research – the exploration of borderlands of the mind. It had shown me the emotional love between two women, where its true significance remained hidden from them because of religious taboos.

I had recognized both the strength and weakness of their situation. I had realized the fortitude and inspiration such unresolved conflicts can produce. But I had not seen that the very strength of inhibitions dictated by religious taboos could lead to religious mania. This was the way Caroline became affected during the last ten years of her life, though she enjoyed her 'illness' rather than suffered from it. Caroline had belonged to the Society of Friends, who have demonstrated a relatively understanding attitude towards homosexuality. But she did not want to have anything to do with their pamphlet: 'Towards a Quaker View of Sex' (1963).

The Quaker image still impresses Christians and non-Christians alike as exemplary. Yet Quakers are a divided crowd. A nucleus of progressive members, among them those who produced the pamphlet, is outweighed by a majority of old-fashioned people, who have not moved with the times, and stick to patriarchal attitudes and beliefs. But trust in their practical Christianity is justified, whether they are old-fashioned or not. And so is their desire to discard sham, be it in religion or human intercourse.

I never found an answer to the question, whether the faithfulness of Caroline and other Friends was dictated by their Quaker values rather than their personal feelings. In the last resort, it does not matter what motives produce a desired result. Yet one's pride is pricked, as if by the thorn of a rose, when one suspects that religious faith rather than love had kept faith with one. It strikes one as an irony of fate. Its decidely comic overtones could be enjoyed in a play, but not by the person concerned. Although ardent lovers cannot avoid bending the truth here and there, the church cannot altogether do without hypocrisy. The Society of Friends made a brave effort to do away with sham, but could not fully succeed because of its religious super-structure. The desire of Friends to be 'real' puts them, however, apart from the conventional church, and secures their special place in religious history.

Reflections touch the far away, and the near, past, as though there were no distance between them. Time folds up or extends as in dreams. It was only two days before writing this, on 20 October 1979, that the Report on Homosexuality of the Board of Social Responsibility of the Church of England came into my hands. It has a double significance for me. It deals with the subject to which I devoted the last ten years of research, and I was one of the 'experts' invited to inform their Working Party about lesbianism.

I compared this Report with the Quaker Pamphlet 'Towards a Quaker View of Sex' and found it wanting. The latter, published sixteen years earlier, was dictated by a Quaker concern, and was a labour of love, while the former has all the ingredients of an intellectual exercise, trying to come to terms with an uncomfortable problem. The pamphlet, pointing out the hypocrisy and arrogance of heterosexuals on this subject, questions their moral code. It has the courage to put the word 'normal' into inverted commas, which is, in itself, an indication of its stance. The group of Quakers who did the work were seekers after the truth, without fear of God or man.

The Report of the Church of England twists and turns this way and that, unable to declare its position. It is a document of uncertainty, which avoids the real issue. It proclaims 'tolerance' of homosexuality but denies it equal status with heterosexuality. With this attitude alone it has shown itself to be an incompetent agency to deal with the subject. It talks of pastoral and moral problems which cannot be adequately dealt with because of Scripture's rejection of homosexuality, which is incompatible with the findings of modern science and psychology. It is a glib and condescending document, essentially different from the outspoken pamphlet of the Quakers. Both religious bodies had the weight of old-fasioned prejudice at their backs, which influenced the Working Party of the Church of England but not that of the Society of

236

Friends. It is the spirit of approach which makes all the difference. Ignorance about female homosexuality is, however, apparent in both documents. In 1963, publications on lesbianism were sparse, but by 1975 considerable material was available. The pamphlet's utterances on lesbian women have no relevance to the real situation. They are repetitions of all the fallacies which had been around for decades. The Report's references, taken from my book *Love Between Women*, are correct, but draw a veil over the most poignant results of my investigation. Neither document shows any appreciation of the importance of lesbianism in modern society, making it appear to be a 'ghostly' side issue. The obvious conclusion to be drawn from both would be that women are regarded as the second sex, and homosexuality is really a concern of men.

Lesibianism cannot really be faced by men or heterosexual women. They are afraid of the utter collapse of the patriarchal society and its codes. In the previous chapter I have given my explanation of why this should be so.

The inadequacy of the Report greatly surprised me, because it did not tally with the impression I had gained of the Working Party when I spoke to its members. I had thought them to be receptive to new ideas. They listened with close attention and nodded approval of my exposition of lesbianism. One legal mind, though, tried to trip me up, suggesting that the whole lesbian situation was a kind of 'false alarm', as more than twenty-five per cent of the women I had investigated were married. He equated this fact with heterosexuality. He has at least read my book, I thought, but failed to draw the right conclusion. I put him right though, and he accepted my explanation reluctantly. The other members appeared to be wholeheartedly with me. I addressed the Working Party as a whole, but had some personal words with the chairman, the Bishop of Gloucester. He impressed me as a man of fine intelligence and wit. Not without amusement, I had to correct him when he remarked after I had finished my talk: 'We must be tolerant towards these people.' I found myself flying at him with the words: 'Don't speak of tolerance, Bishop. Tolerance is condescension, which defeats its object. If you tell homosexual people that one must be tolerant of them, they might answer you "Go to hell". Jews would feel similarly offended if treated in a diminishing fashion.'

The Bishop smiled at me 'tolerantly', but he had taken my

point. He invited me there and then to come and see him in Gloucester whenever I visited his town.

The Report mentions my book but not my visit. Had I been too outspoken, or was it simply an oversight, as I was told? The Bishop of Gloucester allayed my doubt. He apologized for the omission of my name, assuring me he would testify that I had been there if I wished him to do so.

Religion has come into my life since I was six years old. As a child, I felt deprived not to be loved and watched over by Jesus like my schoolmates because I was Jewish. How I prayed to Jesus, not to be discarded by Him! How disappointed I was in the Jewish Sunday School, a sorry surrogate for what I missed at the *Höhere Töchter Schule*. We learned to read Hebrew texts, but were not taught their meaning. This failure was the first stone to bar my way to Judaism. And when, as an adolescent, I paid visits to the synagogue, where I met with over-dressed women talking about nothing at all, I became repelled by Jewish religious service. I don't know whether it was the hollowness of this 'service' that made me turn to the Jewish past. In any event, I became an avid reader of the Old Testament and the history of the Jews. My imagination assimilated these readings, but I did not allow my preoccupation with Jewishness to ferment doubts about my German status. The Prophets inspired my poetry, and the remarkable Jews who lived in Spain during the Middle Ages gave me a sense of pride, glamour and awe. The eleventh and first half of the twelfth century was their time of glory. Jews excelled in the spheres of learning, poetry and statesmanship; indeed, the personal physician of Alphonse VI was a Jew. Greatly respected and admired, they filled high offices at the Muslim Courts. They wrote, in Hebrew and Arabic, philosophical and religious tracts, excelled in poetry and also in the art of medicine.

Jehuda Halevi, a foremost poet of the time, yearned in his odes for Zion, in spite of honours and fame bestowed on him in his native Spain. His close friend Moses ibn Ezra did not forget his roots either. Towards the end of Halevi's life, a fanatic Muslim sect persecuted the Jews, but his longing for the homeland had a deeper origin than the wages of fear. Jews have felt uprooted in good and bad times, ever since Nebuchadnezzar drove them into exile about 2,400 years ago. And so it went on through the ages. Many of the Spanish Jews were physicians, and Halevi himself practised as a doctor in Christian Toledo.

238

It was the sage Maimonides who fired my imagination even more than his predecessors. His learning, his wisdom, the philosophical and religious treatises he wrote at an early age, made him the most exceptional being I had ever heard about. Already middle-aged, he left Spain for Morocco, where he practised medicine and became personal physician to the Sultan Saladin. Maimonides represented to me the finest flower of Jewish perceptiveness and spirituality. I worshipped his image as a disciple) worships his teacher, and made him the model for my own aspirations.

Dreams and day-dreams have their own measure of time. One can vastly extend one's mental and physical size in fantasies. While Maimonides became the image of mental perfection and a symbol of spirituality of times past, the Old Testament fed me with religious wisdom. Ever since my late teens, King Solomon, the Preacher, has meant to me what Christ means to His followers. If I have a religion at all, it is that of the Preacher.

The conflict about my misfired visits to the synagogue also concerned the inferior position of women in Jewish society. Why did they not protest, I wondered. They were, of course, the *eminences grises* at home, yet few men would have liked to be in their place. My indignation was strong enough to question our Rabbi about it. Dr Kaelter, a short figure of a man, bald with only a few blond locks at either side of his head, fully agreed with me that it was scandalous to give women an inferior place in religious service. But he couldn't do anything about an old custom. This man, with his wise eyes and white skin, was a scholar with progressive views on Judaism and women's place in society. We enthused together about Jewish history, and shared our admiration of the spiritual strength and courage of our ancestors in fortunate and disastrous times.

Was it a paradox that I had been unable to discover my own Jewish identity through my readings? A paradox can be a shield against polarizing forces, incompatible with mental and emotional balance. The German language and culture was the ground on which I stood – I would have found myself on quicksands if it had been otherwise.

The shock of Nazi persecution established my Jewish identity, and with one stroke wiped away the belief that I was German. From then on I felt I belonged to a persecuted people, without abiding in their religion.

The interval between my first longing for Jesus and my first reading of the New Testament spanned nearly forty years. Caroline, a born missionary, went on trying to convert me to Christianity. She got me to read the New Testament, but only to please her.

Lady Ottoline's gift of the German Bible twenty-two years earlier had been a token of affection and concern, rather than an inducement to find solace in Christ's teaching. Love alone made me try in earnest to read about Jesus Christ, though I enjoyed the beautiful stories and pearls of wisdom in the Gospels. Listening to me, Caroline smiled wistfully, and went on doing so for twenty-six years without ever giving up her pet wish to make a Christian of me. Every now and then she would say: 'I know that one day you will be a believer.'

It never happened. Instead, she confirmed my conviction that religion is a potential poison like any medicine: when taken in the right dose it can do good, when taken in the wrong one it is destructive. But I am sure that atrophying Christianity in the Western world has led to the disintegration of society. Most people need the ethical code of religion to sustain consideration for others, self-esteem, pride in their work, even vitality. Materialism is the deformed child of irreligion. It has made modern societies fall into the abyss of self-destruction.

Humanism is for the few whose insight and judgment can replace religion in teaching the difference between right and wrong.

Christianity did not catch up with me. My religion had been poetry. Minting words in the joys and pains of a mental birth relegated me to a force beyond my personal Self. For me, poetry was a vocation, philosophy the apex of the hierarchy of learning, and medicine the mongrel child of art and learning.

Neither poetry nor philosophy was a proper profession, certainly not for a woman of the twenties and early thirties. Yet I had wanted to study philosophy, not medicine. But how grateful I was, already in my German past, that I had done so. I realized that medicine could be a feeding ground for poetry, and an antidote against too much inwardness. My rational choice not only equipped me for an independent life, but also nourished my imagination through human experience. I wondered whether my Spanish ancestors, Halevi, Maimonides and ibn Ezra, had come to a similar conclusion in practising medicine side by side with poetry and philosophy.

There seems to be a natural link between literature and medicine. Spanish poets of Jewish descent practised medicine in the early Middle Ages. Chekhov, the playwright and short story writer, did so in the nineteenth – and Somerset Maugham, Gottfried Benn and A. J. Cronin in the twentieth century. One can assume that there were many more of their kind over the centuries.

Religion is in poetry and healing in medicine, which is a para-religion. Doctors are meant to be priests at the altar of body and mind. The Shaman is still at the back of physicians, directing them like puppets on a string, to perform their task artfully rather than authentically. Dress and mannerisms of the 'doctor-priest' have changed, but their aspirations are still the same. Such attitudes worked with people in primitive societies, but failed in the modern world. Physicians have lost much of their prestige through pretentiousness and role playing. Their credentials have been found questionable and wanting. Their sense of superiority and power deprives them of real contact with their patients. Bedside-manners and the false mystery of 'superior' knowledge do not work any longer. Their expertise is limited anyway, and the clumsiness of drug treatment, with its pitfalls of harmful side effects, has made many people turn away from medicine to nature cure and other forms of unorthodox treatment. The image of the physician has undergone an irreversible change for the worse, from jovial paternalism to a computer agent. The worst sin of the profession is the lack of true participation with the patient, the coldness of heart. The most reprehensible members of the profession are those psychiatrists who excel in playing the 'Buddha' role, and indulge in megalomaniac ideas. They presume to 'know' always better than anybody else. There are of course exceptions. R. D. Laing and Thomas Szas, for example, realized the false position and have tried to remedy it in word and deed.

I have tried to treat my patients person to person, shedding the mask of priest of the soul. The word psychiatrist means healer of the psyche, which invests her/him with the mantle of a 'Godlike' person. 'By their fruits ye shall know them' (Matthew VII, 20) is an appropriate motto for the profession. The fruits of healing the mind ripen through the power of love, but cannot develop in an atmosphere of coldness and role playing. This puts psychiatrists into an awkward position. How many can follow the call for love? The answer is – silence.

The one branch of medicine which has improved its image in time is surgery. Its method has become refined through advances in physics and biochemistry. Surgeons work on a safe, scientific basis and can do wonders. But with all their achievements, they still have insufficient knowledge of the inter-relationship between different parts of the body and the brain. Acupuncture could add a new approach and finer technique to their craft.

The declining faith in medicine has worried physicians for quite a time. A kind of revolt against conventional treatment has started among many who realize the dangers of drug treatment, and have begun to take more notice of the best equipped physician: Nature.

In the twenties a different revolution had awakened doctors and others to the need for birth control, which had to include psychological advice. Psychoanalysis had enhanced the insight that medical care cannot be separated from psychological understanding, social welfare and population planning. In those days physicians were acclaimed as a power for good. Now they have lost ground, as the unreliability of their knowledge has diminished faith in their treatment. Medicine and, particularly, psychiatry have to make a U-turn to adapt to modern needs and demands. They claim to be scientific but fail to convince. The same holds good for psychology. Its roots are intertwined with those of philosophy and poetry. The frontiers between science and literature are blurred, if they exist at all.

Conventional medicine and psychology had been suspect to me since I was in my twenties. I yearned for wholeness in medicine, science and the arts. I aspired to investigate unexplored areas of the mind which might reveal unthought-of human capacities. Psychological research was the flashpoint which welded together poetry lost and new ecstasy found in discoveries. It gave me back that breath of life which I needed for my spiritual survival. At the same time it secured my social status and financial security.

Poetry and research have been the pinnacles of my life, highpoints which acted like mental lighthouses, showing the way and giving warnings of the tumultuous traffic on the seas of living. As long as there was direction there was inspiration and hope. But long stretches of existence were passed in darkness, when depression and restlessness pushed creative endeavour into a tight corner.

During such a period my Malvern friends changed the canvas

242

of my experience, and added discoveries in 'real' life to those of research. The Malvern time seemed to stretch endlessly, because it represented the only substitute for home and family I had found since childhood. Yet it was an interlude of a kind because it linked, approximately, the period after the war with the present day. There was a 'before' and an 'after' Malvern. In hindsight, both appear to be restless and unrelaxed times. The point of 'going home' has been missing ever since Caroline's death, when Malvern became stripped of its meaning, a place for sightseeing only. Hazelwood and the house at Malvern Link had served their purpose, whether I had indulged in an illusion about their inhabitants or not. I believe that I did not do so as long as Caroline's sensuous attachment lasted. But the ground started to get shaky when, in the end, her preoccupation turned to her family, Christ and good causes. Old people go back to their roots. Bent backs look at the ground where it all began, as criminals are drawn to the place of their crime. But in time, it did not matter to me whether I came first, second or third. I insisted on remaining anchored, even when the moorings seemed insecure. Illusion is part of life and human relationships. We need it as much as we need oxygen if we are to go on breathing. A nest had been made for me, and I brought some precious gifts to fill its barren spaces. I could be there in peace, to begin or finish a book, to be driven into the countryside, or to take walks in the revivifying air of the Malvern Hills. If, at the end, I became a schemer, I gave affection in return for what I obtained by design.

It is a common assumption that we repeat the same patterns throughout life. Early impressions may be responsible for an underlying mould which is shaped into structured patterns later on. Truth or half truth – that is the question. I settle for the latter. Many things can happen to alter patterns at any age, such as shock experiences, illness, an emotional implosion or mental enlightenment. When the imagination is stirred and enriched, the mind has dominion.

Negative emotions stick fast to the mind: they do not only inflict self-torture but predispose to repetition. When we fall back into old errors and cannot find a way out of a trap, we may get nervously or physically ill. This is the time to ask why we have to imprison ourselves, and spend so much of our life in self-doubt, depression and anxiety. Are we forced to revert to self-destructive fixations of childhood and youth, as psychoanalysts believe? This might be true for some, but by no means for everybody. I believe in a deeper cause for these afflictions: *boredom*, this insidious human disease. Even parental care and an imaginative education may not save either child or adult from this paralysing state of mind. When ego-weakness and neurosis reinforce its lethargizing effect, movements towards others are fraught with difficulties which clamp down on relationships. The desire for protection and parental warmth becomes imperative. Boredom can be both cause and result of depression, and acts as a mental poison in any event. Boredom stands at the head of most social evils, and the main task of any future society will be to deal with its pervading destructiveness. I am convinced that the desire to travel, to explore and engage in love affairs, even creative efforts, are safety valves against boredom.

In my own life, intimate attachments were dictated by a cry for help as well as by boredom. I went from one 'maternal' figure to another to assist me in the humdrum of daily living, while my longing for glamorous people exploded in short and ecstatic meetings, or was relegated to the imagination. Many times I tried to get out of this pattern, which didn't alleviate disappointment and boredom. No other medicine but creative endeavour and love could take off these shackles of mental paralysis. The ecstasy of research alone was not a satisfactory answer; it still left a vacuum. Love and maternal care were needed to assure a more stable equilibrium of body and mind. Only then did boredom take a back seat.

The uniqueness of Malvern was, in a nutshell, my *idea* that I had altered an old and unsatisfactory pattern, and broadened my outlook on others and myself. Yet the need for maternal love and protection had remained. It was, in fact, the same situation in a different setting. True enough, never before had I met people of such sophisticated taste and perfect manners. I had moved up into a different class. Their culture and *savoir vivre* became a school for a refined sybaritism, but could not alter the drawback of a childlike dependency. But I had learnt something new after all. My life with them had taught me to stand aside without anger and the urge to run away, when attention was no more focused on me.

Experience is a hard taskmaster and a bad teacher. Unless it hits us hard enough, we go on repeating the same mistakes. People and nations are equally inept at learning from experience. Take, for example, this country, which has not yet grasped that it is no longer a great power. But Germany had its economic miracle after near destruction through the war. The Germans re-created their country. It rose like a phoenix from the ashes. As the nation, so its members. Without defeat and love for persons or ideas, experience does not leave pertinent traces on the memory. Learning remains superficial and inefficient unless it touches the depths of emotion. Intellectual insight into one's condition cannot change a miserable pattern of life into a good one. Emotional learning is a slow, step-by-step process, where errors and relapses are unavoidable. No outside agency can teach us the art of shedding an uncomfortable skin for a comfortable one. The renewing process can, in the last resort, only come through the Self. Psychoanalysis and other treatments try to effect emotional changes in their clients, but their reported successes are doubtful. New emotions might be experienced in a laboratory situation, but they leave no lasting mark. They vanish in the open air of life, when the crutches of analysis have been taken away. Methods which, of necessity, rely on verbal communication falsify the authenticity of inner happenings. These express themselves in a non-verbal language, and words can never grasp their meaning. Psychotherapy will therefore seldom leave more than an intellectual residuum of broadened self-knowledge. But self-knowledge alone does not produce emotional change. Some therapists, being aware of the dilemma, have tried to find new forms of treatment. Gestalt psychologists, for example, meet their clients person to person and rely on non-verbal language. They watch posture, gesture and facial expression, which are the true indicators of inner events. And they try to shed mannerism and role playing.

Some other methods also apply new forms of treatment, for example, transactional analysis and encounter therapy. They attempt to help clients to help themselves. But I fear that these therapies are as well-meant as they are self-defeating. This is especially so in encounter therapy. An anonymous group of people tries to make sensuous contact with one another, which is a blindfold way of learning about oneself and others. It curtails sensitive awareness rather than develops it. One can only come closer to oneself and others in one's own good time, and not through hot pursuit in an artificial situation. Artificiality and self-consciousness blur the real issue: authentic contact with the 'other' is impossible without personal involvement.

Professional advice on techniques of sexual intercourse also

245

misses the point: emotional love alone saves sexual acts from futility. Without it, the whole razzmatazz of physical acrobatics is an empty shell. An artificial education for successful sexual performance does not touch the nerve centre of the situation. Knowledge of physical delights comes from autodidactic learning in childhood. Early sensuous awareness of oneself and others is what matters. It must not be frustrated or forbidden by parental censorship and religious taboos. Jewish and Christian attitudes to sex are largely responsible for inadequacy of intimate relationships in adults. But the poor ersatz of teaching adults new tricks kills spontaneity and enhances sensationalism.

Lessons in sexual performance as well as religious puritanism have made a mockery of physical love.

'*Il faut corriger la fortune*' (G. E. Lessing, *Minna von Barnhelm*), maxim of the delinquent, describes 'manipulations' man has applied to help himself over the centuries. There is always something amiss, be it in the relationship with others or oneself. A grumbling warning of loss follows human beings like a shadow. It can act as an incentive to heighten one's sights and performance, since without the drive to improve oneself and one's situation we would die of boredom, and society would disintegrate. But the idea of absolute perfection in both is the route to suicide. Much as we resent imperfection in others and ourselves, we could not exist without some degree of it. The Persian carpets of finest quality are always woven with a hardly visible fault because of an unspoken command – intended not to offend God and man. Western society seems less sensitive than the Persian carpet weavers. Engaged in half-baked thoughts and defective behaviour, apology comes too easily to our lips. 'I am sorry' is a refrain most frequently used in the English language, certainly by the older generation. It has become a parrot-like sentence to get absolution for mistakes and wrongdoing without punishment.

Lessing's *bon mot* has stuck in my memory ever since I read his plays at school. Together with my father's motto: '*Tue recht und scheue niemand*' ('do the honest thing and fear nobody') it has provided me with a so-called philosophy of life. Both proverbs have helped me through many vicissitudes. They are contradictory, which is their special attraction. To 'manipulate fate' on one hand and be honest on the other demands inventiveness and flexibility of mind. We don't effect changes in misadventures and unhappiness by blaming ourselves or others. But we might be seduced into believing that we could help *destiny* along with a little 'push'. And we flee to different surroundings to find fresh pastures where our luck might change, or we attempt to correct an uncomfortable situation through diplomacy. Sometimes it works. '*Make* "fortune" turn in your favour, but don't be found out' can be the lever to lift one out of an unbearable situation into a possible one. How often do people apply this diplomatic art to keep a lover they might otherwise lose, or to get one who might otherwise not have reacted to their advances! 'In love there is always one who suffers,' la Princesse Edmond de Polignac told me with a wistful smile, and I suspected that it was *not* she who did.

Our life proceeds with its ups and downs, from one interlude to another. Times in between are either packed full or empty, fruitful or barren, in accordance with patterns we have developed. Some people are fully aware of them, others recognize them vaguely and many not at all.

Life itself is an interlude between birth and death. These two giant pillars hold it together and give it the one meaning which makes sense to me. Before birth there was nothing, and the same is likely after death. Life is a span of time from nothingness to nothingness. The story of our life might be reflected in the memory of those concerned with us. But why do we want permanence and immortality if the human condition is not made that way? We search for 'Gestalt', an imperishable profile of ourselves. We find it momentarily in the ecstasy of love and creativity. Then a sense of omnipotence takes hold of us, and death has no dominion. But probably we are deceiving ourselves in coming to the conclusion that our 'highlights' could have cosmic significance. Yet they might be a spark of the divine flashing through our fragile lives. In any event, we cannot know either their reality or their meaning. I only know from the one experience of this kind I had (in my youth), that its wonder was as unexpected as its meaning was closed to me.

Humanist or not, the older we get the more intense is our desire to find out whether there are laws in the recurrence of events, or the unexpected reappearance of people, as if we came full circle in the space of a lifetime. The mystery of meetings with one's past is like the return of fashions, which happens with almost mathematical precision. If such events do follow a law, it is a law beyond human understanding. Theories of periodicity and

247

biorhythm cannot explain them. I know of pattern-hunters who look out for unexpected connections between either people or situations which seem to reveal a 'planned design' in their lives. They are often successful in finding both. Few persons would deny that these things exist, nor the amazement they feel about them.

When we meet strangers who turn out to be distant relatives or friends of friends, we marvel at 'how small the world is'. Such coincidences occur too often to be dismissed as chance. The idea that we attract other people through psychological kinship, independent of space or time, however, lacks conviction, unless we can believe that God's hand is working in everything that happens. The thought of a collective magnetism which draws certain people together and repels others, seems far-fetched. Its effect would have to encompass different continents. And this idea becomes more odd when the 'intermediary' has nothing in common with us. A theory of collective magnetism remains therefore an open question.

The mystery, illusory or not, makes us all agnostics even when we profess to be atheists. A secret stream of inexplicable mystery seems to run through human destiny. It is the 'ring round the moon' of the imagination.

When there is no answer to the uncanny, the supernatural is called upon for help. The adept of the occult suffers from the same wishful thinking as the religious believer. Both pass the problem on to a higher office. Coincidences of mental and emotional reactions are predictable, and are wrongly believed to be 'uncanny'. They depend largely on learning and imitation, and are accessible to psychological understanding.

But what about physical resemblance between complete strangers who lived many hundreds of years apart, and at opposite ends of Europe? When I strolled one day through the Alte Pinakothek in Munich with a cousin of mine, we stood dumbfounded before the portrait of a courtier at the Court of Philip IV of Spain, painted by Velasquez. We stared at one another. Was this man, who had the same formation of face, lips and eyebrows, the same insertion of hair and beard as my cousin, our ancestor? No member of our families had such a striking resemblance to my cousin. Perhaps the man portrayed had been a Marranne, a converted Jew, unrecognized as such. Had we come across the art of Nature to reproduce the same forms characteristic of a race, independent of time and space? But this could not explain the precision of details of the face, even of the expression of the eyes, so individual a feature of my cousin's. The experience was so powerful that I still feel the shock of recognition it conveyed. Nature can produce unbelievable shapes, but this reflection gives no answer to my experience.

The experience of my youth has a link with a very recent experience which also left me aghast. The early German romantics had always caught my fancy. While I was still at school I read Bettina von Brentano's life of Caroline Günderrode many times. This enigmatic poetess had always fascinated me because she was in advance of her time and probably bisexual. When I heard of Christa Wolf's recent book *Kein Ort. Nirgends* ('No place. Nowhere'), which relates an imaginary meeting between Günderrode and Kleist, I had it sent to me at once. Both poets committed suicide in Winkel am Wannsee, and Christa Wolf projects their characters with such vividness that I could not put the book down before I had finished it. A poetic passage relating to Kleist made me sit up in wonder. Christa Wolf used the same images and practically the same words as I did in my poem 'Jesaias' (see Chapter VI). Here they are:

Charlotte Wolff: *'Durch die Sohlen seiner Füsse, brennt das Herzensblut der Erde.'*

Christa Wolf: *'. . .und fühlte den Herzschlag der Erde unter seinen Fussohlen.'*

We have practically the same surname. She was born in Landsberg (Warthe), not very far from Danzig, and is a citizen of the East German Republic. She probably has no Jewish blood and is thirty years my junior. The same poetic images expressed by two women, apart in all but the German language, is both an elevating and a sobering thought. It is, in my view, miraculous that so similar a poetic expression could be fashioned by two minds. How is such a detailed similarity possible? This question has no answer.

Gertrude Stein uttered on her death-bed the words: 'The answer is in the question.' She was only partly right. Many questions remain, to my delight, unanswered.

IX Berlin Again

Berlin had been a chimera ever since 23 May 1933, when I stood at the Bahnhof Zoologischer Garten, waiting for the train to take me to Paris. It never entered my mind that one day the chimera might turn into a pleasant dream. But it was a long time before that came to pass. Did I not tell myself over and over again that I had left Germany for good, and that nothing would induce me to go back even for a short visit? I had repeated my resolve many a time to Ruth, who did not share my irreconcilable attitude. She had taken every trouble to find Katherine's address in Konstanz am Bodensee, and the two had been reunited in a lively correspondence, soon to be reinforced through a visit by Ruth to Konstanz. Messages went backward and forward between Katherine and myself; she expressed the ardent wish to renew her friendship with me also, and begged me to accompany Ruth. Willy nilly, I had become part of another trio. I had misgivings about the reunion, and about going back to Germany. And how could I see Katherine again after her break of trust and a separation which should have been final? But Ruth coaxed me to fight this aversion to Germany and everything German. In the end, I reluctantly agreed, on condition that she would act as my 'bodyguard' if need be. And in the autumn of 1964 we set out for Konstanz.

Katherine played the role of the German woman who had always loved the Jews, to perfection. But she acted out a melodrama: three old friends reunited at last, and being as close as if they had never been apart, in spite of the Hitler past.

There was Konstanz, still a town of the Middle Ages. We stayed in the ancient hotel where I had spent happy days with the Lubowskis and the Persian poet about forty years ago. There were the luscious gardens bordering Lake Konstanz. One could rest one's eyes on its large surface, and glimpse the small island of Mainau with its sub-tropical plants. One guessed rather than perceived the mountainous other side of the lake, towards which we had rowed in a little boat in my student days. Katherine approached a bench in the gardens, on which a dignified old lady had installed herself. *'Würden Sie erlauben?'* (Would you mind?) Katherine asked her, bowing slightly. The lady didn't seem at all pleased, but with a *'Gestatten Sie'* (do you mind?), the three of us sat down. The same old-fasioned manners were still abroad. It seemed that nothing had changed in this provincial town, which had seen much violence in the Middle Ages and in our own time. The atmosphere of the ancient streets and public buildings, and the old private houses, still suggested another century. Time *had* had a stop. We took afternoon tea in a grand café in the gardens. People bowed to each other in almost Chinese fashion. But their hefty handshakes were truly Germanic. How well I knew this demonstrativeness, hiding hostility and fear! Yes, it was all as it had been, even the band which played Palm Court music, tunes from before the war and waltzes by the brothers Strauss. I was really back, breathing the air of 'home'. I could not help being enchanted by the music, the gardens, the sea- and landscape. Memories of my student days evoked a nostalgia which I would have despised only a week before.

Next day we took the ferry to the ancient town of Meersburg am Bodensee, a mecca for poets. It was the home of Annette von Droste-Hülshoff who had lived and died there, in a house in one of the cobble-stoned streets which climb the hilly town. She was the most celebrated German poetess of the nineteenth century, but she also wrote one novella: *Die Judenbuche,* which I recalled, looking at the plaque in her memory. It is a documentary story of anti-Semitism, where she describes how a good man, a Westphalian Jew, was persecuted by the people of his village. More than thirty years later, George Eliot echoed her sentiments in *Daniel Deronda* on a larger canvas. My memory of Annette von Droste-Hülshoff's book was pertinent to what happened a few hours later. On our trip back to Konstanz I saw a typical 'old-time' German: red-faced, bull-necked, clad in leather shorts and wearing a Tyrolean hat. He stared at me with unconcealed hatred, and I stared back as I had done at the Gestapo officer who arrested me in the underground to Neukölln in 1933. When we reached Konstanz I asked to have our evening meal on the Swiss side of the town. From the moment I had been confronted by that man I found myself looking over my shoulder. The illusion of 'happy days' in Germany had burst like a soap bubble.

After my return to London I swore that I had really finished with Germany for good. But I did not regret my visit: I had faced up to something I had believed I could not do. My idiosyncrasy against the German language became acute again. In any event, I hardly ever spoke it since I had left Helen in Paris. By 1964, I had lived longer in exile than in Germany. I had settled for exile, with no more steps back into the past. During those days I often recalled Heinrich Heine's famous lines:

Denk ich an Deutschland in der Nacht
bin ich um meinen Schlaf gebracht.

His words sounded the right note in me. Perhaps the Germans have always been unlivable with, if a German-Jewish poet of the nineteenth century had felt as he did. It was impossible for a Jew to be at ease with any German, I told myself. There would always be a constraint, a nervous and muscular tension, stiffening body and mind.

That was how I felt for about seven years after my visit to Konstanz. Then something happened to make a crack in my defences. I had to correspond with the German publisher of *On the Way to Myself.* He suggested sending the translator of the book to see me. She came in June or July 1971, and at my first glance at her, scales fell from my eyes. The whole card-house of prejudice against Germans of the younger generation collapsed. A woman in her early twenties, dressed in shapely red trousers and a kind of bolero over a green silk vest, shook hands with me. She could have come from New York or Paris: she was one of that breed which feels at home anywhere, and can make contact with all kinds of people. Her eye had that 'German' blue, but otherwise nothing reminded me of a 'type'. I did not know myself, the way I talked to her as if we had known each other for years. She was a student of philosophy at Hamburg University, and we got together at once on my memories of Walter Benjamin. We had other interests in common also. She was as mad about jazz as I was, and we enthused about it together. She could listen to it by the hour, and so could I. When I showed her my book *Love*

252

Between Women, she looked at it thoughtfully, pondering for a while. Then she said: 'I know someone at Rowohlt's. Would you like me to make enquiries about a German translation?' I agreed. 'I would very much like to translate it myself, if that is all right by you?' I agreed again, on condition that I would supervise and correct her text. She was as good as her word. The book was published in 1973 at Rowohlt's, translated by Christel Buschmann. When she came to see me again to discuss her translation, we became friends. Unbeknown to her, she had been the pathfinder to prepare the way for a different approach to German people which, in the end, led to the two visits I paid to Berlin.

It seemed an odd signal from fortune that in 1977, a lesbian magazine U.K.Z. (*Unsere Kleine Zeitung*), published in Berlin, drew attention to my novel *An Older Love*. It is the mouthpiece of the lesbian group L.74 (L. for lesbos, 1974 for the year it was founded). Lesbian monthlies in Germany, America and this country exchange information and articles of common interest. The U.K.Z. was interested in the interview I had given to Jackie Forster of Sappho about my novel because of the publication of *Love Between Women* (*Die Psychologie der lesbischen Liebe*) in Germany in 1973. The April number of 1977 of the U.K.Z. reproduced a photo of me, and gave a short description of events in my life relevant to my work. *Die Psychologie der lesbischen Liebe* was mentioned as a landmark in lesbian literature. A review of my novel was promised as soon as the book became available in the German translation. I wrote immediately to Käthe Kuse, the founder of L.74 and one of the editors of the magazine. My letter was answered for her by Eva R., informing me of the group's pleasure and satisfaction to be in touch with me. Käthe Kuse, on leave at the time, would write to me on her return. And, soon after, I received a letter of welcome from her, together with a circular she had written some years before. It recounts the first beginnings of the group. I was fascinated to learn about the struggle of German homosexuals to find their collective identity, and form groups to fight the prejudices of society. It had taken them longer than their American and British counterparts because of German history. In any event, the L.74, which became instrumental in bringing me back to Berlin, is a group of professional women in the older age-groups. They believed that they would not fit in with an already existing lesbian group, the L.A.Z. (*Lesbisches Aktion Zentrum*), whose members were mainly young students, employees and nurses. The circular also mentions the H.A.W. (*Homosexueller Arbeitskreis*), which is an organization of homosexual men, established some years before the L.74. Both had been helpful in the foudation of L.74 in providing addresses of prospective members. The painter, Gertrude Sandmann, pupil of Käte Kollwitz, had been godmother to it. Her conviction of the necessity to bring professional lesbians of a 'riper' age together had carried weight, and given it direction. All its founder members happened to be dedicated and remarkable people. And they *made* the U.K.Z. in more ways than one. The quality of its contributions puts it in the forefront of the lesbian journals I have come across. It had been a wise decision to limit membership to professional women aged thirty to eighty and over. They had a deeper understanding of the lesbian situation than the younger generation who were born after Hitler. As the pre-history of my visits to Berlin is linked with German lesbian history in some ways, I want to mention a few of its salient points.

There is a time lag between a lesbian collective in Germany and in this country and America. It is the result of the suppressive influence of the Hitler régime, which many lesbians have not quite overcome. They had considerable difficulty in establishing their identity and an even greater one in proclaiming it. Their feelings of guilt and rejection were more complex and painful than those of lesbians in Anglo-Saxon countries and America. But once the pressure of Germany's historical aberration had been relieved, the voltage of their emotions was very high indeed. The young lesbians had an easier life. They were born after the Nazi régime, which by then was morally discarded by governmental and other official agencies. And they could cope better with parental difficulties than the older generation, still close to the horrors of the past. But whether old or young, German lesbians are all ardent feminists. Their affiliation to the Women's Liberation Movement not only eased their ghetto situation in society, but made them part of an international revolution. Their feminist framework invested them with a sense of self-confidence. Rightly so, as feminism would never have got off the ground without the lesbian influence. The time lag is also reflected in the interest the German media took in the lesbian cause. While the first lesbian television film in England was shown in the late sixties, the first German television film *Zaertlichkeit und Rebellion* ('Tenderness and Rebellion') was seen in August 1973. One of the younger founders of L.74 had the courage to declare publicly that she was a lesbian, and allow her face to be shown on the screen. All other participants had their visages covered.

German lesbians felt that they had been left behind, and in 1977 were still searching for a safer ground under their feet. They turned to foreign sources, American and English publications, to find reassurance and confirmation. Their longing for international solidarity among lesbians was probably the reason why my book on female homosexuality held such appeal for them. The possibility of a personal contact with me seemed to them desirable and promising. And I became intrigued with the idea of meeting German feminists and lesbians. I wanted to make direct contact with them, and get to know their personalities and aspirations. The wish became more urgent through a lively correspondence with two members of the L.74, which made me suggest visiting them in their lair. The idea was taken up with enthusiasm by my correspondents. I don't know why I so impulsively overthrew decades of rejection of everything German, and wanted to see Berlin again. I suppose that my change of mind was due to the fact that I felt 'safe' with lesbian feminists, as no harm could come to me in their midst. Yet I was bound to see other Germans also, hear and speak the language, 'feel' the past which had annihilated many of my family, and nearly caught me in its net of destruction. In spite or because of this odd urgency to see Germany again, I was torn by conflicting feelings about a prospective visit to Berlin. Many times I discarded the idea, but curiosity and an inexplicable nostalgia overruled my inhibitions. Berlin began to look like a 'treasure island', where I wanted to retrieve something precious which I had believed lost.

My correspondents wrote to me about a research project in which they wanted to involve me. They had searched for documents of lesbian life in the twenties, a period they rightly looked upon as the lesbian El Dorado. A magazine, *Die Freundin*, had been published in Berlin from 1924 to 1933, and Eva R. had discovered that the whole set was still intact and lodged in the Staatsbibliothek in East Germany. She had retrieved and photocopied all its numbers. It is difficult to understand how a whole collection of such 'degenerate' literature could have survived the Nazi period, but soon I had thirty photocopies of *Die Freundin* in my hands. I agreed to write a foreword to the project which was to be published in book form. As I was myself a 'period piece', my correspondents wanted to interview me during my visit. They wanted to know about my lesbian experiences, the atmosphere in the night clubs, dance palaces and other meeting places of the twenties. I read these magazines, which are a strange part of German cultural history before Hitler, with amusement, disbelief and absorbing interest. I had never come across *Die Freundin* when it had appeared, a sure proof of the secrecy surrounding its publication, though homosexual films and plays had been en vogue in the twenties. *Die Freundin* had obviously been an 'illegitimate child' which did not dare to show its face openly. The lesbian world which it depicts had little in common with the homosexual women I knew and the places I frequented. Its readers must have been of a different class who loved, wined and danced in a different world. They came together every week in localities on the Alexander Platz and the surrounding district where the poorer people lived. The following advertisement in *Die Freundin* illustrates better than any second-hand description the way those lesbians enjoyed themselves: 'Sonnabend, 30 Juli, 1927. *Nur Damen* treffen sich jeden Mittwoch und Sonnabend im ALEXANDER-PALAIS. 'Ein Sommernachtstraum'. (Only ladies meet each Wednesday and Saturday at Alexander Palace. 'A Summer Night's Dream'.)

Die Freundin published all sorts of advertisements by female and male homosexuals, even 'straights'. And they not only announced places of amusement but also lectures on homosexuality by Magnus Hirschfeld, psychiatrists and lawyers. It was a mixed bag of a publication where the ingredients did not mix. Short stories, poems and drawings were kitsch at its most mannered and ridiculous. *Die Freundin*, catering in its advertisements for both sexes, followed a custom of the time. Females and males were invariably 'seen' together, even in homosexual clubs.

Homosexual women and men have a longing for a history of their own, which had inspired my correspondent to dig for their roots. 'The seventies meet the twenties' was the cry of young Germans, and not only those who were homosexual. They wanted to go back to the past before Hitler in all aspects of cultural life, to build their own future on a Germany which had once been a model of freedom. The project about *Die Freundin* tallied with a general need. The suggestion that I should collaborate in it, and my agreement to write the foreword, gave a definite purpose to a visit to Berlin. But the project, well thought out and prepared, had to be shelved, as one of the collaborators left Berlin. However, the animated correspondence and my involvement with *Die Freundin* had been the vital sparks to get me to Germany on 5 April 1978. The final 'lever' was an invitation to give a reading from my books. I had vacillated and postponed the journey three or four times, until a letter from Christiane put an end to my ambivalence. She invited me in the name of Labrys and the Group L.74 to read from my novel *Flickwerk* (*An Older Love*) and from *Innenwelt und Aussenwelt* (*On the Way to Myself*) at the American Gedenk Library. The invitation to give a reading made me feel that my visit was *meant*. But doubts and fears still abounded. It so happened that Sybille Bedford visited me ten days before I was due in Berlin. I told her of my conflict, and her words put an end to my indecision. 'You must go back in triumph,' she said. 'It will do you good. Do go.' But on the morning of my departure from London, I still wondered whether to cancel the whole thing. Then, all of a sudden my fears vanished. I looked forward to the visit and couldn't wait to be off.

After the overcrowded labyrinth of Heathrow, the airport at Tegel acted like a tranquillizer. The officials had a smooth way of dealing with one's documents, bags and luggage. The building is of a circular shape which has a calming effect on the nervous system. One could have counted the number of people landing or taking off at the aerodrome. But I didn't spend much time watching them. I looked out for Ilse Kokula, one of my correspondents, and her friend who had promised to take us to the Pension where we were staying – a stone's throw from the Kurfürstendamm. My friend Audrey accompanied me because I couldn't face going to Germany alone, and she wanted to see Berlin. In a flash I spotted two smiling faces behind the barrier, that of Ilse with dark, amused eyes, and that of S. with a tense gaze in deep blue eyes. Both waved at us. Soon the barrier was opened and we were together. Ilse presented me with a bouquet of lilies, and after S. had stowed our luggage in the boot of her car, we were off to the Pension Arkona in the Meineke Strasse. I didn't recognize, nor did I even see the streets we passed through. It could have been anywhere in the world. The two women were in their thirties. Ilse, an outgoing person, was obviously pleased to meet me in the flesh. S. had a retiring manner, friendly but distant. Her clear-cut questions fitted with the observant gaze with which she scrutinized me and the crowded streets through which we drove. Her face had the colouring of a red-head, but she had golden-blonde hair. She behaved like an athlete, lifting our heavy suitcases in and out of the car, but there was a delicacy about her physical appearance belying the muscular strength she displayed. We arrived at the Pension in an old house which had withstood the war. Its style and comforts were the same as in my Berlin time. A lift made its journeys up and down at one of the outer walls, stopping midway between apartments. I found this relic of the past a little disconcerting. The wide flights of stairs, typical of old German houses, were not carpeted, but the wood gleamed with cleanliness. When we entered our room in the Pension, I practically fell onto one of the two beds. But I agreed to visit the Group L.74 the same evening in spite of fatigue. We had journeyed on a Wednesday, the day of their weekly meeting, and they expected us to come. Two hours later, S. and Ilse drove us to the Mariannenstrasse 34 in Kreuzberg where the L.74 occupied a small but roomy flat on the third floor. By that time I had shaken off some of the daze of having really arrived in Berlin. I vaguely recognized the shabby houses in the poor district of Kreuzberg which borders on Neukölln, once my place of work.

Our two companions left after depositing us at the door. I was greeted by Käthe Kuse, a handsome woman in her seventies. She led us into the 'parlour' where I met the group. About twenty women in slacks sat at tables along the walls, beer bottles and plastic mugs in front of them. It is customary in Germany to give a present to one's host, but also to a newly arrived guest. Käthe presented me with a bouquet of roses and freesias. Audrey and I sat down and were served with coffee and biscuits. Next to me was an impressive old woman of considerable proportions. Her facial expression was grim, her speech abrupt, but neither surprised me when I was introduced to her. I had recognized her from pictures seen in the distant past. She had been an Alderman in the Weimar Republic, and had lived through the war in a disused railway carriage hidden in a wood. Although of Aryan blood, she had been in danger of her life in the Nazi time because she was a communist. As she was a woman of few words and no courtesies, I soon turned my eyes away from her, asking aloud: 'Is Eva R. here?' No sooner had I spoken her name when a smiling young woman jumped from her seat and was at my side. Her spontaneity and obvious pleasure at seeing me warmed me. I looked at her dark, intelligent eyes in a handsome face as if I had known her a long time. From that moment I felt at home with the L.74, and settled down to take in the rest of the company. They were a chequered crowd: nurses, teachers, lecturers, economists. One had been a cook in a mental hospital near Exeter for twenty years. She was a fat and homely creature, who conversed with my friend in English. All of them wanted to know about London lesbians, their organizations and their doings. I told them all there was to say, in German. Some members of L.A.Z. had come over for the evening – 'to have a look at me'. They asked questions in a slightly aggressive tone, being unsure whether I would be in agreement with their outlook. But they changed their tune after our dialogue and, to the surprise of the L.74, asked me if I would come to their meeting place for a discussion with the whole group. I agreed and an evening was arranged.

Two hours had passed in a pleasant atmosphere. We had exchanged views, and I had answered many questions. The contact with the L.74 and the 'patrol' of the L.A.Z. had been made to our mutual satisfaction. Eva R. took us back by car to the Pension, and suggested fetching us the following morning for a visit to East Berlin. On opening the front door, we were in a badly lit entrance hall, and could hardly find our way to the outside lift. We fell into our beds but, in spite of extreme fatigue, I noticed the well-built double windows and the brass handle on the door, exactly as I had known them in times past.

When I awoke the next morning, I wondered how to cope with the six days packed with events. The flight to Berlin, the meeting with Ilse and S., and a visit to the L.74, all in one day, were parts of a way of life I was not used to. I need not have worried. My vitality grew with the occasions, all of them enjoyable and unusual experiences. The first whole day on German soil started with the visit to East Berlin. Eva R. took us by car to Checkpoint Charlie, which gave us a taste of frontier regulations in a communist country. The elaborate procedure of vetting foreigners took over an hour. In a shed of an office, the size of a prison cell, stood about fifty people, one half separated from the other by a long narrow table, on which one had to fill in forms – if one could get near it. Details had to be noted down of the exact amount of money in one's purse and on one's body. Passports were handed to a young blonde who never smiled and looked bored and exhausted. How could she deal with that crowd, standing cheek by jowl in suffocating air? The passports disapppeared down a chute, and had to be retrieved from another equally unsavoury office. We had to pay for the visa in Deutschmarks, and exchange 6.50DM into the same sum of East German money, a good bargain for the coffers of the Exchequer; it was an order to spend their money in East Berlin. However, we forgot the inconveniences as soon as we entered the Friedrichstrasse, and drove towards the former Schlossplatz. There is the heart of old Berlin, which had either been luckily preserved or skilfully rebuilt in its original shape. The Humboldt University stood where it had always been – unscathed. There I had heard Albert Einstein speak on his theory of relativity, listened to the *Kunsthistoriker* Heinrich Wölfflin, and Ludwig Klages, the founder of scientific graphology. The Schlossplatz, now Marx-Engel's Platz, lay before us in its perfect geometry. I spied the green patina of the dome with relief and joy. 'The dome has survived the war,' I said to Eva. 'No, but it is rebuilt exactly as it was. Even the sarcophagi of the Hohenzollern kings are still preserved in its entrails.' *Das Kaiserliche Schloss* (the imperial castle) had been destroyed, and government offices now stand in its place. The illusion of past splendour was still left. The former Schlossplatz had an atmosphere of dignified stillness. But looking back towards 'Unter den Linden' one couldn't doubt the transformation which had also made streets in East Berlin unrecognizable. The famous Linden (lime trees) had gone, and small stumps planted on each side of the wide avenue were a sorry replacement of past glory. I had hardly seen the prosperous and bustling West Berlin, but East Berlin gave one a sense of relief from the onslaught of noise through so many people and their motor cars. Only few people and even less motor cars were about here, and the men and women we saw looked well-dressed and content. Eva R. took us to the best restaurant of East Berlin in the Ermeler Haus on the Märkische Ufer along the Spree. This street has a romantic atmosphere, with languid willows overhanging the river. The restaurant and the meal had the quality and the trimmings of the best of their kind anywhere in the world, and I thought the food preferable to the offerings in elegant eating places in the West. I had had unnecessary misgivings about drinking Bulgarian red wine as no other was served, but it stood the test of comparison with French wine. After a glimpse at the Karl Marx Allèe, formerly Greater Frankfurter Strasse, we turned back to Checkpoint

Charlie and had less trouble in getting out of than getting in to East Berlin.

During the afternoon I was, for the first time, on my feet in Berlin. The Kurfürstendamm of today was so different from the one I had known in the past that it could have been in a town I had never seen before. The Café Krantzler occupied the place of the legendary Café des Westens. Its proportions and interior architecture were of a different world, stripped of the bohemian charm of the past. One entered a large covered veranda, leading to the main room, with soft carpets, waitresses in uniform, and delicious sweets. Café Krantzler is a meeting place of the prosperous of all ages, and full to the brim from morning to night. The upper floor is given over to variety performances, which has made this elegant establishment go the vulgar way of the world we live in. The *cachet* of that corner of Berlin had gone. It had been a grand first day, and an important evening event was still to come: a party in my honour at the feminist bookshop, Labrys, where I was to meet its owners and other women who had been instrumental in inviting me to Berlin.

Christiane drove us to Labrys, situated in the Kreuzberg district. I had not noticed the streets of Berlin the evening before, but now I became aware of them. I wanted to find points of orientation to link the present with the past. I recognized with satisfaction the Bülowbogen, a significant landmark. I saw the high steel wall around a U-turn where, in the past, the underground had gone overground. Now it runs underneath, and its old wagons, still standing in the empty place, have been transformed into *Trödelläden* (shops selling knick-knacks and occasional 'finds').

Why do we have this desperate need to search for the familiar, the things we know? They constitute the geometry of set patterns in which we feel secure. Without recognition of our surroundings, we are in the air. The sense of orientation makes the ground under our feet safe, which is the basis of physical and mental balance. We have to know where we are in order to know who we are. The sense of space affects our feeling of identity because of its relation to the inner space, which is the geometry of the imagination.

It reassured me to picture, in my mind, the homo-bar underneath the Bülowbogen where I had enjoyed the wild dancing of same-sexed couples in the company of Helen and Franz Hessel.

261

We entered Labrys, and I met feminists who were professional women, artists or senior citizens. One was a woman in her eighties who impressed me greatly. She was hardly five feet tall, had luminous grey eyes and white locks over a high brow. She had not left Germany during the Hitler régime, but had braved her self-imposed 'destiny' with an iron will. She is a Jewess and a painter of considerable talent, a pupil of Käte Kollwitz. She was accompanied by a strange woman who held her head so stiffly that I wondered whether she was in great pain or just very inhibited. An enigmatic smile never left her face, but considerable charm and friendliness emanated from her black eyes. There was a certain *on ne sait pas quoi* about her. I wanted to know her, but she avoided direct contact, and so I kept on looking at her in silence. These two people had an extorardinary 'aura' about them. Tamara, the smiling one, suffered from severe arthritis, but kept on her job as a lorry driver in spite of great pain and progressive immobility of hands and feet. I concluded from her looks that she had already reached retiring age, but she was still in her exacting job. I guessed that she had to go on because she was afraid of 'standing still'. Perhaps also, she wished to provide those extra luxuries for her friend which she had been used to before the German disaster. 'Goodness itself,' Christiane had described her to me. 'Nobody knows anything about her. She never speaks about herself. We only know that she was once a dancer and acrobat.' The painter, Gertrude Sandmann, sat next to me. She had the enthusiasm of an adolescent in spite of her eighty-four years. Nothing was lost to her observing eye. She realized how tired I was, and helped me to get back to the Pension at a reasonable hour. Her friend, Käthe Kuse, had protected her during the Nazi horrors, and saved her life many times. When the Gestapo called, Käthe Kuse had hidden her in a large drawer of a big cupboard. The rather well kept secret of her survival was revealed to me by Ilse. I had met people of unusual devotion to one another, people of rare courage. There had been quite a number of Germans like Käthe who risked their lives for their Jewish friends. Those three old women alone would have made my journey to Berlin worth while.

The young ones I met that evening had their own dynamism and secrets, but without the patina of the other three. The thirteen or fourteen women present were all feminists. Some were lesbians who had had a hard struggle against family and marriage bonds, to find their true identity. All of them were determined to make Germany a country fit for liberated women to live in. Their fervour to change the position of women in Germany has that extra intensity because of the suppression they suffered under Hitler. *Kinder und Küche* had to be changed into 'Women creating a new world'. It is the war cry of feminists all over the world, but with them the battle call is both a reminder of past horror and the hope for a future when women hold the reins. They are prepared to nip any fascistic backlash in the bud. The brand of male chauvinism they had experienced has made them even more radical than feminists in democratic countries. They have their eyes open because the danger of concentration camps and even death was too near to the lesbians under Hitler ever to be forgotten by homosexual feminists.

The women I met at Labrys were either friends or lovers or both. Was it their intimacy which created the extraordinary atmosphere in this candle-lit room? Although their personal bonds may have kindled the emotional atmosphere of the evening, the enthusiasm and warmth towards my friend and me came from another source. Germans have a ceremonial streak which is part of their social conditioning, whatever régime they may be under. They know how to celebrate. And the evening was a feast for the 'prodigal' colleague who had come back to tell the tale of another life and another world. Never did I feel as wanted in any gathering as with the women of Labrys. The warmth with which they embraced me, a stranger, would, by conventional standards, be thought of as over-demonstrative. But their kisses were as natural as their enthusiasm. They had an emotional directness which is taboo in British society. Perhaps feelings are more ambivalent, their emotions less stable than with citizens of more self-assured and powerful nations. But power does not only corrupt, it also makes the heart go cold. The warmth of my hosts was the Alpha and Omega of a happy visit, and counted even more for me than our common goals. It was lucky that this atmosphere never changed. It created the right temperature in which to 'blossom out', which was probably the secret of my renewed vitality.

The following day, Friday 7 April, was the highlight of my stay, its very purpose – the reading at the American Gedenk Bibliothek from my novel and my first autobiography. It was to take place at 8 p.m., but the hours before could not be idled away. There was too much to see, to discover and rediscover. I wanted to get to know Berlin, an international metropolis, once more, but not quite, as glamorous as in the twenties. Accompanied by Ilse, we set out for the Dahlem Museum, built about sixteen years ago. The taxi driver noticed that I was one of those who had come back, and volunteered explanations to my many surprised questions and exclamations. I could not make out where all the streets had 'gone to', the streets I had known in my time. I could not understand how so short a drive took us to the Grunewald, or rather what has remained of it, on our way to Dahlem. And to find myself in Steglitz, having passed the Hohenzollerndamm in minutes after departing from the Meineke Strasse, made me feel confused and distraught. I could not comprehend where I was, nor why it had all shrunk into different proportions during my absence of forty-five years. But there it was – I had to learn a new language of topography step by step.

'Why has Berlin shrunk?' I asked Ilse. She stared at me and had no answer.

'It is the WALL,' the taxi driver answered in her stead.

'Of course not,' I replied. 'I never lived in *that* part of town. My streets have gone or are all different.' I nearly wept with frustration. I felt like a five-year-old at her first reading lessons. Every word was a new word which I had to learn with the help of pictures. But I could not yet make sense of long lines: the streets of Berlin.

Tired from the frustration of not making head or tail of a Berlin changed beyond all recognition, I sat down on the first bench I saw in the Dahlem Museum. But I couldn't possibly miss the opportunity of seeing the sculptures by Riemenschneider. I didn't look at anything but the slim figure of his 'Pope'. Tilman Riemenschneider lived in Würzbrug in the fifteenth and sixteenth centuries. He was one of the greatest sculptors of the Gothic period. His Pope stood on a small base, as if on the point of flying away, a graceful figure, not bound to this earth. I recall his penetrating eyes in an upward-looking face. He seemed to look through and not at one, with the air of a spirituality hardly ever shown in sculpture. I noticed over-sized Byzantine figures in the same hall which Riemenschneider's figure made look like heavy furniture. On the way back, the taxi passed through the Südwest Korso where I had lived and practised for several years. My flat had been in No. 53A. The houses, in a long row, looked the same as before. Or were they re-built imitations? In any event, I had found another mark of recognition. On the other side of the street there had been small allotments for Sunday gardeners. Now they were replaced by another row of houses as similar as Rhesus monkeys. I felt no connection with the street and the house I had lived in. I wanted to get away quickly – and I did.

Perhaps the Riemenschneider sculpture had given me courage for my reading that evening. How odd that I had hardly prepared for it! Even more incomprehensible, I was not preoccupied with the most important event of my visit. Only the thought of being too tired to read well worried me from time to time. On returning from Dahlem we decided to have a good meal, and went into a pub opposite the Pension. I had a typical German dish, *Kassler Rippenspeer mit Sauerkraut*. It put me on my feet again. But first-night nerves didn't come. Languidly I chose some passages from my novel, and the description of my meetings with Virginia Woolf and Walter Benjamin from my autobiography. The former had become the heroine of German feminists, and Benjamin's stature was now legendary in the eyes of German students and intellectuals. An hour before Ilse and S. arrived to take us to the American Gedenk Bibliothek, the *right* nervousness came over me. I was unable to eat or drink, and only wanted it all to be over. I knew that this 'hot' anxiety would see me through. The heightened state of mind opened my eyes to the surroundings. I noted everything in my orbit of vision. We went once more through the Kreuzberg district. The Library, on the Blücher Platz, lies close to the Landwehrkanal, infamous for harbouring the corpses of Rosa Luxemburg and Karl Liebnecht, thrown into it by their murderers in 1917. The Blücher Platz is close to the Berlin Wall, the border of the two Germanys, which was the reason why it was chosen as the site for the library. It was built in 1954 as a present from the American to the German people. The Americans still hoped for a re-unification of East and West Berlin. The architects were chosen through a prize competition; two Germans won, and designed the building on the model of an American public library. In spite of its exquisite façade and interior, the library fits into the poor surroundings. It is built on two floors only, and stands out without sticking out. I only saw it at night, and am fully aware of the tricks memory can play. I recall it as a large brown building, one side spreading higher into the air than the rest, like the wing of an enormous bird. The forecourt is a large meadow, which sets it well back from the street.

I found myself in an auditorium on the ground floor, gently lighted, and the impression of discreet warmth was emphasized by the dark brown colour of the walls. Christiane introduced me to an audience of about 400 people, almost all women. I sat on the platform in front of two microphones. Several people came up to me before I started reading and asked for my autograph. It broke the ice. After Christiane's send-off, I was free of anxiety about the performance and the people who filled the seats and window sills, or sat on the floor. I forgot about my surroundings after I had read the first few words of my novel. The atmosphere of the library drew this large audience together, spreading a sense of privacy over a public meeting place. It may have been due to the colouring of the walls which seemed to have discreetly disappeared, and the soft lighting which made the audience less visible. I had never spoken or listened in such aesthetically pleasing surroundings. As my novel is largely autobiographical, Christiane had indicated that I would answer questions about my life if this was wanted. But after I had finished reading, no questions were asked. I had a few minutes' rest, before I continued with the passages I had chosen about Virginia Woolf and Benjamin from *On the Way to Myself*. By then the audience seemed ready and willing to question me. They were particularly keen to know everything I could possibly tell them about Virginia Woolf. They showed less interest in Walter Benjamin. Several people wanted to know about my research on the human hand. I told them about Julius Spier's course on hand-reading in Berlin, which had given me the idea of methodical research on the subject. I spoke of my work in Paris and London, and mentioned my investigations of apes and monkeys at the London Zoo. A young woman enquired, rather abruptly, why and how I left Germany, and if I was happy in England. Her question moved me, and I became conscious of real contact with my German audience. This was the moment when I rose to the occasion as I had wanted to. I told them how I felt about Hitler and the Nazis, and about my estrangement from Germany. I said (passionately by then) that I had been one of the lucky people who had not only survived, but had found a new life of such possibilities as I could never have met with in Germany. And I continued: 'I have been grieved that your great country was put into the abyss of sadism and inhumanity by that madman Hitler. You lost half your land, and the Jews lost six million people – all through the madness of one man.' The reaction to my

266

words was complete silence. Was the audience stunned? I felt quite weak after my outburst and had to sit down, but recovered after a few minutes. I knew that I had to say these things or I would have felt a traitor to my own people. After having discharged my task, I felt free to speak of my happy days in the Weimar Republic, about which they couldn't hear enough. I ended on a happy note. Many women came up to me, either to ask a personal question or to get my autograph. Among them was the daughter of Julius Spier, a white-haired, gentle woman, whom I liked. I told her how important her father had been for the course my life had taken in exile. A young woman gave me a bunch of violets she had picked before coming to the reading. Another took a leather *étui* out of her handbag; it contained two photos of me which she had cut out from my books. They did not let me go until the lights were dimmed and we were asked to leave the premises. The attentiveness and enthusiasm of the audience made me feel a different person. I had come back to Berlin in the way Sybille Bedford had predicted.

Christiane, Ilse, S. and a few other friends took us to a picturesque restaurant in the Güntzel Strasse. Victorian lamps, obviously meant to produce an old-fashioned and cosy atmosphere, hung from the ceiling. It was a small and poorly furnished place with uncomfortable benches along the walls, which the period trimmings did not make any more attractive. My friends frequented the restaurants out of solidarity with the English woman who owned it. She was unhappily married to a Yugoslav who did the cooking. He must have been particularly spiteful that day because the food was inedible, and we had to make do with ices and red wine. But neither the gimmicks, bad service nor the atrocious meal spoiled the fun. We were happy in each other's company, and talked until the early hours of the morning. At midnight, Gertrude Sandmann and Tamara arrived suddenly, to drink a glass of wine with me. The unexpected appearance of these two brought tears to my eyes. They had lost their way, but had not given up the search for the restaurant, late as it was. Gertrude's luminous eyes spoke more than words of her pleasure that I had come to Berlin, and read to young German women about my life and work. I embraced her, and smiled at Tamara. She couldn't stand any *caress*, however spontaneous. I had experienced a kind of emotional re-birth that evening. We returned to the Pension at 2 a.m., but I didn't want to go to bed

267

and, for another hour, scrutinized some of the books I had received.

We had a date with Christiane and Heidi at 11 a.m. on 8 April, to get a breath of fresh air. They planned to take us by car to a favourite sightseeing spot close to Berlin – the Wannsee. The weather had been sunny and fairly warm so far, and it kept its promise to shine on us also on this day. On our way we passed the Hohenzollerndamm which had worried me before because I didn't recognize its new design. But I became quite dismayed when my eyes fell on the dwarf-like *Lachmaler*, which are sculptures with large faces distorted into expressions of amusement. 'The Berliners need cheering up,' my friends told me. 'They look like gargoyles to me,' I answered. I had not credited the Berliners with such bad taste, as many modern buildings are attractive in design, and the reconstructed streets are aesthetically pleasant and marvellously functional. But the excellence of the new Berlin did not help me to find again the town I had once known like the palm of my hand. On the contrary, the new splendour put a barrier between Berlin and myself. We passed the Grunewald, and once more I was bewildered as I had neither expected it to be where it was, nor could I believe it to be so much thinned out. It looked a quarter of its former size. I decided not to disturb myself any further, but look at the straight autobahn in front of us and enjoy the speedy run.

How well I recalled the Wannsee with elegant villas around it, and little islands close to its shores. It had always been an enjoyable place for weekend outings. Things had not changed by 1978. I once more re-discovered a familiar sight. 'Yes, that is the Wannsee I know,' I said to myself. The place was crowded with people. They walked around the sandy beaches or up the hilly paths. How smart they looked, as clean and well kempt as Berlin's streets and public places. Many boats with colourful sails made the Wannsee resemble an enormous bath for children to play in with sailing boats. We took a ferry to the little island of Lindwerder, close to the shore. We went for a quick *marche active* and breathed the fresh 'sea air' which dusted away every trace of fatigue. Lindwerder owes its popularity to its one and only restaurant, known for its good food. It is, in fact, a magnified pub. We sat down in one of its big, bare rooms with rustic furniture. A group of rustic-looking men arrived with their hounds, as a dog race was going to be run in the afternoon. The dog-owners, heftily-built men, seemed ordinary and unassuming people. They all wore simple suits of similar colour and cut, like men in uniform, 'on the beat', I thought. Luckily they kept their animals under strict control, and we could enjoy a meal of venison with red cabbage and potatoes, followed by Edamer cheese and coffee in a fairly peaceful atmosphere. Still submerged in the events of the evening before, we talked and talked of further collaboration in times to come, and didn't return to the Pension until 5 p.m.

At eight o'clock Eva R. took us to the discussion evening at the L.A.Z. We entered an old shabby house in the Kulmer Strasse in Schöneberg, and went straight through the back door into a large yard, which accommodated three *Hinterhäuser* (houses at the back). The home of the L.A.Z. was in the third, that is – the cheapest one. I wondered whether it was part of a warehouse, as we were led into a place which looked like a large store-room and seated about 200 people. I had a big audience once more. The women of the L.A.Z. started the discussion by asking personal questions. Why did I go on with medicine if I preferred literature? And could I tell them something about my relationship with the friend who had come with me? They wasted no time in getting my 'measure'. They wanted to know first of all if I had a genuine lesbian bond with another woman, which was the test of my solidarity with them. If I had failed the examination, they might have stormed out of the room! But all went well and I could sit down in peace. The audience, mainly university students, included a few university lecturers, and also one woman who had reached a high position in the Civil Service. Close to the little table at which I was seated was a make-shift bar. Lemonade and drinks were served before the discussion got going. The consumption of alcohol must have been moderate because, although the atmosphere became heated, it was not through artificial stimulants, but the natural aggressiveness of the young. They tend to mistrust older people, and like a fight anyway. But it was the public servant of a riper age who put me through the mill, attacking me on one point after another, taken from my book *Love Between Women*. She objected with obvious signs of anger, that a person's endocrine make-up could have anything to do with homosexuality. She declared the idea to be utterly mistaken. I explained that hormones played a part in many, but by no means all, people who became homosexual, and told her to read my book carefully once more. She believed blindly in behaviourism, and so did the majority of the students present. Several supported her, saying: 'The milieu makes people, and we become what society teaches us.' I pointed out that individuality, intelligence and critical faculties were considerable forces of defence against outside influences which go against the grain. I asked them: 'How then have you become lesbians in a milieu which despises lesbianism?' 'Protest,' they shouted, 'we protest.' I left it like that, as the discussion had shifted onto an irrational plane. To my relief, someone who spoke with a gentle voice changed the subject back to the personal, asking me: 'Would you mind telling me about Else Lasker-Schüler? Was she a lesbian do you think?' 'As far as I know, all her lovers were men, but she loved women emotionally, a love she has celebrated in some of her poems. I think of her as bi-sexual.' This gave the clue for the next question: 'Why have you written a book on bisexuality?' I shortly explained why I had and, to my surprise, they didn't probe any further and refrained from belittling the subject, as one would have expected from the response of English lesbians. Questions jumped like yo-yos from the general to the personal, which gave me a few shocks. Some-one asked, with an expression of great curiosity, whether I had had difficulties with my parents about my love for women. When I told them that I came from a loving Jewish family, who accepted me as I was, and never questioned whom and how I loved, I was rudely interrupted by someone shouting: 'Loving Jewish family? Tell that to the marines! Jews despise girls. They adore the male, and no Jewish parent would tolerate a lesbian daughter. The men say prayers of thanks for not being born female.' With these words, she stormed out of the room. Was she anti-Semitic, I wondered. No, she wasn't, Eva told me, only an excitable person who had a grievance, but not against Jews.

We went on agreeing and disagreeing in hot dispute and friendly concord. I conceded the all-important influence of the milieu, but gave them to understand that behaviourism by itself was as dead as the dodo. Someone in the audience loudly declared: 'I don't want to be threatened by an overpowering society. We must be *ourselves*.' I applauded, and others did the same. When the evening came to an end, they asked me to write a few words in their visitor's book. I wrote: 'Children, you are on the right way.' They appeared to be pleased with it, and asked me to come again if I returned to Berlin. I was truly relieved about the harmonious finish at the L.A.Z.

Eva took us back to the Pension. I was wide awake when we passed the Tauentzienstrasse. I stared at the decapitated *Gedächtniskirche*, remembering its former glory. But it had a powerful appeal as it was. It should take the place of the bear as the symbol of Berlin, I said to Eva R.

I had enjoyed the fight and the harmony at the L.A.Z. These young lesbians were fearless, and determined not to be interfered with in their way of life. I did not observe the same freedom in older lesbians who, as writers, used pseudonyms, or had to hide their lesbianism to protect their professional position. Professor Lautmann later confirmed that this masking process was the rule with homosexual women. Several of the co-authors of his book *Seminar: Gesellschaft und Homosexualitat* had not dared to write under their own names. And Ilse had used the pseudonym of Ina Kukuck, for her book *Kampf gegen Unterdrückung* (*Fight against Suppression*), which deals with discrimination against lesbian women in professions and society.

The evening at the L.A.Z. rounded off my official engagements. The visit to Berlin would soon come to an end – only one day was left. Every hour had to be savoured, for who knows if I could ever return. On Sunday morning I went to Ilse's flat in Neukölln, where she interviewed me for at least two hours. Her two-room apartment, in an old house built about ninety years ago, had still a *Kachelhofen*. But the furniture was modern, sparse, simple and functional. It cemented well the present with the past. The whole atmosphere of the place suggested order and hard work. I had not looked forward to this interview, which I felt might put me into an awkward position. I tried hard to remember my pleasurable past which was its *raison d'être*. But my tongue did not function properly. I spoke in bad German about things I either did not want to talk about, or which my memory had either blurred or repressed. Yet I didn't like to disappoint Ilse, who had made all the practical arrangements for my stay, and been with me most of the time. I felt ill at ease, and wanted to get the interview over. At a moment I thought appropriate, I invited her to have lunch with me. And we went back to the pub in the Meineke Strasse where we had lunched before. But my purpose was not only to get a good meal; I wanted to familiarize myself with a few places, to add another crutch to my limping sense of orientation in the new Berlin. I had paid several visits to the Café Krantzler for the same reason. Both places and the people I saw there formed at least a faint design of a selective corner of the town. I had been surprised about the easy contact Germans made with strangers, be they taxi drivers or customers in a restaurant or café. For example, at the Krantzler, two women at a neighbouring table started a conversation without any prompting from me.

The afternoon of this precious last day was spent with Christiane and Heidi, who wanted to show us the poorer districts of Berlin. I had found my bearings on the first part of the tour, when we passed the Gedächtniskirche and the Café des Westens. It still stands as it did in years gone by, but, once we came to the Wittenbergplatz, I was bewildered again. It had been the watershed between Berlin's West End and the less fashionable parts, a sign-post of cross-roads. Its distinction had gone. The place had been stripped of its former identity and only the name had remained. The Nollendorfplatz, where I once lived in a bed-sitter, had undergone the same fate: it had only kept its name. No wonder that I gave a sigh of relief when we entered the Bülowstrasse with the Bülowgen, which was familiar terrain. But Schöneberg, one of my much-frequented beats in the past, had become an alien district. Even the *Rathaus* which looked an old building, unscathed by the war, did not stir my memory. My disorientation was accentuated by the time factor. One went from one district to another so quickly that distances were uncannily reduced. I tried to rationalize this incomprehensible change. I could not believe that it was the speed of a motor car which had clustered the Kurfürstendamm, Schöneberg, Kreuzberg, Neukölln, together. I came to the conclusion that the division of Berlin through the Wall had *mentally* changed the topography of the districts in either part. The taxi driver who told me so had been right. It had a claustrophobic effect, which added to the difficulty of recognizing even streets and places still preserved.

After Schönberg, we drove into Kreuzberg. We entered the Yorkstrasse, passed Labrys but didn't stop. Our friends wanted to get us to a favoured square, where West and East Berlin meet in front of the Wall. And so we arrived at the Chamisso Platz, which immediately took my fancy. It is a beautiful if gruesome square. The Wall stares at one, though no soldiers, with or without bayonets, were to be seen when we looked at it from inside the car. One could spy the houses on the other side. They seemed to be empty, as if the inhabitants had been frozen out of them. One had the sense of retreat into no man's land: the immediate sur-

272

roundings on both sides of the Wall were as silent as death. But the gently ascending Chamisso Platz itself had a stillness and beauty which was by no means dead. On the contrary, it was violently alive. The dirty walls bore calls to arms against fascism like 'Down with fascism' and 'Live Communism'. The atmosphere of stillness in spite of these 'cries of violence' seemed a paradox. Here was one of the few spots in West Berlin where I felt almost at home. The square had been spared the destruction by bombs, and the old houses recalled old Berlin in an oddly unchanged manner, though they had not been maintained as they should. The heavy entrance doors looked as dirty as the outside walls. The inhabitants, mostly Turkish *Gastarbeiter*, were probably content to have a roof over their heads, however neglected the houses. A few Turkish women with scarves over their heads went in and out of them, and children played in a shabby yard made into a poor playground, with a seesaw in the middle and a trapeze hanging from the ceiling of an open shed. The grey wall on one side had anti-fascist slogans written in large black letters. It constituted the outer wall of the Chamisso Café, well known to progressive intellectuals and artists. The interior impressed me greatly. An artist's imagination had made it into a place one was not likely to forget. The long, narrow room was kept in twilight through paintings in pastel colours covering the walls. The café itself reminded me of a ship, with a raised platform at its narrowed end, suggesting the captain's bridge. What cosy retreat, I thought! It might have been planned as such. The owner is an academic, engaged in social work, who wants the café to be a restful meeting place for artists and intellectuals. There is a romantic streak in German people which progressive politics and materialism have not killed. Their imaginative flair makes the *spiritus loci* come to life, and gives at an atmosphere of the unusual or mysterious. This romantic brand of the imagination instils unforgettable impressions, as memory is stirred through its emotional impact. Romanticism, bound up with emotion, is the ingredient of desire and nostalgia. One wants to see again what one remembers nostalgically. No wonder that places like the Chamisso Café leave one with the wish to return. I knew that I would want to go back there at the first opportunity.

On our return we passed Labrys, where Heidi got out of the car to fetch a present for me from the shop. I looked at the elegance of this androgynous woman, who moves with the alertness and skill of an acrobat. Her flexibility of body is not quite matched by her verbal expressions. Her large grey-blue eyes, dreamy and introvert, witness intelligence and depth of feeling which she cannot express with the same eloquence as that of her physique. Early traumatic shocks have diminished her verbal articulation. Heidi put an enormous volume on my lap. I could hardly hold it in my hands: *Tendenzen der Zwanziger Jahre, 15. Europäische Kunstausstellung*, Berlin 1977. It is far more than a catalogue. It explores in several thousand pages the mainstreams of art in the twenties, which come to life through many illustrations and poignant biographical sketches of the artists. This book is one of the most precious gifts I received. Before leaving Labrys on the evening of the reception, Heidi had shown me a collection of books and magazines they stocked, and presented me with a number of both. I had become closely acquainted with Christiane and her, who were the soul of Labrys. They founded it in 1975, and ran it as a collective. It soon became more than a bookshop selling feminist literature. The women who work there cultivate a personal contact with their customers. They advise if asked, they comfort, if comfort is wanted. Salaries had to be kept low to make the enterprise possible. And several women could only work part-time because they had another profession. Labrys counts among its workers teachers, lecturers, journalists, and even a physician. All of them are dedicated to spreading knowledge about feminism.

The generosity of my hosts and audiences had been almost overwhelming. On my visit to the L.74, the members of the group had handed me the first published number of U.Z.K., inscribed by everyone present. Two manuscripts were pressed into my hands. *Der Rosa Winkel* (known also in this country) and a fat letter had also been presented to me. They wanted to spend their goods and themselves, as if they couldn't do enough to make me feel at home. The manuscripts are fascinating documents of Nazi terror. They describe how German people protected their Jewish friends – to a limit. This limit was shown in *Sie Vergessen Keinen* ('They don't forget a single one'): the fear of accompanying them into a concentration camp. This documentary story describes the cruelty of a Gestapo officer who came to arrest an old Jewish woman whom he knew to be hidden in a German house. Told by the inhabitants that his victim was not there and never had been with them, he shouted: 'I shall send everyone who lives here to a concentration camp if that Jewish sow does not show up by to-morrow at the assembly place in the Hamburger Strasse.' The threat changed their attitude. They berated their Jewish friend when she finally arrived at their door. She had guessed what had happened. She brought all the money still in her possession, and every transportable good to the people who had protected her so far. She had gone away without a grudge – and was never seen again. The manuscripts were written by the women who presented them to me. They were tokens of *their* horror of Nazi Germany. They wanted me to know that *they* never had anything to do with Nazism.

I was even more touched by the letter containing sixteen pages which a young member of the group had given me. She tells of a bus ride in 1939, when she was a Hitler *Mädchen* (Hitler girl) in uniform. An old woman entered the bus in which all the places were occupied. She stood up, offering the woman her seat. The whole crowd shouted abuse at her: 'How dare you give your seat to a Jewess!' She saw the yellow star on the overcoat of the old woman, who got off at the next stop. And she, young as she was, felt humiliated. She never forgot that incident, which has worried her all her life. The letter refers to the anti-Nazi attitude of her family, and relates that her father had told her: 'If Hitler wins the war, we shall have to crawl on our bellies to stay alive. We are already suspects.' The letter ended with the information that not only homosexual men, but also lesbians couldn't escape the concentration camps, though no record of their fate exists. *Der Rosa Winkel* tells only of the sufferings and deaths of male homosexuals, and has not a word to say about lesbians, who were physically and mentally humiliated, beaten and raped. When I enquired about the matter, my informant told me that these rumours went around, but could be neither proved nor disproved. The horrors of the documents, which I had only read perfunctorily, did not penetrate my mind during my stay in Berlin. I must have repressed their impact in order not to disturb my equanimity.

I was immersed in the glow of an unexpected happiness. An enterprise which I had feared had become the fulfilment of a cherished dream. The weather had been benevolent, and the five days, filled to overflowing with events, had gone without a hitch. Everybody concerned was satisfied, and the contacts I had made promised to be solid. But I had not seen Berlin on my own. People and their cars were at my disposal any time I ventured to leave the Pension. Audrey and I were fetched and carried from beginning to end of the visit. It had lasted five days, and proved how insignificant the idea of 'length of time' is.

Our plane left at 9.15 a.m., and S. arrived from her home in the suburbs to see us off. She carried our suitcases, put them in the boot of her car, and drove us to Tegel Airport. In spite of an acute indisposition, she came to see us depart safely.

The new Berlin had not yet revealed itself to me, but I had become re-acquainted with some streets and houses not changed beyond recognition. Yet in many places nothing but the *name* had been left. Names are the last station of remembrance when life has gone. History ends up with names. When the substance of life dwindles into oblivion, it can still be recalled by its name. The names of everyone are registered in the Book of Life and are known to God – says the Bible. I had been able to see a faith design developing from familiar points of the town. I tried to re-create them in my mind as a provisory 'pointillist' sketch, which could perhaps become a picture if, one day, I explored Berlin on my own. I thought of Seurat, whose work I admire. His paintings remind me of a score of electrical impulses set down as marks of orientation; they preserve the *status nascendi* in the final result – the picture itself. I had just started to re-enter a world in which I had once lived. Though it had changed, and largely disappeared, I had found a treasure. I had come to know young German women, and I was as sure as one can be that we would keep in contact.

No sooner had I returned to London, than I thought how pleasant it would be to see Berlin again. A lively correspondence with a growing number of acquaintances kept communication going. And contacts were strengthened through visits to London by several of them. They helped to solidify budding friendships, and the wish for further collaboration. Christiane was the most frequent visitor. She came three times before I ventured on my second journey to Berlin. On her last visit she suggested that I should come at the invitation of Labrys, and participate in the events of the Summer University held in the first week of October. I should read from the German translation of *Bisexuality: A Study*, which was going to be published in August 1979. I accepted the invitation with pleasure, as it tallied with my own wishes.

A year and a half passed between my first and second visit to

Berlin. One's time scales alter with age. One cannot gauge changes in circumstances and people much younger than oneself. Those who had opened their minds and arms to me in 1978 might feel differently in 1979. I knew that the German Women's Movement had undergone changes, and the L.74 had not remained static either. Several of the founder members had left. The L.A.Z. had lost its home and seemed astray. I hadn't stood still either, but my 'move' was a move down the hill of life-expectation. I counted my future in terms of a year or two or five, while their future was, in most cases, counted in decades. They are young and I am old, and the difference worried me. Perhaps we wouldn't be in step with each other any more? Meetings in London with those I knew best reassured me up to a point. Nevertheless, doubts about the visit came, went, returned. With age one's physical and emotional 'skins' get more delicate and 'fold up'. One's sensitivity is heightened, one's tolerance level reduced. And I could not avoid reminding myself of a certain opportunism in German people, their over-valuation of social status which adds emotional ambivalence to a rather doubtful sense of loyalty. Loyalty was the trait I had learned to admire and count upon in this country. I had at last found some inner peace in Great Britain through the faithfulness of English friends.

The first visit to Berlin had been perfect. The exuberance and warmth of the audiences, the demonstration of friendship from those who had invited me, had made the stay one of complete harmony. I felt like someone in love who is afraid of a second meeting with the object of her infatuation, fearing the magic might not be there – a second time. The German women, happy as they had been to have me in their midst, were not yet friends, as no conflicts or trials had welded our happy contact into a solid bond of friendship.

During the interlude between the two journeys to Berlin, I had relived my life in writing a new autobiography, which heightened my natural introversion. Any change of circumstances was difficult to imagine. But in spite of this, I knew that I had to go back to Germany. I was still in search of that treasure which had been almost, but not quite, in my hands during the five beautiful days of my visit. The second time things had to be different though. I decided to concentrate my interest more on ideas than people. On a second visit personal flashpoints of enthusiasm would not be enough, even if they returned, which was doubtful.

277

And I wanted to see Berlin on my own, making careful notes of discoveries of things I had known and those which were new. The thought of reading from my new book became an important sideline, but was no more the focus of the journey. I had been asked by Labrys to take part in a podium discussion with three other women, which interested me even more than my own performance. It was announced in the catalogue of the Summer University as *Werkstattgespräch* (seminar) under the title: 'Single women – lesbians – motherhood – and the direction in which the Women's Movement should be going.' This seminar was bound to give me a clearer knowledge of the ideas and reactions of German feminists. I guessed that I would come into an arena of diverging goals and emotions, and more aggression than assent among the audience. I wanted to know the reactions of German 'heterosexual' feminists to lesbians, and to ascertain whether the trauma of the thirties had had an impact on the ideas and way of life of either. Apart from all this, I needed to complete the vague design of a few corners of Berlin. One does not like to leave something hardly begun, lying about in one's mind, unfinished.

The two-fold motivation was strong and urgent enough to take me back to Berlin, however much I might waver. A month before I was due, I did indeed cancel the whole thing. However, a telephone call from Christiane and Heidi talked me round. After all, they had not only organized the programme of my contributions but has already publicized them in the catalogue of the Summer University.

On 1 October I went with Audrey once more to Berlin. We nearly missed the plane – there was no taxi to be had in the Fulham Road. The drivers had to take their lunch at about 12 noon I thought this useless wait was a bad omen. After about fifteen minutes, despair made us reckless enough to hail private cars. Most passed us by, but one did stop when our time had nearly run out. Amazed at our good fortune I explained our predicament to him. We had, in fact, hailed a car for hire who had been on his way to a client, but could manage to get us to Victoria in between.

And we arrived safely once more at Tegel Airport. This time Christiane and Heidi waited for us – with roses. They took us to a hotel close to their apartment in the Pariser Strasse, a street of great moment in my life. I had stayed nearby with the Arinsteins, and Lisa's house was only ten minutes away. It seemed a good omen to be plunged again into the scene of my first visit to Berlin at the age of sixteen, when I was in pursuit of romance. The new hotel was not yet properly furnished but the inconvenience was amply compensated for by the service and friendliness of owners and staff. In the end, we liked it well enough to think of a further stay there, in case we returned once more.

The 1st October happened to be the day after my birthday. We had been expected on 30 September, but were unable to get a flight on that day, and had to postpone the journey. Christiane and Heidi had arranged a birthday party in their home, to be attended by about forty people. Most of them could come on the later date and, only a few hours after our arrival, we were on our way to their flat. The Berlin air is sprightly. The exhausts from the many cars pollute it far less than in this country, and the air alone lifts one's energy and spirit. We went along the Pariser Strasse and entered an old Berlin house. We crossed the entrance hall and went towards the back door to reach the *Gartenhaus* where my friends lived. Many such buildings can be found in the fashionable parts of Berlin. Good houses have back gardens but, space being at a premium in Berlin, *Gartenhäuser* were built. I was quite at home with them, and the one we entered had all the features I knew well: a wide flight of stairs, uncarpeted but not creaking under one's feet. It was a long climb to the flat on the fourth floor, but the staircase was designed for comfort and beauty. The newels of the banisters, of the same solid wood as the stairs, were carved like pieces of old furniture. The spotless cleanliness of the steps also reminded me of old times. But the lighting was dim, and inclined to go out after a few seconds rather than minutes. This parsimony in a good house of prosperous Berlin seemed paradoxical to me. I stopped for a breather on one of the landings between flats, and looked through its large window at the well-asphalted footpath between tall trees, and remembered my student abodes in similar *Gartenhäuser*. I recalled the heavy front doors which seemed to push against one when one tried to open them. Pariser Strasse 37 was in the style I had known, and I enjoyed this link with the past like a child enjoys a Christmas present.

After the contretemps of the difficult departure from London and all that followed, I went about like a sleep-walker. Audrey did not experience that dazed feeling which had got hold of me, but walked briskly up the stairs. At last we were on the top floor.

279

It housed two flats, but it was not difficult to know which the right one was. I stopped in my tracks at the door. It showed the cover of the German edition of my first autobiography. The entire door had been transformed into a picture. It was all there: the white background with grass-green borders, and the black hand-print of Ravel in the middle. Even the letters of the title *Innenwelt und Aussenwelt*, together with my name, were exactly imitated. I stood open-mouthed – the door was ajar, and we could hear the noise of guests who had arrived early. It needed some time to take in the most imaginative welcome I had ever come across. It made me feel still and shy with pride and pleasure. And I was shaken out of my trance-like fatigue.

We went in. Christiane and Heidi, already busy with serving the guests, smiled enchanting smiles. I pointed to the door, speechless, but the emotion I felt transmitted itself. I just asked: 'Who did it?' Christiane's idea, I was told, but the execution of the picture had been the work of two members of the Labrys collective. The surprise at the door made the evening a celebration from the start.

The first person I saw was Käthe Kuse, who greeted me with a bunch of roses as she had done eighteen months ago at the L.74. She brought greetings from Gertrude Sandmann, who was unable to come because Tamara was in hospital, very seriously ill. Gertrude went every two days to see her at the clinic close to the Wannsee – a long way from her home. I talked a great deal to Käthe, and asked her about the times when Gertrude was in danger. I told her that I had heard how she protected her during the Nazi period. Gertrude was her friend, she replied, and it was only natural to do what she could for her. 'It was not so difficult for me as for others to help Jewish friends,' she continued. 'My father was a good person. He was a carpenter, and several workmen helped him in the business. All of them were anti-Nazi, and *one* was always on the look-out for the Gestapo, and gave me a warning sign when they approached the house.' She continued with : 'I have to telephone Gertrude when I return to tell her all about the evening.' Our conversation was concluded with these words from me: 'With people like you, one could survive anything.'

Christiane's flat in a solid old house had the advantage of almost forgotten comforts: high ceilings in large rooms, properly built double windows in big wooden frames. I found myself sitting on a sofa, talking and talking to one person after another, or being conducted from one room to another to meet people. I seemed unable to take in all the faces and names I came across, and asked some women two or three times who they were – I hope to their amusement. Christiane and Heidi feasted us with pâtés, chicken, cheese and wines. And even greater treats were in store. When midnight came a toast to me was drunk in pink champagne. I had never tasted nor seen pink champagne before. It is apparently a product of the south of France. As if this was not enough, I was handed six hand-prints with the signatures of their owners, all members of the Labrys collective, as a token of remembrance of the evening. They had taken great pains to procure the copper dioxide recommended in *The Human Hand* for making hand-prints. It was my turn to end the feast with a speech of thanks. I said that their imaginative surprises had touched me. They made me aware that I had received an invaluable present, namely, to belong with German women again.

Christiane drove us back to the hotel as the clock struck one. We had gone through a day of events and celebration – under her wing – from our arrival at Tegel to the end of a feast at her home! I was much preoccupied with her that day, and during those which followed. Her inventive mind was the admiration of her friends, and had not gone unnoticed in the professional circle in which she moved. How little her appearance reveals of her gifts – at first glance! She is a comely woman tending to corpulence, but as quick in movement as in observation. The deep-set blue eyes in her round face are equally quick to express enjoyment, wit and thoughtfulness. Her swift reactions make her highly sensitive to her surroundings. She senses harmony or disquiet in the atmosphere like a dowser. Her soft skin and impressionability are counteracted by strong muscles and athletic skills. Her imaginative power is matched by excellence in sports, and her fine intelligence is applied to action as well as reflection. Her complex personality poses puzzles to herself and others. She combines virility and physical strength with delicacy of feeling and maternal protectiveness. She is a born fighter *for* the right causes and *against* injustice and discrimination. No wonder that she has an important place in the Women's Movement.

After taking leave of her at the hotel, I decided to have a day of rest, and perhaps a tentative exploration of Berlin. In the morning of 2 October we walked along the Uhland Strasse to the

Kurfürstendamm, and entered the Café Moehring at the corner. I always preferred to sit down rather than walk. And being a café addict, I intended to visit Moehring and Krantzler as often as possible. Both were elegant places with perfect wares and perfect service. But I wondered why they were always full from morning to night. Visitors to Berlin couldn't account for it. Did the industrious Berliners have time to idle away during working hours? But perhaps the many men met business partners there! How different Berlin's smart cafés are from the bohemian places on the *rive gauche*! I am attracted by both, the more so as neither of them has a *pendant* in London.

I made my first 'discoveries' while on the walk to the Café Moehring. I looked at the houses in the Uhland Strasse, carefully sifting the old from the new, and I went as far as to enter one of the most promising old buildings. One could hardly open the heavy front door, symbol of the protective power of capitalism. A slightly winding staircase of marble steps led to the ground floor. A large mirror opposite reflected one's image and the marble steps, but the splendour stopped at this point. All the other stairs were of wood, uncarpeted and not clean. Heavy doors and marble steps were typical of a number of houses I inspected in this part of Berlin. Some were well kept, others not properly maintained. The large metal plate of a consultant psychiatrist could be seen on one, with obvious signs of neglect. I was surprised that a medical man should tolerate such shabbiness at his place of practice. The paradoxical mixture of splendour and parsimony surprised me again and again. But reflecting on it, I realized the reason for an absence of pride and care not in tune with the German character. Berlin is an island, and its vulnerable position had made it unsuitable for the pursuit of big business. While tourism, the arts and science flourish here, big business has left for West Germany proper. Those who own or rent flats in the grand old houses are not rich enough to keep them in up-to-date trim.

The Café Moehring was part of a splendid example of an old house of the late nineteenth century, which had kept its original glory. The impressive façade was decorated with reliefs of cupids and other antique symbols, which looked down on the passers-by from the top of the building. The café itself occupied the ground floor, and had been reconstructed into a modern and elegant place with the comforts of a five-star hotel.

The first attempt to re-discover something of old Berlin had been successful, and my luck held good that day. When I went to the Berliner Bank in the Hardenbergstrasse to cash some money, I was delighted to be confronted with my past in the very street. The *Kunsthochschule*, a few steps away from the Bank, had not lost its original shape and commanding dignity. There Ruth had studied sculpture, and we had both enjoyed the famous *Maskenbälle* of the twenties. It stood in front of the Steinplatz which had not changed beyond recognition either. I recalled frequent visits to a great-aunt who treated me to five-course lunches in one of its fine houses. But more enjoyable had been the visits I paid to my Langfuhr relatives who lived in a side-street nearby, which revivified the friendship between my cousin and me.

The Berliner Bank, a modern building with much glass, was an experience in itself. One could wish it to be the architectural model for *every* bank. Its interior decoration combined good taste with exemplary comfort. One heard no noise in the thickly carpeted hall. I stood in the silence of this temple of Mammon, quite prepared to worship. My business was done with smiles and a few pleasant remarks by a lady employee. Her attitude was customer-directed and efficient. I had an *Ausland Konto*, (account held by foreigners) but her enquiry about my affairs was hardly noticeable, and took about two minutes. The customers behaved in the style of the institution – going about their business without fuss, speaking in low voices. In the ante-room to the 'temple' sat people on easy chairs, reading newspapers. These were fixed in wooden holders, and hung on a stand in the middle of the room. Like the building, so the employees! They perfectly fitted into the surroundings, designed to give the best of the best. Efficiency in the framework of beauty is seductive. Capitalism apparently has its points. Could socialism serve one equally well, with wheels turning fast and in silence, with people on both sides of the counter accepting that we are all cogs in a wheel? Would I join the Mammonites, I wondered, impressed as I was by the Berliner Bank. But I didn't waste much time reflecting on the subject. Hardly out of the building, I was greeted by another familiar sight: the old bridge above the Hardenbergstrasse, leading to the Bahnhof Zoo. It had been fixed in my mind since my departure from Germany in 1933, and its unaltered existence was a relief of a sort. Audrey and I, tired as we were, did not refrain from wandering over the Tauentzin- and Budapesterstrasse to the Café Krantzler on the Kurfürstendamm. We relaxed over tea and cheese cakes before returning to the hotel. Extreme tiredness had, at last, caught up with both of us. The rest of the day was spent indoors, as I had to prepare for my reading the next evening.

The 3rd October was *the* day. Ilse Kokula had a seminar from 12 to 2 p.m. at the university, on the theme: *Lesbianismus und erste Frauenbewegung*. Audrey and I, fetched by a friend of Ilse's, a family judge from Hamburg, attended. I had no eyes for the streets the car passed through, so interested was I to talk to Anke who combined social work with her profession as a judge. She apparently took on many of the tasks of a probation officer. Such a progressive attitude in the field of the law was new to me, and so was the attainment of the high office of judge by a woman in her early thirties.

When we reached the University in Dahlem, I glanced for a moment at the magnificently ugly building we were on the point of entering. It looked like an enormous pre-fabricated house, with a roof of corrugated iron. But once inside, one was enveloped in comfort and warmth. The corridors, leading in criss-cross fashion to the auditoria and *Werkstatträume* (rooms for seminars), were a labyrinth I would not have dared to traverse alone. But Anke brought us safely to Ilse's seminar, which was already in full swing when we arrived. It took place in a large rectangular room, furnished with tables from wall to wall, at which women of different age-groups sat, making notes. Every place was taken, as the theme was the central interest among the feminists who attended the fourth 'Summer University' in Berlin. The audience was a chequered crowd of students, social workers, teachers at progressive schools, university lecturers and other professional women, who had come to learn and discuss. Practically all of them were lesbians who felt secure enough to declare themselves as such. This fact alone was of absorbing interest to me. Ilse, the lecturer on Lesbianism and the Women's Movement, reported her findings, answered questions, discussed doubtful items. But I thought the seminar was no better than most of its kind – a laboratory experiment which lacks the flesh and blood of *life*. I recalled my disappointment in Truffaut's film *Jules et Jim*. The characters it displayed had been my friends. The actors could in no way re-create them as the people they were, and the film was like a weak sketch rather than a portrait. It did not show them in flesh and blood, but only as figments of the

284

director's imagination. At this seminar, many names and deeds of great women in the *Frauenbewegung* of the late nineteenth and early twentieth century were reported and discussed. Early German feminism, which started nearly a hundred years ago, was a model of its kind. The importance of lesbianism for the movement was acknowledged, and the Scientific Humanitarian Committee founded in 1897 regarded female homosexuality as 'normal'. The emancipation of homosexuals had begun. 'Lesbians must be accepted' was the slogan, a rather unfortunate formula because of its condescending undertones. Already in 1829, German lawyers had demanded that homosexual acts between women should not be punishable. Yet lesbians needed courage, if not bravado, to show the world how they felt. At the end of the nineteenth century, Käte Schumacher and Klara Schlecker did so. And a few years later Helene Truschkow and Johanna Gebenkor, lesbian members of the *Frauenbewegung*, even went a few steps further. They wanted the 'final solution' for men, who ought to disappear from the planet altogether.

It was all very interesting, yet told in too low a key to 'see' these great women. Their personalities were camouflaged through the cataloguing of their doings and certain facts of their lives. It was like a history lesson where knowledge of the dates of battles fails to call up the real happenings. The long list of early feminists included the well-known names of Dr Helene Stöcker, Anna Rule and Hedwig Dohm. But one was none the wiser about them as *people*. Some factual information the lecturer gave was, however, of great interest. Working-class feminists of the time disregarded lesbianism, as if it didn't exist. In any case, if they were aware of it, they drew a veil over it.

In spite of the obvious dilemma in trying to bring history to life, the audience was attentive and alert. They questioned the lecturer, and discussed doubtful points with vivacity. I was intrigued by the speedy flow of the well-punctuated arguments of a young woman who is writing her Ph.D. thesis on lesbian history. She not only questioned the lecturer, but put forward counter arguments. I had not been a silent attendant either. I questioned the timing of lesbian feminism, which is in fact over 2,500 years old, and has its roots in the feminine society around Sappho of Lesbos. In the Western world Germany had been the model of feminism. I reminded the audience that social evolution proceeds in waves, like the ebb and flow of the tide. The violent reaction against feminists and lesbians before the First World War proved this point. The lecturer agreed and spoke of the strenuous efforts of the Scientific Humanitarian Committee, under the auspices of Magnus Hirschfeld, Helene Stöcker and others, to save the situation. Otherwise the law against male homosexuality would have been applied to lesbians in 1912. Under the Weimar Republic, the famous paragraph 175 (the law against male homosexuality) was abolished. The golden age of sexual freedom had come. And then, in 1933, Hitler appeared on the German stage and with him the concentration camps. Homosexuals, classed as degenerates, were thrown into them, and probably lesbian women also. I added that German feminism of today was part of the greatest international revolution of the century, which alters the whole picture, and provides the first real chance for its survival. I wondered why German feminists feared right-wing politics now more than in 1978, particularly as this gathering of 7,000 women was sponsored by the Berlin Senate, not only by the allocation of money, but also the acknowledgment of its educational importance and merits.

The seminar came to an end. People moved, and some moved towards me. One, a teacher at the progressive Odenwald Schule, wanted information about early lesbianism in England. The student who had so frequently questioned the lecturer's report had arranged a 'Lesbian Tour' through Berlin the following day, and invited me to join. I gladly accepted. She struck me as being not only very intelligent, but also very imaginative. She had focused the tour on Schöneberg and Wilmersdorf, districts where lesbians of the twenties had lived. We were to look at houses which had seen the comings and goings of lesbian couples of the past. I applauded her imaginative idea. It occurred to me again that we can only catch a glimpse of reality through the imagination. Imaginative writers and poets alone can give history the breath of life – the 'third dimension'. 'We shall at least meet their houses,' I said to her, 'and your plan goes some way towards making the lesbian past come close to the present. Houses are "communal clothes" in which these women shared.' Some 'seers' can reconstruct the past (and foretell the future) of a person through a fragment of their belongings, and we might get a feel of some lesbians of the past by looking at the places which enclosed them.

Eva R. and some women I had met on my first visit came up to me also, and the whole thing started to become a 'party'. I took my leave as the lecturer, Ilse Kokula, and her friends were waiting to get us back to the hotel.

And so we left the Hörsaal. The corridors were filled with women, and large tables exhibited magazines and books. Germany boasts three feminist bookshops and three feminist magazines: the monthlies *Courage* and *Emma*, and *Die Schwartze Botin* which appears quarterly. On our way out, a lanky blonde in jeans accosted me with a charming smile. It was Brigitte Classen, editor of *Die Schwartze Botin*. She led me to their table where I met her partner Gabriele Goettle. They invited me to visit them at their home at the end of the week. Their magazine is the mouthpiece of radical feminism with anarchist leanings. Although eccentricity is a feature of the graphic and literary products of *Die Schwartze Botin*, they count some of the best writers and artists among their contributors.

On our way back, Ilse and the photographer, Edeltraut Veidt, gave me a warning about too optimistic an interpretation of German feminism. They implied that German feminists were not as sure of themselves as their behaviour suggested. Edeltraut is a student of psychology, and spoke of the wobbly sense of identity of German women who *think*. 'How can we ever feel safe with ourselves after Hitler?' she told me. Christiane and Heidi had uttered similar doubts, not about their own stance, but about the world around them which could once more plunge women into a new slavery – feminism or not. Far from being a signal of doom, I took the various misgivings I heard about as a healthy sign of self-searching in radical German feminists of today.

I had repressed the thought of my own contribution to the *Sommer Universität* which was to take place in the evening. So far the day had been of absorbing interest through meeting new people and seeing Eva R. again. But I needed to spend the next few hours on my own, meditating and waiting for the evening to come. Although I had prepared my reading, I had an attack of first night nerves. Ilse and her friend S. were taking me to the university after an early supper. Unfortunately, we set off far too soon because of the anxiety which drove me on to hurry. But on the way I seemed to calm down, and asked S. to drive along slowly. I told her about my eagerness to find out whether I had progressed in recognizing streets and buildings we passed. I couldn't grasp the change of distances and the new physiognomy of the surroundings. I stared helplessly at the wide avenue of the

Hohenzollerndamm, and was even more bewildered by the streets of Steglitz, my playground of past adventures. In my time, it had been a poor district, but the Cinderella had become a princess. The shabby suburb was now the residence of the well-to-do, and hid exquisite restaurants in dimly lit streets and cul-de-sacs. Dusk was falling when finally we approached the university. My eyes were keenly watching the many cars filled with feminists hurrying to the events of the evening. And I was well aware of the beautiful villas of Dahlem, a district just a cut above Steglitz. Berlin had to extend as far as possible into former suburbs, and make the best of being under the ever-threatening hand of the East German Wall.

The university looked like a tramp outside, but was well 'dressed' inside. The labyrinthine corridors were a delight to cross because of the sights to be glimpsed at every step. Women were lying on the carpeted floors, some alone, asleep or reading; and couples could be seen kissing, talking or singing. In the middle of a principal corridor sat a large woman heartily singing an obscene song about the male chauvinist pig. She seemed to address, more personally, her own husband who had 'pushed' seven children into her womb, a fact she couldn't forgive. But she had rhythm and fury in her song of hate.

On a junction with three other corridors, I saw something which made me tell my companions to halt. About fifteen lovely 'nymphs' were engaged in a *Ringelreihen* (a round dance). They formed a garland, holding each other by the hands, moving sideways, forwards, backwards, in slow dancing steps. They bowed to their vis-à-vis, and went on doing the same thing over and over again. They didn't mind being watched, if, indeed, they noticed it, so absorbed were they in the old-fashioned folk dance, performed as a ritual. I wondered if they connected some magic spells with their gyrations.

The thousands of women from all over the country who had gathered here were not a bad certificate for the legitimacy of the Women's Movement and its resolve to make itself felt. These women seemed to have confidence in the durability of feminism. The whole atmosphere from the corridors to the lecture rooms was impregnated with a sense of togetherness. I was reminded of my visits to a lesbian discotheque years ago, when I was thrilled by the erotic atmosphere the women exuded. They danced as if in a trance, and their togetherness left no room for a male either to

288

join in or replace a woman as partner. The sense of belonging among the German feminists had something of the same quality. Many of them were lesbians, and the majority of lectures, seminars, plays and cabarets were about female homosexuality. And many of the lecturers and players were themselves lesbians.

The feminists assembled here reflected every type of woman, but in an accentuated profile. They had come dressed in jeans, flowing caftans, elegant dresses. Some wore Eton crops, others had their hair floating down to their shoulders or further. One could not have picked out characteristic features in their appearance. Some had brought a child or two, even some dogs appeared on the scene and in the lecture rooms. The world and its woman was there, and the absence of men was not only unnoticeable but a true liberation. The 'intruder', man, would not have been able to change the *spiritus loci* of the Summer University. The collective bond between women is one of the great merits of feminism, and has untold consequences. It has proved in action that the stereotyped idea of female dependence on the male is nothing but a social imposition. The understanding that the differences between men and women have been overplayed to absurdity is the matrix of the social homophily between women. Most of them realize that polarized sexual attitudes have shifted onto a better equilibrium of sexual reactions. It was evident at this gathering, even when the quarrels between hetero- and homosexual feminists still roused the two factions to hot blooded fury. The frontiers between them have started to get blurred as the knowledge of human bisexuality is taking root. Bisexual feelings play their part in all relations, and women are less and less inclined to deny them. This realization is basic for the success of feminism, as it ensures the independence and creativity of women, which is its principal goal. When women have realized that they are freed from the fetters society had caught them in, the world is their oyster. Feminism is on the way to transforming woman from an artefact into the individual she is, standing on her own ground, and living her *own* life.

The long walk through the criss-cross corridors and talk with my companions had been a welcome diversion from the anxiety which had gripped me. But we had still arrived an hour early in the auditorium. I felt lost, finding myself alone in an immense extension of space, with steeply ascending rows of seats. The whole place was painted in an ugly yellow. The colour alone was disturbing, and deprived me of that feeling of comfort I had enjoyed so much when I gave a reading at the American Gedenk Bibliothek. Two microphones in front of me and one young woman in the first row were all I could fix my eyes on. The acoustics were not all they should be, according to the technician who asked me to get as near as possible to both these rather frightening magnifiers of speech. No, I had not much confidence in the success of my second performance in Berlin. And tiredness grew greater with every minute that passed. Then Christiane and Heidi came into the lecture hall, and I felt that a good wind had caressed my tired cheeks. They realized that I had made a mistake in getting there so early. Although their presence gave me some support, I had neither the right mood nor spirit for the reading. The portents were not favourable and that was that. Time went on. More and more women entered until the auditorium was almost filled. My spirits rose; I knew by then that I would read to a very large audience. It made all the difference. But I felt uneasy again when some women went out a few minutes after they had arrived. Why this unrest, I wondered. 'Typical of the *Summer Uni*. Too many events at the same time make people wander from one to the other,' Ilse told me. At my first reading in Berlin I had not experienced anything like it. I took it to be a discourtesy, and I worried, remaining unconvinced about the real difference between the two occasions. But the audience of about 500 women settled down the moment Christiane introduced me. Then I started to read from *On the Way to Myself*. I had chosen a very personal extract from the chapter 'A Journey into Russia'. In re-living the events, I forgot the audience. The start of the evening with a personal text provided a suitable contrast to the second part, the reading from *Bisexuality: A Study*. I had been advised to introduce the subject beforehand. By that time I had not only recovered my equanimity, but was almost in high spirits, and fatigue was forgotten. I read extracts from the first chapter, and was pleased when applause greeted my asides about certain passages of the text. I went so far as to break off in the middle of reciting the autobiography of a bisexual woman who had found in her lesbian 'side' a spontaneity and newness of love-making absent in her relations with men. I told the audience that I had chosen this particular autobiography for a special purpose: I wanted to allay false ideas about the physical expression of love between women. I pointed out the mistake lesbians made in

290

imitating heterosexual techniques. Imitation, a form of flattery, makes lesbian love derisory to men. I am not sure if I drove this important point home to everybody, but hope that the majority understood it.

I read another documentary story to show a little-known view about the relevance of fantasy to love, and the place it can take as a substitute for actual experience. I had once more forgotten time and place, which turned out to be to my advantage. There was no time for discussion, as the lights were dimmed and we had to leave the lecture hall, but on the demand of the audience it was arranged for the following day.

Unfortunately, it meant, for me, the cancellation of the Lesbian Tour. Every loss can be a gain, I comforted myself when we went next morning to the Café Moehring. After a pleasant hour of a sit-down and tea, we walked up the Kurfürstendamm towards Henrietta Platz, the former Halensee, where I had once enjoyed circus pleasures at the famous Luna Park. The place had become a busy cross-road, with not one iota of its former 'cachet'. On the way back we looked into several bookshops. The Germans resemble the Russians in one respect: they are both great readers, keen on education and literature. Books of the day were exhibited in glass vitrines on the pavement of the Kurfürstendamm, which is the accolade in advertisement. *Bisexuality: A Study* had not advanced to that eminent stage.

We turned into the Knesebeckstrasse which is the street of booksellers, where we made the round. We entered the feminist bookshop, Lilith. Two young women were in attendance, one of whom had listened to my reading the evening before. Another bookseller had also been there and had even read my book on bisexuality. Their active interest in the wares they were selling surprised me, and reinforced my impression of the educational zeal among German people.

Berlin opened itself up to me more and more. Streets I had trodden over and over in the twenties came into view, and houses, the style of which I have already described, were signals of a familiarity I was looking for longingly.

The discussion in the afternoon, under the chairmanship of Ilse K., lasted two hours. The coincidence with the Lesbian Tour had reduced the audience to about 150 women. They filled the lower rows of the auditorium, but many sat on the floor around me. An atmosphere of intimacy was immediately created, but the proceedings were by no means cosy. The questions turned around the main themes I had read about: the difference between gender and sexual identity, between bisexuality in the Self and as a way of life. Every question was well thought out and to the point. I had no difficulty in making my audience understand the underlying bisexuality in all human beings, indeed, the whole of nature. But the idea of a bisexual society aroused much astonishment and discussion. Doubts were expressed about the possibility of finishing with patriarchal influences inside such a society. The atmosphere was electric. In the end, the audience and myself seemed to have melted into one happy sisterhood. The afternoon had given me the best moments of any public performance ever. I felt so happy that I stretched out my arms as if to embrace my audience, a moment photographed by Edeltraut Veidt as a memento of an event which would, in itself, have made the whole journey memorable. It certainly was the highlight of the whole visit. Dinner at an Italian restaurant in Steglitz made culinary excellence the full stop to an unforgettable day.

The discussion has echoed in my mind until now. I have asked myself why it was so different from the evening before, when a large audience attended my reading and seemed to be with me all the way. Yet I had felt drained beforehand, and afterwards had been unable to enjoy the feast Labrys gave me at a quaint but excellent bistro. I had been disturbed before I started by the coming and going of women who couldn't make up their minds whether to stay with me or try something else, either a conference, a cabaret or a play. Their unrest interfered with the inner rhythm of quietude one depends upon before stepping into the intimate world of an autobiography. My mood and spirit had swung up and down like a fever curve. I was exasperated, then happy, and in the end free and easy enough for extempore asides to the text in hand. At the dinner party late that night, another disturbance clouded my mind. Only a few guests congratulated me on my reading. This made me feel like a boxer who had been beaten in the last round.

It may have been the complete contrast between the two events which made the discussion overshadow the performance proper. Firstly there were fewer people present, and they were not only interested in the subject, but had already had an introduction to it. They were a more homogeneous crowd who wanted to learn about bisexuality, a subject which had been to them as clouded as unclean water. And the smaller size of the auditorium produced an intimate atmosphere from the start. I felt enveloped by their concentrated attentiveness. It produced an instantaneous contact between us, so important for stimulating thought and an easy flow of language. Homo- and heterosexual women had attended in about equal proportions. Some of the latter seemed apprehensive about the lesbian side of bisexual women. They wanted a down-right explanation why lesbian love had a uniqueness that made it incomparable with any other kind of love. I greatly enjoyed their doubts and was much relieved when answers appeared to fall into the right slot. Another bone of contention was the danger of patriarchal influences in society. How could feminists rid them-selves of the evil which male chauvinism had imposed on lan-guage and education, apart from all the violations against them. My proposition of a cultural revolution in the framework of a bisexual society seemed to fall on fertile ground after careful and detailed explanation. But some were not convinced that such a society could work. Big things come from tiny cells, and utopias have an uncanny way of becoming realities, I told them.

The afternoon of discussion came to a close with such warm applause from my audience that I stretched out my arms in response. It was a kind of love. The trite saying that the public must be seduced by the performer has a ring of truth. I was, however, not after 'seduction', but spontaneous contact.

The 4th October had been my lucky day, and had ended in a harmonious evening with Ilse Kokula. When we dined and drank Italian Frascati, which looks like water and tastes like nectar, the conversation was as entertaining as informative. I learned much about the *Summer Uni* and the changes in the German feminist movement. This time the accent had been on lesbianism. It had been decided a year before that female homosexuality must be given a clear-cut profile, so that the invisible lesbian could show her face with confidence. One only needed to scrutinize the catalogue to see that female homosexuality was the foremost theme on the agenda. It permeated most performances, from cabarets, plays, readings, to seminars and conferences on music and the arts. And most of the performers were homosexual women. The same struggle and antagonism between hetero- and homosexual women of the Movement existed in Germany as in other countries, perhaps even more so. And the resentment on both sides spoiled the efficiency of the Women's Liberation

293

Movement. This time the lesbians had their cake, but it remained questionable if they could enjoy eating it.

The lesbian influence on the culture of today had been the preoccupation of the performers. They showed its predominance, for example, in a conference on 'The Other Line', which represents avant-garde efforts in painting and literature. The sense of order and purpose of the organizers impressed me greatly. They had thought of every angle of life in preparing the events and the catalogue announcing them. The conferences ranged from discussions on the need for a 'Frauenpartei' to difficulties in love relationships of homosexual women, psychoanalysis, mysticism, and many other themes already mentioned.

The Women's Movement had been weakened through splits in its ranks and fear of right-wing politics. German feminists have started to put great weight on 'femininity' and motherhood, together with feminization of thought and language. They proclaim the necessity of developing the 'whole woman', whatever that may mean. Another cry is the return to nature, and many of them have chosen to live on the land. Others have developed a penchant for mysticism which, according to them, follows the 'female' way of intuitive thought. The cult of 'womanhood' was probably responsible for the number of children who strutted about in the corridors and lecture halls. The sight of pregnant women, knitting while listening to lectures and discussions, completed the gamut of German feminism as seen at the *Summer Uni*. It included the virago, the maternal woman who wants children and knits wherever she goes, the nature-lover, the folklorist and the superstitious mystic. Women who had retired to the country to 'cultivate their own garden' and eat macrobiotic food were closely akin to those who look out for the occult. They had come from far and wide to gather here – with the exception of female farmers, who seemed to be sparse on the ground.

I had the opportunity to get a first-hand impression of German feminists at the Werkstattgespräch on 5 October. The agenda for discussion focused on four main points: lesbians, motherhood, splits in the feminist movement, and its future development. I sat on the podium with three lesbian feminists. We had the task of introducing the relevant points and leading the discussion to follow. Heidi of Labrys had arranged the seminar, and had chosen a lecturer in philosophy, a director of a broadcasting company and myself to preside over the meeting with her. She introduced the programme with the words: 'This is a conference mainly directed against the repression and oppression of lesbians. But apart from this theme, we shall deal with many aspects of feminism, for example, the political tendencies in this country with threaten all feminists.' I looked at the large audience in the same Hörsaal where I had read two days before. This time I felt at ease, but burning with curiosity to observe the reactions of the audience. From the start, one could sense tenseness in the atmosphere; the women appeared to flex their mental muscles for a fight. Why, I wondered, do they look apprehensive, when they all have the same creed? Yet they gave the impression that they were afraid of being got at by us, the four women on the podium. I enjoyed the 'thick air' of pugnaciousness. I was prepared to give as good as I got – just in case. The first outbreak of hostility came when Heidi argued that lesbians were too inward looking, concentrating on individual problems instead of committing themselves to radical politics as a collective. One heard murmurs of protest, but the open attack came when she spoke of splits inside the lesbian community. There were those who retreated into the country or copped out in other ways, she said. She was bluntly told that lesbians in rural areas had the greatest difficulty in keeping their heads above water emotionally and socially. And she could not compare a provincial setting with Berlin where social conditions were favourable for lesbians. There, they could find their collective identity.

At this point, I gave a warning: 'In town or country, homosexual women must gather together in one "body", and remain in communication with one another throughout the land. They have to be prepared to fight political oppression collectively, otherwise they might one day be in the same position as the Jews were under Hitler. You should not forget', I continued, 'that homosexual men, and probably women also, were thrown into concentration camps, and one never knows what the future has in store.' I caused an uproar. A chorus shouted: 'We don't want to be made anxious. Our situation is quite different from that of the Jews.' I also found opposition from two members of the panel, who could not see the relevance of my point. Only Heidi did. I remained unruffled by the protests.

The radio director stopped further outbreaks of annoyance and aggression by saying that lesbians were regarded as a minority because of a 'sexual' divergence, which was an idiotic standpoint.

295

It was only one aspect of personality. This was agreed to by the majority. Heidi, too, didn't think it either right or wise that lesbians should consider themselves to be outsiders. But the lecturer in philosophy rather blurred the issue. She doubted whether lesbians really knew what they wanted. She thought it was difficult for them to preserve their identity when they were working with other women alongside men. I objected to her viewpoint, and got on my hobby horse, proclaiming that lesbianism was the foundation of feminism. This knowledge had strengthened the self-confidence of homosexual women in the past, and should not be forgotten in the present. My enthusiastic words were acclaimed with loud applause by the lesbians present, but found no acknowledgment from the heterosexual feminists. They felt left out, and accused me of being prejudiced against them. The discussion became heated as my statement had brought the antagonism between hetero- and homosexual feminists into the open. The latter complained of the inequality of service between the two 'factions'. Lesbians went on marches with other feminists to demonstrate against the Paragraph 218 (law against abortion), but do 'heteros' lift a finger for them? Do they demonstrate against the suppression of their gay sisters? They don't. An American voice could be heard saying: 'I come from San Francisco. Gay women actively support all feminist issues and demonstrate for them, but their loyalty is not requited. They are left to fight for themselves. Heterosexual women don't join gay marches. They don't want anything to do with lesbians, as they could be suspected of being homosexual themselves.'

After the sensible remark of someone: 'How can we change that?', the theme turned to the subject of bisexuality. I reported about the efforts of some feminist workshops in England, which tried to 'educate' heterosexual women towards an emotional approach to lesbian feminists, an intelligent method of making them aware of the bisexual nature of everybody. Someone asked in a cynical tone: 'How does that education proceed?' and: 'Is that really possible?' I admitted that I had not been personally involved in the scheme, but knew that both 'factions' collaborated in tasks of a highly emotional nature, like the fight against rapists and support for their victims.

When I spoke of my research which had shown that many lesbians and bisexual women had jumped into marriage without being aware of their 'double' nature, the audience kept a stony silence. I stressed the overpowering influence of the conventional code which delayed people's awareness of their total sexuality. I continued that bisexuality was dismissed by most people in the Western world. But the realization that one can love people of both sexes can come to anybody. I told the audience of several married women in middle age who suddenly fell in love with another woman. From then on they thought of themselves as lesbians or bisexuals as the case may be. The silence was broken by an outburst of aggression. A well-known homosexual maintained that all married bisexual women were lesbians. They only married for reasons of convenience, she continued. I must have been mentally deaf as I did not hear her words which were a contradiction of my research findings. Or had the general uproar drowned her statement? Eva R. supported me with the remark that the borderline between hetero- and homosexuality was blurred, and got more so as time went on. Her words were disregarded. Instead, a small chorus shouted at me that I should refrain from making them unnecessarily anxious, as if they didn't know what their sexual needs were. I objected with the words: 'You have to distinguish between healthy and neurotic anxiety. To be afraid of bisexuality is not a healthy fear. The awareness of one's bisexuality can only lead to inner enrichment and broadening of experience. Why don't you allow for a wider view of yourselves and others?' The idea of two kinds of anxiety was vigorously taken up by two lesbian women, who amplified the point through examples of how 'fury' had strengthened them to fight for the custody of their children.

The attacks of the audience stimulated rather than depressed me. I quite enjoyed a gauntlet thrown at my feet. Aggressiveness can be of considerable value when it is the result of fighting a dawning awareness which the conscious mind refuses to accept. In the lecture hall at the Summer University, I got first-hand proof of how much bisexuality is rejected by homo- and heterosexuals alike.

An old lesbian angrily drew attention to the proletarian women who are not wooed enough into the Women's Movement. 'It is about time,' she said, 'that you broadened your horizon, and didn't stand still in your middle-class isolation.' Her justified statement left the audience cool. The women were probably preoccupied with their own reactions to what they had heard before. They left, thoughtful and anxious, disturbed and apprehensive. I had had new experiences of German feminism, and was delighted with the experience – the arguments, the coldness and the excitement of the audience.

Old acquaintances greeted me, and some I hadn't met before introduced themselves to me. I left the podium to join my friends. On the way out, a young woman addressed me: 'I have a message for you from Gertrude Sandmann. Tamara died yesterday.' I was not really surprised as I knew how ill she had been, but the finality of it disorientated me. In a state of mental anaesthesia, I asked for Gertrude's telephone number, and spoke a few words to the messenger.

The Labrys collective and friends joined us at the Italian restaurant in Steglitz where we had dined the evening before. I felt unable to tell anybody about Tamara's death. It was like a highly confidential secret which must under no circumstances be disclosed. I never spoke of it during the rest of my visit. I would love to have met Tamara again, who had taken herself away for ever. And the secret about her was gone with her into the grave. During the long-drawn-out meal, one of the guests addressed me all of a sudden: 'I didn't want to attack you.' It was the woman who had emphatically denied the existence of bisexuality. I made a mental note of her remark, but didn't then react to the ambivalence of feelings it betrayed.

My engagement at the *Summer Uni* had come to an end with the podium discussion. How different in mood and happenings the second visit had so far turned out to be! I had met with diverging audience reactions, I had seen more of the true character of acquaintances and new friends. The ground under my feet was no more a soft carpet, but hard, solid wood. I was content, though, counting the knowledge I had gained of Berlin and of German feminists as an invaluable broadening of my world. I had been carried along by individual enthusiasm on my first visit. My head had been in the clouds, and the euphoria I felt was shared by those who had been its cause. I might have been no more than a revenant for them, but they took me to their hearts and believed in my work, which gave them another vista of their own goals, and appeared to strengthen their confidence to persist in their efforts. They had to catch up, as their time-table of progress had been delayed through their unfortunate history. This time lag was probably the reason why my appearance in their ranks had been welcomed so warmly eighteen months ago. They received me as if

I had been a present from heaven, and I thought exactly the same about them.

On Saturday 6 October, Audrey and I visited the publishers of *Die Schwartze Botin*. They fetched us from the hotel in the early afternoon, and we drove through the now familiar streets of Steglitz and Dahlem to the still countrified Lichterfelde. The street where they lived hadn't changed since Kaiser Wilhelm's time, with its cobble stones and old houses. They were a mixture of villas and boarding-houses. These hybrid buildings stood in large gardens with tall trees, and cars carefully avoided the street because of the cobble stones. Their house had been reconstructed into flats; they lived on the top floor which seemed very far away from the hustle and bustle of Berlin proper. These two women have their own world, all in one. Two rooms, apparently used for storing the magazine, bordered their private quarters. Books were everywhere. We sat in what was probably their drawing room. It had a large balcony, looking out on the garden which seemed to have run wild. I admired this rural ivory tower of theirs, which was a fortress defying the outside world, but allowing for a good look at what was going on underneath. Brigitte Classen could have been Swedish by her looks, while Gabriele Goettle, corpulent and dark, might have descended from Tziganes. She has the emotionality and shrewdness of the 'travelling people'. I was fascinated by this couple. Brigitte was inclined to take the floor, and I to study her friend. I had the uncomfortable sensation that Brigitte was not quite 'with us', probably preoccupied with the other visitor who was to follow on our heels. My friend Audrey silently watched me getting more and more tense. The conversation in German rather shut her out. As it happened, the afternoon defeated any anticipation I might have had of these two and their milieu. They both have idiosyncratic tastes, which can encourage a lop-sided view of ideas and people. They seemed to listen to me, but I was unsure of how much they took in. Gabriele, less sure of herself than Brigitte, was the better listener. She has a flexible mind, while her partner is not free from prejudice and rigidity of thought. *Die Schwartze Botin* is a messenger of gloom, an élite production which carries neither advertisements nor readers' letters. It is intended to be a perfect mouthpiece for avant-garde ideas, disdaining commercialism. Its publishers are perfectionists in their own way, and looked upon as loners by the feminist movement. They walk with single-mindedness on their chosen path, attacked by many as eccentrics indulging in a sense of superiority. I realized that none of us could come to terms with a kind of communication which seemed to go somewhat astray from the start. Our talk was like a walk out of step. One person was in front, the other behind or sideways. In the end, the two hosts appeared to have turned a corner without my noticing it, and I found myself alone, not knowing where I was. The afternoon dragged on. Suddenly the bell rang and the 'other' guest, an Austrian poet, arrived. This was the signal to leave. What a pity, I thought, in the taxi which took us back to the hotel – we had seen each other but hadn't met. The afternoon had been puzzling, and left loose ends. It had been a hide-and-seek game which nobody won. The thought of the 'failed' visit lingered in my mind. Frustration teases the imagination and memory.

Perhaps I had felt something akin to failure about the walk over Berlin's streets that very morning. I was driven by a compulsive desire to recognize my old haunts, to get back into the world of my past. Audrey and I passed the bookshops in the Knesebeckstrasse, and turned first into the Goethestrasse, and from there into the Schillerstrasse. Why was I drawn to wander along these streets? I had already been distressed by the Mommsenstrasse which had preserved much of its former appearance, but now looked like a neglected old person. But I went on and on until we reached the Bismarck Platz right in Charlottenburg. Then I 'saw' myself, running like a crazed creature the same way on early evenings and late nights to Lisa – forty-six years ago. I stopped, standing quite still, and decided to return to the hotel at once. What was I after, I asked myself. To catch something which had become a museum, and is alive only in the imagination? Yet I had a sound purpose in my tour of recognition: to make sure how I felt seeing the museum pieces of yesterdays still preserved in the new streamlined Berlin. My life was far away from both, but it still fed on the past. I needed to look at what had remained of it. It was a matter of solidifying memories. The new Berlin was a delight in itself, which didn't inflict itself on me negatively. It had everything to do with a new chapter in my life: the meeting with young German feminists, new acquaintances, and budding friendships. The appreciation of my books published in Germany, and my own performances before large audiences, renewed my vitality, and gave me an unexpected outlet in a place I had thought lost to me for ever. The re-vitalizing force which people and ideas

300

of the new Germany have given me is probably one of the most fortunate events I have experienced in a long life.

The chimes of the Ludwigskirche woke us at 8 a.m. on Sunday. The church in red brick, as ugly as sin, had survived the war without a scratch. I had known it for ever, that is, since my first visit to Lisa when I was still at school. This Sunday, S. and Ilse were to take us into the country for relaxation. We went on a glorious tour to the Wannsee and the river Havel which flows through it with greater aplomb than the Liebe went through the Sorgensee in my home town of Riesenburg. We stopped the car close to the place where we had taken the ferry to the Lindwerder island eighteen months ago. 'Health through Joy' had been the Nazi slogan, the hymn to the myth of the German superman. It had been ridiculed all over the Western world. Standing on the sandy shores of the Wannsee, the slogan made perfect sense, bar its sinister implications. One felt invigorated by the bracing air in the beautiful surroundings, only a few miles away from Berlin. One's lungs expanded in the oxygen of this favoured spot, where lake and woods purified the air, as though one holidayed at the Baltic. As before, people had come in their hundreds to walk in the wooded hills, or to sail on the blue waters of the Wannsee. The scene could have been a model for a painting by Dufy. The crowd on the beaches dispersed in all directions, and there was space enough not to feel oppressed by so many people. The Grunewald Turm, built in 1903, taller than the fir trees surrounding it, dominated the landscape, and absorbed many of the people into its bowels, which contained an excellent restaurant. These trees with their naked stems wear their conifers like crowns. They are characteristic of the *Märkische Sandkasten* (the Sandbox of the Mark Brandenburg), but also grow along the shores of the Baltic. They reminded me of Danzig, Zoppot and Gdingen, and my walks along the seafront, either alone or with friends and lovers.

S. had planned the outing carefully. We had an early lunch at the Grunewald Turm before continuing the drive along the Havel. The restaurant is built like an L-shaped room, with a small horizontal, and an enormous vertical, part. One couldn't see the end of the latter, which finished in the kitchens. We got the last available table in the 'foot' of the L. The restaurant was familiar territory to me. The interior decoration imitated the style of the twenties. There were the chequered table cloths fixed with metal

301

clips, the large plates in different colours, and waiters in *Hemds-ärmeln* (shirt sleeves), everything as I had known it. And the German customers seemed familiar also. The men, heavily built with square faces, and the women tending to corpulence, also evoked old memories. Their faces were as unwrinkled as those of wax dolls, and even the younger women among them had this expressionless look. And both sexes seemed to be entirely absorbed in the delicious food in front of them. The most familiar figures of all, however, were the waiters. Most of them had reached middle age; they ran about with admirable concentration for their job. They wore waistcoats but no jackets. They had that appearance of efficiency which doesn't know how to stop for a breather. Their faces, strongly lined, had forgotten how to smile, but it would be a mistake to think of them as depressed or lacking in humour. They enjoyed the hurry, the money they earned and the tips of grateful customers, who appeared not to stint them-selves. The food couldn't have been more carefully prepared nor the wines of better quality. Contrary to my expectation, I was not apprehensive at being cheek by jowl with the German lower-middle classes assembled here. They had once been the ferment and salt of Nazi Germany. Now they peacefully enjoyed them-selves in their own way, and nobody gave me so much as a glance. The weather had been favourable throughout our visit, and on this day it was even warm. We drove through the woods border-ing the river Havel until we reached a famous castle – the Glienecker Schloss. It has been preserved without a blemish: not a scar from the war nor from enterprising officials. It is painted white, except for the wooden frames of the large windows which are a lemon-yellow colour. They have the shape of a cross, divid-ing the small upper from the large lower panes. The castle is set in a magnificent park, with old trees of German and foreign origin. This monument of past glory now houses a restaurant, an art gallery and a concert hall. Many people sat on chairs in front of the restaurant, others walked in the park. It is an irony of fate that the East German frontier is at the doorstep of the castle. We couldn't cross the bridge over the Havel close by, as it belongs to the East German zone. Beyond the bridge lies Potsdam with its famous Sanssouci, built by Frederick the Great of Prussia, adding another 'unseemly' note to the situation. The West Germans seem to have got used to the limitations of their territory. S. didn't show the slightest reaction to an obvious absurdity. We turned into a side road, and passed through Wannseedorf, a little village with a country pub and houses unchanged for more than a hundred years. In this old and old-fashioned German village time had stood still. It made me wonder whether the villagers still use shire horses and oxen to plough their land and to gather their harvests. S. had done us well, and had added some unforgettable hours to a visit of many surprises.

On the way back from Schloss Glienecke we had driven through the Konstanzerstrasse where I had stayed with the Arinsteins in 1916. The street offered no sign of familiarity, but I glimpsed something I knew, when we passed the Duisbergerstrasse.

We had an evening engagement with Christiane and Heidi. They fetched us early to drive us around the quartier, as they knew the part it had played in my youth. I had so far avoided going near the Pariser Platz and the Duisburgerstrasse where I had spent holidays with Lisa and her family. But at my request, Christiane took us there. The Pariser Platz had been left a shambles after several direct hits, and was unrecognizable. My heart fell. But I didn't flinch, and asked to have a look at Lisa's house, in case it was still there. Several of the buildings of 'her' street had been spared. And Duisburgerstrasse 7 was unviolated, but how neglected and abandoned it looked, like a very old person shrunk in stature and showing the blemishes of decline. We rang several of the many bells – without success. When we were on the point of retreat, a young man opened the entrance door and let us in. We took the lift to the top floor where Lisa had lived. I could have wept, so terrible was the nakedness of the destruction I saw. The slightly winding staircase leading to the *Dachgarten* (roof garden) could perhaps still be negotiated without danger, but the whole floor appeared to have been uninhabited for a long time. The ceiling above the staircase had caved in and water stains darkened the walls. Nothing was left to connect the fifth floor of 7, Duisburgerstrasse with the building it had once been. We left in a hurry. How odd that this house should have played a part in my life twice! The lawyer who dealt with my pension claims in 1963/64 had his offices there. And, once again, letters had gone to and fro between that address and mine. The odd sensation of having seen the end, if not the death of a house, disclosed the nonsense of seeking traces of the imperishable in the perishable. Yet I did not mourn. The sight had left me numb, but did not prevent me from pursuing the same hunt a day later.

This experience did not even disturb the happy mood I shared with my friends over dinner. Had I finished with the past, I wondered. Certainly not. I had only realized once more that streets and houses, once alive, were now museum pieces. Yet I still wanted to be confronted with places which had played a part in my former life. They gave a physical dimension to memory, knitting together loose ends which leave one in the air.

It had been a day of contrasts. In our talk at dinner, we were back in the world of feminism, its problems and achievements. There were many of both. An avalanche of literature had come onto the market. With few exceptions, the books were informative, progressive and stimulating, although too much feminist 'culture' could diminish its impact, as Heidi wisely remarked. The two friends gave a vivid account of the phone-in broadcast the night before at R.I.A.S. (Radio International American Sector). It had lasted from 1 a.m. to 4 a.m. The voices of feminists and avant-garde artists had been heard. Poetesses, writers, composers of music, critics, etc., talked and answered questions about their work. Labrys also got a word in. The broadcast was intended to inform about modern trends in the arts and education. About one hundred women were present. Everybody was allowed one minute speaking time – time enough perhaps for a few avant-garde painters to answers questions on the 'Other Line', and for a composer to inform a questioner whether her music was feminist. (Her sensible answer had been: 'No, it is human!') Labrys was asked how they could best serve their customers! They had found it a bit awkward to answer such a mammoth enquiry in one minute. But they had a great time listening to all these earnest professional women who were dedicated to feminists' rights and a feminist culture.

Christiane gave a vivid account of an important development. She told us that radical German feminists are trying to counteract the impoverishment of *collective* feminism through greater activity in single groups. The same was relevant to lesbians. When larger groups had come into some disarray, lesbians had attached themselves to the *Gewerkschaften* (T.U.C.), and a political party (the F.D.P.). And they also organized themselves inside certain professions. The affiliation to the *Gewerkschaften* goes a step further in Germany than here, while professional groupings are more numerous in this country. Germany is also behind in counselling services for lesbians and male homosexuals. Only one such agency has just been started in Kreuzberg by a mixed homosexual group of the F.D.P.

We talked and talked, drank pink champagne, ate Westfälischen raw ham and rye bread until the Ludwigskirche chimed midnight.

The occasion for another test of confrontation with the past came the following day. Ilse Kokula spent the day with us for further exploration of 'hidden' Berlin, and visits to my former haunts. I asked her to drive to Südwestkorso 53A. 'I want to go into the house where I lived and started my medical practice.' Though the façade was familiar, the houses had quite a different atmosphere from before. We entered No. 53A and went to the first floor, rang the bell of my former flat but got no answer. We tried the same on the floor below. This time an old man opened the door and looked askance at us intruders. I explained that forty-four years ago I had lived in the same flat one floor above him. I failed to make an impression; he didn't allow us to enter. But I persisted, telling him about the layout of my former apartment. He did confirm that it was still the same as in my day. 'Let's go to the Laubenheimer Platz,' I suggested when we were outside again. I told my companions that I had lived there for about two years before my flight from Germany. How odd that I had always thought of Südwestkorso 53A as my real Berlin home! Laubenheimer Platz No. 3 had had a balcony and large rooms. An enamel plate with '*Dr med. Lotte Wolff, Praktische Ärztin*' (G.P.) had been fixed to the wall close to the entrance door. How well I remembered all this now! The Gestapo had been there on their search for bombs and communist literature. I had been on my own at the time. I now looked at the beautiful square with a sense of *déjà vu;* the houses had a certain resemblance to those I had known, but were blatantly new. No. 3 was in its old place, and so was the balcony of 'my' flat on the first floor. But not only had the houses been replaced but the name of the square had been changed to 'Ludwig Barnay Platz' (the name of a famous German actor). The house looked as attractive as the old one, but I was not tempted to enter. I did not know that its old name Laubenheimer Platz is not forgotten, but lives on in the revolutionary history of Berlin. Heidi told me the following day that it had housed a colony of revolutionary artists who had prevented Nazi flags from being hoisted on the blocks of flats. Arthur

Koestler, Ernst Busch, the well-known singer, Ernst Bloch, the writer, and several other well-known personalities had been the vigilant guardians of the last ounce of freedom left in Germany. But their efforts were defeated by the end of March 1933. I had never heard of my remarkable neighbours, though one of them, a Russian-born writer, had been my patient. We left Ludwig Barnay Platz and went back to the Südwestkorso. I perceived with acute interest the bus stop near No. 53A, exactly on the spot where I had always stood waiting for transport to come. Now I was compelled to get close to it. I stood still and shut my eyes. A long-forgotten memory came back and hit me with an unexpected emotional force. It was there, where I had stood waiting for the bus in early May 1933, that I felt in danger of my life. I remember that I used to look anxiously over my shoulder, watching for the Gestapo. It was here that I decided to leave Germany as soon as possible. This bus stop had been the signpost of departure for a new life. There I had realized with horror that waiting would be disastrous. For the first time I was emotionally gripped by the past. I paled under the impact of re-living those moments. I took the arms of my two companions, but I didn't tell them what had happened to me. I felt quite ill. Already that morning I had not been quite 'the thing', being troubled by a sore throat. But I hoped that it would pass off during the day. We promenaded along the Süudwestkorso to find another square in the neighbourhood where a certain Dr Goebbels had lived. But it had disappeared from the face of the earth, which was just as well. The morning had gone; we drove back to the West End for lunch. Then we continued the planned tour through Berlin, halting at the Schöneberger Rathaus, getting, I don't know how, to Moabit, famous for its large prison and street fights before the Nazis came to power. We passed old houses in a state of decay, only good enough for *Gastarbeiter* or revolutionaries. They didn't hold much interest for me because I didn't feel up to the tour, but I didn't want to spoil the pleasure of my companions. Only the Chamisso Platz roused me again. I enjoyed sitting in the car staring at the houses, the threatening Wall, the gently ascending square and the café. But it was closed on Mondays, and so we drove on to Labrys, and found Heidi sunning herself outside, sitting on a window sill. She treated us to coffee before showing me their stock of books. I bought one and was presented with others. We didn't stay long as we had a dinner engagement that evening, and needed a rest.

S. had invited us to dine in one of Berlin's most unusual restaurants. Christiane and Heidi fetched us by car, and off we went on a fairy-tale journey. The fairy-tale was 'Die Strasse des 17 Juni' which runs through the Tiergarten. The name refers to the revolt of workers in the D.D.R. on that day in 1953. The statue of Gneisenau (a famous Prussian general) stared at us out of the bushes, as one of the few who had not been beaten into dust by the war. But the magic of the street had nothing to do with past glories of German history. It goes back, I am afraid, to Adolf Hitler who received a most unusual present from Benito Mussolini – street lamps which allowed for a display of light such as I had never seen before. Who was the artist, I wondered, who had invented this illumination? The lamps were arranged in a double row at a certain distance and angle from one another. The orange glow they emitted was skilfully reflected from one to the other. It was like a ball game, one lamp throwing its light to the other, which sends it back again. One couldn't take one's eyes off the display; it had a hypnotic effect. It was a magical game nobody had ever played before.

Christiane stopped the car in front of a 'mansion' in a select quartier of Berlin, a stone's throw from the Tiergarten and looking onto the Spree. We didn't enter the house at once, but stood in silence at the river bordered by willows. It reflected the houses and willows on the other side. The softness of the trees, with their long and slender branches enveloping the trunks like a soft dress, made us feel slightly melancholic. This poetic corner with its romantic atmosphere was the prelude to a strange evening. The restaurant had the distinction of being on the first floor of a superb private building. A marble staircase leading to the ground floor, and a wide staircase to the rest of the house, promised elegance and grandeur inside. It could have been the dwelling of a Bleichröder or Rothschild in its secluded position in a quiet street in the Tiergarten quartier. A restaurant in the private splendour of large and high-ceilinged rooms was surely unique. The proprietor had managed to create the atmosphere of a stately home rather than that of an eating house. One hardly heard the waiters serving customers in three or four of these 'imperial' rooms. The atmosphere of the place was too splendid to be realxing, and I for one was awe-inspired by it from the start. S. and her friend

307

received us with smiles and much expectation of culinary and conversational treats. The food and wines were indeed well matched with the élitist surroundings. We ate and we drank, but the menu was evidently outlandish enough for some of us to make a wrong choice. I certainly did, and pretended to enjoy what in fact I disliked and knew to be indigestible. The first calamity at the dinner started with the stomach. The charming smiles and obvious enjoyment of the hostess didn't wipe away a sense of gloom which attacked the rest of us. She alone was herself. The others became more and more artificial, and were play-acting badly. Our divided minds emanated a sense of disturbance which one could not relate to anything in particular. I felt weak from a sore throat getting sorer by the hour, and the emotional upset of a dinner party gone wrong. We parted with a false show of friendliness, and couldn't get away quickly enough. I wanted nothing more than a bed to be ill in.

I didn't get out of bed for the next two days. A bad cold had provided an enforced rest. It turned out to be a lovely illness. The affection and care of the friends of the Pariser Strasse, the flowers and phone calls from acquaintances, made it worth while to resign oneself to being incapacitated. But we decided to shorten the visit, and flew back to London a day earlier than planned. Christiane and Heidi, who had received us at Tegel Airport on our arrival, saw us off. They had been the central figures of my second visit to Berlin.

This time I had found new ground under my feet. Heartwarming events had been overwhelming enough to make a few disturbances look trivial. German women have a dynamism and vitality which is a prerogative of their race. It gives a colour to their relationships which is missing in England. They have given me once more the assurance of being wanted and sought after as a friend. I had been impressed by Berlin's new splendours, and seen some of my old haunts. I had explored town and people with a zest I had not thought myself capable of a year or two ago. The relationships with new friends had been solidified, and two of them visited me in London only a fortnight after our departure. The lines of communication, which had started in 1976, would not only be continued but broadened out. A third visit to Berlin preoccupied my mind the day I landed at Heathrow Airport.

Berlin had again become a place on my emotional map. It had given me a new lease of life.

Index

309